BUCKS COUNTY TOMBSTONE INSCRIPTIONS

HILLTOWN TOWNSHIP

Compiled by

Frances Wise Waite

BUCKS COUNTY GENEALOGICAL SOCIETY
POST OFFICE BOX 1092
DOYLESTOWN PA 18901

First printing, 1984

Copyright © 1984
Bucks County Genealogical Society

All rights reserved.

Library of Congress Catalog Card Number   84-070129

International Standard Book Number   0-9612804-1-7

Made in the United States of America

TABLE OF CONTENTS

FOREWORD	1
LOCATION OF THE HILLTOWN TOWNSHIP CEMETERIES -- MAP	2
BLOOMING GLEN MENNONITE CEMETERY (next to church)	3
MAP OF BLOOMING GLEN MENNONITE CEMETERY (across the road)	9
BLOOMING GLEN MENNONITE CEMETERY (old section, across the road)	11
CALVARY CHURCH CEMETERY	53
UPPER HILLTOWN BAPTIST CHURCH CEMETERY (1781)	55
MAP OF UPPER HILLTOWN BAPTIST CHURCH CEMETERY	66
LOWER HILLTOWN BAPTIST CHURCH CEMETERY	67
HILLTOWN GERMAN REFORMED CHURCH CEMETERY	79
MAP OF OUR LADY OF SACRED HEART CEMETERY (1919)	81
OUR LADY OF SACRED HEART CEMETERY	83
PERKASIE MENNONITE CEMETERY	91
MAP OF ST. PETER's UNION CEMETERY (next to church)	92
ST. PETER'S UNION CEMETERY (oldest section)	93
MAP OF ST. PETER'S UNION CEMETERY (across the road)	121
ST. PETER'S UNION CEMETERY (newer section)	123
SILVERDALE BRETHREN IN CHRIST CEMETERY	167
TRINITY EVANGELICAL CEMETERY	175
INDEX	179

FOREWORD

<u>Bucks County Tombstone Inscriptions - Hilltown Township</u>, containing all of the known cemetery inscriptions in Hilltown Township, can provide historians and genealogists with insight of the past residents of the area.

Hilltown Township, incorporated in 1722, has had a variety of nationalities and religious groups inhabit its land. The Welsh Baptists came from Philadelphia County and purchased land from the original English land holders, many of whom were non-residents. By 1737, the Welsh built a church and cemetery. They continued to grow and in 1781 built the Upper Hilltown Baptist Church and a cemetery at Naces Corner.

The Mennonites arrived from across the county line and built a log church in 1753 at Blooming Glen, with a cemetery. Other early Hilltown Township Mennonites are buried in Line Lexington Mennonite Graveyard in New Britain Township.

The Lutheran and the Reformed (now known as The United Church of Christ) acquired property in the Township and built St. Peter's Union Church and Cemetery in 1804-1805. They purchased land across the road from the church in 1870 and opened additional cemetery acreage. The St. Peter's Union Cemetery is owned jointly by both congregations. Before 1805, the Lutheran and the Reformed families worshipped in the union churches of nearby townships.

The Methodist Church was constructed about 1842 as the result of the interest created by the first camp meeting held in Upper Bucks County, according to the 1905 <u>History of Bucks County</u> by Wm. W.H. Davis. The cemetery which remains along Green Street is known as the Trinity Episcopal Cemetery.

The Hilltown German Reformed Church was active during the mid-1800s. This cemetery, located behind the present German-Hungarian Club, is maintained by that organization. The building was previously used by the Leidytown Presbyterian Church and as a school.

More recently opened cemeteries include: the Silverdale Brethren in Christ, whose congregation was formed about 1825; Calvary Church, Telford; Perkasie Mennonite Church, with a cemetery containing burials from about 1950; and Our Lady of the Sacred Heart, founded in 1919 for the parish which included most of Hilltown Township and parts of Plumstead, New Britain and Bedminster Townships.

When tombstone inscriptions are used as research tools, the researcher should keep in mind the several stages at which mis-information may appear in the final record. First, the dates and spellings are no more accurate than those given to the stone cutter, and may contain his errors. Second, the quality of the stone and how well it has weathered may have obscured the original intention of its meaning. Third, the transcriber and typist may have mis-read or mis-copied information. The compilers of this book have done their best to keep such errors to a minimum.

The inscriptions in this collection were made during the past three years in co-operation with the Bucks County Historical Society, through the efforts of Terry A. McNealy, Librarian, and Edna Mae Loux, Frances Wise Waite, Roberta Daymon and Jennie Sperling. Assisting with the transcription of tombstone information were: Linda Dyke, James Etters, Joanne V. Fulcoly, Carol Gardner, William and Audrey Heiser, Donna Line, Daniel Metzler, George Morley, Jayne Newman, Lynn Serok, Anna Shaddinger, Helen Urbanchuk, Fletcher Walls, Jennifer Walls and Dorothy Young. Mrs. Young also did the cover art work for this book.

March 1984   Frances Wise Waite

HILLTOWN TOWNSHIP

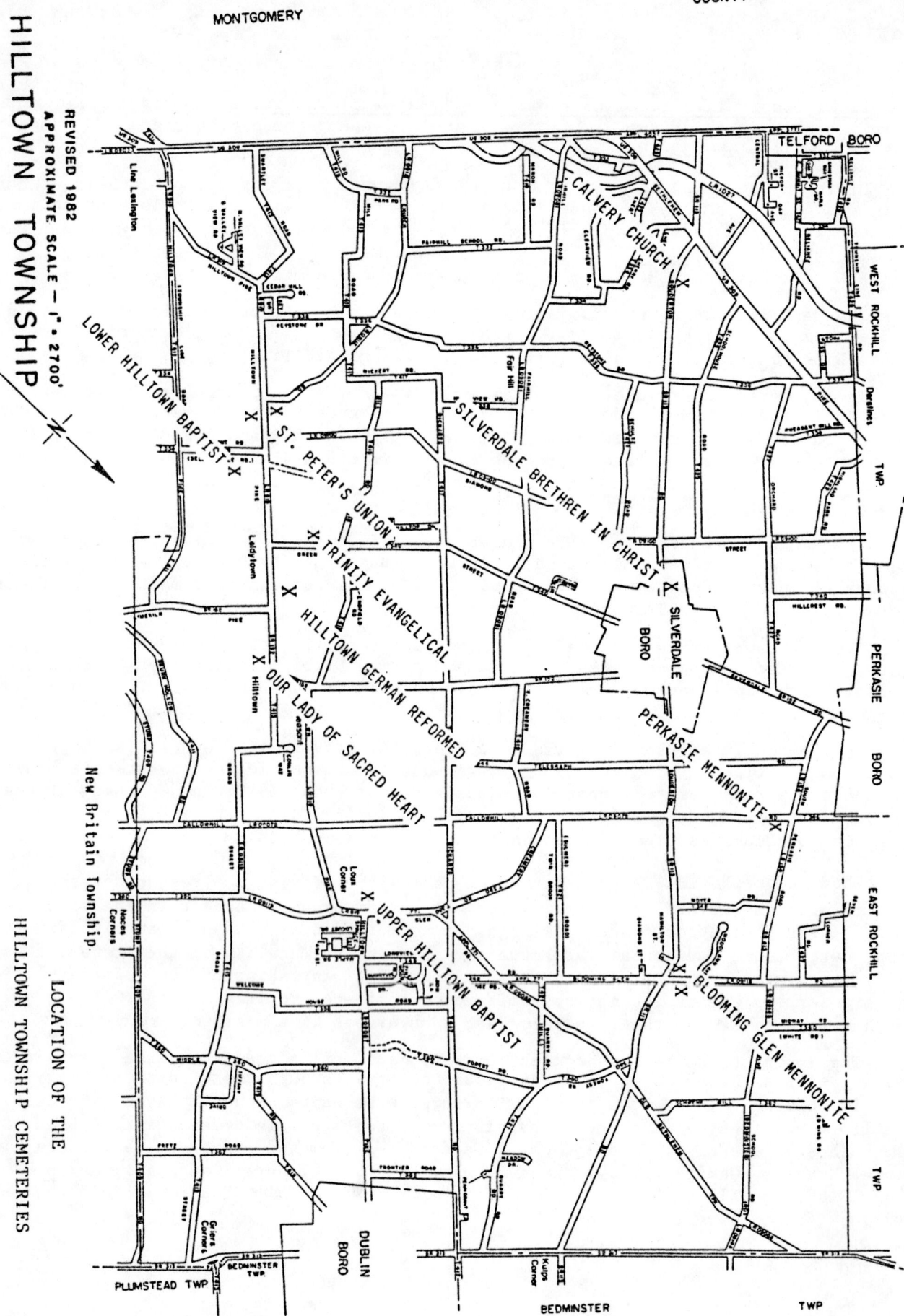

REVISED 1982
APPROXIMATE SCALE — 1" = 2700'

LOCATION OF THE
HILLTOWN TOWNSHIP CEMETERIES

BLOOMING GLENN MENNONITE CEMETERY (NEW SECTION)

The portion of the Blooming Glenn Mennonite Cemetery on the same side of the road as the church building is the newest burial area. It is located on the side of the parking lot fartherest from the town of Blooming Glenn.

Row one was assigned to the row of stones nearest the Blooming Glenn Road. The rows are read from the parking lot toward the west. This section contains eight rows, as of 1983.

Row 1

MEYER - MOYER FAMILY MEMORIAL
   Erected in honor of our forefathers and our pioneers, CHRISTIAN & HANS MOYER, who settled in this vicinity early in 1700.

[space]

YODER, SADIE C.
   15 Oct 1888 - 6 Jun 1873
YODER, LEVI M.
   4 Jul 1885 - 13 July 1959
   [above two on same stone]

[space]

YODER, BESSIE M.   daughter
   10 April 1911 - 23 Aug 1930

DETWILER, ADDIE M.   1891 - 1961
DETWILER, ELMER B.   1888 - 1973
   [above two on same stone]

ROSENBERGER, ALICE M.
   5 Jan 1921 - [blank]
ROSENBERGER, I. STANLEY
   8 Jul 1920 - 16 Feb 1953
   [above two on same stone]

ROSENBERGER, MARILYN
   19 Dec 1941 - 26 Jan 1942
   Daughter of Stanley & Alice Rosenberger

MOYER, TOBIAS   1857 - 1930
MOYER, MARY ANN   1854 - 1948
   [above two on same stone]

MOYER, IDA D.   1889 - 1930
MOYER, H. WARREN   1887 - 1971
   [above two on same stone]

MOYER, TRESSIE S.   1892 - 1952

   [three spaces]

KULP, HELEN LORRAINE
   30 Nov 1930 - 5 Dec 1930
   Daughter of Warren & Lizzie Kulp
   [two spaces]

LEATHERMAN, SALLIE G.   1878 - 1960
LEATHERMAN, JACOB S.   1877 - 1977
   [above two on same stone]

DETWEILER, MARY M.   1875 - 1939
DETWEILER, FRANK G.   1873 - 1853
   [above two on same stone]

BISHOP, KATIE K.
   15 Jan 1864 - 2 Feb 1931
BISHOP, JACOB B.
   10 Feb 1858 - 29 Dec 1931
   [above two on same stone]

LANDIS, HENRY M.
   17 May 1842 - 22 Apr 1932
   age 99y 11m 10d

[Stone is broken off]

LANDIS, ELIZABETH
   wife of Henry M. Landis
   13 Sept 1845 - 25 Jun 1940
   Aged 94y 9m 12d

LANDIS, MARY C.
   13 Dec 1874 - 22 Sept 1942
   Age 67y 9m 9d

MOYER, ANNIE S.   1872 - 1959
MOYER, PETER L.   1870 - 1949
   [above two on same stone]
   [space]

CASSEL, CHARLES S.   1862 - 1932
CASSEL, ELIZABETH H.   1862 - 1955
   [above two on same stone]

GODSHALL, SHIRLEY M.
   daughter of Wilmer & Maimie Godshall
   15 Mar 1934 - 24 Apr 1935
   [four spaces]

YODER, SUSIE L.   Sister
   3 Feb 1914 - 17 Jul 1968

YODER, NORMAN L.   1912 - 1937
YODER, AMANDA M.   1884 - 1969
   [two spaces]

Row 1 continued:

GARIS, INFANT SON
    son of Willard & Shirley M. Garis
    29 Feb 1956

MOYER, LOIS B.   1911 -
MOYER, GARWOOD R.   1907 - 1980
    [above two on same stone]

Row 2

MOYER, MYRTLE Y.   1890 - 1964
MOYER, ABRAM R.   1889 - 1960
    [above two on same stone]

MOYER, SALOMIE H.   1875 - 1944
MOYER, HARRY H.   1873 - 1948
    [above two on same stone]

KRATZ, HENRY M.   1845 - 1934
KRATZ, SOPHIA L.   1844 - 1934
KRATZ, M. Emma   1868 - 1959
    [above three on same stone]

HUNSBERGER, EARL H.   1895 - 19__
HUNSBERGER, ESTELLA M. 1894 - 1934
    [above two on same stone]

BISHOP, LILLIE S.   1889 - 1950
BISHOP, GARWOOD   1888 - 1960
    [above two on same stone]

KRATZ, HILDA S.   1910 -
KRATZ, WALTER M.   1902 - 1979
    [above two on same stone]

KRATZ, GERALD D.
    son of Walter & Hilda S. Kratz
    2 May 1934 - 20 Jul 1934

MOYER, LILLIE B.   1879 - 1954
MOYER, ENOS M.   1872 - 1842
    [above two on same stone]

MOYER, PEARSON K.   1874 - 194?
MOYER, MARY A.   1866 - 1936
    [above two on same stone]
    [space]

YOTHERS, HARVEY K. father 1886 - 1964
YOTHERS, IDA MAE   mother 1886 - 1935
    [above two on same stone]
    [three spaces]

MOYER, DAVID Y.
    son of Dwight & Eliz. Moyer
    20 Nov 1932 - 22 Mar 1935

    [two spaces]

DETWEILER, ANNA L.   1905 -
DETWEILER, WILLIAM G. 1903 - 1956
    [same stone "erected by friends")

SMITH, MAGGIE H.   1873 - 1935
SMITH, ELSIE M.   1891 - 1976
SMITH, WALTER B.   1892 - 1977
    [above two on same stone]

BEIDLER, HENRY D.
    21 Sept 1909 - 19 Mar 1971
BEIDLER, SAMUEL D.
    13 Jan 1895 - 21 Dec 1967
BEIDLER, Mary L.   mother
    27 June 1871 - 27 Dec 1937
BEIDLER, NATHAN G.   father
    25 Feb 1871 - 21 Mar 1940
    [above two on same stone]

STOVER, NORA   1888 - 1970
STOVER, ARTEMUS M.   1886 - 1957
    [above two on same stone]

STOVER, LAURA B.   1891 - 1969
STOVER, ABRAM M.   1892 - 1950
    [above two on same stone]
    [two spaces]

SWARTZ, ANNIE H.   1873 - 1966
SWARTZ, JOHN O.   1870 - 1953

Row 3

GROSS, J. FRANKLIN
    23 Apr 1935 - 9 Oct 1935
GROSS, KATHRYN U.
    17 Jan 1899 - 25 Apr 1958
GROSS, JOHN C.
    15 Apr 1897 - 28 Jul 1961
    [above three on same stone]

MOYER, EDNA F.   1899 - 1940
MOYER, D. CLARENCE   1895 - 1954
    [above two on same stone]
    [two spaces]

DETWEILER, CORA M.
    21 Feb 1886 - 22 Jul 1972
DETWEILER, A. FRANK
    26 Oct 1880 - 25 May 1961
    [above two on same stone]

WORTHINGTON, MARY ELLEN 1878 - 1945
WORTHINGTON, STACY T.   1870 - 1936
    [above two on same stone]

DETWEILER, TERRY BRIAN
    son of Charles and Regina Detweiler
    24 May - 27 May 1936

DETWEILER, JEAN F.   1918 - 1979
DETWEILER, CHARLES B. 1915 -
    [above two on same stone]

BLOOMING GLEN CEMETERY (New Section)

Row 3 continued:

KRATZ, ANNA LAURA	1818 - 1965
KRATZ, OLIVER B.	1879 - 1958

[above two on same stone]

SMITH, ANNA E.	1886 - 1941
SMITH, HARVEY D.	1881 - 1960

[above two on same stone]

HUNSBERGER, RACHEL D.	1895 - 19__
HUNSBERGER, HORACE H.	1887 - 1937

[above two on same stone]

STINLEY, MARGARET D.	1918 - 1966
STINLEY, MARVIN M.	1916 - 1966

[above two on same stone]

STINLEY, INFANT SON
   of Marvin and Margaret Stinley
   4 Oct 1938

BISHOP, MARGARET D.	1914 - 1976
BISHOP, CLAUDE B.	1913 -

[above two on same stone]

BISHOP, GORDON LYNN
   Infant son of Claude and Margaret
   Bishop
   23 Nov 1938
[space]

DERSTINE, MIRIAM K.
   16 Oct 1917 - 9 Jun 1943

DERSTINE, INFANT SON
   of Claude and Miriam Derstine
   24 Feb 1939

GODSHALL, SALLIE M.	1888 - 1960
GODSHALL, ALLEN M.	1884 - 1961

[above two on same stone]
[two spaces]

GODSHALL, INFANT DAUGHTER
   of Warren and Ruth Godshall
   9 Nov 1939

FULMER, LEIDY K.	1901 - 1966
FULMER, FLORENCE D.	1900 - 1965
FULMER, RUTH D.	1938 - 1939

[above three on same stone]
[four spaces]

HOCKMAN, INFANT SON
   of Harold and Gertrude Hockman
   10 Feb 1944

HOCKMAN, SAMUEL F.
   son of Harold and Gertrude Hockman
   10 Aug 1949

BISHOP, JACOB RAY	3 Aug 1948
BISHOP, CRAIG	22 Jun 1954

   sons of Evelyn and Jacob Bishop
[above two on same stone]

BISHOP, EVELYN G.	1919 - 1979
BISHOP, JACOB H.	1916 -

[above two on same stone with
   first names of sons above]
[space]

STOVER, INFANT SON
   of Samuel and Dorothy Stover
   7 Jul - 8 Jul 1960

STOVER, BARBARA M.	1909 - 1976
STOVER, CALVIN M.	1908 - 1971

[above two on same stone]

LANDIS, MAMIE B.	1902 -
LANDIS, EPHRAIM M.	1900 - 1981

[above two on same stone]

YOTHERS, ANNIE R.	1884 - 1967
YOTHERS, ABRAM K.	1881 - 1967

[above two on same stone]

Row 4

ROHR, CAROLINE BIGELOW	1907 - 1961
ROHR, WALTER M.	1890 - 1940

[above two on same stone]

ROHR, CHARLES M.	1892 - 1969

SHELLY, CORA A.	1888 - 1961
SHELLY, ERWIN M.	1886 - 1943

[above two on same stone]

MOYER, VALERIA M.	1891 - 1962
MOYER, WILLIAM O.	1884 - 1972

[above two on same stone]

MOYER, LILLIE L.
   14 Aug 1881 - 27 Oct 1860
MOYER, WILLIAM H.
   16 Sept 1877 - 28 Feb 1944
[above two on same stone]

ROSENBERGER, M. EMMA	1884 - 1968
ROSENBERGER, MARTHA G.	1890 - 1960

[above two on same stone]

FRETZ, KATIE D.	1879 - 1965
FRETZ, E. CLARENCE	1878 - 1944

[above two on same stone]

WILKINSON, KATHRYN FRETZ	1909 -
FRETZ, ELLA AMANDA	1912 - 1982

[above two on same stone]

BISHOP, CLARA G.	1891 - 1970

BUCKS COUNTY TOMBSTONE INSCRIPTIONS - HILLTOWN TOWNSHIP

Row 4 continued:

BISHOP, HENRY A.   1887 - 1966
    [preceeding two on same stone]

GROSS, HANNAH A.
    13 Jun 1891 - 2 Aug 1976
GROSS, ROBERT D.
    19 Sept 1892 - 24 Jan 1946
    [above two on same stone]
    [two spaces]

SMITH, INFANT SON
    of Walter J. and Pearl C. Smith
    15 Sept 1947
    [one space]

LANDIS, ALICE F.   1901 - 1970
LANDIS, HOWARD M.   1896 - 1948
    [above two on same stone]

LEATHERMAN, ELLEN M.
    12 Jan 1874 - 18 Apr 1949
LEATHERMAN, JOHN S.
    12 Dec 1872 - 18 Mar 1954
    [above two on same stone]

HISTAND, ARLENE A.   1926 -
HISTAND, CLAUDE H.   1926 - 1982
    [above two on same stone]

HISTAND, RONALD EUGENE
    5 Apr - 7 Apr 1954
    [five spaces]

HUNSBERGER, STEVEN RAY   1964
    infant son of Arlin and Naomi
    Hunsberger
    [two spaces]

ALDERFER, LIZZIE R.   1895 - 1971
ALDERFER, PRESTON S.   1892 - 1967
    [above two on same stone]

MOYER, KATIE B.   1895 -
MOYER, ERWIN G.   1805 - 1970
    [above two on same stone]
    [one space]

SHELLY, IRENE S.   1912 - 1975
SHELLY, WILMER B.   1915 - 1981
    [above two on same stone]

YOTHERS, EDNA M. mother   1912 -
YOTHERS, HENRY R. father   1913 -
YOTHERS, RICHARD H. son   1951 - 1970
    [above three on same stone]

ROW 5

    [one space]
HUNSBERGER, ROGER LEE   baby   1947

SOUDER, RUTH M.   1899 - 1958
SOUDER, MAHLON A.   1901 -
    [above two on same stone]
    [one space]

SHADDINGER, EMMA H.   1883 - 1958
SHADDINGER, HENRY R.   1881 - 1952
    [above two on same stone]

ROSENBERGER, LYDIA S.   1893 - 1949
ROSENBERGER, HENRY G.   1894 - 1967
    [above two on same stone]

FRETZ, IRENE K.   1908 - 1947
FRETZ, HENRY D.   1907 -
    [above two on same stone]

    [new grave, no marker]
    [space]

WISMER, AQUILLA   1891 - 1948
WISMER, ABRAM M.   1891 - 1969
    [above two on same stone]

    [three spaces]

MOYER, PAULINE   daughter of
    William R. and Dorothy Moyer
    26 Sept 1938 - 4 Jul 1950

MOYER, STELLA A.
    20 Jan 1885 - 7 Mar 1955
MOYER, WILSON R.
    2 Jun 1872 - 25 May 1959
    [above two on same stone]

ANGSTADT, ANNA M.   1982 -
ANGSTADT, J. RAYMOND   1893 - 1959
    [above two on same stone]

SCHMELL, STELLA
    22 Apr 1889 - 8 Aug 1978
SCHMELL, SAMUEL S.
    20 sept 1886 - 29 Apr 1961
    [above two on same stone]
    [one space]

LEWIS, VIOLA A.   1896 - 1966
LEWIS, WILLIAM H.   1899 - 1975
    [above two on same stone]

    [new grave, no marker]

FULMER, MARVIN D.   1923 -
FULMER. KATHRYN H.   1923 -
FULMER, RUTH ANN   1951 - 1967
    [above three on same stone]
    [one space]

MOYER, BLANCHE M.   1898 - 19__
MOYER, WILLIAM A.   1897 - 1972
    [above two on same stone]
    [one space]

Row 5 continued:

MOYER, MILDRED M.
   wife, mother, grandmother
   Feb 1928 - Feb 1973

[two spaces]

SCHWAGER, WILLIAM M., SR. 1896 - 1976
   Cpl. U.S. Army AEF WWI
SCHWAGER, HANNAH R.   1911 -
[above two on same stone]

LANDIS, ESTELLA B.
   2 April 1906 --
LANDIS, ALVIN M.
   16 May 1905 - 1 Feb 1977
[above two on same stone]

[two spaces]

MOYER, MARY G.   1913 -
MOYER, LEROY R.   1912 -
[above two on same stone]

Row 6

DETWEILER, EMMA M.   1882 - 1955
DETWEILER, IRA B.   1882 - 1950
DETWEILER, SARAH M. dau. 1919 - 1975
[above three on same stone]

[four spaces]

HERTZLER, INFANT SON
   of Aldus and Ruth Hertzel
   24 Sept 1951

[two spaces]

MOORE, MARY ELLEN
   26 Jul 1873 - 31 Mar 1959
MOORE, HENRY H.
   26 Dec 1870 - 2 Mar 1952
[above two on same stone]

MOORE, MARY S.
   31 Aug 1894 - 28 Nov 1968

[four spaces]

SCHMELL, BETTY ANNE   daughter of
   Wilmer L. and Jean Schmell
   12 May - 13 May 1955

MUSSELMAN, LIZZIE F.   1897 -
MUSSELMAN, WILLIAM F. 1899 - 1958
[above two on same stone]

MOYER, EMMA K.   1906 - 1961
MOYER, HOWARD E.   1905 -
[above two on same stone]
[two spaces]

MOYER, MABEL S.   1895 - 1962
MOYER, JOSEPH R.   1891 -
[above two on same stone]
[four spaces]

MOYER, DONALD LEE
   20 Feb 1964, 10 hours

[four spaces]

MYERS, DONNA LEE
   5 Feb 1965

[three spaces]

MILLER, DONNA K.   1950 - 1982
MILLER, BENJAMIN W. 1952 -
[above two on same stone]

[two spaces]

MOYER, BABY GIRL   daughter of
   David and Jeanne Moyer
   20 Sep 1967

[three spaces]

GROSS, CATHERINE B. 1922 - 1978
GROSS, J. PAUL   1918 -
[above two on same stone]

[five spaces]

MOYER, CLYDE M.   1917 - 1980
MOYER, MARY K.   1915 - 1978
[above two on same stone]

[two spaces]

MOYER, MAMIE R.   1904 -
MOYER, EDITH R.   1898 - 1979
[above two on same stone]

Row 7

BISHOP, MARGARETH   1894 - 1974
BISHOP, MELVIN A.   1893 - 1953
[above two on same stone]

[two spaces]

MOYER, ALICE K.   1883 - 1953
MOYER, EUGENE M.   1880 - 1955
[above two on same stone]

[two spaces]

SHELLY, BABY GIRL   1955

[two spaces]

ALDERFER, IDA D.   1901 - 1959
ALDERFER, WILLIAM L. 1902 -

[four spaces]

Row 7 continued:

BISHOP, LORIE   infant daughter of
    Marie and Lloyd Bishop
    27 Oct 1961

ALLEBACH, MAMIE D.   1881 - 1975
ALLEBACH, WILSON G.   1877 - 1962
    [above two on same stone]

    [two spaces]

ALLEBACH, MABEL G.   1901 - 1971
ALLEBACH, W. ERNEST   1903 - 1971
    [above two on same stone]

HOCKMAN, LAVERNE W.   1943 - 1976

    [one space]

HOCKMAN, KEVIN M.
    11 Apr 1966 - 3 Jan 1967

YODER, EDITH A.   1890 - 1976
YODER, WARREN D.   1890 - 1969
    [above two on same stone]

HIGH, LIZZIE G.   1889 - 1982
HIGH, ELMER H.   1888 - 1970
    [above two on same stone]

GROSS, MARION B.   1907 - 1972
GROSS, HENRY O.   1911 -
    [above two on same stone]

MOYER, IDA M.
    14 Nov 1892 - 5 Aug 1972
MOYER, NORMAN M.
    17 June 1892 - 9 Dec 1977
    [above two on same stone]

    [five spaces]

KULP, SHERRY LYNN   Apr 1977
    [a metal marker]

    [three spaces]

ALDERFER, ANNA   1906 -
ALDERFER, ARTHUR L.   1905 - 1980

ROW 8

STEINLY, VIRGINIA C.   1894 - 1963
STEINLY, J. CLARENCE   1894 - 1977
    [above two on same stone]

    [two spaces]

BISHOP, GERTRUDE MAY   1893 - 1964
BISHOP, PEARSON M.   1893 - 1978
    [above two on same stone]

DETWILER, L. EDNA   1888 - 1982
DETWILER, IRVIN H.   1886 - 1970
    [above two on same stone]

MOYER, KATIE K.   1903 -
MOYER, CHARLES R.   1902 - 1966
    [above two on same stone]
    [two spaces]

BISHOP, NICOLE MICHAL
    16 Nov 1965 - 9 Mar 1966

WENGER, ETHEL R.   mother 1922 - 1966

    [two spaces]

WEAVER, CATHERINE   1914 - 1982
WEAVER, DAVID J.   1912 - 1967
    [above two on same stone]
    [two spaces]

RUSH, ALVIN L.   1909 - 1968
RUSH, MARY B.   1911 -
RUSH, DAVID R.   1956 -
    [above three on same stone]
    [three spaces]

MOYER, LISA GAYE
    7 Nov 1970 - 6 Oct 1973
    [one space]

SMITH, LAURA H.   1889 - 1969
SMITH, LEIDY D.   1887 - 1970
    [above two on same stone]

    [three spaces]

MOYER, LAURA S.   1902 -
MOYER, ARNON S.   1899 - 1972
    [above two on same stone]

GROSS, LYDIA K.   1910 -
GROSS, CLAYTON O.   1905 - 1975
    [above two on same stone]

    [four spaces]

ALDERFER, MARIA B.
    28 Jun 1897 -
ALDERFER, FRANKLIN L.
    22 Dec 1897 - 11 Aug 1978
    [above two on same stone]

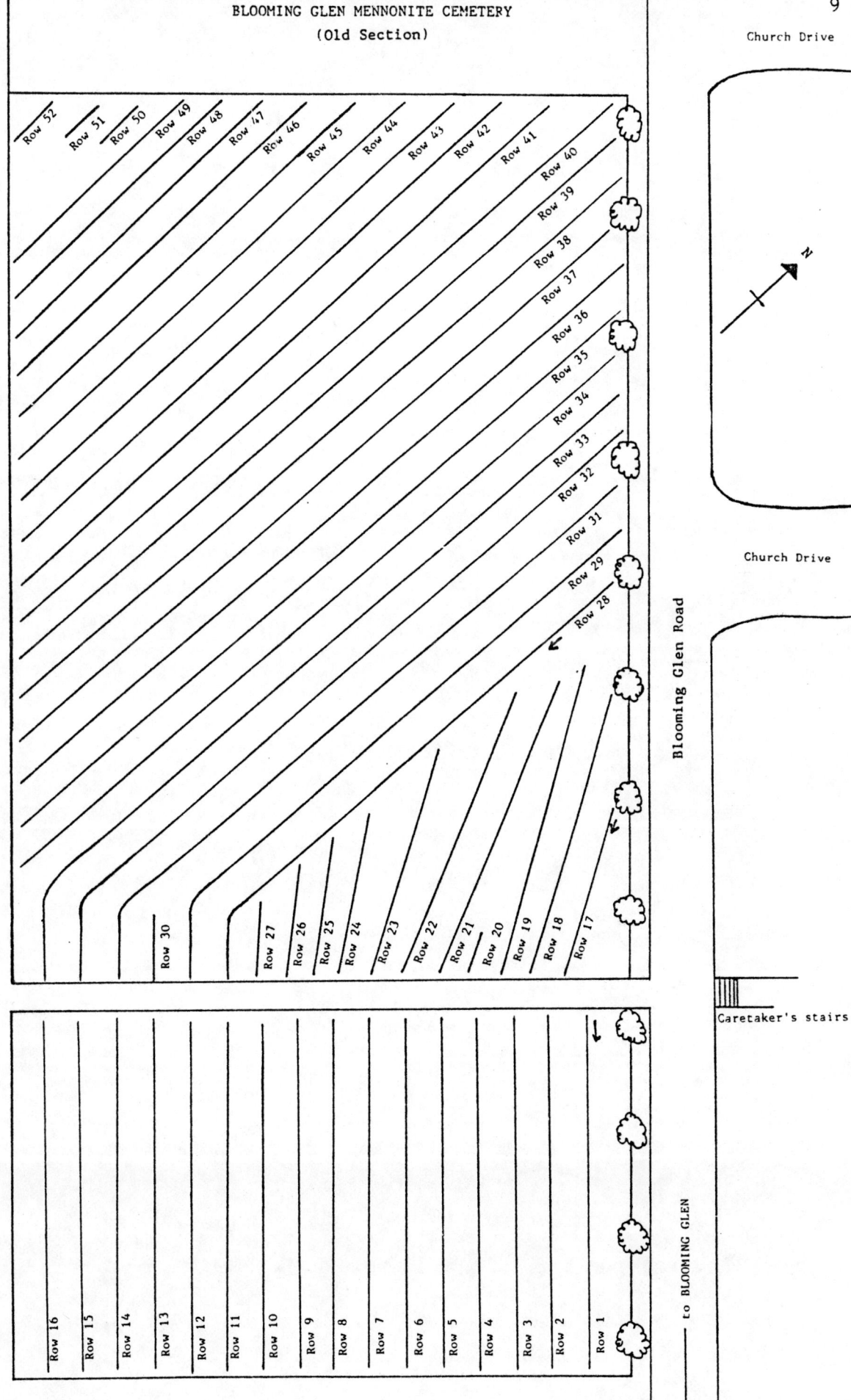

BLOOMING GLEN MENNONITE CEMETERY
(Old Section)

Church Drive

N

Church Drive

Blooming Glen Road

Caretaker's stairs

← to BLOOMING GLEN

Rows 17–52 (diagonal, upper section)
Rows 1–16 (lower section)
Row 30 (upper section)

BLOOMING GLEN MENNONITE CEMETERY -- OLD SECTION

The older part of this cemetery is across the road from the church buildings. The rows are laid out in several different directions, with the older ones facing a more or less easterly direction and the newer ones paralleling Blooming Glen Road.

The first part read was the section closest to Blooming Glen. There is a roadway separating this part from the older section. Each row was read beginning with the stone closest to the cemetery roadway and progressing toward the town. Row one was assigned to the row closest to Blooming Glen Road.

The rows numbered 17 through 27 are adjacent to the above section, and somewhat parallel to Blooming Glenn Road, but less so than the above. They were read, with row 17 being assigned to the row closest the highway, beginning with the stones closest to the crest of the hill and progressing toward the town.

Rows 28 through 52 run more or less in a north-south direction with the stones facing east. The first stone read in each row, was the one closest to Blooming Glen Road and progressing away from the church buildings.

There are several stones in a portion of the cemetery on the southerly side of the cemetery driveway which parallels Blooming Glenn Road. These end the list.

Row 1

MOYER, ADDISON   45y 10m 17d
   4 Dec 1847 - 17 Oct 1893

DETWEILER, ELIZABETH B.   mother
   wife of Jacob L. Detweiler
   25 Nov 1846 - 11 Dec 1924

DETWEILER, JACOB   father
   5 Feb 1847 - 3 Sep 1915

ROGERS, MARY A.
   wife of Edmund Rogers
   20 Aug 1870 - 13 Apr 1895

DETWEILER, MARIA   72y 2m 2d
   wife of John A. Detweiler
   5 Feb 1826 - 7 Apr 1898

DETWEILER, JOHN A.   82y 2m 1d
   9 Mar 1823 - 10 May 1905

MYERS, SARAH   85y 27d
   wife of John G. Myers
   22 Nov 1810 - 19 Dec 1895

MYERS, WILLIAM F.   73y 8m 28d
   1 Jan 1844 - 28 Sep 1917

MYERS, MARIA   57y 2m 1d
   wife of William F. Myers
   8 Nov 1845 - 9 Jan 1903

BILGER, BESSIE M.   8d
   daughter of Samuel and Anna Bilger
   28 May 1900

BILGER, SAMUEL B.   1871 - 1954
BILGER, ANNA M.   1875 - 1953
   [above two on same stone]

MOOD, SARAH M.   mother   1869 - 1929
MOOD, ENOS F.   father   1860 - 1931
   [above two on same stone]

ALDERFER, LINFORD L.   18y 7m 1d
   son of Franklin and Katie R. Alderfer
   9 Apr 1900 - 10 Nov 1918

ALDERFER, KATIE L.
   daughter of Franklin and Katie
   died 9 Sep 1896

ALDERFER, FRANKLIN L.   1864 - 1935
ALDERFER, KATIE R.   1867 - 1948
   [above two on same stone]

LANDIS, LIZZIE M.
   9 Mar 1865 - 9 Aug 1940
LANDIS, REUBEN R.
   12 Oct 1864 - 19 Oct 1951
LANDIS, REUBEN M.   1902 - 1903
LANDIS, INFANT DAUGHTER   1900
LANDIS, INFANT DAUGHTER   1898
   [above five on same stone]

Row 1 continued:

LANDES, INFANT DAUGHTER
    of Reuben and Lizzie Landes
    25 Jan 1898

LANDIS, INFANT DAUGHTER
    of Reuben and Lizzie Landis
    29 Sept 1900

LANDIS, REUBEN M.
    son of Reuben and Lizzie Landis
    4 Aug 1902 - 24 Jun 1903

MOYER, MAMIE E.
    wife of Henry R. Moyer
    16 Jul 1881 - 13 Jan 1917
    age 35y 5m 27d

ALBRIGHT, CHRISTINA
    wife of Reuben Albright
    15 Mar 1852 - 23 Aug 18__
    Age 37y 5m 8d

ALBRIGHT, REUBEN
    11 Mar 1846 - 17 May 1914
    age 68y 2m 6d

ALBRIGHT, INFANT SON
    of Walter and Alta M. Albright
    17 Feb 1919

[two spaces]

M. A. M.

[two spaces]

Row 2

MOYER, DAVID R.   1861 - 1939
MOYER, ELIZABETH M.   1865 - 1922
MOYER, IDA H.   1892 - 1893
    [above three on same stone]

MOYER, CHRISTINE C.   1899 - 1980
MOYER, BESSIE C.   1901 - 1970
    [above two on same stone]
    [space]

MOYER, KATIE   1879 - 1921
MOYER, TITUS K,   1877 - 1955
MOYER, MARGARET   1889 - 1974
    [above three on same stone]

MOYER, JACOB H.   father 66y 5m 20d
    19 Feb 1851 - 9 Aug 1917

MOYER, EMMA MATILDA mother 58y 1m 26d
    wife of Jacob H. Moyer
    3 May 1856 - 29 Jun 1814

HUNSICKER, ANNA   mother 54y 1m 5d
    wife of A. M. Hunsicker
    29 Mar 1855 - 5 May 1909

HUNSICKER, A. M.   father 60y 1m 1d
    24 Jul 1851 - 25 Aug 1911

MOYER, SAMUEL M.   father 1842 - 1897
MOYER, MARY H.   mother 1848 - 1926
    [above two on same stone]

MOYER, WILLIAM M. father 1874 - 1964
MOYER, K. FLORENCE mother 1880 - 1945
    [above two on same stone]

MOYER, KATHRYN B.
    daughter of Wm. M. and Florence Moyer
    26 Dec 1915

MOYER, PAUL B.   8m 25d
    son of Wm. M. and Florence Moyer
    9 May 1913 - 3 Feb 1914

MUSSELMAN, SAMUEL F.   75y 4m 6d
    20 Jan 1867 - 26 May 1942

MUSSELMAN, SALLY W.   45y 9m 3d
    wife of Samuel F. Musselman
    28 Nov 1868 - 31 Aug 1914

MUSSELMAN, SALLY M.   6y 7m 22d
    daughter of Sam'l and Sally Musselman
    4 Jun 1898 - 26 Jun 1905

MUSSELMAN, VERDA M.   1894 - 1973
MUSSELMAN, MELVIN M.   1896 - 1969
MUSSELMAN, EMMA E.   1895 -
    [above two on same stone]

DETWEILER, WILSON C.
    19 Apr 1871 - 13 Jan 1929
DETWEILER, MINERVA H.
    22 Sep 1876 - 16 Dec 1950
    [above two on same stone]

RENNER, WILLIAM   G.A.R. marker
    12 Apr 1843 - 6 Jan 1911
RENNER, SARA
    3 Oct 1844 - 13 Dec 1911
    [above two on same stone]

MOYER, EMMA LOTTIE   1882 - 1954
MOYER, JACOB M.   1876 - 1963
    [above two on same stone]

MOYER, KENNETH A,
    5 Aug - 7 Aug 1924

[two spaces]

BLOOMING GLEN MENNONITE CEMETERY (Old section) 13

Row 2 continued:

ROSENBERGER, ESTHER K.	1915 - 1928	
ROSENBERGER, ISAAC G.	1880 - 1956	
ROSENBERGER, LAURA K.	1884 - 1945	
ROSENBERGER, MARY D.	1880 - 1963	
BEYER, KENNETH L.	13 Dec 1945	

[above five on same stone]

Row 3

KRATZ, ABRAHAM   father   74y 11m 6d
  25 Feb 1823 - 4 Feb 1888

KRATZ, LYDIA E.   mother   80y 6m 7d
  16 Jan 1830 - 22 Jul 1910

KRATZ, ABRAHAM LINFORD   14y 1m
  son of Abraham D. and Sarah Kratz
  22 Jun 1890 - 22 Jul 1904

KRATZ, ABRAHAM O.
  6 Sept 1856 - 6 May 1931
KRATZ, SARAH ANN   his wife
  4 Apr 1860 - 8 Jun 1927
  [above two on same stone]

HENDRICKS, KATE C.   86y 1m 18d
  21 May 1853 - 9 Jul 1939

ANGLEMOYER, HENRY O., Rev.
  6 Jan 1859 - 2 Nov 1908
  aged 49y 9m 26d

DETWEILER, ELI H.   1877 - 1926
DETWEILER, STELLA A.   1885 - 1972
  [above two on same stone]

MOYER, ALICE A.
  24 Jan 1880 - 10 Jun 1950

MOYER, WILLIAM M.   father   1856 - 1926
MOYER, LOVINA H.   1861 - 1925
  [above two on same stone]

MOYER, LUCY ANN   17y 7m
  daughter of Wm. M. and Lovina H.
  5 Sept 1883 - 5 Apr 1901

ANGLEMOYER, JOHN H.   father
  14 Jun 1858 - 19 Oct 1919
  61y 4m 5d

ANGLEMOYER, ANNIE H.   39y 1m 20d
  wife of John H. Anglemoyer
  26 Nov 1859 - 16 Jan 1897

ANGLEMOYLER, LEANNA M.   daughter
  8 Sep 1881 - 5 Feb 1970
  88y 4m 28d

ANGLEMOYER, SAMUEL   father   73y 7m 20d
  28 Oct 1834 - 18 Jun 1908

ANGLEMOYER, LUCY ANN   85y 2m 17d
  mother
  8 Dec 1837 - 25 Feb 1923
  [space]

MUSSELMAN, JOSEPH M.   68y 4m 9d
  father
  19 Feb 1841 - 28 Jun 1909

MUSSELMAN, SARAH   mother   86y 1m 22d
  15 Dec 1842 - 7 Feb 1929

MUSSELMAN, HENRY W.   father
  15 Aug 1874 - 7 Jul 1929

MUSSELMAN, LIZZIE B.
  Wife of Henry W. Musselman
  12 Nov 1870 - 18 Nov 1920

MUSSELMAN, DELILAH F.   10y 7m 5d
  Daughter of Henry W. and Lizzie B.
  23 Dec 1894 - 28 Jul 1905

MUSSELMAN, HENRY F.   young
  son of Henry W. and Lizzie B.
  31 May - 1 Jun 1912

[three spaces]

MOYER, THEODORE F.	1883 - 1967	
MOYER, LUCY ANN	1885 - 1964	
MOYER, LARUE M.	1912 - 1912	
MOYER, LEROY M.	1908 - 1908	

[above four on same stone]

ROSENBERGER, ALVIN K.   1904 - 1982
ROSENBERGER, MARETTA B.   1907 -
  [above two on same stone]

Row 4

BISHOP, INFANT SON
  of Sallie and William Bishop
  [Aug 14?] 189[3?]

[space]

BISHOP, WILLIAM B.   father   1866 - 1927
BISHOP, SALLIE M.   mother   1871 - 1957
  [above two on same stone]

BISHOP, JACOB M.   father   50y 10m 5d
  21 Nov 1845 - 26 Sep 1896

BISHOP, ESTHER   mother   61y 6m 21d
  wife of Jacob M. Bishop
  12 Dec 1846 - 13 Jun 1908

[space]

SMITH, MARGARET K.   1873 - 1956
SMITH, JACOB K.   1875 - 1958
  [above two on same stone]

Row 4 continued:

SMITH, INFANT DAUGHTER   d. 20 Dec 1897
    of Jacob K. and Maggie Smith

SMITH, JOHN M.
    son of Jacob K. and Maggie Smith
    19 Jan 1899 - 18 Jan 1???
    Aged ? years 11m 29d

CROSS, JOSEPH M., Rev.   father
    28 Jun 1866 - 15 May 1921
    Age 64y 10m 17d

CROSS, MARIA   mother   81y 11m 2d
    wife of Rev. Joseph M. Cross
    4 Oct 1869 - 6 Sept 1951

SWARTZ, I. FRANK
    27 Oct 1860 - 18 Mar 1937
SWARTZ, AMANDA E.
    13 Jul 1862 - 4 Jul 1934
    [above two on same stone]
    [space]

HIGH, ALLEN M.   1873 - 1954
HIGH, MARY H.   1875 - 1964
HIGH, SON   1901
HIGH, DAUGHTER   1897
    [above four on same stone]
    [space]

HOCKMAN, JOHN M.   76y 8m 14d
    3 Jun 1846 - 17 Feb 1923

HOCKMAN, ELIZABETH   76y 11m 13d
    wife of John M. Hockman
    5 Feb 1842 - 18 Jan 1919

HOCKMAN, JOHN K.   19y 8m 14d
    son of John M. and Elizabeth
    Hockman
    21 Jun 1880 - 15 Mar 1900

MOYER, ELMER M.
    19 Dec 1876 - 14 Mar 1910
MOYER, BEULAH E.
    25 Jul 1876 - 13 Jun 1942
    [above two on same stone]

MOYER, MARY ANN   mother
    wife of W. C. Moyer
    29 Feb 1855 - 20 Nov 1907

MOYER, W. C.   father
    5 Mar 1854 - 4 Jul 1914

MYERS, SAMUEL A.   1880 - 1974
MYERS, CLARA M.   1884 - 1964
MYERS, CLAUDE M.   1909 - 1934
    [above three on same stone]
    [space]

ROSENBERGER, ALLEN M.   1881 - 1950
ROSENBERGER, ELLA NORA   1889 - 1948
ROSENBERGER, SARA MAE   1912
    [above three on same stone]

MOYER, SAMUEL R.   brother
    15 Nov 1875 - 28 Mar 1932

Row 5

LANDIS, JACOB R.   father 71y 8m 15d
    18 Jul 1822 - 3 Apr 1894

LANDIS, ESTHER ANN mother 71y 1m 29d
    14 Feb 1836 - 13 Apr 1907

ALLEBACH, ROSE L.   mother
    3 Mar 1872 - 17 Sept 1952
ALLEBACH, HARVEY K.   father
    10 Sept 1869 - 8 Aug 1923
    [above two on same stone]

ALLEBACH, NORMAN L.
    son of Harvey and Rosa Allebach
    11 Jul 1890   age 7m 5d

FREED, EMMA   32y 3m 12d
    27 Feb 1883 - 8 Jun. 1915

FREED, MARY C.   61y 5m 20d
    wife of Abram H. Freed
    17 Feb 1862 - 7 Aug 1923

FREED, ABRAM H.   1858 - 1942

HOCKMAN, LEIDY K.   21y 9m 10d
    9 Jan 1876 - 19 Oct 1897

HOCKMAN, CHRISTIAN M.   father
    29 Sept 1848 - 2 Aug 1921
    age 77y 10m 3d

HOCKMAN, AMANDA M. mother 72y 7m 25d
    15 Aug 1856 - 10 Apr 1929

KULP, SARAH J. mother 75y 8m 11d
    27 Nov 1851 - 8 Aug 1927

KULP, JOHN M.   father 50y 10m 21d
    5 Feb 1850 - 26 Dec 1900

MOYER, WILLUS B.   1898 - 1898
MOYER, FLORENCE B.   1900 - 1901
    [above two on same stone]

MOYER, ABRAM B.   1870 - 1936
MOYER, CLARA G.   1873 - 1960
    [above two on same stone]

BISHOP, EDWIN   1864 - 1931
BISHOP, LUCINDA   1867 - 1947
BISHOP, EDWIN   1906
    [above three on same stone]

BLOOMING GLEN MENNONITE CEMETERY (Old Section) 15

Row 5 continued:

KULP, JACOB K.
    31 Oct 1866 - 12 Jun 1923
KULP, SARAH A.
    10 Feb 1869 - 16 Apr 1954
    [above two on same stone]

KULP, JOSEPH F.   1898 - 1978
KULP, WILLIS F.   1896 - 1978
    [above two on same stone]

KULP, ABRAHAM K. father 1871 - 1946
KULP, ELLA L.   mother 1878 - 1951
KULP, J. HARVEY   infant 1907 - 1907
    [above three on same stone]

LANDIS, GEORGE R. father 1828 - 1910
LANDIS BARBARA C. mother 1840 - 1924

GRASSE, INFANT SON   19 May 1948
    son of Anthony M. and Lillian H.
    Grasse

GRASSE, ANTHONY M.   1892 - 1982
GRASSE, LILLIAN L.   1900 -
    [above two on same stone]

LANDIS, JOHN M. father 1876 - 1949
LANDIS, BERTHA H. mother 1879 - 1965
    [above two on same stone]

ROW 6

HIGH, MAIMIE E.   1m 11d
    Daughter of Henry Y. and Mary High
    6 Aug - 17 Sept 1891

HIGH, HOWARD H. son   17y 5m 5d
    20 Feb 1899 - 25 Jul 1916

HIGH, HENRY Y.
    18 Dec 1862 - 8 Jul 1949
HIGH, MARY B.
    1 Mar 1866 - 15 Jan 1943

MOYER, KORES M.   16y 25d
    son of Henry C. and Susanna Moyer
    26 Sept 1879 - 20 Oct 1895

MOYER, HENRY C.   1850 - 1936
MOYER, SUSANNA G.   1854 - 1938
MOYER, DEBORAH M.   1884 - 1963
    [above three on same stone]
    [two spaces]

YODER, ABRAHAM L.   28y 1m 24d
    husband of Rosa M. Yoder
    27 Nov 1870 - 21 Jan 1899

DETWEILER, DAVID A.
    29 May 1876 - 19 Dec 1929

DETWEILER, IDA K.   45y 11m 13d
    wife of David A. Detweiler
    30 Aug 1874 - 13 Aug 1920

DETWEILER, HARVEY H.   5 days
    son of David A. and Ida K. Detweiler
    died 10 Aug 1900

DETWEILER, IRENE H.
    daughter of David A. and Ida K.
    Detweiler   died 19 Oct 1901

DETWEILER, RAYMOND   16 days
    26 Feb 1904 - 14 Mar 1904
DETWEILER, MARY
    26 Feb 1904
    [above two on same stone]
    both children of David A. and
    Ida K. Detweiler

SHADDINGER, JENNIE
    7 Apr 1878 - 8 Feb 1927
SHADDINGER, GRIFFITH
    9 Apr 1873 - 30 Jul 1934
    [above two on same stone]

MOYER, William M.   31y 8m 27d
    28 Oct 1927 - 26 Jul 1909

MOYER, MAGDALENA RICKERT 82y 11m
    Our Mother
    12 Jan 1841 - 12 Dec 1923
    [above two on same style stones]

MOYER, CATHARINE R.
    9 Mar 1870 - 8 Feb 1910
MOYER, TYRUS H.
    7 Nov 1869 - 19 Mar 1943
    [above two on same stone]
    [two spaces]

KRUPP, HARVEY H.   1889 - 1944
KRUPP, MABEL B.   1894 - 19__
KRUPP, HAROLD M.   1914 - 1914
KRUPP, KENNETH M.   1916 - 1916
KRUPP, GERALD M.   1920 - 1921
    [above five on same stone]

BISHOP, CLAYTON A.   1889 - 1957
BISHOP, FLORENCE M.   1892 -
BISHOP, MARIE   1918 - 1923
    [above three on same stone]

LANDIS, HANNAH M.   1y 4m 20d
    daughter of Samuel M. and Eva G.
    Landis
    6 Nov 1922 - 26 Mar 1924

LANDIS, SAMUEL M.   1884 - 1965
LANDIS, EVA G.   1885 - 1965

Row 7

DERSTINE, SOPHIA   57y 11m 12d
  mother, wife of Joseph H. Derstine
  7 Feb 1837 - 19 Dec 1894

DERSTINE, JOSEPH H.   79y 1m 9d
  father
  8 Dec 1820 - 17 Jan 1900

FREED, EMMA JANE   mother
  27 Aug 1865 - 17 Sept 1927

MOYER, HIRAM C.   33y 3m 28d
  13 Mar 1864 - 11 Jul 1897

STOVER, IDA H.   47y 7m 26d
  mother, wife of Edwin F. Stover
  26 Mar 1873 - 22 Nov 1920

STOVER, EDWIN F.   58y 4m 26d
  father
  6 Dec 1889 - 2 May 1928

STOVER, VENA E. MARTIN   70y 11m 12d
  1 Sept 1876 - 13 Aug 1947

MUSSELMAN, SIMON M.   54y 8m 20d
  23 Nov 1845 - 13 Aug 1900

MUSSELMAN, MARY ANN   63y 2m 21d
  wife of Simon Musselman
  18 Feb 1842 - 9 May 1905

GODSHALL, ELIZABETH   72y 11m 27d
  mother
  24 Dec 1844 - 21 Dec 1917

BEIDLER, JACOB   90y 15d
  Father
  25 Sept 1845 - 10 Oct 1935
  Priv. Co. K Reg. 2 D.C. Inf
  [GAR flag holder]
  [space]

MUSSELMAN, JACOB G.   1875 - 1956
MUSSELMAN, DIANNA H.   1874 - 1950
MUSSELMAN, SADIE G.   1901 - 1901
  [above three on same stone]
  [space]

_____, Roy
  [stone is illegible]

GEHMAN, TOBIAS R.   67y 4d
  Father
  4 Oct 18?? - 18 Oct 1913

GEHMAN, MARIA M.   58y 10m 29d
  Mother, wife of Tobias R. Gehman
  17 Mar 1852 - 16 Feb 1911

GEHMAN, EMMA H.   68y 1m 18d
  15 Feb 1879 - 3 Apr 1947

BISHOP, PAULINE   1926 - 1929
BISHOP, CLAUD   1911 - 1913
  Children of Floyd A. and Elizabeth
  Bishop [above two on same stone]

MOYER, EVELYN   24y 28d
  wife of R. Walter Moyer
  29 Nov 1894 - 27 Dec 1918

MOYER, WALTER M.   1917 - 1944
  P. C. C. Co. D 13th U.S. Inft.
  Killed in Action World War II

MOYER, MABEL M.   1896 -
MOYER, R. WALTER   1893 - 1978
  [above two on same stone]

MOYER, RICHARD M.   9m 4d
  son of R. Walter and Mabel Moyer
  28 Apr 1921 - 2 Feb 1922

MOYER, EMMA M.   55y 4m 9d
  Mother, wife of Samuel M. Moyer
  22 Oct 1966 - 1 Mar 1922

MOYER, SAMUEL M.   83y 8m
  Father
  3 Nov 1866 - 3 Jul 1950
  [space]

DETWEILER, CLIFFORD
  son of Ephraim and Florence Detweiler
  9 Feb 1921 - 24 Jun 1927

Row 8

MOYER, EMMA R.
  26 Nov 1869 - 21 Oct 1953
MOYER, ABRAM M.
  5 Oct 1867 - 18 Apr 1939

MOYER, BESSIE S.   30y 5m 3d
  daughter of Abram M. and Emma R.
  Moyer
  5 Nov 1890 - 8 Apr 1921

MUSSELMAN, MAMIE
  daughter of John F. and Katie H.
  24 Aug 1894 - 30 Aug 1899

MUSSELMAN, BESSIE L.
  daughter of John F. and Katie H.
  Musselman
  17 May 1899 - 17 Jan 1900

MUSSELMAN, JOHN F.
  4 Dec 1862 - 29 Jul 1934
MUSSELMAN, KATIE H.
  22 Sept 1874 - 25 Sept 1938
  [above two on same stone]

HENDRICKS, ABRAHAM A.
  20 Aug 1829 - 23 Mar 1925

BLOOMING GLEN MENNONITE CEMETERY (Old Section)

Row 8 continued:

HENDRICKS, ELIZA
    8 May 1852 - 18 Apr 1932
    [preceding two on same stone]

FULMER, JOHN M.   1864 - 1955
FULMER, MARY J.   1862 - 1908
    [above two on same stone]

HOCKMAN, INFANT SON   26 Mar 1902
    son of Jonas and Mame Hockman

HOCKMAN, JONAS G.   1868 - 1944
HOCKMAN, MAME   1872 - 1958
    [above two on same stone]

BARINGER, W. PAUL
    son of W. B. and Bella Baringer
    16 Jun 1901 - 25 Apr 1904

BARINGER, MILDRED M.
    daughter of W. B. and Bella M. Baringer
    4 Feb 1904 - 14 Nov 1905

KULP, LLOYD D.   1910 - 1911
KULP, JOHN K.   1879 - 1954
KULP, ELIZABETH R.   1884 - 1967
    [above three on same stone]

MOYER, HOWARD M.   9m 13d
    son of Wm. H. and Lillie L. Moyer
    died 27 Mar 1917

MOYER, ABRAHAM C.   74y 3m 11d
    father
    14 Nov 1848 - 25 Feb 1923

MOYER, MARY R.   60y 11m 28d
    mother
    17 Apr 1859 - 15 Apr 1940

MOYER, ELIZABETH A.   74y 18d
    12 Mar 1866 - 30 Mar 1940
MOYER, REUBEN C.   87y 11m 26d
    30 Mar 1860 - 26 Mar 1948

MOYER, SARAH E.   1858 - 1940

BARINGER, ELLAMAE
    11 Mar 1907 - 25 Nov 1924

BARINGER, ISABELLA M.   1880 - 1940

MYERS, JOHN H. father 1850 - 1928
MYERS, ANNIE H. mother 1854 - 1942
    [above two on same stone]

MYERS, E. NORMAN   1888 - 1959
MYERS, J. HORACE   1894 - 1969
MYERS, FLORENCE   1891 -

Row 9

MOYER, SAMUEL H. father 52y 4m 14d
    7 Apr 1836 - 21 Aug 1898

MOYER, MARY ANN   68y 11m 5d
    wife of Samuel H. Moyer
    2 Jun 1845 - 7 May 1914

MOYER, ALLEN M. brother 22y 3m 22d
    2 May 1874 - 21 Aug 1896
    [above three same style stones]

MOYER, AMANDA G.   1880 - 1972
MOYER, ABRAM M.   1880 - 1948
    [above two on same stone]

MOYER, LAURA C.   1y 8m 7d
    daughter of A. M. and Amanda Moyer
    6 Mar 1914 - 13 Nov 1915

[two spaces]

GEHMAN, _____
    died 15? ____ 1898 Aged 17 days
    [illegible]

GEHMAN, ABRAM B.   1879 - 1937
GEHMAN, DELLA M.   1880 - 1950
    [above two on same stone]
[two spaces]
MOYER, PAUL M.   3m 21d
    son of Christian? and Sallie ?
    Moyer died 11? Feb 1899

[two spaces]

HUNSICKER, LEIDY D.   1878 - 1954
HUNSICKER, DELLA M.   1879 - 1971
HUNSICKER, ALVIN M.   1904
    [above three on same stone]

HUNSICKER, ISAAC M.   1848 - 1928
HUNSICKER, MARY D.   1848 - 1916
    [above two on same stone]

HOCKMAN, ALICE S.   1911 - 1913
    daughter of Harvey K. and Ella M.
    Hockman

HOCKMAN, HARVEY K.   1884 - 1957
HOCKMAN, ELLA MAE   1888 - 1948
    [above two on same stone]

MOYER, EDWIN M. died 4 Nov 1925
MOYER, JAMES A. died 19 Feb 1927
    sons of J. Arthur and Grace Moyer
    [above two on same stone]

MOYER, GRACE ELAINE 18y 6m 22d
    2 Mar 1930 - 24 Sep 1948

MOYER, J. ARTHUR
    11 May 1903 -

Row 9 continued:

MOYER, GRACE C.
    29 Aug 1907 - 30 Sept 1973
    [preceding two are on same stone]

MOYER, ABRAHAM A.
    28 Feb 1894 - 23 Oct 1965
    P.F.C. Bat. A 314th F. A.
    U.S. Army WWII
    [masonic emblem on this stone]

Row 10

GODSHALL, HARVEY M.   19y 8m 20d
    3 Jun 1877 - 23 Feb 1897

GODSHALL, ISAAC M.   24y 2m 8d
    husband
    1 Dec 1881 - 9 Feb 1906

GODSHALL, MARIA H.   68y 4m 24d
    mother, wife of Samuel Godshall
    14 Mar 1846 - 8 Aug 1819

GODSHALL, SAMUEL L.   80y 4m 29d
    father
    4 Sept 1844 - 3 Feb 1925

KRATZ, William H.   9y 25d
    son of Wm. M. and Elizabeth Kratz
    17 Aug 1893 - 12 Sept 1902

KRATZ, ELIZABETH
    23 Feb 1857 - 24 Oct 1933
KRATZ, Wm. M.
    24 Nov 1837 - 30 Mar 1912
    [above two on same stone]

KRATZ, CLAYTON H.
    Memorial
    born 5 Nov 1896
    "went to Russia 1920"

STOVER, ELLIS S.   2y 6d
    son of Allen and Lizzie Stover
    4 Sept 1901 - 10 Sept 1903

STOVER, ALLEN F.   59y 6m 12d
    17 Oct 1871 - 29 Apr 1831
STOVER, LIZZIE K.   87y 6m 19d
    20 Sep 1869 - 9 Apr 1957
    [above two on same stone]

SMITH, WILLIAM R.   1855 - 1933
SMITH, LYDIA ANN   1857 - 1908
    [above two on same stone]

FRETZ, PAUL H.   WWI 1917-1918
    15 Dec 1893 - 3 Dec 1945

FRETZ, ABRAHAM M.
    15 May 1853 - 1 Aug 1912
FRETZ, SARAH ANN
    26 Jul 1855 - 29 Dec 1943
    [above two on same stone]

MOYER, WALLACE R.   1888 - 1967
MOYER, MYRA F.   1891 - 1969
MOYER, D. LARAINE   1925 -
MOYER, MILDRED   1908 - 1908
MOYER, CHARLES K.   1929 - 1929
    [above five on same stone]

FELLMAN, LAURA D.
    6 Feb 1916 - 21 Mar 1923

FELLMAN, LEIDY B.   1867 - 1931
FELLMAN, ANNIE B.   1875 - 1949
    [above two on same stone]

YODER, JOHN D.   1885 - 1942
YODER, STELLA M.   1885 - 196?
    [above two on same stone]

Row 11

HELERICH, LIZZIE   2y ?m 16d
? ?   ?   1900?
    [two spaces]
    [a stone missing from its base]

MEYERS, TILGHMAN father 1865 - 1943
MEYERS, LIZZIE J. mother 1874 - 1926
    51 years
    [above two on same stone]

HENDRICKS, FANNY T.   77y 8m 12d
    mother
    29 Jan 1840 - 11 Oct 1917

HENDRICKS, JOSEPH   59y 10m 17d
    30 Nov 1842 - 17 Oct 1902

DETWEILER, CHARLES B.   1870 - 1920
DETWEILER, MARY E.   1871 - 1933
    [above two on same stone]
    [two spaces]

SPANNINGER, LAURA G.   1904 - 1949
    nee Detweiler   aged 45y 13d

DETWEILER, PAUL C.   1m 4d
    son of Abraham H. and Ellen M.
    3 Sep 1906 - 7 Oct 1906

DETWEILER, ABRAM H.   1878 - 1928
DETWEILER, ELLEN M.   1875 - 1956
    [above two on same stone]

HUNSBERGER, SOPHIA   1853 - 1913
HUNSBERGER, HENRY   1851 - 1936
    [above two on same stone]

BLOOMING GLEN MENNONITE CEMETERY (Old Section)

Row 11 continued:

HOCKMAN, WILLIAM K.   1888 - 1978
HOCKMAN, MARY L.   1891 - 1978
HOCKMAN, PAUL F.   1914 - 1915
HOCKMAN, JOHN L.   1919 - 1924
   [above four on same stone]

HOCKMAN, JOHN LANDIS
   son of Wm. and Mary F. Hockman
   21 Jan 1919 - 4 Oct 1924

HOCKMAN, PAUL F.   2m 23d
   son of William and Mary Hockman
   18 Nov 1914 - 5 Feb 1915
   [three spaces]

YODER, WILMER R.   1901 - 1963
YODER, EDNA G.   1902 - 1926
   [above two on same stone]

YODER, SAMUEL M.
   22 Apr 1864 - 17 May 1933
YODER, ROSA EMMA
   2 Sep 1866 - 5 Jun 1937
   Father and Mother
   [above two on same stone]

GEHMAN, EPHRAIM D.
   23 Mar 1890 - 8 May 1981
GEHMAN, VALERIA Y.
   9 Sep 1888 - 7 Mar 1951
   [above two on same stone]

Row 12

BISHOP, RUTH C.   2y 25d
   daughter of Howard and Sallie Bishop
   23 Mar 1898 - 17 Apr 1900

BISHOP, SALLIE   60y 8m 12d
   mother, wife of Howard D. Bishop
   18 Nov 1861 - 30 Jul 1922

BISHOP, HOWARD D.   83y 5m 16d
   father
   17 May 1856 - 3 Nov 1939

LANDIS, ELIZABETH   1867 - 1923
   wife of Dr. D. M. Landis

LANDIS, DANIEL M., Dr.   1864 - 1927

LANDIS, Deborah   1894 - 1956
   wife of Dr. D. M. Landis

   [three spaces]

I. H. M.
   [no other information]

DETWEILER, HANNAH H.   69y 8m 17d
   9 Feb 1840 - 26 Oct 1909
   wife of Jacob A. Detweiler

DETWEILER, JACOB A.   75y 5m 7d
   10 Aug 1835 - 17 Jan 1911

DETWEILER, ELLA A.
   22 Sept 1968 - 26 Jun 1935

DETWEILER, HOWARD G.   1883 - 1938

BISHOP, MICHAEL B.   1861 - 1927
   father
BISHOP, MARY M. mother   1866 - 1931
   [above two on same stone]

BISHOP, EMMA   10y 2m 17d
   6 Jul 1906 - 23 Sept 1916

   [two spaces]

MOYER, ANNIE B.
   18 Sept 1866 - 20 Jan 1935
MOYER, DANIEL L.
   17 Feb 1863 - 13 Jul 1927
   [above two on same stone]

   [two spaces]

HUNSBERGER, HENRY L.   1864 - 1939

YODER, AMANDA A.
   30 Sep 1858 - 10 Sep 1933

   [space]

GROSS, ELMER M.   1894 - 1982
GROSS, ELLEN A.   1900 - 1965
   [above two on same stone]

GROSS, CLAUDE M.
   9 Feb 1900 - 27 Feb 1947

Row 13

STOVER, MILTON F.   1866 - 1926
STOVER, AMANDA N.   1868 - 1918
STOVER, LAURA M.   1897 - 1976
STOVER, ALICE M.   1900 - 1901
   [above four on same stone]

STOVER, ELLIS L.
   son of Howard and Mattie Stover
   18 May 1918 - 25 May 1918

MOYER, ANNA MARTHA
   daughter of Gideon and Clara Moyer
   15 Jan 1907 - 19 May 1907

MOYER, ANNA MAY
   daughter of Gideon and Clara Moyer
   3 Dec 1910 - 24 Apr 1917

MOYER, GIDEON S.
   3 Apr 1868 - 29 Dec 1953
MOYER, CLARA B.
   5 Jun 1876 - 11 Nov 1945
   [above two on same stone]

BUCKS COUNTY TOMBSTONE INSCRIPTIONS - HILLTOWN TOWNSHIP

Row 13 continued:

MOYER, FLORENCE 26y 11m 17d
    mother, wife of Howard H. Moyer
    9 Jan 1892 - 26 Dec 1918

MOYER, ELIZA H.
    mother, wife of Benjamin M. Moyer
    2 May 1849 - 14 Jan 1914

MOYER, BENJAMIN M. father
    5 Jun 1847 - 4 Mar 1911

EISENBERGER, VERONICA 46y 1m 9d
    wife of Raymond Eisenberger
    27 Dec 1879 - 6 Fed 1926
    [two spaces]

YODER, EDNA D.
    daughter of Wm. D. and Annie Yoder
    28 Nov 1913 - 4 Nov 1920

YODER, WILLIAM D. 1883 - 1960
YODER, ANNIE A. 1882 - 1960
YODER, IRENE D. 1914 - 1969
    [above three on same stone]

BISHOP, LILLIE M.
    18 May 1892 - 13 Sept 1972
BISHOP, LINFORD M.
    24 Apr 1891 - 27 May 1953
BISHOP, WALTER H. son
    23 Sept 1923 - 13 Feb 1928
    [above three on same stone]

BISHOP, LEON M. 1895 - 1966
BISHOP, LIZZIE H. 1899 - 1939
BISHOP, MARTHA H. 1904 - 1962
    [above three on same stone]

BISHOP, MARVIN L.
    son of Leon and Lizzie H. Bishop
    15 Sept 1920 - 25 Jan 1934

Row 14

HENDRICKS, RUTH S.
    daughter of Abram H. and Ella G.
    Hendricks
    30 Aug 1907 - 8 May 1918

HENDRICKS, ABRAM H. 1872 - 1958
    father
HENDRICKS, ELLA D. 1876 - 1945
    mother
    [above two on same stone]

LOUX, EMMELINE mother 74y 11m 28d
    26 Dec 1860 - 24 Dec 1935

LOUX, JACOB B. father 63y 6m 20d
    14 Sept 1854 - 3 Apr 1918

LOUX, ANNIE 2y 2m 23d
    daughter of Jacob B. and Emaline Loux
    died 13 Sept 1883 ?

LOUX, CLARAY 19y 5m 7d
    daughter of Jacob B. and Emaline
    12 Apr 1891 - 19 Sept 1910

MOYER, EVELYN
    daughter of Harvey and Alma F. Moyer
    19 Feb 1911 - 28 Feb 1916

MOYER, HARVEY R. 1886 - 1968
MOYER, ALMA F. 1889 - 1970
    [above two on same stonw]

LANDIS, ABRAHAM L. our son
    28 Oct 1882 - 5 Jul 1916

BECK, WILLIS B.
    3 Feb 1895 - 26 Jan 1921

BECK, SALLIE S.
    1 Aug 1860 - 4 Mar 1925

BECK, JOHN P.
    18 Mar 1863 - 31 Mar 1933

    [two spaces]

HENDRICKS, SAMUEL
    son of Clarence and Martha Hendricks
    died 14 Jun 1926

    [three spaces]

LAPP, WILLIAM L.
    27 May 1866 - 16 Nov 1933
LAPP, AMANDA M.
    28 Jul 1866 - 5 Apr 1931
    [above two on same stone]

MOYER, HOWARD H.
    13 Aug 1882 - 12 Mar 1948
MOYER, MAYME D.
    18 Sept 1888 - 2 Mar 1947
    [above two on same stone]

Row 15

ROHR, ABRAHAM H. 81y 5m 9d
    father
    10 Aug 1844 - 19 Jan 1926

ROHR, KATE S. 72y 7m 28d
    mother, wife of Abraham Rohr
    14 Jan 1845 - 12 Sep 1917

HEACOCK, LOVINA K. 38y 6m 11d
    wife of Reuben H. Rickert
    14 Mar 1864 - 25 Sept 1902

[RICKERT, LOVINA K. HEACOCK -- as above]

Row 15 continued:

RICKERT, REUBEN H.   58y 5m 21d
    11 Jun 1863 - 2 Dec 1921

RICKERT, SUSAN   61y 5m 10d
    wife of Reuben H. Rickert
    28 Apr 1859 - 8 Oct 1920

    [space]

HUNSBERGER, JONAS S.   1866 - 1952
HUNSBERGER, KATHRYN H.   1868 - 1964
    [above two on same stone]

HEACOCK, AARON   83y 3m 24d
    father
    12 Sept 1831 - 6 Jan 1915

HEACOCK, ELIZABETH   78y 3m 30d
    mother, wife of Aaron Heacock
    31 Jan 1832 - 20 May 1910

HUNSBERGER, DOROTHY M.   2m 18d
    7 Jan 1916 - 23 Mar 1916

    [space]

LANDIS, SARAH M.   1861 - 1933
LANDIS, DANIEL O.   1863 - 1955
    [above two on same stone]

[P. L. ?]
    [illegible stone]

    [two spaces]

DETWEILER, VALENTINE R.   1887 - 1963
DETWEILER, EMMA M.   1887 - 1973
DETWEILER, GARWOOD 5 days   1923 - 1923
    [above three on same stone]

ROHR, ELIZABETH K.
    4 Aug 1869 - 13 Feb 1953
ROHR, SAMUEL B.
    4 Feb 1868 - 21 Jul 1955
    [above two on same stone]

HEUSCHER, CLARA M.   1896 - 1927

    [two spaces]

OPDYKE, MARIA V.   1877 - 1930
OPDYKE, JACOB H.   1878 - 1949
    [above two on same stone]

    [space]

WERNER, IRVIN K.   Daddy
    1901 - 1938

Row 16

SENTMAN, GEORGE C.   1873 - 1951
SENTMAN, ELLA G.   1881 - 1962
SENTMAN, HENRY M.   son   1907 - 1911
    [above three on same stone]

CLYMER, INFANT DAUGHTER
    of Lizzie and Samuel Clymer
    born and died 13 May 1915

CLYMER, LIZZIE   37y 3m 21d
    wife of Samuel B. Clymer
    4 Nov 1879 - 25 May 1917

CLYMER, SAMUEL B.   88y 10m 25d
    9 Jan 1878 - 4 Dec 1966

    [base, with stone missing]

SMITH, HENRY B.   91y 11m 10d
    23 Jan 1843 - 13 Jan 1935

SMITH, HENRY K.
    7 Oct 1884 - 10 Feb 1965

E.F.   [no other information]

    [two spaces]

    [new burial -- not marked]

BISHOP, HARVEY   1863 - 1925
BISHOP, EDNA EARL   1868 - 1947
BISHOP, CORA LEE   1890 - 1981
    [above three on same stone]

SWARTZ, RAYMOND B.   31y 3m 27d
    3 Mar 1898 - 30 Jun 1929

SWARTZ, ABRAHAM O.
    22 Sept 1868 - 27 May 1945
SWARTZ, MARY ANN
    15 Mar 1869 - 17 May 1956
    [above two on same stone]

RICKERT, MARIA   1899 - 1930
RICKERT, LOYD   10 days   1930
    Maria, wife of Henry F. Rickert
    [above two on same stone]

KRONMAIER, HENRY
    11 Jan 1858 - 8 Jan 1944
KRONMAIER, IDA
    8 Oct 1866 - 21 Aug 1955
    [above two on same stone]

    [two spaces]

BISHOP, MERLE
    19 Jul 1932 - 24 Jul 1932

BISHOP, STANLEY
    20 Jun 1931 - 10 Dec 1931

BISHOP, LESTER,   1895 - 1961
BISHOP, ANNIE   1892 - 1975
    [above two on same stone]

Row 17

[GERBER?], MARIA   81 or 84 years
   24 Apr 1846
   [stone difficult to read]

FULMER, CATHARINA   1y 6m 18d
   23 Nov 1861 - 11 Jun 1863

FULMER, SASSAMAN   76y 3m 3d
   30 Aug 1833 - 3 Dec 1909

FULMER, MARY Y.   80y 2m 27d
   wife of Sassaman Fulmer
   9 Dec 1831 - 6 Mar 1912

LUTZ, CAROLINA   65y 10m 14d
   wife of John [K.?] Lutz
   6 Feb 1812 - 20 Dec 1977

HEACOCK, TOBIAS S.   73y 17d
   21 Sept 1807 - 7 Oct 1880

   [two spaces]

SCHLICHTER, MARY   5y 4m 6d
   daughter of Andrew and Caroline
   Schlichter   died 6 [Jun?] 1864

KRAMER, HENRY   69y 11m 20d
   21 Feb 1811 - 13 Feb 1881

LANDIS, JOHN R.   43y 11m 30d
   25 Mar 1832 - 24 Mar 1876

LANDIS, DEBORAH A.
   wife of John R. Landis
   daughter of Samuel and Content King
   late of Hardin Co., Iowa
   born 10 Aug 1842 in Pennsville,
   Morgan County Ohio and
   died 13 Feb 1867 in Hilltown, Bucks
   County while on a visit to her
   father-in-law   aged 24y 6m 3d
   [as written on the stone]

LANDIS, GEORGE M.   84y 8m 8d
   20 Dec 1796 - 28 Aug 1881

LANDIS, MARIA   94y 6m 23d
   12 Aug 1804 - 4 Mar 1899
   wife of George M. Landis

RUSSEL, ELEAZER
   1796 - 3 Apr 1874
   [part of this stone is buried]

RUSSEL, ANNA   68y 26d
   30 Oct 1799 - 23 Jan 1868

ZIEGLER, JACOB B.   75y 7m
   1 Dec 1799 - 1 Jul 1875

Row 18

LICEY, ANNA   72y 3m 5d
   wife of Abraham Licey
   26 May 1812 - 3 sep 1881

LICEY, ABRAHAM   83y 4m 12d
   3 Dec 1808 - 20 Apr 1892

BRYAN, ELIZABETH   50y 7m 13d
   wife of David K. Bryan
   24 Feb 1839 - 12 Oct 1893

BRYAN, DAVID K.   69y 5m 17d
   15 Jul 1835 - 2 Jan 1905

   [six spaces]

JÖKEL, JACOB   61y 1m 18d
   17 Mar 1803 - 5 May 1864

YAKEL, CATHARINE   81y [10m?] 7d
   wife of Jacob Yakel
   [dates are illegible]

KRATZ, BARBARA   73y 9m 15d
   [daughter of Jacob Kratz]
   23 Oct 1807 - 8 Aug 1881

MOYER, LEVI N.   1864 - 1936
MOYER, ANNA Y.   1866 - 1951
   [above two on same stone]

LANDIS, SAMUEL B.
   4 Oct 1849 - 18 Jan 1933
LANDIS, MARY ANN
   3 Jan 1848 - 26 Aug 1934
   [above two on same stone]

SWARTLEY, ELMER D.   30y 3m 21d
   15 Dec 1889 - 6 Apr 1920

___SSEL, ULYSSES GRANT   29 days
   7 Jun 1865 - 6 Jul 1865
   son of J. K. and K. A. [Ca?]ssel

MOYER, ANDREW   9 months
   son of William and Mary Moyer
   28 Jun 1866 - 8 Apr 1967

LANDIS, SAMUEL H.   1y 24d
   son of Samuel and Mary Ann Landis
   31 Jul 1881 - 22 Aug 1882

LANDIS, WILLIAM
   9 Jul 1888 - 4 Aug 1888   25 days
LANDIS, IDA
   9 Jul 1888 - 18 Aug 1888   1m 9d
   twins of Samuel B. and Mary Landis
   [above two on same stone]

BERGEY, SOPHIA   85y 11m 20d
   25 Jan 1806 - 15 Jan 1892
   wife of Jacob Bergey

BLOOMING GLEN MENNONITE CEMETERY (Old Section)

Row 18 continued:

BERGEY, JACOB   82y 4m 16d
   6 Oct 1806 - 22 Feb 1889

LONG, SARAH   1844 - 1937
LONG, DAVID C.   1867 - 1879
   [above two on same stone]

Row 19

SEIBEL, JOHAN HENDRICH
   1818   [field stone]

_____, BARBARA   1y, 1m 3 weeks
   4 May [broken off] -- 26 Jun 1782
   [no last name written on field stone]

_____
   4 Jenner 1785   IN X A X 5 Dag
   [no name on this field stone]

KOLB, CATHARINA
   HN x W x A x 2 x W x 5 x DA
   [as written on red field stone]

_____
   [face of this fireld stone broken off in chips]

FUNCK, JOHANNES   1807
   [field stone]

   [blank field stone]

   [blank field stone]

MOYER, ABRAHAM C.   1856 - 1948
MOYER, SOLOME M.   1859 - 1942
   [above two on same stone]

NASH, ELIZABETH   69y 4m 12d
   wife of Christian Fretz
   17 Aug 1812 - 29 Dec 1881

[FRETZ, ELIZABETH NASH -- as above]

MOYER, ANNA   81y 4m 17d
   wife of Samuel H. Moyer
   5 Aug 1829 - 22 Dec 1910

MOYER, SAMUEL H.   65y 7m 10d
   12 Jun 1818 - 22 Jan 1884

   [face of this grey stone is completely worn off]

BENNER, KATIE S.   37y 6m 20d
   wife of Dr. A. R. Benner
   11 Jul 1849 - 1 Feb 1887

BENNER, BESSIE EVA   aged 1 month
   daughter of Dr. A. R. Benner
   died 9 Jul 1885

BENNER, NELLIE VIOLA   [?] and 1m
   daughter of Dr. A. R. and Katie S.
   Benner   died 9 Jul 1885
   [above two on same stone]

BENNER, HOWARD   3m 7d
   13 Jul 1881 - 20 Oct 1881

BENNER, OSCAR ABNER   0y 3m 13d
   son of Dr. A. B. and Kate S. Benner
   19 Aug 1879 - 2 Dec 1879

[BENNER ?]
   [this stone is broken and part has been removed from lot]

BENNER, ROSA MAY   3y 5m 23d
   daughter of Dr. J. R. and Kate S.
   Benner [why not A. B. ?]
   19 Apr 1875 - 10 Feb 1879

MOYER, ANNA   69y 6m 15d
   wife of Johannes S. Moyer
   30 Mar 1805 - 15 Oct 1874

MOYER, JOHN S.   78y 2m 7d
   30 Dec 1801 - 6 Mar 1883
   [space]

KOLB, MARIA   4y 3m 6d
   11 Feb 1876 - 7 May 1880
   daughter of John and Catharine Kolb

KULP, CATHARINE S.   74y 6m 14d
   24 June 1842 - 8 Jun 1917
   wife of John H. Kulp

KULP, JOHN H.   76y 10m 25d
   28 Oct 1840 - 23 Sept 1917

MOYER, MAHLON D.   24y 6m 20d
   28 Jul 1813 - 18 Feb 1868

Row 20

[short row between row 19 and 21]

ROSENBERGER, JOHANNAH K.   64y 7m 11d
   wife of Joseph D. Rosenberger
   17 Dec 1840 - 28 Jul 1905

ROSENBERGER, JOSEPH D.   78y 6m 15d
   11 Feb 1830 - 26 Aug 1908

ROSENBERGER, INFANT SON   2 days
   son of J. D. and J. H. K.
   Rosenberger
   died 5 Feb 1870

Row 21

KUNFARDIN, ELIZABETH
    Ano 1785
    [field stone]

E. L. S.   [field stone]

LANDES, MARY   3y 4m 24d
    daughter of Simeon C. and Lavina
    Landes
    10 Oct 1878 - 4 Mar 1882

[broken stone, missing]
[LANDIS, ALLEN -- Lizzie Fretz record]
[son of Simeon and L. Landis]
[4 Jun 1876 - 18 Mar 1889]

LANDIS, SIMEON C.   42 years
    son of Jacob and Mary Landis
    23 Dec 1848 - 23 Jul 1891

LANDIS, LEVINA   57y 10m 20d
    wife of Simeon Landis
    10 Feb 1847 - 30 Dec 1904
    [space]

ALLABACH, HENRY B.   14y 11m 15d
    16 Jan 1831 - 31 Dec 1875

ALLEBACK, HANNAH   79y 18d
    wife of Henry B. Alleback
    29 Mar 1835 - 17 Apr 1914

KOOKER, JACOB   75y 3m 24d
    28 Oct 1807 - 22 Feb 1888

KOOKER, CATHARINE   70y 11m 16d
    wife of Jacob B. Kooker
    20 Mar 1814 - 6 Mar 1885

HIGH, HENRY   82y 5m 5d
    26 Oct 1821 - 31 Mar 1904

HIGH, ANNA   49y 6m 17d
    wife of Henrich Hoch
    4 Jun 1831 - 21 Dec 1880

[two spaces]

H. Y. M.

MOYER, HENRY Y.   72y 9m 11d
    12 Sept 1830 - 23 Jun 1903

MEYERS, TOBIAS father 1818 - 1882
MEYERS, MARY   mother 1817 - 1891
    [above two on same stone]

MYER, LIZZIE
    daughter of Tobias and Mary Myer
    23 Feb 1848 - 31 Mar 1883

Row 22

[FUNCH, CHRISTIAN   17?5]
    [this in Lizzie Fretz's transcription
    but no longer in row 22]

MARIA [no last name written on stone]
    Maria x D 1773 30 Juni
    [30 Jun 1773]

[two spaces]

I. H.   [Field stone, nothing else is
    legible --- Lizzie Fretz has I. D.
    1767]

[7 or 8 spaces]
[Lizzie has stones: H. K. and
C E E K in her transcription]

MOYER, JACOB C.   64y 11m 21d
    father
    26 Feb 1853 - 17 Feb 1918

MOYER, BARBARA   70y 9m 23d
    mother, wife of Jacob C. Moyer
    14 Apr 1855 - 7 Feb 1926

MOYER, JOSEPH   b & d 11 Mar 1880
    son of Jacob C. and Barbara Moyer

MOYER, HENRY   b & d 26 Jan 1886
    son of Jacob C. and Barbara Moyer

MOYER, MARY   56y 7m
    wife of Christian F. Moyer
    10 Oct 1825 - 10 May 1882

MOYER, CHRISTIAN F.   75y 10m 27d
    2 Dec 1818 - 20 Oct 1894

HUNSBERGER, JOSEPH B.   66y 1m 5d
    father
    3 Feb 1854 - 8 Mar 1920

HUNSBERGER, BARBARA M. 84y 2m 3d
    mother
    15 Oct 1854 - 18 Dec 1938

[two spaces]

BISHOP, AMY   20y 10m 21d
    daughter of Jacob Bishop
    19 May 1862 - 10 Apr 1883

[two spaces]

SMITH, ADELLA   2m 1d
    daughter of Oliver D. and Amanda
    Smith
    29 Aug 1807 - 30 Oct 1807

J. K. M.

Row 22 continued:

SMITH, OLIVER D.   46y 6m 29d
   26 Dec 1883 - 25 Jul 1930

SMITH, AMANDA O.
   8 Jan 1884 - 20 Apr 1961

Row 23

KEELER, WILLIAM H.   1871 - 19__
KEELER, ELIZABETH J.   1868 - 1941
   [above two on same stone]

LENGEL, ISAAC M.
   son of Samuel R. and Mary A. Lengel
   29 Nov 1880 - 4 Sept 1882

OVERHOLT, MARTIN
   26 Jan 1851 - 26 Feb 1922
OVERHOLT, CATHARINE HUNSBERGER wife
   30 Nov 1854 - 28 Jul 1922
   [above two on same stone]

HUNSBERGER, ISAAC   67y 7m 18d
   2 Oct 1814 - 20 May 1882
HUNSBERGER, ANNA   88y 8m 5d
   wife of Isaac Hunsberger
   17 Feb 1827 - 22 Oct 1895
   [above two on same stone]

HUNSBERGER, HENRY B.   64y 11m 26d
   17 Dec 1849 - 13 Dec 1919

HUNSBERGER, JACOB R.   7y 9m 6d
   son of Joseph and Barbara Hunsberger
   13 Mar 1894 - 19 Dec 1901
HUNSBERGER, KATIE   1m 23d
   daughter of Joseph and Barbara
   Hunsberger
   19 Dec 188? - 11 Jan 188?
   [above two on same stone]

BUTTON, JACOB   90y 8m 1d
   24 Jan 1794 - 25 Sept 1884
BUTTON, ELIZABETH   87y 5m
   wife of Jacob Button
   13 Sept 1799 - 13 Feb 1887
   [above two on same stone]

BUTTON, JOHN   78y 9m 15d
   9 Jun 1821 - 24 Mar 1900
BUTTON, ELIZABETH   71y 2m 13d
   wife of John Button
   29 Aug 1826 - 12 Nov 1897
   [above two on same stone]

SMITH, CLAYTON D.   12y 3m 20d
   son of John R. and Mary D. Smith
   12 Feb 1885 - 2 Jun 1892

SMITH, MARY D.   52y 6m. 4d
   wife of John R. Smith
   21 Jun 1851 - 25 Dec 1903
SMITH, JOHN R.   81y 6m 11d
   father
   20 Feb 1851 - 31 Aug 1932
   [above two on same stone]

Row 24

CASSEL, CATHARINE   74y 1m 16d
   8 Feb 1776 - 24 Jun 1850

CASSEL, ISAAC   82y 3m 11d
   20 Apr 1776 - 31 Jul 1958

[stone - illegible]

[space]

CROUTHAMEL, MARY ANN   27y 5m 22d
   wife of Israel G. Crouthamel
   18 Nov 1854 - 8 Jun 1887

[space]

HENDRICKS, LYDIA   47y 3m 11d
   wife of Abraham A. Hendricks
   daughter of Abraham and Catharine
   Hunsicker
   16 Nov 1838 - 27 Feb 1886

KRATZ, LIZZIE   14y 21d
   daughter of Enos and Hannah Kratz
   18 Aug 1879 - 30 Aug 1893
   [dates as on stone]

KRATZ, KATY   8y 10m 26d
   9 Apr 1874 - 5 Mar 1883

KRATZ, ENOS M.   54y 3m 13d
   6 Jan 1836 - 19 Apr 1890
KRATZ, HANNAH G.   76y 3m 3d
   wife Enos M. Kratz
   23 Nov 1845 - 26 Feb 1822
   [above two on same stone]

STOVER, KATIE M.   6m 1d
   daughter of Milton F. and E. K.
   Stover
   16 Sept 1888 - 17 Mar 1889

STOVER, SALOME F.   13y 8m 28d
   daughter of Ephriam G. and
   Catharine Stover
   28 Oct 1874 - 26 Jul 1888

STOVER, CATHARINE H.   74y 1m 19d
   wife of Ephraim G. Stover, mother
   22 Nov 1844 - 11 Jan 1919
STOVER, EPHRIAM G.   49y 8m 7d
   11 Oct 1840 - 18 Jun 1890

BUCKS COUNTY TOMBSTONE INSCRIPTIONS - HILLTOWN TOWNSHIP

Row 24 continued:

STOVER, ELLA   24y 2m 18d
    wife of Allen F. Stover
    9 Dec 1870 - 27 Feb 1895

HARTZEL, GERTRUDE   4m 10d
    22 Apr 1884 - 11 Oct 1884

Row 25

HUNSICKER, JACOB O.   16y 9m 7d
    son of Abraham and Annie Hunsicker
    28 Mar 1882 - 5 Jan 1899

HUNSICKER, INFANT SON   1 day
    son of Abraham and Annie Hunsicker
    21 Feb [1897 or 1895?]

HUNSICKER, INFANT DAUGHTER   12 hours
    daughter of Abram and Annie Hunsicker
    17 Nov [1890?]

HUNSICKER, ABRAHAM   76y 11m 10d
    8 Dec 1811 - 18 Nov 1888
    [stone is broken]

HUNSICKER, CATHARINE   65y 26d
    wife of Abraham Hunsicker
    3 Mar 1818 - 29 Mar 1883

ANGLEMOYER, HANNAH   16y 11m 28d
    daughter of Samuel and Lucy Ann
    Anglemoyer
    31 Aug 1865 - 29 Jun 1882

HENDRICKS, MARY   55y 24d
    wife of J. A. Hendricks
    2 Dec 1840 - 26 Dec 1895

HENDRICKS, J.A.   88y 2m 29d
    20 May 1827 - 19 Aug 1915

SHADDINGER, EDWARD   1857 - 1884
SHADDINGER, ANNA   1855 - 1888
SHADDINGER, SUSAN   1883 - 1885
    [above three on same card]

PENNYPACKER, ELIZ   mother
    16 Aug 1832 - 29 Jun 1927

PENNYPACKER, AMOS G.   64y 10m 27d
    father
    31 Mar 1827 - 28 Feb 1892

SHATINGER, CATHARINE   75y 5m 29d
    wife of John L. Shatinger
    11 Sept 1821 - 10 Mar 1897

SHADDINGER, John L.   82y 8m 21d
    18 Jul 1818 - 10 Apr 1901

BISHOP, SUSANNA
    mother, wife of W. D. Bishop
    22 Feb 1858 - 28 Aug 1911

BISHOP, WILLIAM D.   father
    12 Jan 1854 - 28 Apr 1922

Row 26

ANDREWS, BARBARA   64y 4m 4d
    wife of Elias Andrews
    27 Oct 1832 - 1 Mar 1897

ANDREWS, ELIAS H.   55y 6m 20d
    5 Jul 1828 - 25 Mar 1884
[stone broken and removed from cemetery]

[space]

MOYER, JACOB   aged 7 days
    son of Isaiah and Mary Moyer
    died 23 May 1887

MOYER, MARY ETTIE   8y 11m 28d
    daughter of Isaiah and Mary Moyer
    died 18 Apr 1885

MOYER, ISAIAH B.   44y 6d
    28 Feb 1853 - 6 Mar 1894

MOYER, MARY L.   mother   1854 - 1928

SWINK, ELWOOD B.   14y 11m 26d
    son of Henry B. and Hannah Swink
    6 Feb 1877 - 2 Feb 1892

SWINK, MARY C.
    daughter of Henry and Hannah Swink
    19 Jul 1892 - 12 Feb 1893

KULP, PHILIP S.
    27 Jul 1845 - 10 Sep 1899
KULP, SOPHIA D.
    20 Jul 1845 - 14 Dec 1926
    [above two on same stone]

Row 27

BISHOP, ERWIN THOMAS   4m 6d
    son of [Abm? and Sally?] Bishop
    17 Apr 18?? - 2? Aug 18?5
    [not in Lizzie Fretz's transcription]

[space]

DERSTINE, HANNAH W. MOYER
    2 Oct 1864 - __ May 1____

MOYER, ALFRED S.   37y 1m 21d
    15 Sep 1852 - 6 Nov 1889

BECK, ANNIE M.   1890

BECK, AQUILLAS   1893   57?

BECK, RUDOLPH   1905

BISHOP, JOSEPH D.
    18 May 1849 - 27 Apr 1925

Row 27 continued:

BISHOP, ANNIE   his wife
   22 Jul 1850 - 7 Nov 1926
BISHOP, ELIZABETH   his wife
   15 Mar 1848 - 28 May 1897
   [above three on same stone]

Row 28

BEYDLER, JACOB   died 1781
   "erected by Henry Beidler,
   a grandson Sept 1891"

BEYDLER, JACOB   1784 - 1787

N_____, _____A

   1778 A B_____
   [stone face broken in chips]
   [two spaces]

Anno
1783   [field stone]
F x R

   [6 spaces]

E. M.   17??   [field stone]

I. H. K. FROENIK   1767
   [field stone]

A. KRAZ   28 Apr 1801
   [field stone]

   [two spaces]

KEELER, CATHARINE   85y 5m 27d
   21 Oct 1886 - 18 Apr 1922

KEELER, ELIZABETH   10m 3d
   10 Dec 1874 - 13 Oct 1873

KEELER, MARY C.   11m 2d
   6 Mar 1876 - 8 Feb 1877

KEELER, SUSAN   10y 7m 25d
   18 Jul 1872 - 13 Mar 1883

KEELER, MARTIN   67y 5m 7d
   28 Jan 1850 - 4 Jul 1917

SCHOLL, MAGDALENA
   15 Apr 1827 - 23 Sept 1911

KRATZ, HENRY   aged 11 years
   [no dates on stone]

KRATZ, AMANDA   5y 8m 10d
   died 1852

   [three spaces]

KRATZ, JOHN L.   73y
   died 23 Oct 1878

MOYER, HENRY C.   87y 23d
   10 Feb 1847 - 3 Mar 1934
MOYER, SARAH G.   72y 6m 17d
   24 Sep 1853 - 11 Apr 1926
   [above two on same stone]

MOYER, HENRY G.   1879 - 1962

ROSENBERGER, SARAH M.   mother
   11 Apr 1852 - 24 Oct 1927

ROSENBERGER, JACOB B.   father
   8 Jan 1847 - 16 Aug 1924

   [two spaces]

MOYER, WILLIAM S.   33y 3m 1d
   11 Feb 1887

MOYER, MARY ESTELLA   4y 1m 13d
   daughter of Wm. and Sarah
   [no date on stone]

MOYER, CORDAN   4m 22d
   child of Wm. and Sara Moyer
   [no date on stone]

   [three spaces]

YODER, ERVIN   1886 - 1891

YODER, SAMUEL Y.
   23 Dec 1846 - 10 Aug 1922
YODER, EMELINE   his wife
   20 Mar 1847 - 28 Jan 1893

Row 29

HENDRICKS, JOHN F.   16y 4m 21d
   son of Benj. D. and Elizabeth
   Hendricks
   25 Jun 1846 - 26 Nov 1862

HOCH, JOHANNES   [2m?] 29d
   19 Jul 1834

MOYER, JACOB of Canada   65y 6m 12d
   5 Jun 1833

HOCH, CATHARINA   64y 3m 1d
   born Grimeiger
   20 Nov 1778 - 21 Feb 1845

HOCH, JACOB   49 years
   19 Apr 1827

S. M.   ANO 1818   [field stone]

C. M.   180__ [nothing on stone]

[Lizzie Fretz includes here:
[T. P. E. CH 1769 --but there is no
[stone in cemetery for it]

MEYERN, BARBARA   1778
   [field stone]

Row 29 continued:

MEIER, JACOB   1778
    [field stone]

MEYERN, ELIZABETH   XNO 1777
    [field stone]

_____   12 M 1767
    [field stone - rest chipped off]

ɪPLCH   1769
    [ɪ = J or I]
    [field stone]

D. M.   1772
    [field stone -- Lizzie says D.M.]

MEIR, SAMUEL
    died 19 Oct 1801

M. M.   [field stone]
[face of field stone chipped off]

MEANS, ANNA ELIZA   80y 1m 16d
    31 Jan 1836 - 16 Mar 1916

FRETZ, MARIETTA   41y 1m 22d
    wife of Levi L. Fretz
    daughter of Sam. and Mary
    Rosenberger   died 17 Mar 1883

FRETZ, LEVI L.   61y 10m 9d
    24 Sept 1820 - 8 Apr 1881

FRETZ, MARY   25y 6d
    wife of Levi Fretz
    daughter of Isaac and Agnes Myer
    died 24 Oct 1861

FRETZ, SARAH ELIZABETH   2m 17d
    daughter of Levi and Marietta Fretz
    8 Apr 1867 - 25 Jun 1867

    [space]

FRETZ, MARY   58y 8m 17d
    wife of David L. Fretz
    daughter of John and Mary Overholt
    1 Feb 1841 - 18 Oct 1899

FRETZ, DAVID L.
    7 Oct 1836 - 12 Sept 1925
    [above two on same stone]

ROSENBERGER, EDWARD   8m 22d
    son of Abel and Mary Rosenberger
    died 28 Dec 1858

ROSENBERGER, MARY GODSHALK
    14 Sept 1852 - 14 Apr 1926

ROSENBERGER, ABRAHAM B.
    27 Mar 1853 - 16 Jan 1916
    [above two on same stone]

ROSENBERGER, SUSANNA   87y 11m
    wife of Isaac Rosenberger
    10 Aug 1820 - 10 Jul 1888

ROSENBERGER, ISAAC   68y 5m 27d
    8 Jun 1818 - 27 Nov 1886

ROSENBERGER, MARY ANN   77y 7m 29d
    wife of Bishop Henry B. Rosenberger
    13 Jul 1847 - 12 Mar 1925

ROSENBERGER, HENRY B., Bishop 76y 11m 2d
    27 Jul 1844 - 29 Jun 1921

MOLL, INFANT   died 1890
    of James and Lizzie Moll

MOLL, ALICE   aged 1 day
    21 Aug 1886   daughter of above

MOYER, AZALIA
    daughter of Jacob M. and Emma M. Moyer
    19 Jul 1875 - 17 Jun 1887
    [stone is broken]

MOYER, ABRAHAM ELMER   3y 2m 20d
    son of Jacob H. and Emma M. Moyer
    25 Mar 1879 - 15 Jun 1882

MOYER, HENRY C.   father
    10 Oct 1852 - 12 Jun 1924

MOYER, HANNAH R.   mother, wife
    14 Apr 1857 - 25 Jul 1935
    [above two on same stone]

MOYER, ISAAC H.   70y 4m 8d
    23 Mar 1891

MOYER, NANCY   72y 6m 25d
    29 Feb 1829 - 24 Sep 1901

MOYER, JACOB H.   74y 6m
    3 Nov 1822 - 3 May 1887

MOYER, FRANCES   80y 7m 19d
    14 Jul 1816 - 27 Feb 1897

BEAN, MARY G.   77y 11m 13d
    mother, wife of David B. Bean
    15 Feb 1836 - 28 Jan 1916

BEAN, DAVID B.   father   62y 6m 14d
    20 Mar 1834 - 4 Oct 1896

Row 30

[Bolirc?], MAMIE M.   2m 15d
    daughter of Samuel and _____
    25 [?] 18[31?]

    [three spaces]

BEAN, ELIZABETH C.   49y 6m 11d
    wife of William B. Bean
    3 Sep 1842 - 11 Mar 1892

BLOOMING GLEN MENNONITE CEMETERY (Old Section)

Row 30 continued:

BEAN, WILLIAM B.   65y 7m 20d
   3 Mar 18?? - 23 Oct 18??

LOUX, ELIZA H.   70y 6m 9d
   wife of Pre. Peter B. Loux
   1 Jul 1846 - 10 Jan 1917

LOUX, PETER B. Bishop   74y 3m 1d
   29 Dec 1847 - 30 Mar 1922

Row 31

HENDRICKS, SARAH   11y 1m 9d
   daughter of Benj. and Elizabeth Hendricks
   11 Sept 1851 - 20 Oct 1862

HENDRICKS, AARON F.   18y 2m 18d
   son of Benj. and Elizabeth Hendricks
   29 Jul 1844 - 17 Oct 1862

HENDRICKS, WILLIAM F.   10y 2m 10d
   son of Benj. and Elizabeth Hendricks
   26 Dec 1848 - 6 Mar 1859

HENRICH, JACOB   86y [6|8m?] 8d
   died 1878

HENRICKS, MARIA   1855

HENRICKS, ELIZABETH   6y 1m 22d
   27 Oct 1851 - 9 Dec 1857

HENDRICKS, ABRAHAM   39y [1|4m?]
   16 Feb 1820

HENDRICKS, JACOB   22y 8m
   27 Aug [1841 or 1853?]

HENRICH, JACOB   [13|1y?] 8m 8d
   died 19 Sep 1846

HENDRICKS, JOSEPH H.   8y 1m 1d
   26 Jan 186[2?]

HENDRICKS, SAMUEL [R|H?]. 15y 5m 12d
   died 13 Mar 1862

I. K.   1815
   [field stone]

[illegible red field stone]

HUNSPERGIN, SUSANA   1828
   [field stone]

_____, JOHANNES
   21 Jan ____9 - 27 Mar 1789
   [field stone]

[illegible field stone]

[illegible field stone]

HOCH, PHILIP
   12 or 20 Oct 1775
   [field stone]

HOCKIN, ANNA
   1 Sep 1715 - 22 Oct 1794
   [field stone]

HOCH, PHILIP
   13 Apr 1712 - 11 Mar 1802
   [field stone]

MEYER, ─Jacr   13y 5m ?d
   12 Mar 1845

MOYER, CATHARINA   2y 3m 26d
   14 Apr 1830

MEYER, JOHANNES   35y
   [5? Mar?] 1827

──────   69y 10m
   20 Feb 1892

MOYER, MARIA   65y 5m 9d
   17 Aug 1801 - 26 Jan 1867

S. D.   [field stone]

YEAKEL, CATHARINE   1y 27d
   died 2 Nov 1863

YEAKEL, CHRISTIANA   1y 5m
   _____ 1862

YEAKEL, ELIZABETH|Emaline [1y 3d ?]
   25 Dec 1861

JEEFEL [Yeakel], SARAH   27y 1m 12d
   nee Rosenberger
   first wife of Henry M. Yeakel
   28 Jun 1837 - 9 Sep 1864

YODER, ANNIE D.   69y 6m 7d
   wife of Jacob A. Yoder
   13 Nov 1860 - 20 May 1930

YODER, OSCAR   4y 8m 29d
   son of Jacob and Annie Yoder
   28 Mar 1879 - 27 Dec 1883

YODER, JACOB A.   66y 6m
   7 Sep 1854 - 7 Mar 1921

[three spaces]

RENNER, LEIDY   7m 24d
   15 Dec 1874 - 9 Aug 1875

RENNER, MAHLON
   son of Michael and Elizabeth Renner
   12 Aug 1876 - 22 May 1876

RENNER, ELIZABETH   68y 3m 1d
   wife of Michael H. Renner
   4 Mar 1844 - 5 Jun 1912

BUCKS COUNTY TOMBSTONE INSCRIPTIONS - HILLTOWN TOWNSHIP

Row 31 continued:

   [four spaces]

MOYER, INFANT
   ? Jan - 5 Feb 1877

MOYER, LILLIE ALICE   1y 6m 15d
   daughter of Henry and Sally Moyer
   4 Jul 1875 - 19 Jan 1877

MOYER, HENRY H.
   5 Sep 1847 - 15 Feb 1925

MOYER, SARAH ANN   his wife
   10 Jul 1851 - 17 Aug 1925
   [above two on same stone]

MOLL, LIZZIE C.   58y 6m 3d
   nee Moyer
   9 Sep 1866 - 12 Mar 1925

MOLL, JAMES D.   47y 7m 27d
   9 Aug 1865 - 6 Apr 1918

MOYER, ABRAHAM C.   91y 2m 9d
   5 Sep 1844 - 14 Nov 1935

MOYER, ANNIE W.   66y 11m 21d
   wife of Abm. C. Moyer
   9 Feb 1843 - 29 Jan 1910

[Stone broken and not in cemetery]

BAUM, ABRAHAM B.   89y 1m 3d
   father
   18 Feb 1836 - 3 Mar 1905

BAUM, ANNIE   52y 8m 5d
   mother, wife of Abraham B. Baum
   1 May 1837 - 6 Jan 1910

BAUM, SARAH G.   mother   1859 - 1929
BAUM, HENRY H.   father   1857 - 1918
   [above two on same stone]

Row 32

HUNSICKER, CATHARINE   72y 11m 3d
   wife of Henry Hunsberger
   16 May 1782 - 19 Apr 1855

_____, OSWIN   4d
   son of Reuben _____
   died 11 Jul 1883
   [last name illegible--stone is in
   back and leaning on above stone]

HUNSBERGER, HENRY, Bishop 86y 1m 29d
   24 Jan 1768 - 23 Mar 1854

HUNSBERGER, CATHARINE   80y 11m 17d
   29 Jan 1813 - 16 Jan 1894

NEUKOMMER, DAVID   46y 3m 17d
   11 Dec 1832

HOCH, ANNA   70y 7m 26d
   25 Jun 1828

HOCH, JOHANNES   71y 5m 4d
   17 Aug 1828

   [space]

HOCH, DAVID   94y 2m 17d
   20 Sep 1847

HOCKIN, BARBARA
   1 Dec 1763 - 3 Jul 1811

[field stone--face crumbled off]
[is this Barbara Hoch
   11 Oct 1761 - 1 May 1801 on the
   Lizzie Fretz transcription?]

D. H.   1801
   [field stone]

HOCKIN, ELIZABETH
   died 1 Nov 1801

[four field stones -- illegible or blank]

MOYER, MARTIN B.   55y 1m 12d
   son of Elizabeth and Abraham Moyer
   23 Feb 1803 - 5 Mar 1858

MEYER, ABRAHAM   73y 1m 10d
   29 Dec 1843

MEYER, ELIZABETH
   1 Jul 1830

[small worn stone -- illegible]

[field stone]

   [two spaces]

MOYER, SUSANNA   36y 11m 2d
   died 7 Mar 1771

MOYER, SAMUEL   81y 7m 2d
   8 Jul 1765 - _____?_____

MOYER, SAMUEL   45y 8m 2d
   4 Aug 1794 - 6 Apr 1840

MAYER, SUSANNA   64y 11m 13d
   5 Feb 1808 - 18 Jan 1873

MOYER, BARBARA   85y 2m 12d
   wife of Samuel Moyer
   11 Aug 1798 - 24 Oct 1883

MOYER, ABRAHAM   49y 4m
   born 9 Oct 1799

HUNSBERGER, MAGDALENA   72y 1m 3d
   wife of John H. Hunsberger
   3 Dec 1819 - 6 Jan 1892

BLOOMING GLEN MENNONITE CEMETERY (Old Section)

Row 32 continued:

HUNSBERGER, JOHN H.   66y 9m 12d
    16 Mar 1871

HUNSBERGER, ISAAC   21 Mar 1847?

HUNSBERGER, WILLIAM   aged 4 days
    [no other information]

HUNSBERGER, SAMUEL   aged 3 days
    [no other information]

[space]

YODER, LIZZIE
    daughter of Jacob and Annie Yoder
    died 12 Dec 1881

YODER, MARIA
    wife of Reuben Yoder
    died 27 Sept _____
    [dates of stone are buried]

YODER, JOHANNES   6y 3m 10d
    son of Reuben and Maria Yoder
    16 May 1856 - 26 Aug 1862

YODER, REUBEN M.   70y 7m 12d
    24 Feb 1825 - 6 Oct 1895

KOLB, JACOB   79y 4m 10d
    14 Aug 1799 - 24 Dec 1878

MOYER, MARY ANN   55y 3m 22d
    wife of Rudolph Moyer
    14 Sep 1848 [1843?] - 5 Jan 1899

KOLP, MOSES   69y 5m 17d
    9 May 1810 - 26 Dec 1879

KULB, MARIA   53y 3m 11d
    wife of Moses Kulb
    24 Nov 1816 - 7 Mar 1870

STOVER, EMMA K.   22y 11m 2d
    wife of Milton F. Stover
    9 Mar 1866 - 11 Feb 1889

MOYER, ALLEN K.   16y 4m 25d
    25 Jan 1868 - 20 Jun 1884
    son of Rudolph and Anna Moyer

MOYER, RUDOLPH H.   56y 5m 22d
    25 Dec 1836 - 17 Jun 1893

MOYER, ANNA   33y 2m 28d
    wife of Rudolph Moyer
    13 Dec 1841 - 11 Mar 1875

MOYER, ANNA
    daughter of Abr. E. and U. Hester Moyer
    born 25 Apr 1867 --
    [other dates are buried]

MOYER, HESTER   48y 4m 19d
    wife of Abraham Moyer
    9 Oct 1824 - 28 Feb 1873

MOYER, ABRAHAM F., Rev.   79y 4m 14d
    ordained at Blooming Glenn
    on 6 Nov 1855
    19 Sep 1822 - 13 Feb 1902

MOYER, ANNA D.   86y 3m 20d
    wife of Abraham Moyer
    daughter of Abraham L. & Anna Moyer
    9 Feb 1837 - 29 May 1923

RICKERT, ALIFIA   79y 5m 6d
    wife of David R. Rickert
    6 Aug 1808 - 12 Jan 1888

RICKERT, DAVID R.   82y 5m 3d
    24 Jun 1818 - 27 Nov 1900

MOYER, ALDA M.   38y 1m 7d
    daughter of Abrm. C. and Anna Moyer
    6 Nov 1888 - 13 Dec 1921

MOYER, REUBEN H.   44y 3m 27d
    son of Abraham F. and Esther Moyer
    24 Mar 1898 - 28 Nov 1853

J. B.   [small stone]

LANDIS, JOYCELYN
    daughter of D. D. M. and Lizzie Landis
    2 May 1892 - 16 Jul 1892

ROHR, SALLIE K.   28y 11m 23d
    wife of Charles B. Rohr, mother
    21 Aug 1873 - 4 Aug 1902

ROHR, CHARLES B.   72y 9m 13d
    17 Jun 1877 - 30 Mar 1949

MOYER, CHRISTIAN C.   47y 10m 26d
    5 Nov 1861 - 1 Dec 1909

MOYER, HANNAH H.   62y 8m 14d
    8 Jun 1863 - 22 Sep 1925

Row 33

FRETZ, MARIA   79y 4m 2d
    9 Jul 1849

FRETZ, JOHNNES   78y 6m 5d
    24 Feb 1842

H. FISHER   [field stone]

FRETZ, MARTIN   71y 1m 18d
    26 Sep 1835

Row 33 continued:

FRETZ, ANNA   74y 2m 23d
    second wife of Martin Fretz
    3 Dec 1843

FRETZ, ANNA   47y 9m 13d
    wife of Martin Fretz
    24 Jun 1816

[field stone -- face froken off]

VERONCA   1801
    [field stone]

_____   1798
    [grey stone - no other information]

M.F.   1790
E.F.   [set of initials on grey stone]

[field stone -- face broken off]
    [large space]

GODSHALL, AMANDA   24y 6m 3d
    9 Aug 1843 - 12 Feb 1868

GODSHALL, ALVIN   7m 2d
    19 Jan 1868 - 21 Aug 1868
    [space]

MOYER, FRANKLIN M.   5m 27d
    son of Abraham and Maria Moyer
    2 Jun 1874 - 29 Nov 1874

MOYER, LILLIE M.   7m 17d
    daughter of Abraham and Maria Moyer
    25 Apr 1878

D. S. A.
    [small stone]
    [three spaces]

YODER, MARY EMMA   16y 11m 24d
    17 Apr 1859 - 11 Apr 1876
    wife of Joseph Yoder
    daughter of Henry and Anna
    Hunsberger

YODER, SARAH   39y 10m 14d
    wife of Levi Yoder
    19 Mar 1834 - 14 Jan 1874

YODER, LEVI   deacon   83y 1m 14d
    27 Jul 1827 - 11 Sep 1910

YODER, LEAH   78y 1m 14d
    wife of Levi B. Yoder
    born Fretz
    15 Mar 1829 - 29 Apr 1907

ROSENBERGER, CHRISTIAN   10m 15d
    son of Titus D. Rosenberger
    17 Mar 1886 - 2 Feb 1887

ROSENBERGER, TITUS D.   35y 3m 24d
    14 Jan 1854 - 8 Apr 1889

ROSENBERGER, ANNA F.   70y 1m 17d
    wife of Titus D. Rosenberger
    19 Nov 1843 - 8 Jun 1920

ROSENBERGER, TITUS B.   3 days
    son of Samuel M. and Bertha
    Rosenberger
    17 May 1907

ROSENBERGER, BLANCHE B.   7y 4d
    daughter of Samuel and Bertha
    Rosenberger
    12 Apr 1910

ROSENBERGER, ANNA VALERIA   1y 1m 17d
    daughter of Samuel M. and Bertha
    Rosenberger
    26 May 1911

ROSENBERGER, GERTRUDE   3m 29d
    daughter of Samuel M. and Bertha
    Rosenberger
    12 Nov 1915 - 11 Mar 1916

GRAHAM, MADILLA   48y 1m 23d
    [Matilda, according to Lizzie Fretz]
    27 Sep 1875 - 20 Nov 1923

KROUT, SUSAN   59y 1m 20d
    10 Nov 1833 - 20 Dec 1892

BAUM, ARTHUR M.   1880 - 1900
BAUM, LILLIE F.   1880 - 1965
BAUM, ARTHUR M.   1908 - 1930
    [above three onsame stone]

Row 34

MOYER, HEINRICH   1m 1d
    6 Dec 1851 - 7 Jan 1852

MOYER, CHRISTIAN   11y 5m 3d
    16 Feb 1855 - 19 Dec 1868

MOYER, CATHARINE   11y 5m 9d
    1 Sep 1858 - 13 Feb 1870

MOYER, ELIZABETH   58y 6m 17d
    wife of Wm. F. Moyer
    11 Mar 1816 - 1 Oct 1875

MOYER, BARBARA   72y 16d
    wife of Wm. F. Moyer
    13 Feb 1821 - 31 Mar 1893

MOYER, HEINRICH
    27 Oct 1774 - 19 Oct 1857

MEYER, SALEME   83y 2m 16d
    11 Nov 1771 - 27 Jan 1855

Row 34 continued:

HUNSICKER, JACOB   85y 11m 21d
   24 [Feb?] 1856

HUNSICKER, BARBARA   81y 5m 14d
   28 Oct 1853

KRATZ, ELIZABETH H.   58y 18d
   wife of Abraham Kratz
   12 Aug 1852

KRATZ, ABRAHAM   64y 8m
   14 Sep 1852

[space]

KRATZ, ELIZABETH   27y 22d
   23 Apr [1831 or 1834?]

KRATZ, ANNA   61y 8m 26d
   wife of Valentine Kratz
   4 Aug 1848

KRATZ, VALENTINE   57y 4m 26d
   18 Sept 1830

[field stone - nothing legible]

J.O. & R. G. HENDRICKS   ANO 1801
   [field stone]

J. H. F.   1793
   [field stone]

PREISZ, HENRICH
   27 Jun 1782 - 9 Nov 1832

PREISZ, JOHANNES
   13 Apr 1796 - 24 Apr 1802

PRICE, JOHANN ELIZABETH
   [? ?] 1780 - 23 [Dec?] 1803
   15.16.   [or 1863?]
   [stone very difficult to read]

J. M.   [field stone]

B. M.   [field stone]

T_____
   [worn field stone]

RUTH, MIENA [MEVH?]
   181?   [field stone]

WENGER, HENRY H.   father
   14 Feb 1856 - 21 Aug 1924
WENGER, SALLIE R.   mother
   26 Nov 1855 - 10 Sept 1919
   [above two on same stone]

E. L.   [field stone]

LICEY, CHRISTIAN   22y 8m 27|28d?
   [11 or 21?] Jul 1839 - 28 Apr 1862

LEICY, HENRY   80y 11m 27d
   11 Jan 1811 - 8 Jan 1882

C. A. M.   1827
   [field stone]

BIBIGHAUS, ANNA B.   78y 10m 2d
   born Leise [Leice?]
   14 Jun 1800 - 16 Apr 1879

KULP, ISAAC H.   64y 2m 11d
   28 Jan 1863 - 9 Apr 1927
KULP, MARY K.   18 Apr 1857
   [no more data for Mary]
   [above two on same stone]

MOYER, AMANDA   5y 7m 25d
   daughter of Samuel and Mary Moyer
   6 Aug 1871 - 1 Apr 1877

MOYER, IDA   1y
   daughter of Samuel H. and Mary Moyer
   17 Aug 1885 - 17 Aug 1886

MEYERS, JACOB   37y 11m 2d
   10 May 1802 - 13 Apr 1878
   [there is an error with dates--
    but this is what was transcribed]

MYERS, HANNAH   61y 7m 26d
   25 Oct 1805 - 26 Jun 1870

DETWILER, LINFORD B.   3y
   son of Elmer and Addie M. Detwiler
   died 6 Dec [1815?]

BAUM, ALICE M.   9y 3m 4d
   daughter of Henry H. and Sarah Baum
   14 Oct 1876 - 18 Jan 1886

BAUM, LAURA H.   6y 8m 28d
   daughter of Abraham and Anna Baum
   4 Jun 1871 - 1 Jun 1878

BAUM, ANNA H.   1m 7d
   daughter of Abraham and Anna Baum
   4 Jul - 11 Sep [1873?]

HUNSICKER, WILSON   1y 3m 6d
   son of Isaac and Sarah L. Hunsicker
   3 May 1892 - 9 Aug 1893

HUNSICKER, JACOB   1y 11m 7d
   17 Nov 1876

HUNSICKER, ALLEN   1y 4m 9d
   son of Isaac and Sarah Hunsicker
   17 Oct 1877 - 26 Feb 1879

HUNSICKER, SARAH C.   30y 29d
   wife of Isaac Hunsicker
   25 Aug 1848 - 24 Sep 1878

HUNSICKER, ISAAC   76y 14d
   26 Dec 1846 - 9 Jan 1925

HUNSICKER, SUSANNA   53y 6m 10d
   wife of Isaac Hunsicker
   4 Oct 1852 - 23 Apr 1896

Row 34 continued:

YODER, SAMUEL M.   4m 7d
    son of Christian and Susanna Yoder
    30 Jun 1898 - 7 Nov 1898

YODER, SARAH   22y 2m 8d
    wife of Christian Yoder
    16 Sept 1857 - 24 Nov 1870

YODER, CHRISTIAN B.   59y 5m 28d
    father
    25 Feb 1855 - 23 Aug 1914

YODER, SUSANNA N.   78y 10m 5d
    mother
    15 Mar 1859 - 20 Jan 1938

LOUX, SUSANNA DIRSTINE   62y 7m 28d
    mother, wife of Enos B. Loux
    5 Jan 1861 - 3 Sept 1923

RICKERT, SARAH E.
    wife of Abram Rickert
    2 Jul 1847 - 10 Dec 1927

ROSENBERGER, ELIZABETH   78y 9m 24d
    wife of Martin D. Rosenberger
    27 Jan 1808 - 21 Nov 1886

ROSENBERGER, MARTIN D.   81y 7m 11d
    24 May 1805 - 5 Jan 1887

MYERS, MARY   85y 4m 19d
    mother, wife of Enos W. Myers
    9 Nov 1827 - 28 Mar 1913

MYERS, ENOS W.   82y 10m 3d
    father
    4 Apr 1826 - 7 Feb 1909

MOYER, CHRISTIAN F.
    20 Jun 1852 - 23 Mar 1915
MOYER, LIZZIE
    27 May 1851 - 12 Dec 1936
    [above two on same stone]

NORDERSHAUSER, PETER   82y 3m 4d
    8 Aug 1825 - 14 Nov 1907

Row 35

MUSSELMAN, SIMON   2m 22d
    4 Apr 1837 - 23 Nov 1837
    [as written on stone]

[space]

MUSSELMAN, SIMON   80y
    30 Mar 1791 - 30 Mar 1871

MUSSELMAN, SAMUEL   [36y 4m 24d?]
    29 Oct 1839

MUSSELMAN, HENRY K.   38y 4m 15d
    27 Jul 1821 - 11 Dec 1859

MUSSELMAN, REUBEN   3m 22d
    son of Joseph and Sarah Musselman
    18 Jun 1872

SMITH, FRANY   70y 11m 20d
    mother, wife of Jacob Smith
    16 Nov 1825 - 6 Nov 1896

MOYER, MARY   75y 1m 27d
    mother, wife of Isaac H. Moyer
    8 Jan 1835 - 5 Mar 1910

MOYER, ISAAC H.   father   65y 3m 17d
    20 Jul 1833 - 7 Nov 1898

MOYER, BARBARA   19y 3m 21d
    died 22 Feb 1862

MOYER, SAMUEL A.   71y 2m 24d
    died 28 Feb 1869

MEYER, ELIZABETH   45y 20d
    died 26 Apr 1852

HUNSICKER, ISAAC   89y 3m 19d
    died 18 Sep 1860

HUNSICKER, LYDIA   65y 1m 17d
    died 8 Oct 1849

HUNSBERGER, ISAAC F.   23y 8m 27d
    died 17 Apr 1848

DETWEILER, DANIEL   12y 5m 19d
    31 Jan 1821 - 10 Jul 1833

[four or five spaces]

[broken field stone]   FH. B.
    January 1813

[two spaces]

DIRSTEIN, ESTER   84y 6m 22d
    died 4 Jan 1851

HUNSICKER, ELISABETH   1825

HUNSICKER, JACOB   1812

A. M.   1807
    [field stone]

MEYER, JOSEPH   40y 11m 26d
    died 15 Jun 1815

MEYER, BARBARA   85y 10m 3d
    died 11 Feb 1856

MEYER, CATHARINA   22y 2d
    7 Mar 1839 - 9 Mar 1861

[two spaces]

MEYER, LYDIA   3y 6m 25d

BLOOMING GLEN MENNONITE CEMETERY (Old Section)

Row 35 continued:
    daughter of Samuel and Catharina Meyer
    10 Jun 1859 - 11 Feb 1863

LOUX, [illegible]   7y 3m 13d
    died 1? Nov 18?6

LOUX, MARTIN [T.]   17y 1m 13d
    died 1 Feb 1832

LOUX, SILES
    [stone is mostly buried]

LOUX, PETER   66y 7m 9d
    13 Dec 1788 - 22 Jul 1855

LOUX, AGNES   72y 1m 11d
    10 Aug 1790 - 21 Sept 1862

MOYER, MILTON   26d
    son of Sam. H. and Mary A. Moyer
    [no dates given]

MOYER, ANNA MARY   2y 9m 29d
    daughter of Samuel H. and Mary Ann
    Moyer
    10 Nov 1869 - 9 Sep 1872

MOYER, ELLEN   11y 8m 22d
    daughter of Samuel H. and Mary Ann
    Moyer
    27 Apr 1865 - 20 Jan 1877

HENDRICKS, MARY H.   6 days
    died 21 Jan 1862|63?

  HENDRICKS, MAGDALINA   45y 2m 8d
    7 Mar 1865

HENDRICKS, HENRY B.   84y 9m 24d
    30 Aug 1813 - 24 Jun 1898

GOTWALS, BARBARA   82y 10m 18d
    died 20 Dec 1877

KOCH, WILLIAM   3y 3m 5d
    13 Nov 1821 - 18 Feb 1825
    son of Balzer and Barbara Koch

KOCH, BARBARA S.   mother   75y 8m 19d
    1 Jun 1840 - 20 Feb 1916

KOCH, BALZATHERS M.   78y 4m 19d
    father
    16 Jan 1840 - 5 Jun 1918
    [above two on same stone]

GODSHALL, MARION B.
    daughter of A. M. and Sallie M.
    Godshall   died 26 Nov 1912

DETWEILER, DIANNA   10y 10m 3d
    daughter of Jacob A. and Hannah
    Detweiler
    11 May 1866 - 7 Apr 1877

DETWEILER, KATIE   2 days
    daughter of Jacob A. and Hannah
    Detweiler   died 15 Mar 1878

MOYER, MILTON   1y 4m 1d
    10 Oct 1866 - 11 Feb 1868

MOYER, WILLIAM H.
    son of Ephraim and Susannah Moyer
    25 Sept - 16 Oct 1871

MOYER, WILSON H.   1y 14d
    son of Ephraim and Susannah Moyer
    24 Apr 1876 - 8 May 1877

MOYER, JACOB H.   5m 22d
    son of Ephraim and Susannah Moyer
    16 Nov 1868 - 8 May 1877

MOYER, IDA MAY   5m 21d
    daughter of E. H. and Susanna Moyer
    21 Feb 1886 - 12 Aug 1886

MOYER, EPHRAIM A.   64y 11m 16d
    22 Sept 1841 - 16 Sept 1906

MOYER, SUSANNA
    29 Sept 1846 - 26 Mar 1934

LOUX, ANNA   36y 26d 2m
    wife of Enos B. Loux
    daughter of Levi and Sarah Yoder
    26 Aug 1859 - 22 Dec 1895

LOUX, LEAH Y.   1y 9m 5d
    daughter of Enos B. and Anna Loux
    5 Aug 1891 - 10 May 1893

LOUX, LEVI Y.   1y 2m 12d
    son of Enos B. and Anna Loux
    20 Dec 1886 - 13 Mar 1888

LOUX, MARIETTA Y.   12y 5m 17d
    daughter of Enos B. and Anna Loux
    25 Apr 1889 - 12 Oct 1906

LOUX, CATHARINE B.   41y 10m 1d
    wife of Enos B. Loux
    daughter of Jacob and Mary
    Hunsberger
    4 Sep 1862 - 5 Jul 1904

LOUX, PAUL H.   3y 4d
    son of E. B. and C. B. Loux
    30 Oct 1903 - 4 Nov 1906
    [above two on same stone]

LOUX, ENOS B.   78y 6m 14d
    13 Jan 1856 - 27 Jul 1934

HANGEY, HARVEY H.   3y 3m 19d
    son of Enos and Eliz. Hangey
    died 28 Mar 1888

Row 35 continued:

HANGEY, William H.   1y 4m 11d
    son of Enos and Eliz. Hangey
    died 1 Feb 1890

HANGEY, ALLEN H.   2y 5m 15d
    son of Enos and Lizzie Hangey
    died 12 Oct 1896

HANGEY, ENOS L.   54y 6m 2d
    14 Nov 1857 - 16 May 1906

HANGEY, ELIZABETH   88y 2m 3d
    wife of Enos C. Hangey
    6 Jun 1857 - 9 Aug 1945

HENGEY, JOHN A.   31y 11m 14d
    son of Enos and Elizabeth Hengey
    5 Jul 1891 - 19 Jun 1928

Row 36

MEYER, EPHRAIM   1y 7m 22d
    20 Aug 1856 - 12 Apr 1858

MUSSELMAN, JACOB K.
    25 May 1818 - Dec 1894
    [no day of death given]

MUSSELMAN, HANNA   50y 4m 1d
    28 Aug 1821 - 27 Dec 1871

MUSSELMAN, WILLIAM
    13 Oct 1849 - 25 Dec 1869
    [stone partially buried]

HOCH, PHILIP   80y 9m 12d
    3 Mar 1783 - 15 Dec 1863

HOCH, MARIA   85y 1m 22d
    died 14 Jan 1871

KOLB, MARIA   45y 8m ?d
    21 Mar 1821 - 11 Dec 1867
    [stone was repaired]

KULP, ANNIE   91y 9m
    wife of Isaac Kulp
    6 Apr 1816 - 6 Jan 1868
    [dates as recorded]

KULP, ISAAC   33y 10m 6d
    10 Apr 1803 - 16 Feb 1837

KULP, FRANICA   20y 1m 8d
    7 Oct 1842 - 15 Nov 1862

KOLB, JACOB   70y 11m 16d
    23 Mar 1806 - 8 Mar 1876

KOLB, BARBARA   45y 3m 21d
    10 Oct 1808 - 30 Jan 1851

KOLB, ANNA   87y 2m 29d
    died 2 Jan 1870

KOLB, HENRICH   76y 11m 4d
    died 1 Jan 1855

    [space]

MEYER, MARIANN   27y 10m 10d
    2 Apr 1853

MOYER, SARAH   3m 14d
    died 23 Jul 1844

    [four spaces]

[illegible stone]

    [four to five spaces]

SAUDER, ABRAHAM   88 y
    died 25 Jul 1811
    [field stone]

SAUDER, ABRAHAM   1815
    [field stone]

MAYER, S.   1844
    [field stone]

    [two spaces]

HUNSBERGER, ELIZABETH   18y 10m
    died 14 Nov 1845

HUNSBERGER, SUSAN   4m 20d
    1823 - 1823

    [three spaces]

MEYER, SAMUEL
    17 Nov 1807 - 4 Oct 1832

MOYER, MARIA   28y 3m 2d
    died 2 Jun 1842

MOYER, JOHANNES H.   25y 7m 6d
    son of Samuel and Mary Moyer
    04 Dec 1036 - 30 May 1061

MOYER, ERWIN Y.   42y 9m 5d
    son of Henry S. and Mary Ann K.
    Moyer
    31 Mar 1875 - 6 Jan 1919

MOYER, HENRY S.   71y 9m 3d
    25 Aug 1810 - 28 May 1882

MOYER, MARY ANN K.   84y 3m 26d
    wife of Henry S. Moyer
    17 Sept 1839 - 13 Jan 1924

MEYER, MARIA   44y 11m 27d
    born Clemmer
    29 Nov 1861

E. H. T.

Row 36 continued:

[red stone, no marks]

HENDRICKS, CATHARINE   15y 4m 12d
     daughter of Abraham and Catharine
     Hendricks
     18 Sep 1856 - 30 Jan 1871

HENDRICKS, BARBARA   28y 6m 28d
     daughter of Abraham S. and Catharine
     Hendricks
     21 Sept 1864 - 19 Apr 1893

NACE, JONAS M.   3y 8m 10d
     son of Francis and Mary Nace
     29 Feb 1864 - 9 Nov 1867

NACE, MATILDA
     daughter of Francis and Mary Nace
     born 12 Oct 1871

NACE, FRANCIS   61y 9m 10d
     3 May 1836 - 17 Aug 1898

NACE, MARY   81y 9m 8d
     wife of Francis Nace
     9 Nov 1836 - 17 Aug 1918

NACE, LYDIA   58y 1m 27d
     wife of Jonas Nace
     1 Nov 1813 - 28 Dec 1871

NACE, JONAS   79y 4m 23d
     12 Dec 1811 - 5 May 1891

NACE, MARY ANN   74y 8m 10d
     wife of Jonas Nace
     27 Jun 1835 - 7 Mar 1910

SHATTINGER, SARAH   74y 5m 15d
     wife of Jacob Shattinger
     18 Aug 1831 - 3 Feb 1906

FRETZ, CATHARINE   74y 23d
     born Benner
     7 Dec 1795 - 30 Dec 1869

FRETZ, HEINRICH   71y 3m 26d
     28 Feb 1800 - 24 Jun 1871

FRETZ, JOSEPH   71y 21d
     18 Aug 1831 - 9 Sept 1902

FRETZ, ESTHER   37y 3m 28d
     wife of Joseph Fretz
     23 Sept 1840 - 21 Jan 1878

FRETZ, EMMA JANE   4y 7m 18d
     daughter of Joseph and Esther Fretz
     11 Apr 1872 - 6 Dec 1876

     [space]

MOYER, MARY ANN   37y 11m 29d
     wife of Jacob C. Moyer
     9 Jan 1851 - 8 Jan 1889

MOYER, EDWARD M.   10m 6d
     son of Jacob C. and M. D. Moyer
     21 May 1888 - 27 Mar 1889

BISHOP, WILLARD H.   21 days
     son of Warren A. and Ida H. Bishop
     13 Nov 1911 - 4 Dec 1911

BISHOP, WARREN A.   1885 - 1951
BISHOP, IDA H.   1886 - 1971
     [above two on same stone]

Row 37

KRATZ, ISAIAH   3m 24d
     died 31 Jun 1851

BRUNNER, BARBARA   40y 4m 11d
     wife of Isaiah S. Brunner
     30 Nov 1850 - 13 Apr 1891

     [space]

KULP, ELIZABETH   72y 7m 2d
     wife of Joseph Kulp
     29 Jan 1819 - 1 Sep 1891

KULP, JOSEPH   86y 5m 1d
     26 Mar 1811 - 27 Aug 1897

     [two spaces]

KULP, HENRY L.   89y 3m 18d
     10 Oct 1813 - 28 Jan 1903

KULP, CATHARINE   73y 5m 22d
     wife of Henry L. Kulp
     22 Sep 1826 - 18 Mar 1900

KULP, ELIZABETH H.   60y 4m 15d
     sister
     9 Oct 1845 - 24 Feb 1906

DIRSTINE, GRANVILLE LEWIS   1y 9m
     son of Henry and Susan Dirstine
     28 Jun 1855 - 28 Feb 1857

DIRSTINE, HENRY   aged 81
     died 12 Apr 1900

DIRSTINE, SUSAN   aged 76
     died 5 May 1900

ROSENBERGER, ISAAC   4y 6m 1d
     25 Sep 1851 - 26 Mar 1856

ROSENBERGER, ELIAS
     died 29 Oct 1849

ROSENBERGER, MARY   21y 4m
     daughter of Isaac and Susanna
     died 6 Apr 1880

Row 37 continued:

FISHER, MARY   aged 39
    died 3 May 1844

FISHER, ABRAHAM
    11 Apr 1815   [1845?]

FISHER, SAMUEL D.   36y 5m 22d
    son of Abraham & Mary Fisher
    9 Aug 1828 - 31 Jan 1865
    died in Philadelphia

M.D.   [field stone]

HENDRICKS, H__?__   2y 5m 1d
    died 11 Oct 1831

HENDRICKS, CATHARINA A.   12y 4m 1d
    died 7 Nov 1862

HENDRICKS, S___?___   80y 5m 2d
    died 10 Jun 1845

HENDRICKS, BENJAMIN   70y 9d
    died 21 Jan 1831
    [Rev. War flag]

BECHTEL, MARTIN   53y 3m 29d
    died 7 Dec 1842

BECHTEL, ENOS   1836

[field stone -- nothing legible]

M. B T   1830
    [field stone]

S. T.
    [field stone]

MOYER, JOSEPH   39y 11m 21d
    died 1 Nov 1812

MOYER, ELIZ   77y 6m 29d
    wife of Joseph Moyer
    15 Oct 1803 - 14 May 1881

J. D.   ?y 10m 20d
    __?__ Sep 1846

A. D.   6m 23d
    15 Feb 1848

HUNSBERGER, BARBARA   77y 18d
    wife of Jacob Hunsberger
    26 Jul 1813 - 11 Aug 1890

HUNSBERGER, JACOB   70y 7m 1d
    28 Oct 1809 - 28 May 1880

THOMAS, ELIZABETH P.   79y
    daughter of Isaac and Mary Schlighter
    8 Apr 1815 - 11 Oct 1824

THOMAS, ELI H.   50y 20d
    19 Jan 1813 - 11 Feb 1863

[field stone -- nothing legible]

UNGERCH, DAVID   69y 2m 28d
    23 Feb 1811 - 21 May 1880

UNGERCH, ELIZABETH   78y 3d
    30 Jun 1815 - 3 Jul 1893

HENDRICKS, SOPHIA   36y 10m 27d
    daughter of Abraham S. and Catherine
    Hendricks
    15 Dec 1876 - 12 Nov 1900

LANDES, HENRY   10y 2m 21d
    son of Ephraim and Catharine Landes
    23 Aug 1853 - 13 Nov 1865

LANDES, JOHN R.   12y 4m 21d
    son of Ephraim and Catharine Landes
    22 Mar 1862 - 12 Aug 1874

LANDES, EPHRAIM   76y 9m 20d
    13 Dec 1824 - 3 Oct 1901

LANDES, CATHARINE   83y 3m 8d
    wife of Ephraim Landes
    29 Jun 1828 - 7 Oct 1911

KULP, JOHN
    twin son of Henry and Fannie Kulp
    17 Feb 1875

KULP, AARON
    twin son of Henry and Fannie Kulp
    17 Feb 1875

KULP, ELIZABETH A.   7m 8d
    10 Feb 1809 - 12 Sep 1919
    [dates as recorded]

KULP, SUSANNA   26y 2m 14d
    wife of Henry Kulp
    26 May 1846 - 3 Aug 1872

KULP, HENRY M.   81y 1m 27d
    12 Sep 1842 - 9 Nov 1923

KULP, FANNIE   51y 7m 7d
    wife of Henry Kulp
    daughter of Moses and Mary Kulp
    21 Aug 1845 - 28 Mar 1897

MOYER, CHRISTIAN S.   76y 3m 7d
    14 Nov 1809 - 21 Feb 1886

MOYER, MARY   88y 10m 1d
    wife of Christian S. Moyer
    18 Jul 1815 - 19 May 1904

MOYER, D. SIMON S.
    18 Nov 1806 - 10 Jul 1890

MOYER, EMMA   33y 7m 10d
    wife of Dr. Simon S. Moyer
    21 May 1868 - 31 Dec 1901

BLOOMING GLEN MENNONITE CEMETERY (Old Section)

Row 37 continued:

BARNABY, LYDIA   27y 1m 2d
    wife of William Barnaby
    19 Mar 1866 - 21 Apr 1893

[space]

KOCH, HENRY H.
    1 Aug 1873 - 7 Nov 1938

Row 38

OBERHOLZER, ELIZABETH   70y 25d
    wife of Isaac Oberholzer
    died 26 Apr 1891

OBERHOLZER, ISAAC   72y 9m 17d
    6 Dec 1887

[two spaces]

KRATZ, JACOB   8y 8m 20d
    3 Jun 1814 - 23 Feb 1903
    [as recorded]

PROCTOR, THOMAS   77y 7m 24d
    11 Feb 1784 - 6 Oct 1861

PROCTOR, CATHARINE   77y 1m 14d
    wife of Thomas Proctor
    27 Apr 1793 - 11 Jun 1870

[two spaces]

MOYER, SUSANNA   62y 7m 23d
    13 May 1832 - 6 Jan 1895

MOYER, ABRAHAM H.   64y 6m 28d
    28 May 1825 - 26 Dec 1889

MOYER, SUSANNA
    died 16 Aug 1874

MOYER, EMMA   8m 7d
    22 Jun 1867 - 29 Feb 1868

MOYER, HENRY   1y 5m 9d
    21 Mar 1861 - 2 Sep 1862

MOYER, CHRISTIAN   1y 6m 13d
    30 Sep 1856 - 11 Apr 1858

FRETZ, ABRAHAM,   80y 6m 7d
    12 Jan 1794 - 19 Jul 1874

FRETZ, SUSANNA   53y 1m 11d
    died 10 Sep 1853

ROSENBERGER, HEINRICH M.   23y 11m 22d
    son of Joseph and Catharine
    Rosenberger
    9 Feb 1826 - 31 Jan 1850

HENDRICKS, JOSEPH   80y 3m 4d
    23 Jul 1804 - 27 Oct 1884

HENDRICKS, ELIZABETH   62y 9m 16d
    8 Apr 1809 - 24 Jan 1872

HENDRICKS, MARIA   1y 4m 9d
    died _____ 1811 [1841?]
    [stone has more, illegible words]

HENDRICKS, SUSANNA   8 years
    died 11 Sep 1886

HENDRICKS, SUSANNA   1y 5m 12d
    died 19 Mar 1835

KRATZ, MARIA   66y 4m 23d
    18 [May?] 1800 - 11 Oct 1866

KRATZ, WILLIAM   [10y?] 7m 2d
    [16 Mar 1851|1854?]

B. K.   3 days
    died 1833

KRATZ, WILLIAM P.   9m 28d
    son of V. and S. Kratz
    died 16 Mar 1859

[Field stone -- no marks visible]

HUNSPERGERIN, ANNA   1826
    [field stone]

HUNSBERGER, JOSEPH M.
    [field stone -- no dates]

HUNSBERGER, VERONICA   2y 7m
    [field stone -- no dates]

HUNSBERGER, LYDIA A.   9y 1m
    1 Nov 1853 - 24 Mar 1863

[space]

HUNSICKER, LEANNA   14m 23d
    [no dates on stone]

HUNSICKER, LEA   6m 26d
    [no dates on stone]

HUNSICKER, LYDIA   5y 1m 6d
    [no dates onstone]

HUNSBERGER, ELMER E.   10y 6m 14d
    son of John M. and Barbara
    Hunsberger   died 6 Jul 1878

MOYER, BARBARA   38y 8m 7d
    wife of Jacob H. Moyer
    26 Jun 1838 - 3 Mar 1875

HUNSBERGER, JOHN M.   40y 2m 21d
    14 Dec 1830 - 4 Mar 1871

Row 38 continued:

HUNSBERGER, ENOS   3m 1d
    son of John and Barbara Hunsberger
    28 Apr 1864 - 29 Jul 1864

HUNSBERGER, EMMA   1y 24d
    daughter of John and Barbara
    Hunsberger
    27 Mar 1862 - 21 Apr 1863

HUNSBERGER, MARY JANE   2y 6m 23d
    daughter of John and Barbara
    Hunsberger
    26 Aug 1860 - 19 Mar 1863

[stone with top missing]

HUNSBERGER, ABRM K.   54y 5m 22d
    father
    1 Mar 1811 - 23 Aug 1865

HUNSBERGER, MARY   82y 2m 12d
    3 Dec 1812 - 15 Feb 1895

HUNSBERGER, ISAIAH M.   27y 1m 26d
    5 Apr 1850 - 31 May 1877

J. M. P.

HUNSBERGER, ENOS   60y 7m 22d
    1 Sep 1805 - 24 Apr 1866

HUNSBERGER, MARY   68y 4d
    wife of Enos Hunsberger
    28 Sep 1810 - 2 Oct 1878

HUNSBERGER, ABRAHAM M.   40y 3m 27d
    3 Mar 1837 - 30 Jun 1877

HUNSBERGER, MAHLON M.   53y 10m 22d
    22 Feb 1835 - 14 Jan 1880

HUNSBERGER, ANNA MARY
    daughter of M. and Elizabeth
    Hunsberger
    7 Apr 1865 - 20 Dec 1867

HUNSBERGER, ELIZABETH   73y 11d
    born Hunsberger
    24 Jan 1844 - 5 Feb 1917

DETWEILER, ANNIE A.   62y 6m 29d
    wife of Henry K. Detweiler
    1 Sep 1850 - 29 Mar 1913

DETWEILER, HENRY K.   81y 9m 20d
    father
    16 Nov 1847 - 6 Jul 1929

DETWEILER, DANIEL
    infant son of Henry and Annie
    Detweiler [no dates given]

DETWEILER, MARY   died 20 Mar 1884
    daughter of Henry and Annie Detweiler

DETWEILER, SAMUEL   died 30 Mar 1885
    son of Henry and Annie Detweiler

Row 39

LOUX, SAMUEL F.   76y 5m 17d
    20 Aug 1825 - 7 Feb 1902

LOUX, SAMUEL
    24 May 1863   9 months 12 days
    son of J. and R. Loux

LOUX, ISAAC   5 months
    son of J. and R. LOUX
    died 12 May 1869

LOUX, MARIA   5y 8m
    daughter of Jacob and Rachal Loux
    9 Mar 1858

LOUX, RACHAEL   56y 9m
    28 Aug 1822 - 4 Jun 1879
    wife of Jacob Loux

LOUX, JACOB   69y 4m 11d
    7 Feb 1817 - 18 Jun 1886

DETWEILER, JACOB   60y 1m 26d
    born 30 Oct 1839 - 26 Dec 1873
    married 6 Oct 1839 to
    BARBARA BERGEY
    married for his second wife
    on 8 Mar 1859
    ELIZABETH BENNER

DETWEILER, LIZZIE   10m 17d
    1 Sep 1862

DETWEILER, BARBARA   38y 6m 18d
    wife of Jacob Detweiler
    6 Sep 1857

SCHLICHTER, MARY   79y 6d
    5 Sep 1793 - 11 Sep 1869

SCHLICHTER, ISAAC   66y 2m 21d
    29 Jun 1781 - 23 feb 1851
    [dates as recorded from stone]

[approximately 9 spaces]

M. K.

[space]

HUCH, CAROLINN   12y 1d
    1834
    [stone difficult to read]

HOCK, MARIA   61y 1m
    wife of John Hock
    21 Jul 1797 - 15 Dec 1858

HIGH, JOHN   78y
    20 Sep 1795 - 20 May 1874

BLOOMING GLEN MENNONITE CEMETERY (Old Section)

Row 39 continued:

[two spaces]

[BECHTEL?], JACOB
? Aug 1828 - 8 Apr 1829
[difficult to read]

[space]

I & B   1828
[field stone]

[two spaces]

[Bechtel?], JOHN
13 Sep 1834 - 13 Apr 1836

HALDEMAN, JOEL A.   4y 6m 19d
31 Aug 1861

ALLABOUGH, JOHN   10y 4m 18d
27 May 1845

[three spaces]

HOCK, JACOB   26y 5m 13d
29 Aug 1863

[five spaces]

HUNSBERGER, ISAAC S.   26y 7m 7d
13 Nov 1842 - [23 or 29?] Jun 1869

P. K.

HUNSBERGER, JOHN   61y 3m 11d
19 May 1869

PROCTOR, MARY   19y 9m 17d
  daughter of John and Hannah Proctor
  17 Dec 1845 - 4 Oct 1865

PROCTOR, HANNAH   62y 3m 20d
  wife of John M. Proctor
  4 Sep 1814 - 24 Dec 1876

PROCTOR, JOHN M.   80y 9m
  4 Aug 1819 - 4 May 1900

[three spaces]

E. M. M.

[small blank field stone]

LANDIS, EDWARD M.   1875 - 1883
  brother

LANDIS, ABRAHAM   1823 - 1886
  father

LANDIS, ELIZABETH M.   1837 - 1889
  mother

[three spaces]

CRESSMAN, PAUL
  son of Wm. H. and Katie Cressman
  24 Apr 1907 - 11 Sep 1907

ANGENEY, INFANT SON
  son of J. K. and Catherine Angeney
  [no dates]

ANGENEY, ANNA S.   9m 9d
  daughter of J. K. and Catharine
  Angeney
  27 Oct 1888 - 6 Aug 1889

ANGENEY, DAVID S.   25y 2d
  son of J. and Catharine Angeney
  10 Mar 1879 - 12 Mar 1904

HENDRICKS, CATHARINE D. 1835 - 1925
  wife of Abraham S. Hendricks

HENDRICKS, ABRAHAM S.   66y 11m 4d
  27 Jan 1837 - 1 Jan 1904

Row 40

HALDEMAN, DANIEL A.   4m 15d
  17 Mar 1867 - 1 Aug 1867

HALDEMAN, HIRAM A.
  7y 3m 10d
  8 Dec 1861

HALDEMAN, WILLIAM A.   6y 2m 1d
  15 Dec 1861

HALDEMAN, WINFIELD S.   2y 6m 18d
  17 Dec 18[61?]

HALDEMAN, ABRAHAM   6m 26d
  15 Aug 18[6?]

HAUFMAN, SUSANNA
  wife of Johannes   64y 10m 15d
  12 Oct 1817 - 27 Aug 1882

HAUFMAN, JOHANNES   50y 9m 13d
  1 Jun 1812 - 21 Mar 1863

ANGELMOYER, EMMA   11y 10m 15d
  1862

HAUFMAN, SUSANNA   15d
  died 1859

ANGELMEYER, MARIA   71y 1m
  wife of Heinrich Angelmeyer
  9 Jan 1788 - 9 Feb 1859

ANGELMÄUER, HEINRICH   79y 2m 19d
  1 Jan 1786 - 23 Mar 1865

ANGLEMEYER, ELIZABETH   28y 9m 10d
  6 Jun 1831 - 25 Mar 1860

ANGLEMEYER, JAMES   1m 6d
  [21 or 2?] Aug 1860

ANGLEMOYER, JACOB M.   1y 7m 29d
  son of Henry and Anna Anglemoyer
  died 10 Oct 1879

Row 40 continued:

ANGLEMOYER, LIZZIE M.　　　2y 8m 18d
　　daughter of Henry and Anna Anglemoyer
　　28 May 18[80?] - 16 Aug 18[83?]

YODER, PETER Y.　　　　　　59y 2m 1d
　　21 Aug 1843 - 22 Oct 1902

YODER, MARY ANN　　　　　　28y 10d
　　wife of Peter Yoder
　　died 12 Oct 1877 [dates as recorded]

YODER, HANNAH M.　　　　　19y 4m 13d
　　daughter of Peter and Mary Ann Yoder
　　8 Apr 1872 - 21 Aug 1891

HUNSBERGER, ANNA　　　　　83y 7m 29d
　　4 Oct 1818 - 3 Jun 1902

HUNSBERGER, ESTER　　　　77y 10m 10d
　　9 Jan 1817 - 19 Nov 1891

HUNSBERGER, ANNA　　　　　69y 8m 6d
　　8 Jan 1794 - 14 Sep 1883

HUNSBERGER, ABRAHAM　　　73y 3m 26d
　　12 Oct 1786 - 8 Feb 1860

HUNSBERGER, REMANDES　　13y 8m 28d
　　13 Apr 1849 - 31 Dec 1862

HUNSBERGER, MARTIN　　　　31y 9m 2d
　　27 Oct 1852

HUNSBERGER, ABRM F.　　　67y 7m 16d
　　19 Nov 1831 - 5 Jul 1898

ANGENY, CATHARINE S.　　　87y 2m 25d
　　wife of Abrm F. Hunsberger
　　22 May 1835 - 17 Aug 1922
[HUNSBERGER, CATHARINE S.]

KOLB, MARIA　　　　　　　　78y 8m
　　1850

KOLB, ISAAC　　　　　　　　1847

KOLB, ELIZABETH　　　　　26y 10m 1d
　　10 Apr 1839 - 11 Feb 1866

KULB, ISAAC　　　　　　　　75y
　　22 Mar 1762 - 9 Aug 185[5?]

KOLB, ISAAC　　　　　　　　1836

KOLB, MARIA　　　　　　　　1836

I. D.　　　　　　　　　　　1834
　　[field stone]

HAGEY, ELIZABETH　　　　　94y 1m 28d
　　born Gerhart
　　23 Apr 1777 - 21 Jun 1873

HAGEY, JACOB　　　　　　　59y 4m 17d
　　24 Apr 1775 - 11 Sep 1834

[broken field stone -- no legible inscriptions]

SILFUSS, ELIZABETH　　　　84y 5m 20d
　　1 Dec 1778 - 21 May 1863

MEYERS, CATHARINE　　　　30y 8m 19d
　　26 Jun 1837 - 11 Mar 1868

HUNSBURGER, HENERY　　　　80y 5m 28d
　　26 Feb 1809 - 24 Jul 1889

HUNSBERGER, MARIA　　　　85y 5m 23d
　　wife of Jacob Hunsberger
　　9 Apr 1800 - 2 Oct 1885

HUNSBERGER, JACOB　　　　89y 9m 21d
　　8 Jun 1788 - 29 Mar 1878

HUNSBERGER, HENRY M.　　　41y 4m 7d
　　6 Nov 1833

HUNSBERGER, ANNA　　　　　25y 28d
　　21 Jan 1838 - 18 Feb 1863

HUNSBERGER, BARBARA W.　　1877 - 1962
HUNSBERGER, JACOB A.　　　1867 - 1946
HUNSBERGER, CATHARINE H.　1860 - 1912
[above three on same stone]

MEYERS, ISAAC　　　　　　　72y 8m 7d
　　18 Feb 1802 - 25 Oct 1874

MEYERS, HANNA　　　　　　　83y 24d
　　wife of Isaac Meyers
　　7 Feb 1807 - 1 Mar 1890

[space]

FRETZ, CHRISTIAN　　　　　44y 10m
　　5 Nov 1821 - 5 Sep 1866

FRETZ, MARIA　　　　　　　86y 11m 7d
　　wife of Christian Fretz
　　11 Jun 1826 - 18 May 1913

FRETZ, ELIZABETH　　　　　81y 8m 15d
　　wife of Christian Fretz, Sr.
　　5 Dec 1793 - 20 Aug 1875

[II IFAI. F?] [Hifai?]　　A.D. 1861
　　[small worn and broken stone]

FRETZ, ALLEN C.　　　　　　7y 5d
　　son of Jacob M. and Lizzie Fretz
　　24 Aug 1889 - 29 Aug 1896

[two spaces]

RENNER, CATHARINE H.
　　daughter of Wm. and Sarah Renner
　　20 Apr 1884

[four spaces]

BISHOP, JACOB　　　　　　　75y 5d
　　30 Mar 1890

BLOOMING GLEN MENNONITE CEMETERY (Old Section)

Row 40 continued:

BISHOP, ELIZABETH   88y 5m 4d
    wife of Jacob Bishop
    died 6 Aug 1913

[two spaces]

ANGENEY, JACOB K.   68y 8m 29d
    father
    11 Sep 1845 - 10 Aug 1913

ANGENEY, CATHRYN F.   73y 2m 23d
    wife of Jacob K. Angeney
    20 Dec 1848 - 23 Mar 1922

Row 41

HUNSBERGER, MARIA   47y 5m 11d
    23 Oct 1823 - 4 Apr 1871

HUNSBERGER, JACOB   2m 27d
    26 Aug 1860

HUNSBERGER, JACOB   77y 3m 5d
    1 Mar 1819 - 6 Jun 1896

[Bottom half of stone only]

JOHNSON, ABRAHAM   1y 9m 21d
    son of Joseph and Hannah Johnson
    died 19 Dec 1862

JOHNSON, HEINRICH   4m 4d
    died 7 Sep 1859

JOHNSON, SALOME   22y 9m 19d
    died 25 May 1859

HOCH, ANNA   63y 1m 11d
    22 Jul 1797 - 2 Sep 1860

HIGH, JACOB   86y 11m 2d
    30 Oct 1785 - 1 Oct 1872

KRATZ, SIMEON   58y 3m 11d
    5 Jun 1865

KRATZ, CATHERINE   93y 3m 26d
    wife of Simeon Kratz
    3 Dec 1813 - 29 Mar 1907

[space]

MOYER, ENOS O.   21y 10m 7d
    12 Mar 1851 - 19 Feb 1873

BUTTON, MARY ANN   4y 8m 1d
    daughter of John and Elizabeth
    Button
    2 Mar 1857 - 3 Nov 1861

KULP, HENRY M.   76y 1m 21d
    11 May 1836 - 2 Jul 1912

KULP, MARY ANN   81y 9m 9d
    wife of Henry M. Kulp
    12 Jun 1834 - 21 Mar 1916

MOYER, HENRY B.   74y 11m 5d
    21 May 1818 - 26 Apr 1882

MIRER, MARIA   59y 6m 25d
    wife of Heinrick B. Mirer
    7 Jun 1821 - 2 Jan 1881

MEYER, MARIA ANNA   3y 2m 23d
    died 21 Apr 1857

ANGELMEYER, JOSEPH   16 days
    [no other dates]

ANGELMEYER, MARIA ANNA   10 days
    [no other dates]

KOLB, ENOS   3y 16d
    26 Sep 1849 - 14 Oct 1852

KOLB, CHRISTIAN   9y 11d
    2 Oct 1843 - 21 Sep 1852

BUTTON, HEINRICH   39y 17d
    20 Nov 1815 - 7 Dec 1854

MOYER, HANNAH   95y 4m 8d
    wife of Samuel B. Moyer
    died 9 May 1914

MOYER, SAMUEL B.   37y 9m
    died 7 Nov 1852

MOYER, ISAAC   11y 5m 25d
    died 2 Jun 1855

MOYER, SARAH   34d
    1847

RICKERT, ABRAHAM   5m 27d
    10 Feb 1860 - [??] Aug 1860
    [data as recorded from stone]

HIGH, ANNA   77y 5m 24d
    wife of Jacob H. High
    19 Apr 1819 - 13 Oct 1896

HIGH, JACOB H.   80y 9m 19d
    30 Oct 1819 - 18 Aug 1900

HAUFMAN, C.   15 days
    26 Apr 1856

ANGELMEYER, J.   6m 1d
    [no dates given on stone]

ANGELMEIER, CATHARINA   14y 9m 2d
    28 Jan 1929 - 9 Oct 1843

HAUFMAN, J.   1851
    [no other data on stone]

MOYER, MARY O.   79y 4m 4d
    wife of Jacob H. Moyer
    10 Oct 1843 - 14 Feb 1923

MOYER, JACOB H.   70y 10m 17d
    10 Sep 1835 - 27 Jul 1906

Row 41 continued:

MOYER, MAGDALENA   32y 5m 21d
    wife of Jacob H. Moyer
    29 Dec 1839 - 20 Jun 1872

MOYER, MARY MALINDA   1y 9d
    daughter of Jacob H. and Magdalena
    Moyer
    13 Jul 1864 - 22 Jul 1865

[space]

LOUX, HENRY E.   1y 2m 18d
    22 Apr 1863

LOUX, WILLIAM M.   3y 5m 11d
    died 3 Mar 1863

LOUX, OLIVER S.
LOUX, ALFRED H.
    both died 8 mar 1863
    both aged 5y 6m
    [as on stone -- both names and one
    set of dates]

LOUX, ABRAHAM F.   6y 9m 21d
    3 Mar 1863

LOUX, LEVI   28y 2m 13d
    died 18 Mar 1863

MORRIS, BARBARA   60y 3m 11d
    wife of Samuel T. Morris
    5 Apr 1834 - 19 Jul 1894

MOYER, ABRAHAM C.   36y 11m
    26 Sep 1837 - 26 Aug 1874

MOYER, ANNIE   81y 7m 26d
    16 Feb 1842 - 12 Oct 1923

YODER, WILMER L.   3m 20d
    son of Henry L. and Lizzie Yoder
    13 Jun 1918 - 12 Oct 1918

YODER, JACOB L.   1m 10d
    son of Henry M. and Lizzie S. Yoder
    died 5 Apr 1915

WISMER, SALLIE   3y 3m 10d
    daughter of Joel and Mary Wismer
    [no dates recorded]

WISMER, MARY   15y 10m 27d
    [no dates recorded]

[three spaces]

MOYER, SALLIE E.   76 years
    died 11 Jun 1848

RUSH, ANNIE M.   72y 8m 2d
    wife of Remandus Rush
    8 Aug 1846 - 10 Apr 1919

CHARLES, OLIVER H.   38y 10m 11d
    14 Jul 1851 - 25 May 1890

[space]

DETWEILER, DAVID R.   32 years
    1886 - 1918
DETWEILER, SADIE   his wife   32 years
    1886 - 1918
[above two on same stone]

KELLER, FRANK
    22 Apr 1832 - 21 Aug 1906
KELLER, MARIA G.
    11 Nov 1832 - 23 Aug 1913

S. S.   [No other information on stone.]

Row 42

KROUT, BARBARA   76y 3m 12d
    29 Aug 1827 - 11 Dec 1903

ANDREWS, AARON   37y 6m 15d
    29 Oct 1823 - 13 Aug 1861

ROSENBERGER, ALLEN G.   8m 29d
    son of Jacob and Catharina Rosenberger
    24 Feb 1860

ROSENBERGER, JACOB M.   22y 4m 7d
    son of Jacob and Catharina Rosenberger
    21 May 1837 - 28 Sep 1859

ROSENBERGER, CATHARINA   65y 11m 29d
    wife of Jacob Rosenberger
    29 Aug 1796 - 27 Aug 1862

ROSENBERGER, JOSEPH W.   74y 4m 13d
    20 Mar 1801 - 3 Aug 1875

BERGEY, ELIZABETH   56y 9m 29d
    wife of Nathan Bergey
    7 Jun 1839 - 6 Apr 1896

BERGEY, MARY MAGDALENA   3y 5m 15d
    daughter of Nathan and Elizabeth
    Bergey
    25 Dec 1865 - 9 Jun 1869

ROSENBERGER, ERWIN G.   3y 5m 29d
    son of J. M. and Anna Rosenberger
    20 May 1863

ROSENBERGER, CHARLES F.   5y 6m 7d
    son of J. M. and Anna Rosenberger
    died 23 May 1863

[Rucker?], JACOB   8y [6?]m 10d
    7 [Mar or May?] 1839

RUCKER, SUSANNA   17y 1m 19d
    25 Mar 1848 - [1 or 4?] Aug 1865

BLOOMING GLEN MENNONITE CEMETERY (Old Section)

Row 42 continued:

HENDRICKS, JOHN 86y 9m 17d
   20 Dec 1764 - 7 Oct 1881

HENDRICKS, MARIA 61y 1m 13d
   1 Feb 1861 [or 18 Feb ?]

HENDRICKS, HANNAH 1y 26d
   8 Mar 18[38 or 58?]

HENDRICKS, JACOB 32y 7m 23d
   died 28 Dec 1837

HENDRICKS, ANNA 70y 3m
   wife of Jacob A. Hendricks
   and wife of Reuben A. Yoder
   25 Jan 1830 - 25 Apr [1900?]
   [This stone is broken and
    partly buried]
[YODER, ANNA HENDRICKS]

MYERS, SALOME 11y 1m 28d
   daughter of Samuel W. and Salome
   Myers
   died 15 Oct 18[02?]

MYERS, MARY
   daughter of Samuel and Salome Myers
   died 22 Oct 1845

GEORGE, SUSANNA
   daughter of Jacob and Sophia George
   2 Sep 1852 - 25 Jul 1854

RICKERT, ENOS 3y 2m 1d
   [?] 185[9?] - 18??

[Rickert?], HANNAH 1y 2m
   1? [?] 184[?]

RICKERT, CATHARINA 2y 1m 29d
   died 20 Feb 1858

WATZ, JOHN [61?]y 4m 26d
   died 16 Feb 1862

WATZ, MAGDALENA
   died 28 Jul 1849

RICKERT, ISAAC 34y 7m 27d
   9 May 1797 - 5 Jun 1832

L. Y.
   [field stone]

B. R. 1832
   [field stone]

H. L.
   [field stone]

RICKERT, L[INN?] 8y ?m 10d
   daughter of [?] Rickert

RICKERT, ELIZABETH 47y 10m 12d
   wife of Henry Rickert
   6 Feb 1833 - 18 Dec 1880

RICKERT, HENRY R. 79y 8m 8d
   father
   22 Dec 1829 - 25 Mar 1909

RICKERT, CATHERINE 87y 11m 3d
   wife of Abraham Rickert
   2 Dec 1798 - 5 May 1886

RICKERT, ABRAHAM 83y 2m
   13 Oct 1785 - 13 Oct 1868

HUNSBERGER, MILTON M.
   9 Mar 1860 - 13 Oct 1863

HUNSBERGER, ABRAM [K.?]
   29 Aug 1834 - 7 Oct 1863

HUNSBERGER, SARAH 56y 1d
   wife of Abraham Hunsberger
   12 Oct 1833 - 13 Oct 1890

[space]

HENDRICKS, BENJAMIN D.
   8 Feb 1818 - 3 Nov 1898

HENDRICKS, ELIZABETH 65y 3m 29d
   wife of Benj. D. Hendricks
   1 Jan 1812 - 30 Apr 1877

[space]

YODER, HENRY M. 1888 - 1945
   father
YODER, LIZZIE S. 1881 - 1919
   mother
   [above two on same stone]

FRETZ, ERNEST Y.
   10 Aug 1918 - 18 Nov 1918
FRETZ, PAUL Y.
   22 Aug 1924 - 30 Sep 1824
FRETZ, WILBUR Y.
   10 Jul 1926 - 10 May 1930
   All children of William D. and
   Hannah M. Fretz
   [above three on same stone]

FRETZ, ELIZABETH
   daughter of Wm. D. and Hannah Fretz
   25 Jun 1912 - 5 Sep 1913

HUNSBERGER, JOHN 11y 8m 19d
   son of Simeon and Eliz Hunsberger
   died 6 Mar 1883

HUNSBERGER, SUSAN 11y 10m 22d
   Daughter of Simeon and Eliz
   Hunsberger   died 14 May 1883

HUNSBERGER, ELIZABETH H. 70y 4m 13d
   wife of Simeon Hunsberger
   15 Dec 1838 - 29 Apr 1909

Row 42 continued:

HUNSBERGER, SIMEON   78y 9m 16d
    26 Nov 1836 - 12 Sep 1915

[two spaces]

Row 43

FUNK, SAMUEL   76y 6m 25d
    14 Apr 1795 - 10 Nov 1871

FUNK, EDITH   73y 3m 12d
    died 25 Mar 1860

FUNK, SUSANNA
    27 Sep 1800

FUNK, SAMUEL
    son of John and Mary Funk
    11 Dec 1861

CASSEL, SAMUEL K.   64y 7m 18d
    20 Jul 1820 - 18 Mar 1891

CASSEL, ELIZABETH   59y 5m 11d
    wife of Samuel K. Cassel
    20 Aug 1837 - 1 Feb 1897

CASSEL, ALVIN   6m 6d
    son of S. K. and E. Cassel
    15 Mar 1877 - 2 Sep 1877

CASSEL, MARY ANN   6y 1m 19d
    daughter of S. K. and E. Cassel
    28 Jan 1871 - 11 Jun 1877

CASSELL, ELIZABETH   10m 25d
    daughter of S. K. and E. Cassell
    24 Sep 1867 - 19 Aug 1868

CASSEL, JOSEPH   7m 15d
    son of S. K. and E. Cassel
    12 Jan 1865 - 27 Aug 1865

CASSEL, ALLEN   5y
    son of Samuel and Elizabeth Cassel
    18 Jan 1857 - 12 Sep 1862

CASSEL, WILEMINA   1y 6m 11d
    daughter of Samuel and Elizabeth
    Cassel
    26 Jun 1860 - 7 Jan 1862

MOYER, EMMA   77y 4m 18d
    22 Feb 1781 - 12 Jul 1858

[four spaces]

FRETZ, ELIZABETH
    2 Jun 1790 [birth date]

FRETZ, JACOB   71y 5m 7d
    25 Feb 1848

FRETZ, SUSANNAH   [53 or 33?]y 10m 12d
    died 20 Feb 1848

FRETZ, ELI   [33y 3d?]
    2 Jan 181? - 11 Jan 18[73?]

FRETZ, ELIZABETH H.   84y 5m 4d
    23 Nov 1823 - 27 Apr 1908

[illegible stone]

[seven spaces]

J. S.

YEAKEL, SAMUEL S.   72y 9m 8d
    20 Sep 1807 - 28 Jun 1880

YEAKEL, ANNA   70y 10m 25d
    wife of Saml. Yeakel
    10 Sep 1810 - 5 Aug 1881

[four spaces]

[no name]   A.D. 1819
[field stone]

E. D.   [1789 ?]
[field stone]

SPRINGER, ELIZABETH   17y 1m 18d
    died 15 Nov 1863

[no name]   A D 9 Jun 1867
[field stone]

HIGH, CATHARINE W.   31y 11m 15d
    daughter of Jacob high
    20 Sep 1832 - 10 Sep 1864

LANDES, BARBARA   74y 7m 7d
    wife of Jacob Landes
    14 Sep 1806 - 21 Apr 1881

LANDIS, JACOB S.   83y 7m 24d
    19 May 1817 - 13 Jan 1901

MYERS, SALOMA   72y 1d
    wife of Samuel W. Myers
    30 Jan 1820 - 31 Jan 1892

MYERS, SAMUEL W.   72y 4m
    23 Sep 1819 - 23 Jan 1832

MYERS, ELIZABETH   71y 6m 1d
    wife of Jacob H. Myers
    21 Jan 1850 - 22 Jul 1921

MYERS, SARAH   25y 5m 10d
    wife of Jacob H. Myers
    6 Apr 1845 - 16 Oct 1870

MYERS, JACOB H.   94y 1m 27d
    16 Oct 1843 - 13 Dec 1837

[two spaces]

BLOOMING GLEN MENNONITE CEMETERY (Old Section)   47

Row 43 continued:

DERSTINE, AMANDA   37y 5m 14d
    wife of Henry Derstine
    daughter of Henry and Susan Harwick
    died 26 May 1884

SPRINGER, JESSE   80y 1m 14d
    father
    21 May 18[00?] - 5 Jul 1889

SPRINGER, HANNAH   82y 7m 15d
    mother, wife of Jesse Springer
    22 Sep 1808 - 7 May 1891

SPRINGER, ABRAM D.   59y 5m 17d
    husband
    16 Dec 1842 - 2 Jun 1902

Row 44

HIGH, ADDISON   1m 8d
    died 7 May 186[6?]

HIGH, JOHN   1m 5d
    died 2 Dec 186[0 or 8?]

HIGH, SAMMUEL   2m 11d
    died 11 May 186[1|4|7?]

HIGH, ELIZABETH   25y 4m 5d
    29 Aug 1835 - 3 Jan 1866

STOVER, GIDEON S.   62y 3m
    1 Mar 1838 - 1 Jun 1900

STOVER, SARAH   70y 4m 2d
    wife of Gideon S. Stover
    25 Dec 1833 - 27 Apr 1904

STOVER, IDA   15 days
    daughter of Gideon and Sarah Stover
    died 30 Apr 1874

STOVER, REUBEN D.   9y 4m 26d
    son of Gideon and Sarah Stover
    died 21 Apr 1873

STOVER, HANNAH D.   1y 7m 20d
    daughter of Gideon and Sarah Stover
    22 Jan 1862 - 21 Sep 1863

FLUCK, MARY ANN   died 1857

FLUCK, HIRAM   1y 2m 21d
    [no other dates]

[field stone -- nothing legible]

MOYER, ELIZABETH   17y 10m 16d
    died 23 Apr 1838

MOYER, ISAIAH   4y 10m 2d
    7 Sep 1849

MOYER, LEVI   13 days
    died 2 Sep 186[4|1?]

MOYER, MALON   7m ?
    died 2 Dec 1852

BECHTEL, SUSANNA   38y 8d
    died 31 Mar 1859

BECHTEL, CATHARINA   75y 1m
    15 Nov 1862

[BECHTEL?], ISAAC   56y 18d
    17 Jul [1847?]
    [dates worn off -- 1847 from
    Lizzie Fretz's transcription]

[space]

FLUCK, ENOS G.   1866 - 1944
FLUCK, LYDIA M.   1869 - 1965?
FLUCK, ARLO   1908 - 1916
    [above three on same stone]

[space]

J. S.

YEAKEL, LOUIS   30 days
    son of Abraham and Sarah Yeakel
    8 Nov 1885 - 8 Dec 1885

MOYER, IRWIN G.
    son of Samuel K. and Missoura Moyer
    5 Feb 1887 - 24 Jun 1887

MOYER, HOWARD B.   7y 8m 10d
    son of Samuel and Missoura Moyer
    23 Aug 1884 - 13 May 1892

DETWEILER, SARAH   66y 4m 16d
    wife of Joseph A. Detweiler
    9 Jun 1838 - 25 Oct 1901

DETWEILER, JOSEPH A.   72y 8m 18d
    24 Oct 1838 - 12 Jul 19[03?]

DETWEILER, WILLIAM HENRY 8m 16d
    son of Joseph and Sarah Detweiler
    8 Apr 1870 - 13 Dec 1878

GEORGE, MARTIN   68y 8m 18d
    31 Mar 1803 - 18 Dec 18[71?]

GEORGE, MARY
    wife of Martin George
    [stone broken and buried]

FRETZ, MARY   48y 5m 15d
    ?   ? 1832 - 18 Jul 1880
    [stone broken and buried]

FRETZ, WILLIAM M.
    21 Nov 1826 - 1? May 18[8? or 36?]

BUCKS COUNTY TOMBSTONE INSCRIPTIONS - HILLTOWN TOWNSHIP

Row 44 continued:

FRETZ, MARIA   55y 11m 22d
    mother, wife of William H. Fretz
    15 Feb 1840 - 7 Feb 1896

FRETZ, NOAH   76y 2m
    20 Nov 1820 - 20 Jan 1900

FRETZ, MARY   67y 9m 19d
    wife of Noah Fretz
    23 Dec 1846 - 12 Oct 19??

FRETZ, MARY E.   23y 10m 15d
    sister
    16 Jul 1876 - 1 jun 1900

[three spaces]

Row 45

RUTH, LEAH   52y 6m
    6 Apr 1862

GODSHALL, MARY   80y 2m 13d
    wife of Aaron Godshall
    12 May 1820 - 10 sep 1900

GODSHALL, AARON   65y 1m 1d
    28 Nov 1813 - 2 Mar 1879

DETWEILER, ELIZABETH   77y 19d
    wife of Joseph Detweiler
    14 Feb 1798 - 3 Feb 1875

DETWEILER, JOSEPH   63y 8m 5d
    26 Dec 1797 - 1 Jul 1861

GODSHALL, REUBEN   6y 2m 29d
    son of Aaron and Maria Godshall
    died 10 Feb 1857

[space]

KRABEHL, CATHARINE   66y 24d
    wife of Philip Krabehl
    22 Sep 1822 - 16 Oct 1888

KRABEHL, PHILIP   63y 7m 11d
    14 Jun 1812 - 25 Jan 1876

KRABEHL, MARY   8m 17d
    28 Jan 1842 - 12 [Jan?] 1842

KRABEHL, MARGARET   4y 6m 7d
    30 ? 1858 - 8 Oct 1862

KRABEHL, JOHN   8y 1m 22d
    died 2 Oct 18[69?]

KRABEHL, HANNAH   11y 6m 9d
    17 Mar 1851 - 26 Sep 1862

PENNAPACKER, DANIEL   1y 9m 24d
    son of Amos and [Eliza?] Pennapacker
    12 Mar 1851 - 5 Jan 1853

[HESSE?], ANNA   74 years
    died 17 [Oct?] 1852
    [last name has five letters [HE?FE]

LICEY, HENRY   83y 1m 21d
    died 23 Feb 1861 [64?]

[two spaces]

SCHRAGER, MAGDALENA   60y 1m 2d
    wife of Jacob Schrager
    4 Dec 1814 - 6 Jan 1875

SCHRAUGER, JACOB   89y 10m 10d
    8 Jun 1811 - 18 Apr 1901

SCHRAUGER, JACOB, Jr.   52y 1m 12d
    31 Oct 1854 - 13 Dec 1906

HUNSBERGER, A. E.
    daughter of J.B. and S. M. Hunsberger
    died 23 Jun 1879

HUNSBERGER, [? six letters]
    daughter of J. B. and S. M. Hunsberger
    born and died 12 Apr 1880

[three spaces]

KRABEHL, CATHARINE   60y 11m 28d
    15 Feb 1851 - 14 Aug 1911

KRABEHL, HENRY   25y 2m 20d
    6 Nov 1863 - 26 Jan 1889

B. L.

GEHMAN, HANNAH   94y 1m 10d
    wife of Samuel D. Gehman
    11 Dec 1839 - 21 Jan 1934

GEHMAN, SAMUEL D.   84y 4m 11d
    8 Dec 1837 - 19 Apr 1922

BECHTEL, NOPHIAH   81y 2m 7d
    wife of Martin Bechtel
    11 Aug 1807 - 18 May 1889

BECHTEL, MARTIN   33y 2m 29d
    22 Jan 1797 - 14 Apr 1830

GEHMAN, MARY ANN   28y 10m 13d
    daughter of Samuel D. and Hannah
    Gehman
    5 May 1865 - 18 Mar 1894

HOFF, HENRY   1853 - 1911
HOFF, AMANDA   1855 - 1935
    [above two on same stone]

[space]

HAUFF, FANNIE S.   17d
    20 Dec 1881

HAUFF, CLARENCE S.   7d
    14 Apr 18[96?]

BLOOMING GLEN MENNONITE CEMETERY (Old Section)

Row 45 continued:

KLINE, CAROLINE   66y 4m 12d
    mother
    1 Apr 1856 - 13 Aug 1922

DERSTINE, HENRY F.   65y 8m 19d
    13 Mar 1843 - 2 Dec 1908

KLINE, HERMAN   78y 8m 13d
    father
    2 Apr 1849 - 15 Dec 1927

HAINES, JOHN F.   56y 3m 23d
    father
    13 Jun 1845 - 11 Oct 1901

HAINES, MATILDA   102y 3m 25d
    mother
    27 Dec 1831 - 22 Apr 1934

Row 46

HIGH, DAVID K.   75y 2m 4d
    3 Aug 183[2?] - 7 Oct 1908

HUNSBERGER, HENRY W.   52y 6m 11d
    13 Jul 1831 - 24 Jan 1882

HUNSBERGER, CATHARINE   26y 11m 20d
    wife of Henry W. Hunsberger
    16 Jul 1833 - 5 Jul 1860

HUNSICKER, MARIA   72y 6m 2d
    daughter of Jacob Hunsicker
    30 Dec 1799 - 1 Sep 1872

HUNSBERGER, ABRAHAM   72y 3m
    11 Jul 1795 - 11 Dec 1867

HÜNSICKER, ANNA   75y 10m 19d
    29 May 1795 - 31 Mar 1871

BERGE, JOSEPH   89y 9m 17d
    13 Mar 1791 - 30 Dec 1880

BERGE, ELIZABETH   ?y 8m 12d
    wife of Joseph Berge
    15[Aug?] 1789 - 11 J? [?]

BERGE, SUSANNA   47y 1m 25d
    Nov 1852

    [space]

BERGE, CATHARINA   22y 5m 13d
    Oct 1832

    [space]

HUNSICKER, SALLIE   1y 20d
    daughter of Isaac and Betty
    Hunsicker
    17 Jul 1870 - 11 Aug 1872

    [two spaces]

SPIEGELHATTER, JOHN S.   3y 11d
    son of John and Mary Spiegelhatter
    11 Aug 1883 - 22 Aug 1886

    [three spaces]

GODSHALL, SAMUEL   6m 19d
    son of John and [Elizabeth?]
    Godshall   died 20 Mar 1866

    [four spaces]

YEAKEL, HENRY M.   84y 9m 28d
    father
    17 Sept 1838 - 14 Jul 1921

YEAKEL, SARAH   72y 3m 21d
    mother
    21 Dec 1846 - 25 Mar 1916

M. B. F.

I. H.

    [four spaces]

SMITH, JOHN L.   1874 - 1929

GERHART, JAMES M.   67y 9m 26d
    30 Aug 1861 - 26 Jun 1929

GERHART, MARY ANN   73y 1m 25d
    wife of James Gerhart
    27 Jun 1848 - 22 Aug 1921

RICK, JOSEPH   80y 6d
    3 Jan 1833 - 9 Jan 1913
RICK, ROSA   [no dates]   75y
HOFF, ALICE S.   1883 - 1949

MOYER, IRENE   11m
    daughter of Arthur and Ada Moyer
    31 May 1909 - 8 May 1910

SCHRAUGER, CATHERINE   88y 3m 15d
    3 Apr 1846 - 18 Jul 1934

Row 47

DELP, GEORGE   35y 11m 3d
    30 Oct 1867

ALDERFER, CATHERINE   61y 9m 24d
    formerly Catherine Delp
    25 Apr 18[92?]

NUNNEMACHER, SOLOMON   1786 - 1861
NUNNEMACHER, ANNA   1781 - 1862
    nee Landis
    [above two on same stone]

[KRATZ?], SUSANNA   69y 3m? 8d
    12 May 1781 - 20 Aug 1833

OBERHOLZER, MARIA   71y 8m 3d
    ?8 Sep 1781 - 11 May 1853
    wife of Abraham Olberholzer

Row 47, continued:

BERGEY, MINERVA　　　　5y 1m 17d
　　daughter of Isaac and Mary Ann
　　Bergey
　　18 Sep 1880 - 5 Nov 1885

BERGEY, MARY ANN　　　71y 11m 15d
　　wife of Isaac Bergey
　　24 May 1837 - 9 May 1909

BERGEY, ISAAC　　　　　92y 5m 22d
　　5 Jul 1823 - 27 Dec 1915

[small stone with no inscription]

DETWEILER, CATHERINE
　　wife and mother
　　26 Dec 1861 - 18 Sep 1832

DETWEILER, HENRY G.
　　father
　　20 May 1861 - 9 Oct 1927
　　[above two on same stone]

WURSTER, WILLIAM
　　23 Jun 1884 - 27 Dec 1951
WURSTER, HARRIET F.
　　22 Feb 1884 - 8 Apr 1932
　　[above two on same stone]

MOYER, CLARENCE L.　　　1m 10d
　　son of Mr. and Mrs. Maynard F. Moyer
　　12 Jan - 2 Mar 1910

Row 48

BISHOP, ENOS　　　　　53y 5m 27d
　　1 Jul 1826 - 28 Dec 1879

BISHOP, MARY ANN　　　80y 1m 18d
　　wife of Enos Bishop
　　7 Dec 1827 - 25 Jan 1917

DELP, AMANDA　　　　　34y 1m 1d
　　wife of Samuel G. Delp
　　died   30 Mar 1880

DELP, SAMUEL G.　　　　father
　　9 Dec 1842 - 23 Jan 1890

DELP, SARAH　　　　　　mother
　　9 Feb 1848 - 11 May 1928

[four spaces]

FRETZ, LIZZIE D.
　　daughter of Noah and Mary
　　22 Aug 1882 - 23 Jan 1970

[two spaces]

FRETZ, WILLIAM D.
　　17 Jul 1879 - 17 Dec 1969
FRETZ, HANNAH M.
　　2 Mar 1882 - 19 Apr 1952
　　[above two on same stone]

HILL, JOHN A.　　　　　1884 - 1942
HILL, MARTHA R.　　　　1884 - 1958
　　[above two on same stone]

WENGER, ELIZABETH L.　　1887 - 1970

[two spaces]

Row 49

KRATZ, SARAH　　　　　31y 6m 2d
　　1 Feb 1831 - 3 Aug 1865

[space]

KRATZ, W. A.　　　　　2y 1m 6d
　　son of K. and S. Kratz
　　1861

KRATZ, T.　　　　　　　2y 1m 4d
　　son of K. and S. Kratz
　　1866

KRATZ, EMMA E.　　　　8m 13d
　　daughter of K. and S. Kratz
　　died 21 Feb 1872

KRATZ, SARAH　　　　　45y 8m 4d
　　wife of Valentine Kratz
　　died   29 Mar 1877

KRATZ, MARY ANN　　　　37y 3m 3d
　　22 Nov 1856 - 29 Feb 1891

KRATZ, VALENTINE　　　82y 23d
　　24 Feb 1822 - 17 Mar 1910

HUNSBERGER, HOWARD M.　　1895 - 1973
HUNSBERGER, ALVAH R.　　 1868 - 1958
HUNSBERGER, MARY M.　　　1862 - 1956
　　[above three on same stone]

HUNSBERGER, VERA M.　　　1901 - 1975

[three spaces]

HILDEBRANDT, WILLIAM B.　1872 - 1971

Row 49, continued:

HILDEBRANDT, ANNIE   1877 - 1939
HILDEBRANDT, ALBERT   1910 - 1974
    [previous three on same stone]

Row 50

HUNSBERGER, ABRAHAM   79y [3m?] 6d
    28 Aug 1803 - 3 Feb 1883

HUNSBERGER, ELIZABETH   81y 5m 21d
    24 Oct 1804 - 14 Apr 1886

[eight spaces]

Row 51

MARTS, CATRINA   19d
    daughter of Nicholas and Margaret Martz
    died 24 Mar 1911

[five spaces]

Row 52

SWINK, IRWING H.   48y 10m 7d
    24 Aug 1852 - 1 Jul 1901

FEASTER, CHRISTIAN   about 65y
    died 12 Oct 1891

[no surname], ALLIE   1885 - 1890

SECTION

    Across the driveway along the back of the stones which have just been transcribed are two markers. They are located across the driveway and slightly south of row 52.

REYNOLDS, RONALD   1858 - 1979

LANDES, JOHN T.   1903 -
LANDES, HANNAH B.   1906 - 1979
    [above two on same stone]

CALVARY CHURCH CEMETERY

Calvary Church, Souderton-Dublin Pike, near Souderton is located on the northwest side of Route 113. The new cemetery is directly behind the church and its parking lot. Row one is closest to the path. All the inscriptions are on flat plaques and were read left to right by Jennie Sperling during July 1983.

Row 1

KNAPP, BABY GIRL
    22 Aug 1966

BECHTEL, JOSHUA AARON "our son"
    30 Mar 1979   1 day

MOYER, ROBERT M.
    4 June 1913 - 1 May 1959
MOYER, GRACE S.
    12 Mar 1915 - [just buried]
    [these two on same plaque]

KEMMER, RAY RONALD "Baby"
    12 Aug 1957

NYCE, MADELINE L.   1905 -
NYCE, LOYD G.   1906 - 1979
    [above two on same plaque]
    [there may be a new grave here]

MYERS, MARJORIE   June 1956

[space]

JORDAN, STEVEN MICHAEL "our son"
    18 Oct 1967 - 17 Feb 1979

Row 2

MILLER OLGA   1907 -
MILLER, WALTER L.   1908 - 1981
    [above two on same plaque]

RICE, GORDON S.
    7 Mar 1943 - 19 Jul 1966

[space]

NYCE, DAVID LEE
    5 Mar 1960 - 27 Aug 1960

[spaces]

ZOLLER, FRANK J.   1885 - 1958

ALDERFER, DAVID ALAN
    24 Nov 1953 - 23 Mar 1957

[two spaces]

STAUFFER, EDWIN S.   1912 - 1983
    Flag - WWII
    [marker]

Row 3

NISBIT, DAVID N.   1976 - 1983
    [marker]

FREED, BABY   Aug 1965

[two spaces]

ALBRIGHT, ALTA M.
    19 Sept 1893 - 9 Aug 1963
ALBRIGHT, WALTER H.
    27 Feb 1891 -
    [above two on same plaque]

[space]

BRANDENBERGER, BETTY S.   1924 -
BRANDENBERGER, EZRA J.   1918 - 1962
    [above two on same plaque]

BRADFORD, KATHARINE   1885 -
BRADFORD, HARVEY DERR   1885 - 1970
    [above two on same plaque]

BRADFORD, SARA R.   1919 - 1961
BRADFORD, THEODORE W.   1913 -
    [above two on same plaque]

Row 4

NASE, CHAD RICHARD "our boy"
    24 Aug 1975 - 8 Mar 1980

[space]

LEDERACH, EDWARD G.   1920 - 1976
LEDERACH, MARIE   1923 -
    [above two on same plaque]

[space]

GERRARD, STEPHEN WILLIAM "Father"
    11 Jan 1948 - 5 Aug 1972

RICE, BLANCH H.   1919 - 1971
RICE, ELMER D.   1915 - 1981

SHALLCROSS, EDNA   1894 - 1969
SHALLCROSS, LEONARD R.   1890 - 1973
    [above two sets, each on same plaque]

LANDES, BLANCHE A.   1898 -
LANDES, HARRY T.   1897 - 1968

Row 4, continued

LANDIS, ANNA L.
   29 May 1891 -
LANDIS, ABRAM B.
   10 Apr 1890 - 4 Jan 1968
   [above two on same plaque]

MOYER, JANELLE K.
   26 Sept 1955 - 19 Jun 1972
MOYER, GLENN R.
   27 Mar 1952 -
   [above two on same plaque]

Row 5

WARNER, RACHEL LEHIGH
   13 - 18 Jan 1976 "baby"

LANDIS, WESLEY M.
   20 Mar 1949 - 10 Nov 1978
   Sp 4 US Army Vietnam

THOMPSON, MARY S.   1902 -
THOMPSON, ROBERT E.   1900 - 1976
   [above two on same plaque]

NASE, ALICE L.   1908 -
NASE, ROBERT M.   1901 - 1975
   [above two on same plaque]

RIPLEY, HELEN L.   1897 - 1980
RIPLEY, GLENN Q.   1897 -
   [above two on same plaque]

WAMBOLD, MARIAN   [blank]
WAMBOLD, OSCAR H.   1928 - 1972
   [above two on same plaque]

LANDIS, ALMA   [blank]
LANDIS, ELLIS
   8 May 1911 - 20 Jul 1971
   [above two on same plaque]

RICKERT, MARGIE A.   1946 -
RICKERT, Capt. GLENN D.   1945 - 1970
   [above two on same plaque]
   [Vietnam flag holder]

Row 6

GROSS, MARY   1917 -
GROSS, HIRAM   1907 - 1978
   [above two on same plaque]

[space]

DIMMICK, JEFFREY LYNN "son" 1959 - 1972

NASE, HELEN D.   1909 - 1981
NASE, PAUL M.   1903 -

[space]

DETWEILER, GLADYS   [blank]
DETWEILER, ISAAC F.   1918 - 1972

[space]

THE UPPER HILLTOWN BAPTIST CHURCH CEMETERY - NACE'S CORNER - NEW CEMETERY

The newest portion of the Upper Hilltown Baptist Cemetery is located adjacent to the following older section. It begins eleven paces in from the telephone pole at the sixteenth parking space. The stones in this part are all level with the ground.

Row one was assigned to the row closest to the church, and read toward the fields.

Row 1

CRAWFORD, ALFRED E.
    Pvt. Co. F 38th Infantry 3 Div.
    World War I
    20 Jan 1895 - 14 Aug 1960

CRAWFORD, DEBORAH CHESTER
    nee Torricellos
    13 Dec 1906 - 27 Jun 1980

[seven spaces]

GROTH, HAROLD   1912 - 1974
GROTH, NETTIE M.   1915 - 1970
    [above two on same stone]

[five spaces]

STOPKA, IRENE H.   1888 - 1958

STOPKA, ROBERT HARRY
    Pennsylvania AS USNR World War II
    17 Apr 1927 - 24 Apr 1960

HOIROCKS, WARREN E.   1910 - 1972
HOIROCKS, ISABEL L.   1914 - 1977
    [above two on same stone]

KERNER, PHOEBE I.   1882 - 1963

[three spaces]

LAWN,
    [living 1983]

[four spaces]

LEUZ, CHRISTOPHER   1893 - 1963
LEUZ, ELLA E.   1891 - 1963
    [above two on same stone]

ROBERTS, NORMAN LEE
    10 Mar 1949 - 19 Mar 1982

[three spaces]

NEUBERT, JOHN B., Jr.   1922 - 1967

[eight spaces]

TAYLOR, W. THEODORE, Rev. Dr. 1903 - 1981
    Pastor: Hilltown Baptist 1929 - 1933
    Pastor: Central Baptist, N.Y.C.
    1933 - 1973

TAYLOR, IRENE A.   1907 -

[15 spaces]

HENDRICKS, PAUL S.   1903 - 1978
HENDRICKS, DOROTHY M. 1910 -
    [above two on same stone]

RUARK, ERNEST   1911 - 1979
RUARK, VIRGINIA R.   1914 -
    [above two on same stone]

Row 2

[sixteen paces from church driveway
  and telephone pole]

LAKE, GEORGE W. III   1938 - 1960

[five spaces]

KREISHER, ARTHUR W.   1912 - 1980
KREISHER, EDITH E.   1919 -
    [above two on same stone]

[eight spaces]

NEWSOME, IRMA G.   1921 - 1969

[eight spaces]

SCHOLL, PAUL ANDREW
    30 Mar - 13 Nov 1967

[fourteen spaces]

NEUBERT, JOHN F., Sr. 1899 - 1969
NEUBERT, ELIZABETH   1902 - 1971

[eight spaces]

LOCKE, PAUL G.   1903 - 1979
LOCKE, ANNA T.   1908 -
    [above two on same stone]

[twenty-three spaces]

PETERSON, MARY C.   U.S. Army
    8 Sep 1923 - 6 Aug 1977

Row 3

[thirteen spaces from church driveway]

SCHENCK, MAE	1885 - 1965
SCHENCK, JOHN H.	1891 - 1965

[four spaces]

HINKLE, JOSEPH L.	1903 - 1981
HINKLE, CHRISSIE W.	1907 - 1958

[ten spaces]

DERBYSHIRE, ANNE M.	1901 - 1970
DERBYSHIRE, LOUISA	1879 - 1971

McKENZIE, JOHN D.
    Ohio PFC US Army World War II
    21 Aug 1919 - 11 Aug 1973

[eight spaces]

RICKERT, CAROL LYNN	1962 - 1963

[four spaces]

ZUKOW, PAUL J., Jr.	1921 - 1973

[four spaces]

EDWARDS, ROBERT M.   1925 - 1979
    Pvt. US Army World War II

[ten spaces]

NICE, JOSEPH S.	1920 - 1980
NICE, DOROTHY C.	1921 -

[above two on same stone]

Row 4

[Begins eighteen paces from church driveway, in line of J. Hinkle of last row]

GARGES, HARRY L.	1910 - 1973

[five spaces]

CONDICT, CORA H.	1928 - 1960

WEISS, TIMOTHY EDWARD
    22 Oct 1957 - 13 Dec 1958

[twenty-one spaces]

SMITHERS, JAMES	1905 - 1966
SMITHERS, FRANCES L.	1907 - 1973

[above two on same stone]

Row 5

[row begins 10 spaces from edge of the church driveway.]

TEXTER, IDA HELEN	1897 - 1980

[five spaces]

LAPP, HOWARD C.	1883 - 1969
LAPP, EDITH M.	1882 - 1959

[six spaces]

LOUX, HOWARD PEARSON	1902 - 1967

LOUX, HOWARD PEARSON, Jr.
    23 Feb 1927 - 10 Dec 1980

[six spaces]

GEESAMAN, BEVERLY K.	1944 - 1967

[four spaces]

BOLIG, LOIS ARLENE
    23 Jul 1958 - 6 Mar 1980

BOLIG, PAULINE G.
    26 Jul 1931 - 6 Jun 1970

[two spaces]

ZEIGLER, GEORGE W.	1905 - 1974
ZEIGLER, ELLA F.	1906 - 1978

[five spaces]

KULP, HAROLD	1903 - 1974
KULP, LAURA	1905 - 1981

[above two on same stone]

Row 6

[stones start at curbing of drive]

WAUD, IRA B.	1913 - 1973
WAUD, CLAIRE T.	1915

[above two on same stone]

[thirteen spaces]

LOUX, H. MONROE	1905 - 1981
LOUX, LAURA H.	1905 -

[above two on same stone]

[three spaces]

TOMLINSON, ALFRED	1923 - 1973

[three spaces]

TITUS, JOSEPH O.	1923 - 1973

[eight spaces]

MOOREHEAD, ADELAIDE M.	1921 - 1971

THE UPPER HILLTOWN BAPTIST CHURCH CEMETERY - NACES CORNER

The Upper Cemetery at Nace's Corner, Stump and Church Roads, is located on the westerly side of the Hilltown Baptist Church. It is adjacent to the Upper Church Road and the parking lot at the old church building.

The rows are at an angle to the road and face in a more or less easterly and westerly direction. Row one was assigned to the row farthest from the church. All rows were read from left to right as they are faced from the church. Thus the first stone read is the one closest to the baseball field and farthest from the church and Upper Church Road.

Row 1

MUHE, EDITH TYSON   27y 5m 22d
    wife of Louis S. Muhe
    died 14 Jul 1897

MUHE, LOUIS S.
    2 Apr 1895 - 11 Jul 1898

MUHE, HENRY L.   1834 - 1898
    aged 64 years

MUHE, MARY A.   1835 - 1916
    aged 80 years
    [above two on same stone]

Row 2

OPDYKE, REUBEN F.   46y 6m 11d
    father
    1 Nov 1849 - 12 May 1892

Row 3

SIMMON, MATILDA   23y 10m 10d
    wife of Malachi Heaton
    6 Oct 1865 - 16 Aug 1889
    [Heaton, Matilda Simmon]

M. H.

HEATON, JENNIE
    daughter of Malachi & Matilda Heaton
    15 Sep 1888 - 19 Feb 1912

HEATON, MARY   69y 2m 28d
    19 Mar 1827 - 16 Jun 1898

FELL, SUSANNA S.   7y
    died Feb 1843

AARON, SAMUEL   60y
    Deacon of the Hilltown Baptist
    Church for 17 years.
    husband   died 27 Dec 1892

AARON, BELINDA   1832 - 1922

DETTERER, CHARLES   [47?]y
    died 17 Sep 1882

AARON, AMELIA

DETTERER, AMELIA AARON
    wife of Chas. Detterer
    22 Aug 1826 - 7 Dec 1913

Row 4

WINKLER, LIZZIE   50y 3m 25d
    mother, wife of Jesse Winkler
    7 Oct 1842 - 1 Feb 1893

WINKLER, EYRE   19y 4m 23d
    son of Jesse and Lizzie Ann Winkler
    21 May 1868 - 14 Oct 1887

WINKLER, JESSE   father
    7 Oct 1835 - 17 Feb 1899

WINKLER, ELIZABETH   33y 8m 22d
    wife of J. Winkler
    9 Mar 1839 - 1 Dec 1872

WINKLER, WILLIAM HENRY   7m 4d
    son of J. and Elizabeth A. Winkler
    26 Aug 1866 - 30 Mar 1867

OWEN, HENRY
    son of John Owen
    25 Aug 18[45?] - 16 Aug 18[?]4

OWEN, JANE
    wife of Griffith Owen
    [no other information]

OWEN, GRIFFITH   81y 11m [?]d
    [?] Feb [1810?]

KREAMER, ELIZABETH   78y 1m 4d
    wife of Abraham Kreamer
    daughter of Ebenezer and Sarah Owens
    16 Jan 1777 - 20 Feb 1855

KRAMER, ABRAHAM   70y 4m 16d
    24 Oct 17[89?] - 11 May 18[69?]

Row 4 continued:

AARON, DEROSTUS   53y 7m 9d
    died 30 Nov 1859

DETTERER, INFANT   21d
    daughter of Charles and Amelia
    Detterer
    died 20 Nov 18[50?]

[broken stone - illegible]

AARON, MILLIE   10m 22d
    daughter of Hughes and Harriet Aaron
    died 13 May 18[79?]

AARON, OBED HUGHES
    25 Nov 1847 - 29 Oct 1912

Row 5

FELIX, SAMUEL   1883 - 1940

    [two spaces]

HEATON, JANE F.   22y 7m
    died 30 May 1868

BITTING, JOSEPHINE   21y 9m 7d
    wife of Jack E. Bitting
    daughter of Owen and Peninnah Heaton
    10 Feb 1839 - 6 Dec 1860

HEATON, OWEN   77y 27d
    1 Nov 1800 - 28 Nov 1877

HEATON, PENNINAH   53y 7m 11d
    wife of Owen Heaton
    13 Apr 1801 - 27 Nov 1854

A. W.

HEATON, E. R.
HEATON, E.
    [these are together -- stone broken]

YOCUM, BARRILLA   28y 11m 21d
    wife of G. Yocum
    daughter of Robert and Mary Heaton
    died 10 Apr 1836

S. M. Y.

HEATON, EDMUND R.   72y
    died 23 Jul 1826

HEATON, MARY   50y
    died 1 Dec 1816

HEATON, ROBERT   about 80y
    died [11?] Dec 1851

JAMES, ABEL N.   67y 4m 10d
    1 Jan 1771 - 11 Jun 1838

JAMES, OWEN [N. or Y.]   7y
    [?] Jul [?]

JAMES, CATHERINE
    died 19 Aug 1810

OWEN, OWEN   77y
    died 12 Mar 1809

OWEN, CATHERINE   [71 or 74?]y
    wife of Owen Owen
    died 15 Mar 1809
    [above two on same stone]

AARON, [CYII?]   74y
    died 7 Apr 1817

AARON, SARAH   50y
    died 11 Sep 1817

AARON, JOHN   20y 3m 9d
    died 11 Sep 1818

AARON, OBED   77y
    died 22 Apr 1837
    [Rev. War Flag]

AARON, HORATION B.   7y 10m
    son of Derostus and Caroline Aaron
    died 17 Nov 1838

AARON, OWEN   6y 1m 15d
    son of Derostus and Caroline Aaron
    died 11 Apr 1864

Row 6

PETERMAN, ALBERT   1896 - 1897
PETERMAN, CARRIE   1898 - 1898
PETERMAN, CLARA   1899 - 1899
PETERMAN, ANNIE   1891 - 1892
PETERMAN, FRANK   1895 - 1895
    [above five on same stone]

FU[?]STON, JOS., Sgt.
    Co. L   6th PA Cavl.
    [no dates on stone]

MOYER, JONAS D.   66y 1m 28d
    4 Nov 1825 - 1 Jan 1892

MOYER, CAROLINE H.   58y 7d
    wife of Jonas D. Moyer
    25 Jan 1828 - 1 Feb 1886

JONES, SARAH   [17 or 47?]y
    wife of Aaron Jones
    died 11 Sep 18 [31?]

JONES, AARON   67y [?]m [22?]d
    died [17?] Jun 18[42 or 12?]

    [seven or eight spaces]

JONES, MARGARET   95y
    died 9 Apr 1807

JONES, EDWARD   65y
    died 26 Nov 1772

UPPER HILLTOWN BAPTIST CHURCH CEMETERY -- NACES CORNER

Row 6 continued:

   [2 or 3 spaces]

OWEN, OWEN   aged [16?]
   died 29 Dec 1786

Row 7

   This row contains 8 stones. The fifth and sixth are out of line and the last two bisect the right angle corner of the cemetery at Upper Church Road.

   This row and row 8 fill in a change of direction which the rows make.

DANENHOWER, EUPHEMIA   71y 3m 2d
   wife of John Danenhower
   died 27 Jul 1890

DANENHOWER, JOHN   84y 1m 4d
   25 May 1903

MEANS, WILHELMINA   17y 10m 24d
   wife of Levi Means
   daughter of Alfred and Mary Carver
   2 Jun 1842 - 27 Apr 1860

CARVER, ALFRED S.   66y 11m 17d
   29 Aug 1819 - 7 Aug 1886

   [six or seven spaces]

FRY, SUSANN[E?]   in 40th year
   wife of Joseph Fry
   died 20 Sep 1842

   [five or six spaces]

HEATON, JONATHAN   [86?] y
   died [8?] Jan 1849

   [about 24 spaces]

KENEDY, RACHEL   [?y ?m] 11d
   1 Mar 1771 - 12 Jul 1821

KENEDY, JAMES   [?]y 10m [?]d
   27 Nov 179[?] - 1[?] [?] 1826

Row 8

VAIL, CATHERINE   1y [?]m 19d
   died [?]

VAIL, PETER K.   9y 6m 15d
   died 16 Aug 184[?]

VAIL, IRENE   1y 3m 29d
   died 2 Aug 1840
   [three spaces]

ECKERT, HANNAH ELIZZIE   13y 7m [?]d
   daughter of Jesse and Ellen Eckert
   9 Feb 1862 - 26 Sep 1875

ECKERT, ELLEN   65y 7m 14d
   wife of Jesse Eckert
   31 Jan 1831 - 15 Sep 1896

ECKERT, JESSE   82y 6m 14d
   29 Jan 1820 - 13 Aug 1902
   Civil War 174 Reg. of PA

   [three spaces]

ECKERT, HENRY L.   37y 10m 21d
   14 Apr 1854 - 5 Mar 1892

   [three spaces]

ECKERT, DANIEL L.
   son of Henry L. and Ruth L. Eckert
   17 Jun 18[88?] - 15 Feb 18[89?]

ECKERT, WARREN L.
   son of Henry L. and Ruth L. Eckert
   17 May 1883 - 12 Feb 1884

ECKERT, WILLIAM L.
   son of Henry L. and Ruth L. Eckert
   5 Aug 188[6?] - 25 Jul 188[7?]

Row 9

BUSSEL, JENINA   97y 11m 20d
   died 7 Jan 1859

BUSSEL, THOMAS
   died 7 Dec 18[2?]
   [rather illegible]

CLARK, VERNON M.   1875 - 1942
CLARK, VIVA L.   1876 - 1976

WILLIAMS, AMY   11y 1m 11d
   died 1 Jan 18[?]

   [space]

DANENHOWER, PHILIP   72y 8m 19d
   died 9 Mar 1861

DANENHOWER, JOSEPH   4m
   son of John and Euphriana Danenhower
   died 23 Aug 1855

DANENHOWER, ELIZABETH H.   71y 8m
   died 21 Oct 1851 wife of Philip

DANENHOWER, WILSON   2m
   son of John and Euphania Danenhower
   died 20 Mar 1854

[broken stone - illegible]

Row 9 continued:

WILLIAMS, ELEANOR   77y 5m 9d
     wife of Thomas Williams
     died   31 Mar 1856

WILLIAMS, THOMAS
     14 May 1776 - 8 Dec 1841

JAMES, ANN[?]
     daughter of [Thomas?] and Elizabeth James
     13 [?] 1801 - 2 Jan 18 [2?]

[illegible stone]

WILLIAMS, JONES
     son of William Williams
     2 Jan 1808 - 12 Aug 1808

Row 10

     This row starts in from the edge of the cemetery rows several spaces.

KELLY, JANE J.
     wife of Erasmus Kelly
     daughter of Amos and Rachel Jones
     born in Hilltown 28 Jun 1807
     died in Philadelphia   4 Feb 1882

KELLY, ERASMUS
     son of Erasmus and Janira Kelly
     born in Hilltown 11 Jul 1802
     died in Philadelphia   4 Feb 1881

KELLY, LYDIA MAY
     daughter of Amos J. and Lydia S. Kelly
     born and died in Philadelphia
     21 Jan 1872 - 21 Aug 187[?]

KELLY, ERASMUS D.   22y 6m 12d
     son of Erasmus and Jane Kelly
     born in Philadelphia   6 Jan 1812
     killed in [Frin of Peiersl?]
     27 Jul 1864
     [Civil War Flag holder]

[illegible stone]

KELLY, CHRISTIAN KNEASS   4m 26d
     son of Amos J. and Lydia A. Kelly
     born and died in Philadelphia
     5 Mar 1864 - 31 Jul 1864

[illegible stone]

KELLEY, ERASMUS   4y 9d
     son of Erasmus and Jane Kelley
     died   26 Jan 1857

KELLEY, HANNAH ANN   1y 1m 27d
     daughter of Erasmus and Jane Kelley
     died   27 Jan 1857

KELLEY, ERASMUS   6y
     died   4 Jan 1855

KELLEY, [?NIR?] Y.   30y
     died   14 Apr 1891

[space]

SLIFER, JACOB   2m 22d
     son of Abraham Slifer
     died   2 Jun 1800

KELLY, HANNAH   [90?]y
     died   19 Feb 1822

KELLEY, ERASMUS   52y
     died   15 Nov 1783
     [Revolutionary War Flag]

[space]

KELLY, ELEANOR   [74?]y
     died   27 Sep 1777

KELLY, JOHN
     died [?] [?] 176[6?]

EDWARDS, SUSANN   79y
     died   8 Oct 17 [60?]

KELLEY, THOMAS   1749
     [mostly illegible]

Row 11

PATTERSON, JOHN
     30 Nov 1837 - 12 Mar 1893

PATTERSON, HARRY J.
     24 Jul 1876 - 14 Aug 1876

PATTERSON, INFANT SON
     born and died   7 Jul 1877
     children of John and Rachel F. Patterson   [above two on same stone]

FLY, MARY   mother   1801 - 1890

FLY, SAMUEL   father   1799 - 1876

FLY, ARTIS M.   26y 4m 24d
     son of Samuel and Mary Fly
     died in Lancaster County
     died   4 May 1861

M. F.

S. F.

WORTHINGTON, SARAH   66y 7d
     wife of Seth Worthington
     died [23?] [?] 1841

WORTHINGTON, JONATHAN   57y 6m 7d
     died   7 Feb 18 [15?]

UPPER HILLTOWN BAPTIST CHURCH CEMETERY - NACES COUNER

Row 11 continued:

WORTHINGTON, SETH   85y 10m 20d
    died 16 Jan 1856

[21 spaces]

JONES, MARGARET B.   in 70th year
    died 28 Dec 1861

Row 12

MYERS, MARY GILL
    11 Mar 1893 - 5 Oct 1893

[15 spaces]

SELLERS, CHARLOTTE   79y 7m 19d
    daughter of [?   ?   ]
    died 25 Oct 1885

LUNN, ZILLAH   75y 2m 27d
    daughter of Elisha and Amy Lunn
    died 14 Feb 1880

BEER, ELIZABETH   about 90y
    mother
    died 6 Mar 1886

[3 spaces]

BEER, JOHN   [71 or 74?]y 10m
    died 10 Dec 1856

LUNN, EURY   81y 6m 11d
    daughter of Elisha and Amy Lunn
    died 27 Mar 18[79?]

LUNN, AMY   in 85th year
    died in 1861
    widow of Elisha Lunn

LUNN, ELISHA
    died 12 Jun 18[4?]

LUNN, JOSEPH   26y
    26 Sep 1831

[?], SIDNEY
    died [?] May 18[?]

LUNN, ALICE
    died 31 [?] [?]

LUNN, LEWIS
    died 18 May 18[?]

LUNN, LEAH   88y 6m 14d
    25 Sep 18[1?]8

LUNN, JOSIAH   7y 8m 28d
    [?] Feb 1821

Row 13

JONES, HA[?]Y   2y 6m 18d
    Died 17 Dec 18[85?]

LAKE, AZARIAH M., Capt.   in 85th year
    12 Feb 1814 - 23 Jan 1899

LAKE, JANE   61y
    wife of Capt. Azariah M. Lake
    daughter of James and Frances Jones
    died 29 Aug 1879

JONES, FRANCES   91y
    mother, wife of late James Jones
    7 Apr 1870

JONES, JAMES   Father
    25 Dec 1771 - 11 Dec 1851

JONES, RACHEL   in 76th year
    mother, wife of Amos Jones
    died 11 May 1862

JONES, AMOS   18y
    died 17 Sep 1851

JONES, JAMES   33y
    12 Jul 1827

[four spaces]

JONES, MARY   29y 7m 19d
    [?] Nov 1825

JONES, AMOS   21y 10m
    died 19 Aug 1824

JONES, SUSANNA   in 80th year
    wife of Thomas Jones
    died 12 Jul 1850

JONES, THOMAS   60y 6m 16d
    died 9 Jan 1824

[5 spaces]

JONES, WILLIAM   53y
    died 29 Dec 1817

JONES, JANE   49y
    wife of Thomas Jones
    died 29 Jan 1797

JONES, THOMAS   65y 5m 16d
    died 21 Sept 1801

JONES, JONATHAN   25y
    died 12 May 1790

[nine spaces]

JONES, THOMAS [?]
    [any other information?]

JONES, THOMAS   67y
    7 Feb 177[?]

Row 14

RICKERT, D. CLAYTON   1874 - 1954
RICKERT, KATHRYN   1875 - 1941
    [above two on same stone]

RICKERT, CHARLES   1917
    son of D.C. and Kathryn Rickert

[five spaces]

RENNER, FRANCIS   83y 2m 23d
    father
    14 Mar 1835 -13 Jun 1918

RENNER, ANNIE ELIZABETH   [64/61?]y 9m 21d
    wife of Frank Renner
    6 Aug 1831 - 27 May 1893

[two spaces]

GRASS, IRA W.   1871 - 1954
GRASS, MARTHA J.   1873 - 1947
    [above two on same stone]

[four spaces]

NACE, INFANT SON
    son of Amos and Lydia Nace
    Born 11 May 1890

NACE, AMANDA ANN ELIZABETH   2y 8d
    daughter of Amos and Lydia Nace
    3 Feb 1895 - 11 Feb 1897

NACE, HOWARD M.
    son of Amos and Lydia Nace
    13 Sep 1896 - 24 Feb 1902

NACE, LEVI   5y 3m 9d
    son of Amos and Lydia Nace
    3 Jul 1901 - 12 Oct 1908

NACE, PENROSE   20y 5m 22d
    son of Amos and Lydia Nace
    26 Nov 1892 - 18 May 1913

NACE, LYDIA N.
    27 Feb 1865 - 1 Oct 1940
NACE, AMOS B.
    8 Feb 1861 - 31 Mar 1944
    [above two on same stone]

GRASS, ANTHONY B.   1841 - 1930
GRASS, ANNIE E.   1845 - 1922
    [above two on same stone]

GRASS, LEIDY   20y [?]m 20d
    son of Anthony B. and Annie E. Grass
    11 Feb 1868 - 1 Apr 1888

SEARCH, JOHN HENRY   7y 7m 3d
    son of John and [Harr?] Search
    10 Mar 1876 - 13 Oct 1883

[small white stone - illegible]

Row 15

TEXTER, ANNA GRACE "GRACIE"   9y 1m
    daughter of Wm. H. and Susan L. Texter
    died   1 Apr 1905

TEXTER, RALPH
    son of Wm. H. and Susan L. Texter
    died   3 Jan 1905

TEXTER, WILLIAM H.   1870 - 1950
TEXTER, SUSAN L.   1869 - 1958

[four spaces]

BARNES, LAURA M.
    27 Mar 1871 - 3 Mar 1939

BARNES, JOHN H.
    13 Mar 1851 - 10 Dec 1914

BARNES, [?]   aged 19y

BARNES, ELSIE
    daughter of John H. and Laura Barnes
    26 Jun 1901 - 3 Apr 1902

[seven spaces]

GRASS, LEIDY R.   1898 -
GRASS, ROSETTA, L.   1897 - 1972
    [above two on same stone]

FULTON, ELIZABETH   mother
    [Jun or Jan?] 1796 - 27 Apr 188[0/1?]
    [stone is broken]

FULTON, BENJAMIN   in 82nd year
    died   25 Sep 1871

FULTON, ANNA
    daughter of Benjamin and Elizabeth
    Fulton
    7 Apr 1836 - 3 Sep 1911

[field stone - nothing legible]

JONES, JOHN J.
    died [?] Sep [?]

JONES, THOMAS
    died 18[44?]

[small stone - illegible]

JONES, SUSANNAH   80y 2m 13d
    wife of Ashbel Jones
    died   29 Mar 1847

[broken stone - illegible]

[broken stone - face toward ground]

[broken base of stone under ground]

[stone - illegible]

[?], CATHARINE   6y
    died   24 [?] 18[12 or 42?]

Row 15 continued:

[ten spaces]

[?], JOHN   98y
[1773?]
[stone broken - mostly illegible]

[brown field stone - nothing legible]

Row 16

WYDOMINICK, ALEXANDER   1888 - 1956
WYDOMINICK, MARY   1888 - 1959
    [above two on same stone]

BLAHUT, MARY   1860 - 1927

JONES, THEODORE
    father, son of James and [?] Jones
    16 Dec 1818 - 18 Mar 1905

JONES, SALLIE S.   mother
    wife of Theodore Jones
    1 Feb 1853 - 2 May 1898

JONES, CLARENCE   their son
    3 Apr 1898 - 17 May 1898
    [above two on same stone]

GRASS, OLIVER H.   1865 - 1960
GRASS, HANNAH   1868 - 1942
    [above two on same stone]

    [six spaces]

GRASSE, JOHN M.
    11 Oct 1900 -
GRASSE, BLANCHE L.
    2 Jul 1902 - 10 Oct 1970
    [above two on same stone]

    [five spaces]

BUTLER, MARTHA P.   1864 - 1911

    [seven spaces]

M.A.R.

M. R.

RICKERT, DAVID A.
    20 Jul - 8 Oct 1920

RICKERT, ESTHER BEATRICE 1929 - 1930

RICKERT, EMMA S.   1891 - 1963
RICKERT, PETER S.   1880 - 1952
    [above two on same stone]

MILLER, JAMES H.   in 27th year
    26 Jan 1811 - 5 Jul 1870

MILLER, WASHINGTON
    [dates illegible]

MILLER, LYDIA A. J.
    [no other information]

[blank stone]

MILLER, HENRY L.
    [rest illegible]

[small stone - illegible]

MILLER, [?]
    [illegible]

MILLER, PHILIP
    [illegible]
    [Revolutionary War flag]

[18 spaces or more to the road]

Row 17

    [stones begin 9 spaces in from edge]

[broken stone in the ground in fromt of Theodore Jones' stone]

SHELLY, LEVI   62y 8m 27d
    2 Jul 1887 - 29 Mar 1930

SHELLY, ANNIE L.   28y 24d
    wife of Levi Shelly
    22 Feb 1871 - 16 Mar 1899

SMITH, CHARLES R.   1867 - 1953
SMITH, ADELINE A.   1879 - 1949
    [above two on same stone]

    [three spaces]

SMITH, ELVIN A.   1879 - 1980
SMITH, SUSIE S.   1901 - 1971
    [above two on same stone]

SMITH, IDA A.   1900 - 1922
    [nee Hellerman]

SMITH, INFANT DAUGHTER
    of Elvin A. and Isa A. Smith
    died 15 Apr 1922

    [seven spaces]

YODER, ADALINE A.   61y 3m 21d
    wife
    3 Feb 1857 - 24 May 1918

YODER, WILLIAM D.   25y 8m 8d
    17 Apr 1853 - 25 Dec 1879
    [above two on same stone]

    [five spaces]

KRATZ, JAMES M.   16y 3m 6d
    6 Jan 1862 - 12 Apr 1878

J.M.K.

KRATZ, WILLIAM H.   45y 9m 11d
    26 Jul 1825 - 7 May 1871

Row 17 continued:

KRATZ, MARTHA I.　　　　　　51y 4m
　　wife of Wm. H. Kratz
　　12 Sep 1821 - 12 Jan 1876

KRATZ, JOSEPH J.　　　　　　9y 4m 17d
　　son of Wm. H. and Martha I. Kratz
　　died　28 Sep 1862

KRATZ, WILLIAM H.　　　　　　7y 5d
　　son of Wm. H. and Martha I. Kratz
　　died 24 Sep 1862

KRATZ, EMELY E.　　　　　　11y 5m 28d
　　daughter of Wm. H. and Martha I.
　　Kratz　　died　21 Sep 1862

　　[two spaces]

WORTHINGTON, WILLIAM H.　54y 6m 13d
　　husband
　　12 Jan 1848 - 25 Jul 1897

WORTHINGTON, CATHARINE
　　wife of William H. Worthington
　　[no other information]

　　[long space to road]

Row 18

　　[this row starts at the Yoder stone
　　in row 17]

RICE, MARGARET　　　　　daughter
　　2 Aug 1869 - 17 May 1944

RICE, MOSES H.　　　　　father
　　14 Feb 1834 - 18 Mar 1920
RICE, SUSAN J.
　　22 Oct 1837 - 11 Mar 1910
　　[these two stones share same base]

RICE, [　?　]
　　11 Feb 18[68?] - 19 Jan 18[70?]

JONES, JOSEPH　　　　　　92y 22d
　　1 Mar 1780 - 26 Mar 1872

JONES, ELIZABETH
　　wife of Joseph Jones
　　11 Dec 1788 - 8 Feb 1871

JONES, ELIZABETH　　　[71?]y 11m 18d
　　wife of Abel Jones
　　28 Sep 1781 - 18 Sep 1836

JONES, ABEL　　　　　　　84y 5m 15d
　　18 Nov 1782 - 3 May 1867

　　[four spaces]

JONES, JOHN M.　　　　　　37y
　　died　30 Nov 1839

JONES, ALICE　　　　　　in 89th year
　　22 Sep 1799 - 21 Apr 1888

[　?　], MARY
　　[illegible]

JONES, GRIFFITH
　　4 Mar 1772 - [13?] Sep 1818

　　[seven spaces]

[JONES ?]
　　[illegible]

[JONES?], CATHARINE
　　[illegible]

Row 19

　　[row begins six spaces in from edge]
HOFFORD, JOHN　　　　　　97y
　　died　20 Feb 1919　　husband
HOFFORD, ORPHA B.　　　　wife
　　20 Nov 1831 - 10 Nov 1911
　　[above two together]

　　[six spaces]

BISHOP, JAMES H.　　　　1883 - 1962
BISHOP, PEARL M.　　　　1887 - 1971
　　[above two on same stone]

　　[two spaces]

BISHOP, CARROLL
　　son of James H. and Pearl M. Bishop
　　2 Jul 1911 - [1 Jan 1920?]

BISHOP, INFANT DAUGHTER
　　of James H. and Pearl M. Bishop
　　died　23 Jan 1905

　　[five spaces]

FLY, MATTIE E.　　　　　1877 - 1878

FLY, KATIE E.　　　　　　1871 - 1878

FLY, MARY GIBBONS　　　1836 - 1924
　　mother

FLY, SETH W.　　　　　　1828 - 1880
　　father

FLY, SETH W.
　　25 Feb 1828 - 11 Mar 1880
FLY, MARY G.
　　17 Jun 1835 - 16 Jan 1924
FLY, FRANK W.
　　30 Aug 1874 - 7 Mar 1904
FLY, KATIE E.
　　14 Mar 1871 - 15 Jan 1878
FLY, MATTIE E.
　　[5/6?] 1877 - 15 Jan 1878
　　[above five on same monument]

UPPER HILLTOWN BAPTIST CHURCH CEMETERY - NACES CORNER

Row 19 continued:

FLY, ANNIE ELIZABETH	1866 - 1941
FLY, SAMUEL IRVIN	1873 - 1963
FLY, FRANK WESLEY	1874 - 1904
FLY, JULIETTE E. RENOUX	1876 - 1942

    wife of Henry K. Fly

FLY, HARVEY K.   1879 - 1970

[four spaces]

McLAUGHLIN, TACY   in 37th year
    wife of the Rev. [?] McLaughlin
    died   12 Dec 1803

Row 20

    [stones begin in five spaces from edge at the Bishop stone of row 19]

UHRICH, DEBORAH DARLINE
    28 Aug 1952 - 28 Dec 1952

DUCKLOE, AARON S.	1841 - 1917
DUCKLOE, MARTHA J.	1836 - 1903
LAPP, ANNA	1872 - 1929

    sister

LAPP, DEBORAH	1878 - 1933
LAPP, IDA	1874 - 1958
LAPP, EMMA	1877 - 1958

DUCKLOE, FRED S.
    12 Dec 1861 - 22 Feb 1919
    [broken stone and base]

DUCKLOE, GRACE M.
    1 May 1872 - 19 Jul 1931

[foot stone for Tacy McLaughlin]

LEWIS, MARGARET   [55y 1m 21d?]
    wife of Dr. T. Lewis
    daughter of Wm. and M. Shaddinger
    died   25 Dec 1861

SHADDINGER, MARY   mother
    [illegible]
    died 15 [?] 1881

SHADDINGER, SAMUEL M.   21y 4m [?]d
    husband of M. Shaddinger
    died   12 Sep 18[58?]

SHADDINGER, MATHIAS   11y [? ?]
    son of [? ?] Shaddinger
    died   [11?] Feb 1853

LEWIS, EMMA   died [1854?]
    daughter of Dr. T. and M. Lewis

Row 21

    [row starts in front of the Emma Lapp stone of preceeding row toward the driveway]

DUCKLOE, JACOB B.
    7 May 1838 - 12 Apr 1909
    [Civil War marker]

DUCKLOE, ELIZABETH
    4 Nov 1844 - 17 May 1930

DUCKLOE, WILLIAM   in [71?] year
    died   29 May 1878

DUCKLOE, CATHARINE   in 80th year
    died   16 Oct 1890

[small stone - illegible]

[?], MABEL M.
    [illegible]

GEIL, [?]   11m
    [illegible]

Row 22

    [This row parallel's the church. It is adjacent to the driveways and is the only row parallel to church.]

WILLIAMS, RALPH E.
    son of Raymond and Betty Williams
    19 Dec - 21 Dec 1960

[three spaces]

WILLIAMS, RAYMOND R.	1908 - 1955
WORTHINGTON, CHARLES A.	1879 - 1951
WORTHINGTON, IVA B.	1882 - 1968

    [above two on same stone]

WORTHINGTON, IVA C.   1912 - 1936

[six spaces]

LEUZ, LAURA E.
    30 Sep 1918 - 4 Jan 1947

[six spaces]

GRASS, WALTER N.	1896 - 1947
GRASS, GRACE M.	1897 -

    [above two on same stone]

[six spaces]

REDLOW, JOHANNA	1887 - 1948
REDLOW, WILLIAM	1884 - 1953

    [five spaces]

JOHNSON, MAX	1896 - 1949
TEMOSHCHUK, MICHAEL	1893 - 1960
TEMOSHCHUK, MARY D.	1890 - 1950

UPPER HILLTOWN BAPTIST CHURCH
CEMETERY

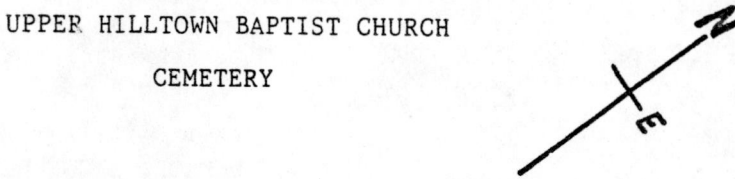

N E

Row 1
Row 2
Row 3
Row 4
Row 5
Row 6
Row 7
Row 8
Row 9
Row 10
Row 11
Row 12
Row 13
Row 14
Row 15
Row 16
Row 17
Row 18
Row 19
Row 20
Row 21
Row 22

New section of Cemetery ←

(stones are level with the ground)

Upper Church Road

UPPER HILLTOWN BAPTIST CHURCH

THE LOWER HILLTOWN BAPTIST CHURCH CEMETERY -- FRICKS

The Lower Hilltown Baptist Cemetery at Fricks is located near the Hilltown Pike on the northerly side of Sellersville Road. The first Baptist Church in Hilltown Township once stood on the property which is now maintained by the Upper Hilltown Township Baptist Church.

Row one was assigned to the row most distant from Sellersville Road. Each row was read from left to right as the stones were faced from the driveway. Thus, the first stone transcribed was in the far left corner of the cemetery.

Row 1

P. M.
   [may be foot stone of Peninah Mathias]

HINES, MILLER   4y 7m
   died 11 Sep 1815

HINES, HERVEY   3y 5m
   died 19 Sep 1817

HINES, ISAAC   56y
   died 10 Dec 1829

HINES, MARGARET   [51/57?]y 5m 8d
   widow of Isaac Hines
   died 7 Jul 1857

SUMMERS, ELIZA   33y
   died 27 Mar 1832

SUMMERS, ENOS M.   [21/24?]y 4m 20d
   died 17 Sep 1843

SUMMERS, ELIZABETH   2y 3m 6d
   died 3 Jan 1853

SUMMERS, ELIZABETH G.   63y 7m 25d
   died 8 Dec 1868

SUMMERS, JOHN   78y
   died 28 Aug 1873

Row 2

MATHIAS, ROWLAND   44y
   died 23 Jan 1810

MATHIAS, MARY   35y
   wife of Rowland Mathias
   died 1 Dec 1836

MATHIAS, PENINAH   25y 10m
   wife of Ashbel Mathias
   died 2 Nov 1815

[illegible -- flat stone]

MATHIAS, ENOCH   84y
   died 2 Jun 1856

MATHIAS, ANNA
   wife of Enoch Mathias
   [illegible]

MATHIAS, CHARLES
   son of [illegible]
   [dates illegible]

MATHIAS, MORGAN
   died 15 Dec [1813?]

MATHIAS, ELIZABETH
   died [?] Mar 1812

MATHIAS, ALICE   73y
   died 6 Jan 1853

JAMES, GAINOR   54y
   wife of John James
   died 20 Sep 1822

MATHIAS, JOHN   80y
   died 8 Sep 1813

MATHIAS, ALICE   74y
   wife of John Mathias, Sr.
   died 23 Oct 1810

MATHIAS, THOMAS   in 41st year
   died 10 Jan 1806

MATHIAS, MARGARET   79y 8m 20d
   widow of Thomas Mathias
   died 8 Apr 1848

MATHIAS, THOMAS, Jr.   in 44th year
   26 Jul 1806

M x 1812 x 5
J x M   [brown stone]

MATHIAS, AMOS G., M.D.   in 28th year
   16 May [1871?]

Row 3

TRIMBEE, CATHARINE
   29 Mar 1860 - 31 Jan 1871

LEWIS, RACHEL, Aunt
   4 Sep 1801 - 22 May 1891

LEWIS, HENRY   in 89th year
   died   19 Jan 1869

LEWIS, MARGARET   in 92nd year
   died   1 Feb 1854 wife of Henry L.

FRANKS, REBECCA   54y 12d
   wife of William D. Franks
   12 May 1808 - 10 Jun 1862
   daughter of Henry & Margaret Lewis

LEWIS, JOHN   49y 2d
   son of Henry and Margaret Lewis
   10 Oct 1805 - 12 Oct 1851

[Brown stone - nothing inscribed]

PHILIPS, CATHARINA   [81 or 84?]y
   died   22 Jun 1819

LEWIS, HENRY   81y
   died   18 Jan 1797

LEWIS, MARGARET   80y
   died   8 Nov 1798

LEWIS, WILLIAM   56y
   [7 or 17?] Apr 1815

[brown stone - nothing inscribed]
[brown stone - nothing inscribed]

MATHIAS, ANNA   55y
   died [?] Jul 1797 wife of Thomas

MATHIAS, THOMAS, Sr.   68y
   died   29 Apr 1799

MATHIAS, ELIZABETH   in 86th year
   died   15 Dec 1821

MATHIAS, MARIA   9m
   died   28 Oct 180[1?]

MATHIAS, JOHN   29y
   died   21 Nov 1803

MATHIAS, ELEANOR   32y
   died   Apr 180[4?] wife of John

Row 4

LEWIS, HENRY   9y 2m 23d
   son of Uriah D. and Mary Lewis
   died   14 Mar 1853

LEWIS, ELIZABETH   4y 3m 1d
   sister, daughter of T. J. and
   Caroline Lewis
   9 Oct 1848 - 10 Jan 1853

LEWIS, WILLIAM HENRY   3y 6m 18d
   brother, son of T. J. and Caroline
   Lewis
   died   27 Oct 1846

JONES, EDWARD
JONES, REBECCA
   [above two on same stone - no dates]

JONES, DAVID   25y
   son of Abel and Rachael Jones
   died 12 Nov 1835

JONES, REBECCA
   died 17 Nov 18 [27 or 37?]

LEWIS, NANCY   77y
   died   17 Mar 1829

LEWIS, JAMES   72y
   died   7 Mar 1828

JONES, EDWARD   82y
   died   1 Sep 1823

LEWIS, MARY   about 78y
   wife of Isaac Lewis
   [no dates on stone]

LEWIS, ISAAC   80y
   Revolutionary soldier under
   Washington
   born 1 Aug 1751
   [no death date given]

LEWIS, MARY   9y
   daughter of Henry and Margaret Lewis
   died   in 1821

Row 5

JONES, ANDREW J.   66y 11m 26d
   4 Jul 1815 - 30 Jun 1882

JONES, JOHN   83y 10m 16d
   22 Jun 1800 - 8 May 1884

JONES, ELIZA   71y 5m 1d
   26 Dec 1797 - 27 May 1869

JONES, MARY   in 67th year
   sister, daughter of Abel and Rachel
   Jones
   died   3 Mar 1869

JONES, RACHEL   73y
   mother
   died   10 May 1848

JONES, ABEL   in 85th year
   died   13 Mar 1850

MATHIAS, ANN   in 85th year
   died   27 Mar 1861

LOWER HILLTOWN BAPTIST CHURCH CEMETERY - FRICKS

Row 5 continued:

YOUNG, JOHN   50y 8m 8d
    died   4 Dec 1851

YOUNG, HARVEY   in 38th year
    died suddenly 12 Apr 1845

YOUNG, JOHN   55y
    died 19 Apr 1815

YOUNG, MARY   in 81st year
    died 26 Mar 1819

Row 6

HARDING, WILLIAM   78y
    died   4 Jan 1855

HARDING, ELIZABETH   75y
    died 15 Feb 1860

M. M.   [possible foor marker for Malinda Mathias in next row]

MORRIS, JOHN D.   56y
    9 Apr 1811 - [15 or 5?] Jan 1868

MORRIS, RACHEL   85y 5m 7d
    wife of Isaac Morris
    died 1 Aug 1856

MORRIS, BURGISS A.   40y 11m 8d
    died 20 Dec 1847

MORRIS, MARY   21y
    wife of Burgiss Morris
    died 20 Jun 1837

MORRIS, OLIVER   19y
    died   2 Feb 1826

MORRIS, MORRIS   in 56th year
    died 11 Nov 1767

MORRIS, GWENTLEY THOMAS in 56th year
    wife of Morris Morris
    daughter of Rev. William Thomas
    died 11 Nov 1767
    [this date is wrong according to a
     family member]

MORRIS, WILLIAM
    died [illegible]

MORRIS, ELIZABETH   10m
    infant daughter of Mathias and
    Wilhemina Morris
    died 14 Aug 1831

MORRIS, MATHIAS, Esquire   52y
    died   9 Nov 18[3 or 5?]9

MORRIS, ISAAC   79y 4m 8d
    died 13 Sep 1843

MORRIS, ELIZA   38y
    wife of Isaac Morris
    died 28 Aug 1803

MORRIS, JUSTUS   6y 4m
    died 16 Mar 1802

MORRIS, WM. I.   15y
    died 14 Oct 1814

ROWLAND, REACHEL   26y
    wife of Thomas Rowland
    died 13 Feb 1802

MORRIS, [?]
    [no other information on stone]

MORRIS, HANNAH   40y
    wife of Abner Morris
    died   7 Oct 1822

Row 7

[brown field stone]   B.

[brown field stone]

[brown field stone]

[grey stone - illegible]

MILLER, ISAAC   59y
    died 11 Oct 1828

THOMAS, ASA   in 82nd year
    died 10 May 1839

THOMAS, MARTHA   in 89th year
    wife of Asa Thomas
    died 11 Apr 1854

THOMAS, MARIA   21y 7m 21d
    wife of John Thomas
    died 19 Dec 1839

HENDRICKS, CHARLES   in 50th year
    died 31 Oct 1844

[brown field stone]

[brown field stone]

THOMAS, SILAS
    [illegible -- has foot stone]

THOMAS, SARAH
    wife of Silas Thomas
    [?] Nov [?] - [?] Feb [?]

[several more brown stones in row]

Row 8

MATHIAS, BENJAMIN, Junior   20y
    died 12 May 1808

BUCKS COUNTY TOMBSTONE INSCRIPTIONS - HILLTOWN TOWNSHIP

Row 8 continued:

MATHIAS, ABEL   teacher   27y
    died 17 Jun 1816

[?], Mary   31y
    wife of Robert [?]
    died 10 Aug 1822

MATHIAS, THOMAS   in 87th year
    teacher
    died 8 Oct 1821

MATHIAS, ANNA   29y
    wife of Thomas Mathias
    died 5 Sep 1826

MATHIAS, JARED M.   11y
    died 18 May 18[38?]

MATHIAS, JOHN   75y
    died 31 May 1838

MATHIAS, ANNA   82y
    wife of John Mathias
    died 14 Mar 1841

[brown field stone - no information]

[brown field stone - no information]

[gray stone - "elder" illegible

[three brown field stones - no information]

E. T.   [Revolutionaey War flag]
    [large brown stone - no dates]

[brown field stone - no information]

THOMAS, INFANT
    of Issackar and Ann Thomas
    [no other information]

[brown stone - no information]

THOMAS, [ELLIS or ELIAS ?] 69y 5m 11d
    died 25 Jun 18[14 or 11?]

THOMAS, ELIZABETH   80y 8m 5w 15d
    wife of Elias Thomas
    [15?] Oct 1740 - 6 Jul 1821

THOMAS, JONATHAN   in 6th year
    son of Ephriam and Sidney Thomas
    died [17 or 27?] Oct 179[3 or 5?]

THOMAS, BENJAMIN   in 3rd year
    son of Ephriam and Sidney Thomas
    died 20 Apr 1796

THOMAS, JOSEPH   53y
    died 8 Dec 1841
    [rest illegible]

THOMAS, ABNER   31y
    died 8 Mar 1816

THOMAS, SARAH   [23 or 25?]y
    died [9 or 16?] May [1847?]

THOMAS, SARAH   60y
    died 22 Mar 1837

[stone - no markings]

Row 9

MILNOR, AARON   27y
    died 6 Sep 1813

MORRIS, SARAH   in [35 or 37?]y
    wife of Seneca C. Morris
    died 3 Jun 1864

M. R.   [may be foot stone of Mary
    Rowland in row 10]

THOMAS, MALINDA   74y 8m 3d
    daughter of Issachar and Ann Thomas
    20 Nov 1825 - 23 Jul 1900

THOMAS, REBECCA
    daughter of Issachár and Ann Thomas
    born 16 Aug 1814
    [rest isillegible]

THOMAS, MARIA
    daughter of Issachar and Ann Thomas
    25 Mar 1808 - 24 Apr 1878
    [rest illegible]

THOMAS, JOHN, Rev.   79y
    died 31 Oct 1790

THOMAS, SARAH   94y
    widow of Rev. John Thomas
    died 2 Apr 1805

THOMAS, MANASSEH   in 81st year
    died 7 Feb 1802

[brown field stone - no information]

THOMAS, EBER   36y
    died 16 Oct 1807

HEATON, ZILLAH   69y
    died 4 Aug 1844

MATHIAS, ANN   44y 5m 5d
    wife of Ashbel Mathias
    died 15 Oct 1840

[small stone - illegible]

HEACOCK, SALLY   19y 5m 8d
    wife of Richard Heacock
    died 8 Oct 1800

Row 9 continued:

THOMAS, JOSIAH
    13 Apr 1784 - 20 Aug 1856

THOMAS, ELIZABETH,   in 69th year
    11 Nov 1786 - 6 Nov 1855
    wife of Josiah Thomas

THOMAS, MARY   in 29th year
    12 Sep 1822 - 10 Apr 1851

THOMAS, MAHLON   in 29th year
    16 Apr 1826 - 11 Mar 1855

Row 10

ELTHAM, THOMAS   in 87th year
    Revolutionary Soldier under
    Washington
    died 12 Apr 1939

ROWLAND, MARY   in 70th year
    widow of Owen Rowland
    daughter of Job Thomas
    died 18 Aug 1857

THOMAS, EPHRAIM   in 69th year
    son of Elias Thomas
    died 24 Oct 1847

THOMAS, ESSACHAR   in 80th year
    son of Elias Thomas
    died 24 Jan 1860

THOMAS, ANN   in 78th year
    wife of Issackar Thomas
    died 30 Mar 1866

THOMAS, WILLIAM   79y
    licensed minister of the Gospel
    died 6 Oct 1757

THOMAS, ANN   72y
    wife of William Thomas, licensed
    minister of the Gospel
    died on the Lord's Day
    5 Nov 1752

ROWLAND, ANNA   40y
    wife of Stephen Rowland
    died [?] May 1759

[brown field stone - no information]

VASTINE, MARTHA   in 66th year
    [no date inscribed]

[six brown field stones - no information]

BITTING, MARY   in 66th year
    consort of Eleazer Bitting
    died 16 Apr 1840

BITTING, ELEAZER   84y 11m 15d
    24 Apr 1778 - 8 Apr 1863

BITTING, THOMAS R.   72y 8m 25d
    8 May 1808 - 5 Feb 1881

BITTING, ALFRED
    5 Sep 1805 - 1 Oct 1846

Row 11

ROWLAND, MARTHA LOUISE   1y 8m 20d
    daughter of Artemas and Martha
    Rowland
    died 1 Aug 1852

ROWLAND, ARTEMUS T.   44y 10m 12d
    died 28 Feb 1857

ROWLAND, MARTHA R.
    wife of Artemus T.
    born 26 Jan 1812
    died 18 Sep 1873

ROWLAND, ANNA MARIA
    daughter or Artemas T. and Martha
    Rowland
    8 Oct 1841 - 30 Jul 1879

ROWLAND, EMMA
    daughter of Artemus T. and Martha
    Rowland
    1 Jan 1850 - 2 Sep 1901

BARTHOLOMEW, ALBERT R.   4m
    son of Samuel and Martha Bartholomew
    died 22 May 1860

BARTHOMOMEW, MARY MARTHA   2m
    daughter of Samuel and Martha
    Bartholomew
    died 15 Dec 1862

BARTHOLOMEW, SAM'L   husband
    Nov 1826 - 2 Sep 1863

SLEIGHT, MARY ELIZABETH
    wife of Samuel Sleight
    4 Mar 1838 - 8 Dec 1913

SLEIGHT, HARRY A.
    4 Feb 1870 - 26 Dec 1936

SLEIGHT, MARGARET E.   1872 - 1958

SLEIGHT, ROWLAND   1878 - 1858

BUCKS COUNTY TOMBSTONE INSCRIPTIONS - HILLTOWN TOWNSHIP

Row 11 continued:

MORRIS, BENJAMIN   84y 6m 5d
    died 2 Apr 1833

MORRIS, MARY   62y 1m
    wife of Benjamin Morris
    died 7 Jan 1813

MORRIS, JOHN   41y 7m 23d
    died 14 Mar 1833

MORRIS, CATHARINE   60y 1m 17d
    died 27 Oct 1838

SELLERS, MICHAEL   87y 29d
    died 29 Oct 1859

SELLERS, MICHAEL   68y
    died 31 Oct 1844

SELLERS, SAMUEL   42y
    died 21 Feb 1849

SELLERS, JOEL J.   in 37th year
    died 21 Mar 18[?]1

PUGH, DANIEL   82y
    died 7 Sep 1813

PUGH, REBECCA   in 80th year
    died 19 Jun 1819

RIALE, DAVID E.   in 40th year
    died 15 Sep 1836

RIALE, JOEL H.
    6 Sep 1840 - 27 Jul 1864

RIALE, SARAH E.
    12 Jun 1852 - 11 Jun 1872

CASSEL, JOSEPH   died 23 Jul 1889
CASSEL, HOWARD   died 25 Jul 1889
    twin children of J. M. and Lauressa
    Cassel
    [above two on same stone]

Row 12

J. H. R.

M. L. B.

S. D. C.

[brown field stone -- no information]

WRIGHT, EDWIN   2y
    son of Jacob Wright
    died 22 Jul 1851

ALBRIGHT, INFANT DAUGHTER
    of Dr. T.A. and Lizzie Albright
    27 Jul 1893 - 28 Jul 1893

LEWIS, ZILLAH
    wife of William Lewis
    died 5 Apr 1858

LEWIS, WILLIAM   83y 9m 2d
    7 Mar 1793 - 9 Dec 1976

ECKEL, MARY EMMA
    daughter of Horace V. and Carrie
    Eckel
    28 Dec 1896 - 9 Jan 1898

ECKEL, WILLIAM LEIDY
    son of Horace V. Eckel
    9 Mar 1886 - 8 Nov 1891

ECKEL, CARRIE M.   51y 10m 5d
    26 Feb 1863 - 4 Jan 1914

ECKEL, HORACE V.   42y 9m 4d
    27 Feb 1858 - 1 Dec 1900

ECKEL, MARY L.   62y 2m 21d
    wife of J. Leidy Eckel
    19 Sep 1830 - 9 Dec 1892

ECKEL, J. LEIDY   76y 7m 28d
    28 Apr 1830 - 26 Dec 1906

EVANS, MARY
    daughter of Robert and Susanna Evans
    died 6 Feb 1821

EVANS, ROBERT
    4 Aug 1791 - 14 Aug 1834

EVANS, SUSAN
    23 May 1790 - 12 Aug 1870

MATHIAS, ABEL   [82?]y
    died 11 Apr 1850

MATHIAS, SARAH   88y 6m 13d
    wife of Abel Mathias
    died 26 Aug 1858

MATHIAS, JOHN
    son of John H. and Jane Mathias
    died 28 Dec 1852

MATHIAS, JOHN H.
    elected Deacon 21 Jul 1855
    Baptized 24 Feb 1839
    22 Jun 1811 - 30 Oct 1881

MATHIAS, JANE MASON
    28 Oct 1819 - 28 Dec 1897

KELLER, SALLIE   mother   1857 - 1922
KELLER, ABRAHAM   father   1863 - 1922

Row 13

ROWLAND, MATILDA   88y 25d
    8 Mar 1802 - 3 Apr 1890

LOWER HILLTOWN BAPTIST CHURCH CEMETERY - FRICKS

Row 13 continued:

ROWLAND, SARAH
    wife of William H. Rowland
    [dates illegible]
    [earlier transcription read it as:
      died 3 Jun 1841 aged 66]

ROWLAND, WILLIAM H.   67y
    died 29 May 1844

ROWLAND, JOSEPH   2y
    son of Newton and Elizabeth Rowland
    died 2 May 1841

ROWLAND, STAUGHTON
    son of Newton and Elizabeth Rowland
    died 17 Jan 1846

[?], Tillie R.
    [stone is broken and illegible]

EVANS, EMILY ROWLAND
    wife of Rev. T. R. Evans
    daughter of I.N. and T. Rowland
    born 2 Jan 1847
    graduated
    baptized 27 Mar 1857
    married 11 Aug 1875
    died 21 Nov 1880

TAYLOR, ASENATH R.   50y 3m 23d
    wife of Lamuel Taylor
    8 May 1831 - [?] Sep 1881

ROWLAND, ELIZABETH MATHIAS
    wife of I. Newton Rowland
    20 Dec 1809 - 27 Mar 1882

ROWLAND, NEWTON   85y 7m 12d
    6 Jun 1806 - 18 Jan 1892

MATHIAS, JOSEPH, Rev.
    [?] May 1778 - 12 Mar 1851

MATHIAS, DINAH
    wife of Rev. Joseph Mathias
    died 9 Jul 1870

MATHIAS, THOMAS, M. D.   22y 6m 7d
    son of Joseph and Dinah Mathias
    died of small pox in Berks County
    died 2 Jun 1830

MATHIAS, LYDIANNA   20y
    died 17 Nov 1831

MATHIAS, BENJAMIN   22y
    son of Joseph and Dinah Mathias
    died 30 Mar 1835

MATHIAS, JOSEPH   [12?]y
    died 17 Apr 1842

MATHIAS, RACHEL M.
    daughter of Rev. Joseph and Dinah Mathias
    died 11 Dec 1814 - 13 Aug 1886

MATHIAS, JOHN N.   62y 11m 20d
    died 29 Mar 1883

MATHIAS, AMANDA MALVINA   90y 1m
    wife of John N. Mathias
    died 13 Apr 1916

MATHIAS, ELLA   1858 - 1938
    daughter of John H. and Amanda Mathias

MATHIAS, ELLEN   8 weeks
    daughter of J. N. and A.M. Mathias
    died 6 Dec 1852

MATHIAS, INFANT
    [illegible]

MATHIAS, EMILY R.   20y 6m 15d
    daughter of J.N. and A.M. Mathias
    died 18 Oct 1882

MATHIAS, FANNY   30y 21d
    daughter of J.N. and A.M. Mathias
    died 11 Nov 1886

MATHIAS, M. IDA   36y 3, 13d
    daughter of J.N. and A.M. Mathias
    died 13 Sep 1892

MATHIAS, ANN   38y 1m 5d
    daughter of J.N. and A.M. Mathias
    died 5 Aug 1903

MATHIAS, JOSEPH   1870 - 1950

THOMAS, JOHN EDWARD
    son of John and Livia Thomas
    died 4 Oct 1864

THOMAS, LIVIA   34y
    wife of John Thomas
    died 2 Feb 1862

THOMAS, MARGARET   36y 9m
    wife of John Thomas
    died 8 May 1852

THOMAS, JOHN   54y 3m 2d
    died 24 Oct 1866

THOMAS, ALIVIA   19y
    daughter of John and Margaret Thomas
    died 1 Mar 1868

Row 14

HARR, GEORGE C.   1876 - 1945
    husband

DUNN, MARY B.   1879 - 1966

Row 14 continued:

GREENWOOD, PETER F.
    19 May 1839 - 22 Dec 1902

GREENWOOD, MARGARET R.
    3 Oct 1858 - 2 Jun 1953

PHILLIPS, GRACE GREENWOOD
    28 Oct 1883 - 20 Oct 1970

GREENWOOD, WILLIAM F.
    8 Sep 1887 - 5 Jan 1906

AARON, JULIET ROWLAND
    wife of John P. Aaron
    15 Dec 1839 - 9 Jan 1907

AARON, JOHN P.
    18 Feb 1839 - 9 Aug 1923

AARON, MARTHA CAROLINE
    30 Apr 1867 - 7 Apr 1947

AARON, ROBERT
    son of John P. and Juliet Aaron
    7 Mar 1875 - 20 Aug 1875

Row 15

GODSCHALL, HOWARD
    8 Jun 1869 - 24 Jun 1950

GODSCHALL, ELIZABETH AARON
    26 Oct 1870 - 27 Jan 1933

BUSWELL, DELLA ROWLAND
    30 Aug 1874 - 1 Sep 1854

[brown field stone - no inscriptions]

SELLERS, JOHN
    died 15 Nov 1879

SELLERS, EMMALINE
    daughter of John and Catherine
    Sellers
    died 15 May 1875

SELLERS, CATHERINE
    wife of John Sellers
    died 15 Feb 1877

COURTER, EMMA L.
    wife of Uriah D. Coulter
    30 Nov 1852 - 17 Nov 1881

Row 16

COURTER, URIAH D.   1850 - 1929

COURTER, MARIAH A.   1859 - 1938

COURTER, MINERVA   4m 28d
    daughter of Uriah D. and Emma S.
    Courter
    died 2 M[?] 1876

COURTER, GEORGE, Rev.
    12 Sep 1855 - 8 Mar 1901

COURTER, SARAH JANE
    wife of Rev. George Courter
    1859 - 1949

COURTER, NORMAN C.   1892 - 1983
COURTER, GEORGE W.   1899 - 1979
COURTER, BERTHA W.   1881 - 1976
COURTER, GAYNOR R.   1886 - 1890
COURTER, CLARA W.   1888 - 1949
COURTER, RAYMOND NORMAN   1918 - 1922
    [above six on same monument]

RUTH, JOHN CLINTON   74y 11m 6d
    son of Joseph and Mary Procktor Ruth
    husband of Lillie Rowland Yost Ruth
    18 Feb 1863 - 27 Jan 1937

RUTH, LILLIE ROWLAND YOST 74y 10d
    wife of John Clinton Ruth
    daughter of Remandes and Sarah
    Rowland Yost
    28 Sep 1862 - 8 Oct 1936

Row 17

MELLOR, MARION   1919 - 1938
    wife of John W. Mellor

HAENN, FREDERICK G.   1885 - 1949
HAENN, EVA   1888 -
    [above two on same stone]

RUTH, JOHN CLINTON
    18 Feb 1863 - 27 Jan 1937
RUTH, LILLIE R. YOST
    28 Sep 1862 - 8 Oct 1936
    [above two on same stone -- also a
    memorial for them in row 16]

ROWLAND, LYDIA A.
    daughter of Artemus T. and Martha P.
    Rowland
    20 Aug 1845 - 25 Nov 1927

ROWLAND, SARAH A.
    wife of Remandus Yost
    21 Apr 1848 - 2 Dec 1871

YOST, REMANDUS
    20 Dec 1834 - 31 Jan 1879

COX, JOSEPH   4m 5d
    son of Rev. S.L. and S.D. Cox
    died 10 Aug 1866

LOWER HILLTOWN BAPTIST CHURCH CEMETERY - FRICKS

Row 17 continued:

COX, SARAH D.   31y
    wife of Rev. S.L. Cox
    died 9 Jan 1868

KERN, JACOB   79y
    died 16 Jan 1866

KERN, SUSANNAH HILL
    mother, wife of Jacob Kern
    3 Oct 1738 - 14 May 1888
    [dates as recorded]

KERN, HIRAM E.
    22 Nov 1820 - 16 May 1822

LEWIS, THOMAS W.
    2 Mar 1845 - 5 Sep 1914

LEWIS, ELIZABETH A.
    18 Oct 1853 - 15 Aug 1951

Row 18

HUNSBERGER, H. RUSSEL
    son of Abraham and Mary Hunsberger
    died 10 Oct 1801

THOMAS, MELINDA   73y 4m 4d
    wife of Levi Thomas
    7 Nov 1812 - 11 Mar 1886

THOMAS, LEVI   77y 11m 28d
    23 Sep 1809 - 21 Sep 1886

HARR, JOHN   1837 - 1898

HARR, MARGARET J.
    wife of John Harr
    1843 - 1908

HARR, LIZZIE   1871 - [?]

HARR, J. HARRY   1867 - 1897

HARR, MARGARET   1894 - 1899
    daughter of J. H. and Ida Harr

HARR, WILLIAM M.   1892 - 1900
    son of J. H. and Ida Harr

HARR, CHARLES E
    4 Nov 1881 - 15 Nov 1920

MORGAN, SAMUEL G.   10y
    son of George and Maggie Morgan
    22 Aug 1876 - 27 Feb 1887

Row 19

SWARTZ, A. LINCOLN   1866 - 1941

SWARTZ, ELLA AMANDA   1869 - 1949

SWARTZ, MAIMIE C.   1894 - 1894

MORRIS, CHARLES M.   1909 -

MORRIS, JULIA F.   1908 - 1980

HAMILTON, MARY M.   1870 - 1940

MORRIS, ARTHUR S.   1877 - 1886
MORRIS, ALLISON M.   1866 - 1866
MORRIS, JOHN D.   1861 - 1864
MORRIS, SUSANNA S.   1840 - 1913
MORRIS, OLIVER G.   1837 - 1918

Row 20

KLINE, JOHN F.   1833 - 1868
KLINE, LYDIA   1833 - 1927

KLINE, CHARLES A.   1859 - 1927
KLINE, EMMA J.   1868 - 1937

KLINE, FLORENCE M.
    3 May 1892 - 16 Aug 1978

FRETZ, INFANT SON
    of H. L. and Wilhelmina Fretz
    [no other information]

ERWIN, JOHN B.
    son of W.B. and M.J. Erwin
    [dates illegible]

ERWIN, WILLIAM B.   1853 - 1929
    son of James and Emaline Erwin

ERWIN, MARY J.   1854 - 1943
    wife of W.B. Erwin
    daughter of Uriah and Mary Lewis

LEWIS, MARY E.
    wife of Uriah Lewis
    27 Feb 1812 - 19 Jul 1889

LEWIS, URIAH
    15 Aug 1811 - 21 Aug 1890

LEWIS, ISAAC   1809 - 1875

LEWIS, ANNA ECKHART
    wife of Isaac Lewis
    died 23 Nov 1873

SCOTT, MICA
    died 10 May 1881

SCOTT, JANE LEWIS   1804 - 1886

Row 21

MAGARGAL, SAMUEL H.   1863 - 1942
MAGARGAL, LAURA L.   1862 - 1940
MAGARGAL, SHELDON G.   1888 - 1913
MAGARGAL, LAURA   1900 - 1900

Row 21 continued:

GARNER, JACOB F.	1836 - 1904
GARNER, EMMA C.	1839 - 1921
GARNER, SHELDON	1861 - 1924
GARNER, MARY C.	1866 - 1893

ROWLAND, WILLIAM D.	1837 - 1918
ROWLAND, MARTHA	1835 - 1906
ROWLAND, MARK T.	1843 - 1844
ROWLAND, JUSTIS	1800 - 1870

ROWLAND, LETITIA   1814 - 1844
    wife of Justis Rowland

COURTER, PETER L.   1840 - 1926

COURTER, REBECCA M.
    wife of Peter Courter
    11 Mar 1846 - 21 Oct 1910

COURTER, GEORGE H.   18d
    son of Peter L. and Rebecca Courter
    died 17 Dec 1868

COURTER, WILLIAM CALVIN   1884 - 1887
    son of Peter and Rebecca Coulter

COURTER, SALLIE ELINDA
    daughter of Peter and Rebecca Coulter
    2 Jan 1877 - 26 Aug 1898

COURTER, EMMA MAY
    daughter of Peter L. and Rebecca Courter
    27 Sep 18[79?] - 26 Apr 1899

COURTER, JACOB   45y 11m 4d
    died 4 Oct 1861

COURTER, GAYNOR
    wife of Jacob Courter
    1 Jun 1818 - 4 Sep 1906

[stone - illegible]

HEDRICK, SAMUEL   83y 1m 24d
    21 Jun 1804 - 15 Aug 1887

HEDRICK, HANNAH   98y 2m 10d
    31 Dec 1800 - 11 Feb 1899

HEDRICK, WILLIAM H.   81y 4m 21d
    [no dates given]

HEDRICK, SARAH   81y 9m 3d
    wife of W.H. Hedrick
    died 13 Oct 1911

HEDRICK, HARVEY   1874 - 1957

HEDRICK, MARY E.   33y 6m 7d
    wife of Lycurcus Hedrick
    12 Apr 1863 - 3 Oct 1896

HEDRICK, LYCURCUS L.   58y 10m 27d
    10 Jan 1852 - 7 Nov 1910

HEDRICK, JOSEPHINE W.   9m 20d
    daughter of Lycurcus and Mary Hedrick
    12 May 1888 - 2 Mar 1889

HEDRICK, ELMER
    son of L. and M. Hedrick
    [?] Aug 1894 - 30 Aug 1895

Row 22

CHRISTINE, JOHN S., Rev.
    13 Oct 1800 - 21 May 1875
    second pastorate of Hilltown
    Baptist Church

LEWIS, CARRIE
    daughter of Lot and Hannah Dettra
    Lewis
    died 25 Jul 1878

KUNZ, ANNA M.   1854 - 1914

LEWIS, MORRIS P.   [81y 1m 25d ?]
    husband of Anna C. Lewis
    son of Thomas J. and Caroline Jones
    Lewis
    8 Apr 1838 - 2 Mar 1920

LEWIS, ANNA C.   33y 2m 14d
    wife of Morris P. Lewis
    born in Eastern Shore, Maryland
    died in Philadelphia
    16 Jan 1844 - 30 Mar 1877

LEWIS, MORRIS P.   1871 - 1938

LEWIS, GERTRUDE E.   1875 - 1962
    wife of Morris P. Lewis

LEWIS, THOMAS JEFFERSON   84y 3d
    25 Mar 1803 - 28 Mar 1887

LEWIS, CAROLINE   83y 6d
    wife of T. Jefferson Lewis
    27 Aug 1813 - 3 Sep 1896

LEWIS, MARGARET R.   75y 9m 7d
    sister
    3 Mar 1835 - 8 Dec 1916

LEWIS, JOHN E.   39y 1m 1d
    father
    18 Jun 1855 - 19 Jul 1894

ECKERT, RUTHETTA   59y
    wife of Henry L. Eckert
    21 Jan 1847 - 4 Sep 1906

LEWIS, MORRIS A.   1903 - 1981

LOWER HILLTOWN BAPTIST CHURCH CEMETERY - FRICKS

Row 22 continued:

LEWIS, MINERVA H.	1910 -
LEWIS, WILLIAM H.	1866 - 1926
LEWIS, ELIZABETH	1867 - 1948

    wife of William H. Lewis

LEWIS, LIZZIE   2y
    daughter of William H. and Lizzie Lewis
    2 Apr 1892 - 8 Apr 1894

Row 23

CONDICT, DAVID   D x D   1926

CONDICT, NEWTON PARSONS
    28 May 1896 - 7 Sep 1937

CONDICT, MAY HINKLE
    7 Apr 1893 - 15 Jul 1875

DINGEE/SIGAFOOS, HOWARD C.
    1882 - 1930

MOFFETT, JOSEPH
    2 Dec 1850 - 6 Mar 1916

MOFFETT, FLORENCE   1860 - 1936

CROWELL, THOMAS   father
    5 Nov 1835 - 1 Dec [1900?]

CROWELL, MARGARET
    mother, wife of Thomas Crowell
    15 Aug 1841 - 14 Mar 1896
    [above two on same stone]

KRAMER, WILLIAM M.
    27 May 1875 - 30 Jan 1947

KRAMER, BLANCHE
    25 Dec 1878 - 24 Dec 1953

HECKLER, IRWIN S.	1888 - 1934

HECKLER, SARAH B.
    wife of Irwin Heckler

HECKLER, FLORENCE	1908 - 1908
HECKLER, C. ALBERT	1915 - 1920

C.R.C

LEWIS, HARVEY W.	1874 - 1953
LEWIS, MAGDALENA B.	1871 - 1947

    wife of Harvey W. Lewis

CROWELL, FRANK   [no dates]

Row 24

PARKER, ROBERT L.	1929 - 1982
CROWELL, ANDREW J.	1866 - 1929
CROWELL, FLORA R.	1865 - 1940

CROWELL, ESTHER L.
    daughter of Andrew J. and Flora Crowell
    15 Oct 1894 - 4 Jul 1895

COURTER, EMMA S.
    daughter of Lewis C. and Mary Courter
    20 Jul 1901 - 14 Jun 1902

COURTER, LEWIS C.
    14 May 1871 - 26 Jun 1922

GODOWN, HENRY N.
    7 Jun 1860 - 27 Feb 1914

GODOWN, CORA
    20 Sep 1867 - 14 Jan 1946

Row 25

LUCAS, CLINTON H.	1888 - 1967

COURTER, JACOB H.   father
    15 Oct 1852 - 1 Feb 1909

COURTER, SARAH E.   mother
    7 Oct 1855 - 28 Jun 1917

COURTER, WILLIAM W.	1880 - 1947
COURTER, SUSANNA K.	1881 - 1964

WOOD, ELMA L.   68y
    25 Dec 1913 - 25 Jan 1982

Row 26

TEASDALE, CHARLES W., Rev.
    1 Jan 1850 - 10 Apr 1920

TEASDALE, ELVA P.
    19 Jul 1868 - 10 Nov 1918

HINKLE, EDWARD THOMAS	1866 - 1923
HINKLE, MARY ELIZABETH	1865 - 1934
HINKLE, ANNA LAPP	1909 - 1949
HINKLE, LESTER	1899 - 1977
CROUTHAMEL, HENRY A.	1888 - 1945
CROUTHAMEL, EMILY M.	1890 - 1957

ALBRIGHT, CHARLES MILTON
    21 Oct 1882 - 4 Dec 1961

ALBRIGHT, FLORA MAY COURTER
    wife of Charles M. Albright
    23 Jul 1884 - 8 Jan 1957

Row 27

SLIFER, ABIGAIL C.   1881 - 1937

Row 28

GREENE, THOMAS J.   1879 - 1941
GREENE, MARY S.
    8 May 1882 - 16 Dec 1960

HILLTOWN GERMAN REFORMED CHURCH CEMETERY

The German Reformed Church Cemetery is located behind what is now the German-Hungarian Club on Hilltown Pike, just south of the junction with route 152.

The German Reformed Church building, located adjacent to the cemetery, was later occupied by the Leidytown Presbyterian Church. It then was used as a school building and is now the home of the German-Hungarian Club.

The Club receives a small amount of money to maintain the cemetery.

Row 1 is closest to the building. The stones were read beginning with the one closest the building and reading away from it.

Row 1

BAKER, ANNA   1841 - 1869

SELLERS, DAVID   73y 5m 22d
    4 Mar 1807 - 26 Aug 1880

SELLERS, SARAH   68y 2m 27d
    wife of David Sellers
    died 31 Dec 1894

SELLERS, MAHLER   7y 11m 22d
    son of David and Sarah Sellers
    22 Feb 1849 - 22 Jan 1856

ROSENBERGER, HOWARD   aged 3m
    son of Joel and Sallie Rosenberger
    died 1 Aug 1877

Between Row 1 and 2

MOYER, JOSEPH, Dr.   40y 3m 2d
    10 Jan 1822 - 12 Apr 1862

Row 2

UMSTEAD, ELIZA ANN   47y 7m 13d
    wife of Richard Umstead
    17 Feb 1824 - 30 Sep 1871

UNSTEAD, RICHARD   69y 7m
    25 Apr 1805 - 30 Nov 1874

J. S. H.

HUNSBERGER, [Harry?]   1y 5m
    died 19 Jan 1863

HUNSBERGER, MARY M.   41y 5m 1d
    wife of J. S. Hunsberger
    died 23 Dec 1861

HUNSBERGER, JOHN S.   43y 1m 15d
    25 Feb 1828 - 10 Apr 1871

BRAND, JOHN
    3 Dec 1817 - 11 Apr 1877

[?], MAGGIE   aged 38y
    died June [?]

HUNSBERGER, ISAAC M.
    in his 34th year
    died 13 Jul 1881

SINE, GEORGE   77y 2m 1d
    14 Jan 1795 - 15 Mar 1872

SINE, ANNA
    wife of George Sine
    31 May 1799 - 18 Feb 1869

Row 3

SELLERS, ELIZABETH
    died 19 Sep 1886

SELLERS, EPHRAIM   aged 83y
    24 Oct 1801 - 7 Feb 1885

SELLERS, HANNA
    daughter of Ephraim and Elizabeth
    Sellers   died 6 May 1856

HACKMAN, SAMUEL   55y 5m 12d
    13 Aug 1822 - 25 Jan 1880

HACKMAN, MARY
    [illegible]

HACKMAN, ISABELLA   64y 6m 1d
    wife of Samuel Hackman
    14 Dec 1823 - 15 Jun 1888

HACKMAN, MARY   1y 8m 5d
    [no other dates]

HACKMAN, JOHN   aged 73y
    [no other dates on stone]

BUCKS COUNTY TOMBSTONE INSCRIPTIONS - HILLTOWN TOWNSHIP

Row 3 continued:

HACKMAN, CATHERINE   aged 72y
    [no other dates on stone]

HACKMAN, ARTHUR M.
    son of Valentine and Maggie D. Ruth
    21 Mar 1878 - 21 Feb 1879

HACKMAN, MARY LUCINDA   29y 7m 13d
    Daughter of John & Catherine Hackman
    died 13 Sep 1865

Row 4

MORGAN, TERRESSA   25y 28d
    wife of David D. Morgan
    daughter of A. S. and Maria Carver
    died 10 Sep 1878

MORGAN, ALLEN D.   1y 18d
    died 12 Jun 1875

MOYER, E. C.   31y 7m 6d
    died 5 Sep 1879

Row 5

MOYER, Wm. M.   33y 11m
    died 1 Dec 1886

McCRORY, JOHN   33y 1m 11d
    11 Jan 1836 - 25 Feb 1869

KOCH, LAURA ETTA
    daughter of Lewis and Caroline Koch
    1 Jun 1880 - 19 Apr 1882

Between Row 5 and 6

McINTYRE, CATRINA
    daughter of James and Catherine
    McIntyre
    28 Nov 1869 - 12 Dec 1871

Row 6

DEFRATIS, FRANCIS   61y 1m 14d
    13 Oct 1816 - 27 Feb 1880
    [G.A.R. flag]

C. A. S.

C. S. S.

Row 7

E. S.

T. H. S.

SMITH, TOBIAS H.   22y 11m 29d
    died 3 Jun 1871

SELLERS, GILBERT S.   27y 25d
    8 Jul 1831 - 2 Jun 1862
    P. Co. 1 Ringgold Reg. 101 P. V.
    died at Rose College Hospital

Row 8

LOUX, KATHARINE A.   76y 8m 28d
    24 Jun 1846 - 22 Mar 1923

LOUX, MAHLON B.   68y 7m 23d
    27 May 1838 - 19 Jan 1907
    A Sgt. in Civil War 1860 - 1864

SELLERS, JOHNY C.   1y 7m 8d
    3 Feb 1880 - 11 Sep 1881

SELLERS, ELIZABETH   4y 2m 10d
    daughter of Josiah and Catherine
    Sellers
    8 Dec 1886 - 9 Feb 1891

SELLERS, CATHERINE A.   49y 9m 29d
    wife of Josiah Sellers
    28 Aug 1853 - 26 Jun 1903

SELLERS, JOSIAH   68y 7m 29d
    11 Dec 1842 - 10 Aug 1911

OUR LADY OF SACRED HEART CEMETERY, HILLTOWN

Hilltown Township, Bucks County, Pennsylvania

OUR LADY OF SACRED HEART CEMETERY

SECTION A

Section A, containing five rows, is located perpendicular to Hilltown Pike (Route 152) and parallel to the lane in the cemetery. Located on the southeast side of the cemetery, this section was read with row one being closest to the lane and the first stone being nearest to Hilltown Pike in each row.

Row 1

JAVORKA, PAUL	1879 - 1937
JAVORKA, ELIZ	1879 - 1928

[three spaces]

PEKAR, JENNIE	1924 -
PEKAR, MARY	1898 -
PEKAR, JOHN	1891 - 1968

[eight spaces]

SWOYKOWSKI, JOSEPHINE	1861 - 1925
FRAY, MARTHA	1891 - 1977
FRAY, WILLIAM	1888 - 1967

[space]

BOLD, NICHOLAS	1869 - 1940
BOLD, MAGDALENA	1871 - 1954
BOLD, JACOB KIRSCH	1901 - 1921

[eight spaces]

OREMUSZ, KATHERINA
   26 Oct 1863 - 19 Apr 1928

SCHILLINGER, THERESIA
   (Gattin Theresia Meingeliebte)
   30 Jul 1884 - 5 Oct 1921

OREMUSZ, STEPHAN
   31 Dec 1858 - 13 Sep 1925
   [eight spaces]

USALIS, URSULA	1876 - 1925
USALIS, ADAM	1877 - 1960

Row 2

LUKESCH, FRANK	1879 - 1964
LUKESCH, ROSE	1894 -
LUKESCH, EDWARD	1865 - 1950
LUKESCH, APOLONIE	1864 - 1938
PIECUSKI, FRANK	1902 - 1964
PIECUSKI, CONSTANCE	1899 - 1979
PIECUSKI, STANLEY HELHOWSKI	1921 - 1930

DARRAR, AMELIA F.
   27 Dec 1890 - 14 Nov 1949

DARRAR, HARRY A.
   10 Sep 1873 - 10 Nov 1930

HOLCINGER, ANNA RECHNER	1850 - 1932
RECHNER, FRANK	1909 - 1932
RECHNER, MARY	1897 - 1938
WILWERT, NICK	1881 - 1961
WILWERT, EVA	1887 - 1955
WILWERT, ANTHONY	1915 - 1932

WHODARCZYK, WALTER L.
   13 Dec 1875 - 23 Dec 1938

WHODARCZYK, ANTONIA L.	1888 - 1949
POMA, KATHIE	1889 - 1972
POMA, ROBERT	1883 - 1959
POMA, JEANNETTE	1939 - 1942
granddaughter	
POMA, ROBERT G., Jr.	1910 - 1963

Row 3

LUECKE, CHARLES H.	1887 - 1967
LUECKE, ELIZABETH	1903 - 1955
LUECKE, JENNIE DAVERN	1902 - 1961
CLEMENTS, GEORGE T.	1913 - 1982
Sgt. U.S. Army W.W. II	

FLORKOWSKI, STANLEY FRANCIS, Jr.
   son of Stanley and Naomi Florkowski
   27 Sep 1949 - 14 Jul 1967

RECHNER, STEPHEN	1872 - 1966
RECHNER, MARY	1877 - 1953
RECHNER, CATHERINE	1913 -
WINKLER, MARGARET	1905 -
WINKLER, RICHARD C.	1902 - 1970
BONGART, HELEN A.	1932 - 1979
WOLF, PETER	1885 - 1970
WOLF, ANNA	1886 - 1960

Row 3 continued:

TREACY, DOROTHY M.	1925 - 1971
TREACY, WILLIAM E.	1924 -
CIMORELLI, RAYMOND A.	1934 - 1974

Row 4

DEMBROSKY, ARTHUR W.	1932 -
DEMBROSKY, SUSANNE R.	1933 -
DEMBROSKY, WALTER J.	1911 - 1981
DEMBROSKY, MARGARET	1911 -

[nine spaces]

JONCZYK, MARY E.
   14 Dec 1904 -
JONCZYK, STANLEY
   2 Mar 1896 - 3 Dec 1975

JONCZYK, STANLEY P.
   22 Jun 1937 - 18 Jan 1973

    space]

Row 5

CONNELLY - HANDSDIN, CATHERINE A.
   1892 - 1975
CONNELLY - HANDSDIN, HERBERT
   1925 -
CONNELLY - HANDSDIN, SAMUEL
   1911 -
CONNELLY, HANDSDIN, MARIE
   1914 -
   [both names on stone]

McCURLEY, LANSING C.
   9 Feb 1899 - 16 Oct 1958
   Pennsylvania
   Pvt. USMC 5 Division W.W. I

PISCHL, VINCENT, Sr.	1893 - 1970
FROIO, FRANK P.	1931 - 1976
KAHLE, MARGARET M.	1911 -
KAHLE, WILLIAM F., Sr.	1910 - 1977
DePHILLIPO, WILLIAM J.	1923 - 1978

   Cpl. USMC W.W. I

DePHILLIPO, CATHERINE V.	1923 -
PALOVCAK, STEPHEN G.	1910 - 1979
SCHMIDT, FRITZ A.	1896 - 1980

ESPOSITO, GLORIA
   30 Jan 1981

| CAMPBELL, MARY ELLEN | 1933 - 1982 |
| KUTLER, LORETTA | aged 42 years |

   5 Feb 1840 - 28 Apr 1982

SECTION B

Section B, on the northeast side of the cemetery lane, contains eleven rows of tombstones plus a twelfth row of stones which face Hilltown Pike instead of the lane. Row one is closest to the lane. All rows are read beginning with the stones nearest to Hilltown Pike.

Row 1, section B

ANDERSON, FRANCES   1894 - 1975

PEKAR, MICHAEL
   1 Aug 1863 - 19 Jun 1929
PEKAR, MARY
   14 Feb 1867 - 12 Feb 1959

[two spaces]

BALCO, MARY ETHEL	1919 - 1928
daughter	
BALCO, MARY PIECUSKI	1882 - 1926
mother	
MAY, SAMUEL J.	1889 - 1924
MAY, MARGARET	1891 - 1974
POLZER, IGNATIUS	1876 - 1923

[four spaces]

HALEY, WILLIAM G.   1902 - 1982

[five spaces]

ROHS, ANNA ROSE
   1 May 1892 - 14 Aug 1926

| ROHS, ANNA | 1865 - 1933 |
| ROHS, JOHN | 1860 - 1938 |

ROHS, JOSEPH J.
   2 Jun 1914 - 24 Jun 1933

WAGNER, HERMAN B.   1923 - 1979
   [blank space on this stone]

| CRAIG, JOSEPH J. | 1910 - |
| CRAIG, JULIA V. | 1915 - 1977 |

Row 2, section B

NEMEC, RUDOLPH
   18 Nov 1886 - 23 Jul 1926
   [six spaces]

KONSOWITZ, STEPHEN J.   1922 - 1968
   Flag 1941 - 1945
   [this stone has a blank space]

| LESH, THERESA | 1885 - 1966 |
| ROHS, STEPHEN | 1892 - 1965 |

OUR LADY OF SACRED HEART CEMETERY   85

Row 2, section B continued:

   [space]

ROHS, HERTA M.
   20 Mar 1925 - 13 Mar 1958

Row 3, section B

LORIS, JOSEPH	1887 - 1933
LORIS, KATIE	1889 - 1970
LORIS, MARGARET	1919 - 1928

   [space]

ERMLER, JOHN J.
   30 Jul 1901 - 26 Aug 1927

   [space]

SCHEIDEL, GUSTAVE G., Sr.
   11 Jul 1887 - 17 Feb 1960
SCHEIDEL, GUSTAVE G., Jr.
   25 Aug 1915 - 26 Feb 1927
SCHEIDEL, ROSE B.
   27 Feb 1889 - 13 Jul 1974
DONIS, NICHOLAS, Sr.   1860 - 1938
DONIS, ANNA E. [3 space] 1866 - 1927
McKNIGHT, JOHN H.   1895 - 1975
   [space on stone for two more names]

   [space]

McCARTHY, RICHARD F., Jr.	1932 -
McCARTHY, MARGARET J.	1933 -
McCARTHY, JOSEPH G.	1960 - 1980

   [sixteen spaces]

SMOLA, JOHN T.	1917 -
SMOLA, EDNA K.	1921 - 1974
GRASSO, EDWARD K.	1935 - 1977
GRASSO, JANE M.	1938 -

Row 4, section B

KUCIKAS, JOSEPH J.	1874 - 1932
KUCIKAS, PETRONELLA	1882 -
KUCIKAS, EDWARD R.	1917 - 1928

   [two spaces]

LORIS, FRANK N.   1914 - 1975
   T|Sgt U.S. Army W.W. II
LORIS, FLORENCE R.   1921 -

   [five spaces]

WALTERS, ALBERT F.
   18 Sep 1926 - 2 Apr 1970
   PA Sgt Mil Police Corps
   World War II - Korea

   [five spaces]

VENETZ, JOHN L.	1937 -
VENETZ, HELEN M.	1941 - 1973

   [space]

WAGNER, ANTON	1889 - 1978
WAGNER, LEONTINA	1892 - 1981

   [space]

PASSANTE, ANGELA MARIE
   16 May 1968 - 7 Feb 1970

   [two spaces]

WALDSPURGER, DAVID A.
   25 Sep 1952 - 29 Oct 1972
   PA AIC US Air Force Vietnam

[metal marker -- information missing]

   [space]

CLOAK, JOSEPH E.	1906 - 1973
CLOAK, CATHERINE E.	1909 -

   [three spaces]

CLIFFORD, ROBERT J.	[blank]
CLIFFORD, ANNA M.	1906 - 1973

   [two spaces]

STRONG, CHARLES D.	1930 - 1974
STRONG, CATHERINE M.	1925 - 1981
RABBONI, LOUISE M.	1903 - 1980

   [above three on same stone]

   [two spaces]

ROWLETT, HAMILTON C.	1912 - 1982
ROWLETT, MARGARET A.	1910 - 1979

Row 5, section B

REUBA, BOLESLO
   9 Aug 1888 - 16 May 1967
REUBA, ONA B.
   26 Jul 1877 - 29 Apr 1946
REUBA, VERONICA
   13 Oct 1916 - 28 Aug 1933

   [six spaces]

WALTERS, ALBERT F.	1926 - 1970
HATTON, JOHN J.	1900 - 1971
HATTON, SOPHIA	1910 -
DAMM, EDWARD J.	1906 - 1972
DAMM, MADELINE D.	1907 -
NEUBERT, ROBERT E.	1932 - 1969
NEUBERT, NANCY A.	1936 -

   [space]

RYMDEIKA, FRANK	1892 - 1969
RYMDEIKA, JOSEPHINE	1901 - 1975

Row 5, section B continued:

[two spaces]

ALFF, MARY LOUISE   1954 - 1969

[four spaces]

KELLER, CHARLES E.
    12 Oct 1920 - 22 Aug 1973

[space]

[HIEGER?], JOSEPHINE S.   1886 - 1973
    [plastic marker from Jay C. Kriebel Funeral Home]

[three spaces]

BETANCOURT, BEATRICE   49 years
    18 Jun 1928 - 16 Jun 1978
    [metal funeral home marker]

RIVEST, KATHRYN L.   1920 - 1977
RIVEST, H. PAUL   1924 -

Row 6, section B

MICH, DAVID LEO
    son of Kenneth and Isabella Mich
    29 Apr 1949 - 12 Jan 1969

SCHADL, ANTON   1877 - 1965
SCHADL, MARY   1886 - 1976

HARBER, LEONARD J.   1908 - 1978
HARBER, IRENE L.   1916 - 1966

GLICK, HENRY A., Sr.   1901 - 1967
GLICK, GWENDOLYN M.   1894 -

CLIME, THOMAS E.   1916 - 1968

BEDNARZEWSKI, KAROL   1892 - 1973
BEDNARZEWSKI, MARY ANNA   1894 - 1975

YOVISH

FITE, JOSEPH B.   1901 - 1970
FITE, MARIAN S.   1896 - 1972

GLUCK, JOSEPH F.   1900 - 1971
GLUCK, MARGARET M.   1909 - 1981

CHESNUS, GEORGE   1899 - 1973
CHESNUS, ELIZABETH   1886 - 1973

KURIAN, FRANK G.   1914 -
KURIAN, ANNA M.   1914 - 1976

Row 7, section B

MAUGER, FRANK J.   1889 - 1953
MAUGER, GERTRUDE   1889 - 1952

JURIN, EDWARD A.   1924 - 1972
    Pvt. U.S. Army World War II

ZOELLER, WILLIAM J.   1892 - 1955
ZOELLER, EMMA L.   1900 - 1960

RECKNER, WILLIAM A.   1895 - 1975
    Sgt. Co. 3 153rd DB World War I
RECKNER, IDA   1891 - 1970
    Nurse Med. Corp. World War I

VOLPE, ANTHONY J.   1915 - 1980
VOLPE, ANNE L.   1921 -

Row 8, section B

RAWA, AGNES JOAN   1942 - 1944
RAWA, JOSEPH   1944 - 1945

JURIN, ANNA S.   1893 - 1969
JURIN, IVAN G.   1889 - 1947

KRAMER, JOHN   1883 - 1968
KRAMER, GERTRUDE   1886 - 1964

RAWA, ADAM   1877 - 1952
RAWA, MARY   1880 - 1948

NACE, GERALDINE   baby
    16 Jul 1949

SOBOCINSKI, IGNACZ   1895 - 1949

POSAVEC, PETER   1888 - 1951
POSAVEC, KATHERINE   1889 - 1969

RAUSCH, MATHIAS   1981
RAUSCH, MARY   1964
RAUSCH, HELENA   [no dates]

LESH, FRANK P.   1909 - 1973
LESH, ELIZABETH M.   1912 -

LESH, ELIZABETH
    22 Nov 1934 - 26 Aug 1952

LONG, HARRY S.   1873 - 1954
LONG, SOPHIE B.   1883 - 1959

KAZLER, ANNA K.   1892 - 1955
KAZLER, PETER   1891 - 1977

Row 9, section B

WALCH, FRANK J.   1878 - 1934
WALCH, JOSEPHINE   1881 - 1969
WALCH, JOHN I.   1919 - 1940

BALCO, LOUISE M.   1916 - 1945
BALCO, JOSEPH G.   1915 - 1981

[space]

OUR LADY OF SACRED HEART CEMETERY

Row 9, section B continued:

ROUNAN, ANNA	mother	
29 Apr 1883 - 23 Mar 1948		
ROUNAN, JOSEPH J.		1878 - 1960

[three spaces]

CHOROMANSKI, MARIANNA	1887 - 1947
KAUNAS, EDMUND	1878 - 1948
KAUNAS, MARY	1887 - 1953
PECKICONIS, ANDREW	1892 - 1965
PECKICONIS, CAROLINE	1895 - 1949

[space]

GORCZYCA, JÓZEF K.	1882 - 1958
GORCZYCA, KLARA	1891 - 1977
NAGURNY, JOHN	1886 - 1950
NAGURNY, FANNIE	1896 - 1958
NAGURNY, ANDREW	1927 - 1948

[space]

FRANCIS, GEORGE	1879 - 1948
FRANCIS, ROSE	1888 - 1955
VITKUS, EDWARD J.	1914 - 1955
VITKUS, HELENE	[blank]
VOGEL, STEPHEN	1883 - 1955
VOGEL, MAGDALENA	1877 -
MATTSON, WALTER W., Jr.	1916 - 1957
MATTSON, ANNA M.	1915 - 1977
GREGG, ROBERT G.	1936 - 1958
GREGG, ROBERT G.	1956 - 1970
COONEY, RICHARD T.	1893 - 1964
COONEY, ADELIA M.	1886 - 1973

MATTSON, NICHOLAS J.   1946 - 1968
   Sgt. A Brty 6/29th Arty.
   Vietnam Era

[space]

THOMSON, JAMES C.   1924 - 1973
   T/5 255th Inf.
   U.S. Army World War II

Row 10, section B

[space]

WIETECHA, THOMAS J.	1887 - 1954
WIETECHA, CAROLINE wife	1888 -
KOWALCZUK, JOHN	1888 -
KOWALCZUK, MARY wife	1890 -

DURSA, GEORGE
   1 Jul 1888 - 19 Sep 1960
DURSA, MARY
   10 Jan 1895 -

[space]

SCHRAMM, GEORGE C.	1888 - 1957
SCHRAMM, KATHERINE F.	1892 - 1966
GRABOWSKI, HELENA	1890 - 1957
GRABOWSKI, JULIAN	[blank]

[space]

SENIOR, PETER J.   1894 - 1961

DORSANEO, MARIA F.
   24 Jul 1920 - 1 Oct 1957
   PA S Sgt 304 Signal OPR BN
   World War II

STRUG, JOHN	1887 - 1961
STRUG, ANNA	1887 - 1959
STRUG, ADELA H.	1915 - 1960
daughter	
PRYKAZ, HELEN K.	1885 - 1960
PRYKAZ, ANDREW	1878 - 1967
WIDMANN, PAUL J.	1938 - 1961
WIDMANN, REINHOLD	1900 - 1969
WIDMANN, MARY T.	1900 -
BUEHNER, ANTONIA	1887 - 1961
BUEHNER, JOSEPH	1887 - 1970
CAHILL, TERESA M.	1951 - 1962
CAHILL, ALMA E.	1909 - 1967
MITNIK, CATHERINE	1916 -
daughter	
MITNIK, MARY	1877 - 1963
mother	

[three spaces]

FULGINITI, CLARA T.   1920 - 1961
   [metal funeral home marker]

MATHIAS, JOHN	1895 - 1981
MATHIAS, MARIA	1894 -
SHULICK, ANDY	1899 - 1972
SHULICK, JULIA	1900 -

Row 11, section B

BERNOTAS, CECELIA	1888 - 1959
BERNOTAS, ANTHONY J.	1890 - 1971
BERNOTAS, FREDERICK W.	1942 - 1968

Row 11, section B continued:

BERNOTAS, EDWARD, Jr.	1942 - 1960
BERNOTAS, GREGORY A.	1952 -
BERNOTAS, ANNA H.	1918 -
BERNOTAS, EDWARD, Sr.	1917 -
BRAQUEHAIS, CECILE U.	1880 - 1962
BRAQUEHAIS, LOUIS A.	1881 - 1962
PIERZCHALA, THERESA	1903 - 1962
PIERZCHALA, PETER	1893 - 1965
SIMONS, SARAH M.	1888 - 1962
SIMONS, JOSEPH L.	1889 - 1967

GUTHERMAN, GEORGE A.
    23 Nov 1886 - 21 Nov 1962
    PFC HA Co. 315 Inf 79th Div
    Pennsylvania   World War I

GUTHERMAN, JENNIE F.	1903 - 1978
OLSEWSKI, ROSE	1882 - 1971
OLSEWSKI, ADAM	1886 - 1962
JAWORSKI, JOHN F.	1914 - 1963
JAWORSKI, ANASTASIA	1922 -
NOWAKOWSKI, STANLEY	1893 - 1969
NOWAKOWSKI, ANNA	1894 - 1964
LUTKAVAGE, STELLA	1887 - 1964
LUTKAVAGE, JOSEPH A.	1892 - 1974

GAGAS, SYLVIA   wife
    5 Apr 1909 - 18 Aug 1968
GAGAS, FRANK   husband
    26 Oct 1907 -
GAGAS, AGNES   sister
    26 Apr 1909 -

MITNIK, CHARLES J.	1909 - 1978
MITNIK, BLANCHE C.	1922 -

Row 12, section B

MIKETTA, IGNATIUS	1886 - 1981
MIKETTA, NOTHBURGA	1886 - 1972
BALCO, JOHN	1881 - 1968
BALCO, ANNA	1891 - 1972

SIMONS, GERALD L.
    18 Apr 1925 - 28 Sep 1978
SIMONS, FLORENCE M.
    14 Nov 1926 -

SECTION C

Section C, located on the southeast side of the circle and fartherest from Hilltown Pike, contains two rows plus a stone. The rows were read beginning with those nearest the circle and reading toward the field.

Row 1, section C

MITNIK, DAVID E.
    27 Aug 1955 - 29 May 1878

MALACH, FRANK A.	1911 - 1980
HEVERLY, TERENCE S.	1964 - 1980
son	
HOBART, JOSEPHINE A.	1915 - 1981
HOBART, CHESTER W.	1909 -
VAN KLEEF, PETER	1862 - 1932
father, husband	

O'LEARV, DENISE MARIE   stillborn
    3 Apr 1981 - 3 Apr 1981
MANNINO, CATHRINE MARIE   daughter
    8 Oct 1980
CLIME, KEVIN MICHAEL
    30 May 1981 - 31 May 1981
COURSEY, BRIAN J.   son
    25 Sep 1979
LEO, THERESA JO
    15 Nov 1978 - 22 Nov 1978
GRANAN, CHRISTOPHER JOHN
    11 Jan 1976 - 16 Jan 1976
REINHARD, THOMAS RANDOLPH
    22 Dec 1974 - 24 Dec 1974

BASGIL, ANGELA M.	1980 - 1980
baby	
SMITH, WILHEM baby boy	29 May 1971
SIDEL, BABY GIRL	1968 - 1968
[reed Funeral home marker]	
KRUK, JAMES L.	9 Jul 1965

WAGNER, ERIK
    14 Jun 1964 - 7 Jun 1965

STAEHLE, ANN M.	1920 - 1957
mother	
CONTE, JOSEPH	24 Apr 1952

CASSEL, KAREN THERESA
    25 Oct 1954 - 28 Mar 1955

Row 2, section C

SIEGRIED, ANNA K.   1905 - 1973
SIEGRIED, ELLWOOD M.   1900 -

KIESTER, CARL A.   1927 - 1977
    FC3   US NAVY   World War II

KORMANSKI, MARIE C.   1921 - 1977
    Y3   US Navy   World War II

ROJINSKY, FLORENCE A.   1927 - 1978

VENETZ, JOHN J.   1908 - 1976
VENETZ, BERNETTA E.   1914 - 1974

MULLMANN, THEODORE M.
    4 Jul 1933 - 16 Dec 1974

GRUBB, EDWARD C.   1909 - 1978
GRUBB, MARGARET F.   1904 -

YORK, STANLEY E.   1903 - 1975

McCAUSLAND, WILLIAM V.   1928 - 1978
    SFC   US Army

NEYRA, JULIA F.   1985 - 1980

NEWSOME, CATHERINE V.   1903 - 1979
NEWSOME, HAROLD W.   1903 - 1975

GRUB[?], EL[?]G   1962 - 1980

GRUBB, EDWARD C.   1936 -
GRUBB, EARLENE R.   1938 -
GRUBB, MICHAEL G.   1962 - 1980
GRUBB, KATHLENE L.   1969 - 1969

HELVESTON, EDNA M.   1912 - 1975
HELVESTON, CHARLES H.   1899 - 1978

WISNIEWSKI, LAURA M.   1893 - 1980

HAFFEY, ANNE M.
    28 Oct 1929 -
HAFFEY, FRANCIS P.
    2 Apr 1909 - 27 Oct 1975

McGRATH, LOUIS J., Jr.
    3 Mar 1931 - 17 Sep 1980
McGARTH, EMMA M.
    20 Aug 1931 -

BRENNAN, THOMAS J.   1968 - 1976

SLEAR, RENO J.   1911 - 1980
SLEAR, SARAH R.   1912 -

PRYKAZ, ADAM   1902 -
PRYKAZ, CAROLYN   1902 - 1982

ROHS, AGNES C.
    5 Feb 1915 -
ROHS, STEPHEN J.
    20 Mar 1912 - 24 Feb 1977

JORDAN, MILDRED I.   1916 - 1975
    mother

SCHMIDT, JOSEPH J.   1907 - 1974
    PFC Co. B   322 Engr
    US Army   World War II

KALMAR, ANTAL
    13 Jun 1892 - 7 Aug 1963

PAGE, MARY KALMAR   1885 - 1966
PAGE, WILLIAM J.   1878 - 1972

CHESNES, DAVID P.   1956 - 1973
    son

HENNESSY, CLIFFORD J.   1904 - 1973
HENNESSY, AMELIA A.   [blank]
HENNESSY, EDWARD F.   [blank]

ALEXANDER, BRANDT E.   1966 - 1976
ALEXANDER, MARK W.   1970 - 1976

ACKERMAN, GEORGE L.   1894 - 1978

Before Row 1, section C

WAGNER, RICHARD S.
    23 Sep 1932 - 10 Oct 1932
WAGNER, JOSEPHINE
    18 Dec 1928 - 11 Nov 1933

BEDNARZEWSKI, JOHN   son
    29 Apr 1921 - 17 Apr 1923

PEKAR, ROBERT   1921 - 1922
    son of Robert and Hedwig Pekar

Row 3, section C

BACHURSKI, JOSEPHINE A.   1921 - 1982
BACHURSKI, EDWARD   1916 -

PERKASIE MENNONITE CEMETERY

The Perkasie Mennonite Cemetery is located on the northeast side of the Callowhill Road, just before it crosses Pleasant Spring Creek and Perkasie (Branch) Road. This cemetery was begun in 1950. Before that time interments for that church were made in Blooming Glen Mennonite Cemetery.

Row 1

BENNER, INFANT DAUGHTER
    of Norman & Ethel Benner   1952

BENNER, STEVEN KIRK
    24 - 27 Dec 1974   "Our Baby"
    (This stone is behind the first one between rows one and two.)

BENNER, NORMAN B.	1911 - 1970
FOUNDS, JOHN R.	1948 - 1952
LAPP, STANLEY W.	1927 - 1953
LAPP, MABEL W.	1900 - 1977
LAPP, [blank]	
STROUSE, WILLIAM H.	1891 - 1956

[flag, but no service information]

STROUSE, FRANCENA	1895 - 1971
DELP, JACOB ALAN	1850 - 1962
GOOD, FANNIE	1885 - 1964
DETWEILER, LILLIAN C.	1901 - 1976
DETWEILER, ELMER M.	1901 - 1965
[HUNSBERGER, HILDA A.]	1917 - 1977

EBERSOLE, HILDA A. HUNSBERGER

HUNSBERGER, HENRY L.	1919 - 1968
KULP, CLIFFORD T.	1941 - 1973
KULP, IDA	1916 -[blank]
KULP, JOSEPH A.	1914 - 1971

[These two on same stone]

Row 2

LEATHERMAN, CLARA W.	1893 - 1974
LEATHERMAN, WALTER H.	1892 -[blank]

[above two on same stone]

ROSENBERGER, L. ELAINE	1930 - 1974
COLE, SHIRLEY R.	1935 - 1960
COLE, VIOLA R.	1905 - 1977
KUHN, JAMES "infant son"	1964 - 1964

UHLIG, OLGA LISA "infant daughter"
    1969

KLINE, MAMIE	1902 -[blank]
KLINE, CLINTON WWI	1898 - 1970

[above two on same stone]

HOCKMAN, SARA	1911 -[blank]
HOCKMAN, ELMER	1910 - 1977

[above two on same stone]

ALLEN, JAMES HENRY   19 - 21 Jan 1977
ALLEN, SUSAN RUTH
    21 Dec 1978 - 27 Feb 1979
    [above two on same stone]

MERRILLS, BOAH LEE   24 - 25 May 1971
    infant daughter of Ronald & Ruth
    Martin   [notes read Martin]
    a second placque reads 26 May 1971

KRAINIAK, MICHAEL
    27 Oct 1924 - 28 Nov 1970
    PA PFC 572 AAAAW BN CAC WWII

Row 3

WENDTLAND, CAROL A.	1850 -
WENDTLAND, MARY J.	1924 -
WENDTLAND, WILLIAM B.	1918 - 1978
WENDLAND, SHERRY SHIELA	1979
REINOSO, FRANCISCO O.	1891 - 1974
ALVAREZ, C. LINO	1901 - 1971
HOCKMAN, GEORGE L.	1899 -
HOCKMAN, EVA M.	1902 -
MOHN, KENNETH W. "son"	1938 -
MOHN, MELLA S.	1918 -
MOHN, ALBERT W. [WWII flag]	1913 - 1980

[above two on same stone]

Row 4

MOHN, ALBERT W.
    28 Mar 1913 - 7 Jun 1980
    AMM 2 US Navy WWII

HILLTOWN UNION CEMETERY (OLD CEMETERY)

St. Peter's U.C.C. Church

to Line Lexington ---

HILLTOWN PIKE

Church Parking Lot

a, b, c, d, e, f, g, h, i

row 1
row 2
row 3
row 4
row 5
row 6
row 7
row 8
row 9
row 10
row 11
row 12
row 13
row 14
row 15
row 16
row 17
row 18
row 19
row 20
row 21
row 22
row 23
row 24
row 25
row 26

row 29
row 30
row 31
row 32
row 33a
row 34
b, c, d
row 35
row 36
row 37
row 38
row 39
row 40
row 41
row 42
row 43
row 44
row 45
row 46
row 47
row 48
row 49

ST. PETER'S UNION CEMETERY -- HILLTOWN UNION CEMETERY

The first section of this cemetery to be recorded is adjacent to the Saint Peter's United Church of Christ parking lot. Row one is next to and parallel to the church. The stones were read beginning at the parking lot and reading toward the Hilltown Pike.

Row 1

REEDER, MARY   91y 4m 19d
    wife of John Reeder
    6 Dec 1771 - 25 Apr 1863

SCHEETZ, CATHARINE   78y 7m 8d
    mother, wife of Andrew Scheetz
    5 Sep 1807 - 13 Apr 1880

SCHEETZ, ANDREW   80y 1m 1d
    father
    25 Aug 1803 - 26 Sep 1873

YEARICK, CALVIN H.   15y 1m 1d
    son of Rev. W. R. Yearick
    died 23 Feb 1870

YEARICK, PHILIP HARPEL   22y 10m 23d
    5 May 1868 - 28 Mar 1891

YEARICK, ANGELINE CHRISTINA
    daughter of Rev. W. R. and W. B.
    Yearick   1867

YEARICK, SUSANNAH M.   36y 2m 0d
    wife of Rev. W. R. Yearick
    daughter of H. Huchunburg?
    died 8 Apr 1862

YEARICK, JOHN N.   15y 1m 0d
    son of Rev. W. R. and S. M.
    Yearick   died 9 Apr 1862

YEARICK, Rev. WM. R.   71y 1m 3d
    died 4 Dec 1888
    14 years of the Gospel
    Reformed Church and 18 at Hilltown

YEARICK, WILHELMINA B.   62y 11m 0d
    wife of Rev. Wm. R. Yearick
    1 Aug 1833 - 17 Jul 1896

YEARICK, TALITHA ANN   50y 1m 28d
    10 May 1852 - 8 Jul 1902

YEARICK, ADALINE   40y 1m 22d
    daughter of Rev. Wm. ans Susanna M.
    18 Jan 1851 - 10 Mar 1890

FULMER, JACOB G.   [0?]y 3m [1?]d
    27 Jan 1851 - Apr 1866

[Fallen stone]

FULMER, MARY
    mother, wife of Jacob Fulmer
    29 Jun 1805 - 16 Aug 1885

YEARICK, LEVI EDWARD   10 years
    died 7 Jul 1875
    [between row 1 and 2]

Row 2

KELLY, LOVINA H.
    wife of John E. Kelly
    daughter of Jacob & Mary A. Dimmig
    20 Jul 1874 - 21 Jul 1891

SCHNAVEL, JONATHAN FRANKLIN   7m 8d
    died 6 Mar 1864

SCHNAVEL, RACHEL   39y 4m 15d
    daughter of Henry & Mary Ann
    Schmoyer
    5 Oct 1821 - 22 Feb 1861

SNOVEL, JONATHAN   80y 7m 27d
    12 Aug 1821 - 9 Apr 1902

BERINGER, MARY ANN   1y 7m 0d
    daughter of Amos and Barbara
    Beringer
    20 Jul 1859 - 20 Feb 1861

BERINGER, BARBARA   ?y 5m 15d
    wife of Amos Beringer
    daughter of Henry S. and Mary
    Anglemoyer
    21 Mar 1827 - 5 Sep 1862

BERINGER, AMOS   61y 6m 5d
    died 4 Dec 1885

B. B.

BERINGER, EPHRAIM A.   22y 6m 25d
    27 Jun 1849 - 22 Jan 1872

BERINGER, SOPHIA   aged 93
    9 Aug 1830 - 15 Nov 1923

SNYDER, CAREY   35y 0m 12d
    Verse - E. Snyder
    13 Aug 1827 - 25 Aug 1862

EARLEY, ELLEN JANE   12y 6m 3d
    21 Jan 1853 - 21 Jul 1865

Row 2 continued:

DANNEHOVER, ABRAHAM T.   38y 6m 10d
   26 Apr 1823 - 6 Nov 1861

DANNEHOWER, ABRAHAM   aged 85
   7 Jul 1786 - 12 Jul 1871

DANNEHOWER, BARBARA
   wife of Abraham Dannebower
   12 Mar 1789 - 10 Dec 1878

DANNEHOWER, HANNAH   78y 7m 0d
   17 Aug 1817 - 10 Mar 1896

SNYDER, INFANT DAUGHTER
   of Franklin and Amanda Snyder
   died 6 Jan 1866
   [buried between rows 2 and 3]

Row 3

SCHOOL, EDGAR   7m 3d
   son of Leidy and Amanda School
   15 Aug 1894 - 18 Mar 1895

SCHOLL, LEIDY
   9 Jul 1849 - 11 Sep 1930

SCHOLL, AMANDA
   8 Jun 1852 - 9 Jun 1928

SCHOLL, LEA   42y 11m 17d
   died 23 May 1865

SCHOLL, CATHERINE   63y 2m 7d
   wife of William School
   daughter of Jacob and Susanna
   Appenzeller
   17 Dec 1824 - 21 Feb 1888

SCHOLL, WILLIAM   63y 7m 11d
   20 Mar 1826 - 10 Nov 1889

WEISEL, LEVI   7y 3m 20d
   son of Aaron & Maria Weisel
   died 26 Feb 1865

WEISEL, DIANNA
   daughter of Aaron and Maria Weisel
   13 Jun 1865 - 19 Aug 1865

WETZEL, WILLIAM FRANCIS   6m 3d
   son of Aaron and Maria Wetzel
   1 Sep 1870

SHERM, BARBARA   63y 11m 15d
   wife of John Sherm
   31 Aug 1805 - 16 Aug 1869

SHERM, JOHN   83y 5m 14d
   4 Jan 1806 - 18 Jun 1889

STEINBACH, WILLIAM H.   24y 2m 25d
   son of Frank and Catharina Steinbach
   1 Sep 1838 - 26 Dec 1862

NUNNAMAKER, CATHARINA MARIA   21y 10m 19d
   daughter of Mich and Maria Nunnamaker
   3 May 1841 - 22 Jan 1863

NUNNEMAKER, MARIA   72y 9m 18d
   wife of Michael Nunnemaker
   15 May 1812 - 2 Mar 1885

NUNNAMAKER, MICHAEL   71y 9m 19d
   3 Apr 1812 - 22 Jan 1884

ELLENBERGER, ?   [no dates given]
   son of J. M. and M. A. Ellenberger

ELLENBERGER, HENRY   1y 3m 6d
   son of J. M. and M. A. Ellenberger
   died 3 Jul 1867

ELLENBERGER, MARY ANN   88y 8m 16d
   4 Nov 1832 - 20 Jul 1921

ELLENBERGER, J. MARTIN   46y 6m 15d
   14 Mar 1824 - 29 Sep 1870

ELLENBERGER, INFANT SON
   child of J. M. and M. A. Ellenberger
   died 29 Nov 18[68?]

ELLENBERGER, INFANT SON
   child of J. M. and M. A. Ellenberger
   1867

[between row 3 and 4 are two stones with illegible german script]

Row 4

ECKERT, MARIA   aged 45
   wife of Isaac Eckhart
   died 29 Jun 1879

KOBER, SARAH C.   74y 11m 16d
   died 31 Aug 1914

KOVER, ELIZABETH C.   30y 4m 13d
   daughter of John and Mary Kover
   20 Nov 1832 - 3 Apr 1863

KOBER, MARY   97y 3m 8d
   wife of John M. Kober
   19 Jan 1802 - 27 Apr 1899

KOBER, JOHN M.   81y 10m 15d
   father
   11 Oct 1800 - 26 Aug 1882

FLUCK, MARY   83y 6m 12d
   daughter of John Ott
   wife of Philip Fluck
   23 Dec 1792 - 5 Jul 1870

ST. PETER's UNION CEMETERY (Old Section)   95

Row 4 Continued:

FLUCK, LEIDY   44y 9m 22d
    son of John and Cath Fluck
    died 15 Jan 1863

[small stone]

FLUCK, EMMANUEL   3y 5m 28d
    son of John and Cath Fluck
    died 28 Jan 1867

FLUCK, CATH   2y 2m 27d
    daughter of John and Cath Fluck
    died 1 Feb 1863

BROOM, LYDIA ANN
    wife of John J. Broom
    daughter of John & Hannah Hoffman
    23 Dec 1831 - 27 Oct 1869

HEDRICK, MARY   75y 8m 13d
    wife of Jacob Hedrick
    21 Jul 1835 - 4 Apr 1911

HEDRICK, JACOB   63y 4m 23d
    23 Jan 1839 - 16 Jun 1902

HEDRICK, ELMINA   3y 2m 12d
    daughter of Jacob & Mary Hedrick
    8 Jan 1859 - 21 Mar 1862

HEDRICK, WILLIAM HENRY 25y 10m 4d
    son of Jacob and Maria Hedrick
    5 May 1861 - 9 Jun 1887

ELLENBERGER, JAMES   22y 5m 19d
    son of Martin and Mary Ann
    Ellenberger
    3 Nov 1865 - 22 Apr 1889

ELLENBERGER, SUSANNA 46y 1m 13d
    daughter of Martin and Mary Ann
    Ellenberger
    8 Jan 1860 - 21 Feb 1906

Row 5

CLYMER, LOVINA OTT   76y 3m 15d
    wife of Levi R. Clymer
    31 Jan 1824 - 16 Nov 1900

CLYMER, LEVI R.   [50y 1m 14d?]
    22 Apr 1822 - 11 Jun 1878

PRIESTER, HEINRICH   24y minus 6d
    Son of Anton and Anna Maria
    Priester
    28 Dec 1840 - 22 Dec 1864

PRIESTER, ANNA MARIA
    Born in Europe
    died 4 Oct [?]

PRIESTER, ANTON
    born Holzappel Herzogthun Nassau
    died in Philadelphia
    23 Mar 1809 - 17 Mar 1871

SWARTLEY, MARY ANN   41y 6m 2d
    daughter of Sam and Eliz Ott
    6 May 1829 - 8 May 1870

SWARTLEY, CHARLES R.   28y 1m 7d
    14 Feb 1860 - 21 Mar 1888

SLIFFER, DANIEL   15y 1m 13d
    22 Jan 1848 - 4 Mar 1863

Row 6

KRAMER, HANNAH   65y 1m 3d
    wife of Enos Kramer
    9 Aug 1800 - 12 Sep 1865

KRAMER, ENOS   79y 5m 8d
    13 May 1797 - 8 Nov 1876

DIETERICH, MARY   68y 11m 24d
    wife of John F. Dieterich
    10 Dec 1823 - 13 Dec 1888

DIETERICH, JOHN F.   28y 7m 26d
    4 Mar 1835 - 30 Oct 1863

SNYDER, HANNA M.   21y 1m 12d
    daughter of Peter and Maria Snyder
    26 Jul 1844 - 8 Sep 1865

SNYDER, MARIA   74y 5m 5d
    wife of Peter L. Snyder
    daughter of Jacob Bachman
    died 5 Mar 1897

SNYDER, PETER L.   55y 9m 21d
    12 Feb 1819 - 3 Dec 1874

SNYDER, MARY   66y 7m 21d
    wife of John Snyder
    23 Jun 1800 - 12 Feb 1867

SCHNEIDER, JOHANNES [56y 10m 10d?]
    1805 - 1863

Row 7

WEEBER, CHRISTINA CATHRINA 72y 2m 6d
    31[Oct? 1876?] - 6 Jan 1856

WEAVER, GEORGE FREDERICK   71y 7m 15d
    2 Jan 17[93?] - 17 Aug 1864
[two footers--no stone remaining]

KLINE, IRA   1y 10m ?d
    son of Siman P. and Lucy Ann Kline
    11 Oct 1866 - 17 Aug 1868

KLINE, HENRY A.   2y 1m 10d
    son of Siman P. and Lucy Ann Kline
    18 Mar 1861 - 28 Apr 1866

Row 7 continued:

KLINE, LUCY ANN   mother
   22 Jan 1841 - 20 Oct 1917
KLINE, SIMON P.   father
   26 Mar 1836 - 26 Dec 1910

CASSEL, INFANT   1 Oct 1864
   daughter of Isaac and Christ Cassel

CASSEL, INFANT

CASSEL, INFANT

CASSEL, CHRISTIANNA   40y 7m 11d
   wife of Isaac Cassel
   7 Jul 1839 - 18 Feb 1871

CASSEL, ISAAC   81y 2m 19d
   died 7 Jan 1911   father

CASSEL, MAGDALEN   aged 40
   died 24 Sep 1881   mother

Row 8

WEBER, GEORGE F.   1793 - 1864
WEBER, CHRISTIANNA C.   1793 - 1866
WEBER, C. CATHARINE
   14 Feb 1821 - 11 May 1896
WEVER, R. BARBARA
   16 Jan 1828 - 19 May 1901
   [above four on same stone]

CASSEL, INFANT   Isaac's Child
   14 Jun 1875

CASSEL, GEORGE
   son of Isaac and M. Cassel
   14 Jun 1875 - 1 Apr 1876

CASSEL, EMMA
   daughter of I. and M. Cassel
   17 Sep 1881 - 24 Sep 1881

Row 9

MOSER, ARVILLA H.   22y 1m 8d
   24 May 1874 - 2 Jul 1896

SPANGLER, AMANDA
   mother, wife of Franklin Spangler
   22 Feb 1858 - 9 Jan 1899

HESS, ELIZ   26y 7m 23d
   daughter of George and Maria Hess
   died Oct 1867

HESS, ELIZ   78y 2m 12d
   wife of Dan Hess
   20 Nov 1822 - 1 Feb 1901

HESS, DANIEL   aged 71
   17 Dec 1841 - 20 Mar 1895

[R?]EALER, GIRDA MAY   1y 7m 9d
   daughter of Frank and Hannah
   [R?]ealer   1877 - 1878

HESS, LITTLE CHILD
   of Christianna and John Hess
   died 19 Feb 1864

SAVACOOL, ELIZ ANNA   43y 0m 29d
   mother, wife of Mahlon Savacool
   16 Jun 1839 - 25 Mar 1881

SAVACOOL, MAHLON   39y 2m 8d
   father
   22 Sep 1832 - 30 Dec 1871

FELLMAN, BEATA   76y 6m 25d
   13 Sep 1829 - 8 Mar 1906

FELLMAN, ABRAHAM   80y 9m 0d
   8 Dec 1817 - 8 Sep 1876

SHOEMAKER, CHARLES   0y 1m 21d
   son of M. and H. Annie Shoemaker
   died 12 Jan 1870

FELLMAN, HESTER   10y 6m 6d
   daughter of Ab and Beada Fellman
   died 26 Jan 1862

Row 10

FREY, SUSANNA   45y 1m 16d
   wife of Wm. Frey
   daughter of E. and L. Summers
   9 Feb 1835 - 25 Mar 1880

FREY, WILLIAM   72y 0m 9d
   2 Mar 1839 - 11 Mar 1911

SUMMERS, LIZZIE   6m 17d
   2 Sep 1864 - 19 Mar 1865

KNAELY, AMANDA   10m 2d
   daughter of John and Catherine Knaely
   5 Aug 1866 - 7 Jun 1867

KNAELY, FRANKLIN   2y 7m 18d
   son of John and Catherine Knaely
   18 Jun 1860 - 1 Apr 1863

Row 11

[SCHEIP?] INFANT DAUGHTER [1809?]

SCHEIP, J. L.   aged 10 m

SCHEIP, MARY ELIZABETH   8m 23d
   daughter of Leidy and Susanna Scheip
   19 May 1858 - 11 Feb 1859

SCHEIP, C. CLINTON   2y 8m 7d
   son of Leidy and Susannah Scheip
   died 4 Sep 1862

ST. PETER'S UNION CEMETERY (Old Section)

Row 11 continued

SCHEIB, ISAIAH   15y 1m 15d
    son of John and Maria Scheib
    20 Oct 1858 - 5 Dec 1865

SCHEIB, MARIA   70y 4m 29d
    mother, wife of John L. Scheib
    daughter of Jacob and Cath Scholl
    19 May 1825 - 18 Oct 1895

SCHEIB, JOHN L.   79y 4m ??d
    9 Aug 1824 - 22 Dec 1899

GROSS, HARYEY S. [Harry or Harvey?]
    son of A. B. and A. E. Gross
    died 5 Aug 1864   aged 2 months

RUTH, JOSEPH
    26 Apr 1824 - 24 Sep 1863
[RUTH?] MARY PROCTOR
    26 May 1831 - 21 Oct 1872
    [above two on same stone]

Row 12

REIDENAURER, DANIEL M.   51y 8m 0d
    16 Jul 1810 - 16 Mar 1865

REIDENAUR, RACHEL   56y 2m 21d
    wife of Daniel Reidenaur
    1 Mar 1810 - 25 Dec 1866

HEDRICK, CATHARINE ANNA   88y 4m 14d
    wife of Peter Hedrick
    daughter of Daniel & R. Ridenaur
    22 Jan 1832 - 6 Jun 1870

HEDRICK, PETER   77y 0m 24d
    6 Apr 1832 - 30 Apr 1909

HEDRICK, MARY A.   88y 3m 19d
    wife of Peter D. Hetrick
    12 Feb 1837 - 31 May 1925

BARNABY, ERWIN   12 days
    died 1 Sep 1850

BARNABY, FRANCES   16y 8m 15d
    son of Sammuel and Margaret Barnaby
    15 Apr 1871 - 20 Dec 1888

ERNY, ANNA ELIZABETH   4m 25d
    daughter of Joseph and Mary Erny
    21 Mar 1879 - 16 Aug 1879

BARNABY, CATHERINE
    daughter of Samuel and Mar. Barnaby
    16 Jun 1864 - 30 Jul 1865

BARNABY, ANNA MARY   3m 1d
    died 28 Aug 1869

ERNY, MARGARET   64y 4m 3d
    wife of Joseph Erny
    25 Nov 1839 - 28 Mar 1904

ERNY, JOSEPH   58y 8m 6d
    19 Feb 1849 - 25 Oct 1901

BARNABY, SAMMUEL   40y 1m 3d
    13 Oct 1833 - 16 Nov 1873

MUMBAUER, JOHN   1817 - 1879

MUMBAUER, MARTHA   31y 3m 15d
    died 19 Apr 1865

MILLER, FIETTA   1845 - 1932

MILLER, MARGARET   1808 - 1900

Row 13

KILE, HENRY   father   68y 5m 17d
    28 Feb 1829 - 15 Aug 1897

KILE, EMALINE   mother   29y 19d
    28 Dec 1836 - 16 Jan 1866

KILE, INFANT   child of H. and E. Kile
    [no dates on stone]

BLOOM, HARVEY   14y 3m 7d
    son of Peter and Christiana Bloom
    8 Apr 1824 - 15 Jul 1868
    [dates as recorded]
    cause of death - Sim Sixalle

BLOOM, CATHERINE
    mother, wife of Peter Bloom
    29 Mar 1805 - 22 Mar [1872?]

BLOOM, PETER   77y 2m 9d
    father
    26 Oct 1792 - 30 Jun 1875

H. H. B.

M. C. B.

_____?_____, SON
    of Charles and Maria   ?
    29 May 1866

CROUTHAMEL, ABBE BERTHA   19 days
    died 11 Aug 1871

SCHINLEAVER, DAVID   21y 11m 13d
    7 Jan 1860 - 20 Dec 1882

SCHINLEVER, MAGDALENA   59y 1m 0d
    wife of David Schinlever
    30 Sep 1821 - 30 Dec 1880

SCHINLEVER, DAVID   56y 9m 27d
    17 Apr 1816 - 11 Jan 1873

Row 13 continued:

SCHINLEVER, LEIDY
[no dates on this small stone]

HACKER, CAROLINE   2y 4m
daughter of Augustine and Henrietta Hacker
11 Nov 1859 - 8 Apr 1862

Row 14

ZIEGLER, ROSINA   36y 3m ?d
8 Mar 1830 - 27 Sep 1866

BEHRINGER, JULIANNA   21y 2m ?d
8 Dec 1851 - 14 Aug 1873

HEDRICK, HANNAH   34y 8m 20d
wife of Peter Hedrick
daughter of Frederick and Julian Baringer
28 Mar 1811 - 18 Dec 1878
[dates as recorded]

BARINGER, JULIAN   85y 11m 12d
wife of Christian Baringer
16 Aug 1806 - 28 Jul 1892

BARINGER, CHRISTIAN F.   83y 2m 14d
1 Jan 1806 - 15 Mar 1882

[stone fallen on its face]

KING, GEORGE
19 Aug 1832 - 20 Mar 1899

KING, MARY   64y 1m 6d
27 Nov 1802 - 3 Jan 1867

ECKHART, JOSEPH   61y 3m 2d
21 Apr 1807 - 26 Jul 1868

HEASTAND, ELIZ   61y 10m 13d
27 Jun 1805 - 10 May 1867

MILLER, JOHN HENRY   5m 20d
son of Ephraim and Catherine Miller
9 Mar 1866 - 29 Aug 1866

MILLER, CATHERINE   53y 11m 21d
wife of Ephraim Miller
19 Apr 1835 - 19 Apr 1889

MILLER, EPHRAIM F.   58y 4m 3d
31 May 1840 - 4 Oct 1898

SOUDER, SARAH J.
wife of Jonas Souder
23 Jul 1811 - Sep 1867

KRAMER, MATHIAS W.
9 Feb 1829 - 25 Feb 1864

DEUSCHLE, JULIANA REGENA
1 Mar 1801 - 24 Jan 1806

CUGEL, JOHANN   66y 3m 6d
1 Dec 1806 - 13 Mar 1873

BARTLES, CHRISTIAN   aged 87 years
26 Oct 1865

Row 15

RENNER, WILLIE A.   son of S. A. Renner
10 Dec 1864 - 21 Aug 1865

RENNER, ISAAC A.   son of S.A. Renner
9 Jan 1873 - 18 Feb 1879

RENNER, HANNAH   23y 6m 16d
wife of Michael Renner
2 Aug 1802 - 18 Jan 1826

RENNER, MICHAEL   85y 1m 10d
10 Dec 1810 - 20 Jan 1896

GERIS, JOHANNES   68y 8m 10d
8 Aug 1797 - 11 Apr 1866

[?], SARAH   72y 4m 17d
born Young
12 Jul 1798 - 29 Nov 1870

FELLMAN, LYDIA S.   mother
1830 - 1900

FELLMAN, JACOB   father
1821 - 1889

MOYER, JOHN M.   [32?]y 4m 2d
25 Apr 1829 - 27 May 1866

MOYER, MARIA   [4m 14d ?]
daughter of John and Barbara Moyer
1858 - 22 Dec 1862

MOYER, ANN   5y 9m 4d
daughter of John and Barbara Moyer
18 Jan 1857 - 22 Oct 1862

KRAMER, ANNA MARIA   [1y 7m 12d ?]
died 11 Sep 1862

BURKHART, LAURA GINNA   6m 21d
daughter of Anthony and Mary Burkhart
19 Oct 1877 - 6 May 1878

Row 16

STEAR, TOBIAS   42y 4m 9d
2 Jan 1825 - 11 May 1867

STEAR, MARY
wife of Tobias Stear
23 Jan 1832 - 27 Mar 1906

TREFINGER, REUBEN   12y 6m 29d
died 21 May 1867

ST. PETER'S UNION CEMETERY (Old Section)

Row 16 continued:

TREFFINGER, MARY [E.?]   8? 6m
   daughter of Frederick and Caroline
   Treffinger   [no dates on stone]

TREFFINGER, FREDERICK   69y 1m 14d
   father
   26 Jan 1829 - 12 May 1898
            [Mar?]

TREFFINGER, CAROLINE   75y 4m 11d
   mother
   1 Oct 1837 - 12 Feb 1918

[HILLWICK ?], ANNA   3y 11m 20d
   daughter of Frederick and Sarah
   Hillwick
   died 6 Jun 1865

[GERYS?] [GEBYS|GEEYS], EMMANUAL
   son of John and Sophia
   3 Jan 1865 - 18 Sept 1869

[?   ], JOHANNES
   son of ?
   [stone is broken]

NEUBOLD, JOHANNAS   17y 10m 27d
   son of Joseph and Catharina Neubold
   9 Jan 1852 - 6 Dec 1869

NEUBOLD, CATHARINE
   wife of Joseph Neubold
   8 Sep 1801 - 6 Aug 1883

NEUBOLD, JOSEPH   [aged 76?]
   21 Dec 17[91?] - 1 Jul 18[68?]

SCHEIRENBRAND, ELIZABETH
   8 Sep 1838 - 30 Apr 1867

SCHEIRENBRAND, WILLIAM   7y 11m
   son of William and Elizabrth
   Scheirenbrand
   27 Oct 1863 - 15 Oct 1871

SCHRIENBRAND, WILLIAM   27y 1m 14d
   17 Apr 1839 - 31 Aug 1866

Row 17

STEER, CHRISTIANA   71y 11m 4d
   wife of Philip Steer
   10 Apr 1802 - 6 Apr 1875

STEER, PHILIP   76y 10m
   22 Jun 1870

MAUERER, JOHN   12y 3d
   _? [?] 1829 - [25?] Jun 1841

KLOPFER, PHILIP   4y 3m 16d
   son of George and Magdalena Klopfer
   18 Sep 18[66?] - June 18[71?]

KLAPFER, ANNA
   daughter of George and Magdalena
   Klapfer
   12 Feb 1876 - 18 Jan 1878

KLOPFER, GEORGE
   son of George and Magdalena Klopfer
   [stone is chipped away]

KLOPFER, SAMUEL
   son of George and Magdalena Klopfer
   10 Aug 1872 - 28 Jan 1878

KLOPFER, HENRY   12y 1m 4d
   son of George and Magdalena Klopfer
   11 Dec 1877 - 15 Jan 1890

KLOPFER, MAGDALENA   50y 7m 16d
   wife of George Klopfer
   28 Nov 1841 - 14 Jul 1882

KLOPFER, GEORGE   76y 26d
   15 Nov 1836 - 11 Dec 1912

Row 18

KELL, LYDIA K.   88y 13d
   wife of Charles Kell
   26 Mar 1836 - 9 Apr 1924

KELLER, CHARLES   61y 11m 17d
   31 Dec 1832 - 18 Nov 1891

C. K.

M. A. K.

C. E. K.

KELLER, MARY AMANDA   10y 11m 20d
   daughter of Charles and Lydia Keller
   died [3 ?] Feb 1868

KELLER, CATHARINE ELIZABETH   8y 2m 3d
   daughter of Charles and Lydia Keller
   died 26 Mar 18[68?]

MILLER, GRACE   3m [5d ?]
   daughter of Noah and Cath Miller
   3 Aug 1883 - 10 May 1884

MILLER, JENNIE EVA   3m 7d
   daughter of Noah and Cath Miller
   [21?] Oct 1888 - [Feb   ?   ]

MILLER, AMMANDA ELIZABETH   1y 2m 12d
   daughter of Noah and Catharina
   Miller
   [27?] Dec [1873?] - 9 Mar [18??]

MILLER, ANNA LAUREA   7 days
   daughter of Noah and Cath Miller
   died 17 Jan 1870

WINKLER, JOSEPHINE   died 1870
   wife of Tobias M. Winkler   aged 70y

BUCKS COUNTY TOMBSTONE INSCRIPTIONS - HILLTOWN TOWNSHIP

Row 18 continued:

WINKLER, THOMAS   87y 5m
    5 feb 1797 - 5 Jul 1884

LEY, TOBIAS   Aged 62
    born in Waldecl__?__, Germany
    died 7 May 1870

[this row continues into row 35]

Row 19

WEISS, CHARLES HENRY
    son of Charles S. and Debra S. Weiss
    18 Feb 1869 - 19 Feb 1878

WEISS, KATY ELIZABETH   1y 1m 15d
    daughter of Charles and Debra S. Weiss
    12 Jun 1867 - 22 Oct 1868

WEISS, CHARLES S.   24y 5m 27d
    23 Apr 1844 - 20 Oct 1868

WEISS, HANNAH   Aged 16
    daughter of Michael L. and Sarah Weiss
    13 Dec 1855 - 13 Dec 1871

WEISS, MICHAEL   70y 5m 13d
    5 Apr 1810 - 19 Sep 1880

MOYER, MARY   69y 2m 9d
    wife of John Moyer
    11 Jan 1818 - 20 Mar 1887

MAURER, JOHANN   56y 6m 7d
    18 Jan 1815 - 25 Jul 1871

TRINKLEY, MARY   5m 3d
    daughter of Martin and Anna Trinkley
    1 Oct 1877 - 4 Mar 1878

TRINKLEY, AARON WILSON   1y 10m 20d
    son of Martin and Anna Trinkley
    18 Apr 1876 - 9 Mar 1878

SWARTZ, SALLIE B.   19y 8m 14d
    daughter of Sammeul and Sarah Swartz
    20 Aug 1875 - 10 May 1894

SWARTZ, ALLEN   14y 6m 25d
    son of Sammuel and Sarah Swartz
    23 May 1868 - 18 Oct 1882

SWARTZ, LICENDA B.   5y 2m
    son of Sam and Sarah Swartz
    3 Oct 1872 - 18 Dec 1877

SWARTZ, CHRISTIANA   8y 11m 6f
    27 Jul 1851 - 1 Jul 1863
    [1854?]

SWARTZ, ELIZABETH   75y 1m 8d
    wife of Elias Swartz
    11 Jun 1815 - 27 Apr 1890

SWARTZ, ELIAS   82y 9m 11d
    20 Nov 1811 - 31 Aug 1894

Row 20

[These four stones are midway between rows 19 and 21 inside a fence]

BISTING, EDNA   6m
    28 Feb 1887 - 26 Aug 1888

BITTING, EDDIE   8m 3d
    son of Simon and Mary Jane Bitting
    2 Jan 1881

BISSING, THEODORE   4y 3m 24d
    son of Simon and Mary Bissing
    11 Feb 1862

BISSING, WIHLAMMA   9y 1m 4d
    daughter of Simon and Mary Bissing
    14 Sep 1860 - 18 Oct 1869

Row 21

EIM, ELIZA   24y 7m 24d
    sister
    died 29 Aug 1867

SEHER, ALBERT A.   [Plaque]

SEHER, JACOB   1870

SEHER, EMILY   1872

SEHER, FENSNER   1874

MILL, WILLIAM   aged 27
    4 Apr 1868
    [inside Seher plot]

SEHER, ANTHONI   4y 4m 19d
    son of Anthoni and Maria Seher
    29 Sep 1865 - 10 Feb 1870

SEHER, AUGUSTE M.   20y 10m 6d
    30 Nov 186? - 6 Oct 1881

SEHER, ALBERT A.   46y 3m 15d
    Son of Anthoni and Maria Seher
    20 Dec 1852 - 4 Apr 1900

SEHER, ANTHONY
    9 Nov 1822 - 26 Aug 1902

SEHER, MARY P.   83y 1m
    wife of Anthony Seher
    born in Germany 18 Jan 1823
    died 18 Feb 1906

POHLE, HARMON   aged 16
    died 9 Dec 1869

ST. PETER'S UNION CEMETERY (Old Section)

Row 22

[CURLIE ?], JESSE ELMER
    son of William and Lizzie [Curlie?]
    28 Dec 1871 - 10 Mar 1872

CROUTHAMEL, ELIZ   33y 3m 7d
    mother, wife of Isaac O. Crouthamel
    14 Apr 1839 - 21 Jul 1872

CROUTHAMEL, ISAAC O.   69y 7m 22d
    father
    30 Jul 1836 - 22 Mar 1906

CROUTHAMEL, SARAH   89y 8d
    mother, wife of Isaac O. Crouthamel
    18 Nov 1843   26 Nov 1932

CROUTHAMEL, HARVEY   20 days
    son of Isaac O. and Sarah Crouthamel
    25 Aug 1875 - 17 Sep 1875

SMITH, MARGARETTE
    11 Jul 1797 - 9 Aug 1887

SMITH, HENRY
    11 Jun 1806 - 20 Oct 1872

GEISEL, CHRISTIAN   6y 10m 16d
    3 Nov 1806 - 21 Sep 1871
    [dates as recorded]

HOTZEL, CATHERINE   76y 1m
    wife of Joseph Hotzel
    22 May 1805 - 22 Jun 1881

[ROTZEL ?], JOSEPH   Aged 72
    31 Jun 1800 - 10 Jun 1873

[?], CATHERINE
    1808

NACE, AARON
    son of John and Barb Nace
    29 Aug 1844 - 18 Nov 1882

ROSENBERGER, JOSEPH D.   aged 57
    9 Jun 1828 - 21 Feb 1886

BAKER, WILHELMINA   42y 6m 15d
    wife of Frank Baker
    26 Jun 1858 - 11 Jan 1901

BAKER, ELIZ ZIEGLER   57y 5m 25d
    wife of Leidy Baker
    1 Sep 1821 - 26 Feb 18[55?]

BAKER, LEIDY   63y 4m 23d
    12 Sep 1828 - 5 Feb 1892

BAKER, CATHERAINE   24y 2m 3d
    daughter of Leidy and Eliz Baker
    1 May 1857 - 4 Jul 1881

BAKER, CATHARINE   91y 2m 10d
    wife of Henry Baker
    12 Feb 1795 - 22 Apr 1886

BAKER, HENRY   77y 4m 9d
    11 Nov 1797 - 18 Mar 1875

MOYERS, SUSANNA   88y 9m 20d
    wife of John Moyers
    23 Apr 1789 - 12 Feb 1878

HILLWICK, FREDERICK   father
    24 Sep 1833 - 16 Nov 1903

SWILER, CARRIE R.
    daughter of Charles and Mary Hecken Swiler
    3 Dec 18[87?] - 27 Aug 1887

BOEHNER, MADDELENE   59y 22d
    wife of Henry Boehner
    died 10 Dec 1897

BOEHNER, HENRY   aged 58
    died 12 Dec 1891

BOEHNER, CHRISTIANNA L.   70y 4m
    21 Dec 1809 - 20 Apr 1880

BOEHNER, [SARAH?]   73y 2m 4d
    16 Jan 1794 - 29 Mar 1877

SMITH, LYDIA   54y 2m 19d
    wife of Frederick Smith
    died 11 Sep 1894

SMITH, FREDERICK   54y 8m
    died 11 Jun 1872

BOEHNER, GILBERT
    1 May 1890 - 14 Mar 1892

BOEHNER, HENRY
    24 Sep 1892 - 6 Mar 1893

BOEHNER, MAY
    17 Sep 1893 - 18 Sep 1893

BOEHNER, EMMA   mother
    23 Feb 1870 - 2 Dec 1913

BOEHNER, JOHN   father
    12 Jul 1863 - 23 Mar 1946

BOEHNER, HENRY
    8 Aug 1861 - 28 Aug 1925

WEAND, CLARENCE E.
    son of Eugene and Emma Weand
    [no dates on stone]

[?], NEVEN E.
    2 Nov 1883 - 25 Nov 18[87?]

[?], ARLINGTON N.
    28 Nov 1877 - 24 Nov 1880
    [G. A. R. Flag]

Row 22 continued:

ROHR, CHRISTIANA BARBARA   52y 30d
    wife of Henry Rohr
    18 Feb 1832 - 28 Mar 18[83?]

ROHR, HENRY   60y 3m 29d
    27 Mar 1833 - 26 Jul 1896

FREY, FLORENCE K.   mother
    3 Mar 1889 - 19 Feb 1927

KERN, CHRISTIAN   1844 - 1932
KERN, CATHARINE   1852 - 1928
    [above two on same stone]

Row 23

SLIFER, WILHELMINA   1 month
    daughter of Sammuel and Mary Ann
    Slifer   [no date on stone]

SLIFER, ANNA MARY   4y 2m 24d
    daughter of Sam and Mary Ann Slifer
    12 Oct 1874 - 6 Jun 1878

SLIFER, SAMMUEL   38y 10m 4d
    3 Mar 1819 - 6 Jan 1878

SLIFER, ELLADORA   5y 10m 26d
    daughter of Sam and Mary Ann Slifer
    17 Dec 1878 - 13 Nov 1884

BITTNER, ANNIE E. [Bitting?]
    born and died 18 May 1870

BITTNER, WINFIELD S.   1y 3m
    21 Aug 1872 - 20 Nov 1873

THEROLF, ERVIN   4 years
    son of Adam and Mary Therolf
    28 Nov 1872 - 25 Sep 1877

THEROLF, PIERSON
    son of Adam and Mary Therolf
    21 Jul 1876 - 4 Oct 1877

HERING, HARRISON
    son of Philip S. and Christina
    Hering
    10 Oct 1889 - 7 Aug 1890

HERING, CHRISTIANNA   35y 3m 9d
    wife of Philip S. Hering
    25 Jul 1854 - 12 [Oct?] 18[89?]

MILLER, SERBIA   60y 1m 2d
    wife of George Miller
    3 Feb 1817 - 5 [Mar?] 1877

MILLER, GEORGE   64y 6d
    15 Mar 1817 - 21 Mar 1881

MARTIN, INFANT
    son of Adam and Magail Martin
    [no dates on stone]

STIPE, LAURA   4m 26d
    daughter of Christian and Catharine
    Stipe   Died 12 Jul 1878

STIPE, CHRISTIAN   47y 6m 1d
    24 Nov 1834 - 25 May 1882

STIPE, CATH   53y 1m 16d
    wife of Christian Stipe
    30 Jun 1837 - 15 Aug 1890

DIMMIG, KATE   59y 2d
    wife of Aaron Dimmig
    16 Feb 1822 - 18 Feb 1881

DIMMIG, AARON   85y 9m 12d
    12 May 1821 - 1 Mar 19[02?]

SNOVEL, MAGDALENA   88y [6?]m 17d
    wife of Abraham Snovel
    19 Apr 17[93?] - 16 Mar 18[81?]

SNOVEL, ABRAHAM   91y 1m 8d
    25 Sep 1791 - 3 Nov 1882

SNOVEL, MIRIA   mother
    28 Sep 1826 - 28 Oct 1918

SNOVEL, JONAS   father
    20 Sep 1827 - 24 Dec 1907

[broken stone -- illegible]

KRATZ, SARAH A.   42y 9m 5d
    wife of Isaac B. Kratz
    11 Jan 1841 - 19 Oct 1883

Row 24

KERN, INFANT
    daughter of John and Lydia Kern
    [no dates on stone]

KERN, HOWARD WILMER   1876 - 1877

KERN, LYDIA DAVIS   mother   1854 - 1906

DAVIS, SOPHIA   1812 - 1900
    mother, wife of John Davis

KLINE, RACHEL   83y 7m 17d
    wife of David Kline
    4 Aug 1796 - 21 Mar 1880

WEISS, JOSEPH
    25 Mar 1856 - 3 Feb 1945

WEISS, RACHEL   79y 7m 5d
    wife of Alfred Weiss
    14 Apr 1827 - 19 Nov 1906

ST. PETER'S UNION CEMETERY (Old Section)

Row 24 continued:

WEISS, ALFRED   59y 7m 15d
    15 Mar 18[23?] - 30 Oct 1884

ROHR, JACOB H.   89y 6m 2d
    28 Jul 1798 - 30 Jan 1888

ROHR, SARAH A.   79y 11m 10d
    8 Dec 1801 - 18 Nov 1881

ROHR, SUSAN   48y 6m 21d
    28 May 1841 - 19 Dec 1889

SEIBEL, ANNA   68y 17d
    wife of Jacob Seibel
    [3?] Jun 1820 - [20?] Jan 1888

SEIBEL, JACOB   aged 73
    [20?] Mar 1820 - 20 Mar 1893

SCHLOSSER, SARAH   70y 2m 24d
    Wife of John Schlosser
    1 Jun 1817 - 25 Aug 1887

SCHLOSSER, JOHN   84y 10m 25d
    3 Jun 1829 - 28 Apr 1914

ROTZEL, CATHARINE   89y 3m 10d
    31 Jan 1795 - 19 May 1884

MILLER, SAM   36y 11m 3d
    died 6 Feb 1880

REEDER, LEVI   85y 6m 8d
    father
    9 Aug 1841 - 17 Feb 1927

REEDER, EMMA O,   71y 8m 21d
    mother, wife of Levi Reeder
    14 Mar 1845 - 5 Dec 1916

REEDER, EMMA O.   12y 3m ?d
    daughter of Levi and Emma Reeder
    31 Jan 1881 - [11?] May 1897

REEDER, ANNA ELIZ   16y 9d
    daughter of Levi and Emma Reeder
    10 Mar 1875 - 19 Mar 1891

MARTIN, ANNA F.
    daughter
    8 Jul 1869 - 19 May 1913

MARTIN, AMANDA
    daughter of George and Theresa Martin
    12 Oct 1887? - 25 Oct 188[1?]

MARTIN, THERESA   82y 2m 15d
    mother, wife of George Martin
    19 Oct 1823 - 31 Mar 1906

MARTIN, GEO   father   82y 2m 15d
    1 Dec 1822 - 16 Feb 1905

STEEB, CARI A.   15y 6m 14d
    son of Frederick and Louise Steeb
    6 Dec 1866 - 20 Dec 1882
    [G. A. R. flag]

STEEB, FREDERICK   father
    21 Nov 1844 - 4 Nov 1915

STEEB, LOUISE H.   mother
    2 May 1848 - 15 Dec 1938

STEEB, FREDERICK G.   1880 - 1951

BITTING, SOPHIA   80y 1m 3d
    10 Jun 1834 - 13 Jul 1914

BITTING, RACHEL   86y 8m 13d
    mother, wife of Michael Bitting
    14 Jun 1808 - 27 Feb 1895

BITTING, MICHAEL M.   82y 30d
    father
    31 Dec 1804 - 30 Jan 1887

ELLENBERGER, MATILDA   42y 6m 28d
    wife of John Ellenberger
    10 Jan 1844 - 8 Aug 1886

[stone, face down]

SEIPLE, JOHN B.
    5 Mar 1818 - 15 May 1897

SEIPLE, SARAH   aged 85
    wife of John Seiple
    died 11 Jun 1922

VIEBEL, BENEDICT   aged 77
    1838 - 16 Apr 1915

Row 25

KERN, CASPER   81y 27d
    died 11 Feb 1890

KERNS, CATHARINE E.   aged 65
    wife of Casper Kerns
    died 6 Feb 1872

SWARTLEY SUSANNA   1y 11m 14d
    daughter of Abraham D. and Sarah Swartley
    died 30 Apr 1871

SWARTLEY, ABRAHAM D.   80y 6m 27d
    father
    died 26 Jan 1917

SWARTLEY, SARAH   mother   84y 2m 14d
    died 17 Oct 1928

RENNER, EMELINE   died [? Aug ?]
RENNER, INFANT   died 17 Sep 1903
    Children of Edward A. Renner

BUCKS COUNTY TOMBSTONE INSCRIPTIONS - HILLTOWN TOWNSHIP

Row 25 continued:

RENNER, OUR BABE   1900
    child of Mr. and Mrs. E. A. Renner

RENNER, SALLIE A.   1890 - 1910

HABERLE, MARTHA H.   26y 3m 27d
    nee Renner
    22 Dec 1894 - 19 Apr 1921

KNEULE, CATHARINE A. ROHR   74y 20d
    wife of John Kneule
    16 Sep 1885 - 6 Oct 1909

KNEULE, JOHN   75y 7m 3d
    father
    19 Jun 1831 - 22 Jan 1907

SNOVEL, MONROE   30y 5m 6d
    11 Mar 1872 - 17 Aug 1902

PFEFFER, JACOB F.   48y 4m 27d
    21 Jun 1834 - 18 Nov 1882

BILGER, MARY   85y 1m 2d
    wife of John Bilger
    10 Jun 1805 - 1 Mar 1890

BILGER, JOHN H.   1y 6m 7d
    20 Jul 1882 - 27 Jan 1884

BILGER, MARY JANE   32y 11m 12d
    wife of John H. Bilger
    22 Nov 1856 - 4 Nov 1889

BILGER, SARAH F.   1843 - 1910

BILGER, LEVI H.   1848 - 1912

MYERS, LAURA   1881 - 1892
MYERS, DORA   1884 - 1885
MYERS, MARTHELLA   1886 - 1886
MYERS, ERWIN   1888 - 1892
MYERS, ALLEN   1890 - 1890
    [above five on same stone]
    All children of William and Eliz

NEWBOLD, CATHARINE   72y 24d
    mother, wife of Joseph Newbold
    died 27 Sep 1897

NEWBOLD, JOSEPH   58y 1m 23d
    father
    21 Dec 18[27?] - [14?] May 18[86?]

FISHER, CHRISTINA   aged 90y
    wife of Bernard Fisher
    died 24 Jun 1913

FISHER, BERNARD   91y 7m 24d
    died 27 May 1917

VOID, EDNA C.
    [29?] Jan 1897 - 14 Sep 18[97?]

VOID, MABEL   [3?]y [11?]m
    daughter of F. B. and Mary Void
    died 21 Dec 18[87?]

VOID, DELLA   9m 24d
    daughter of Frederick and Mary Void
    25 May 1894

VOID, BERTHA   12y 1m 9d
    daughter of Frederick and Mary Void
    14 Apr 1882 - 23 Aug 1894

ROMIG, CHARLES FRANKLIN   19y 24d
    son of James A. and Angeline Romig
    13 Jun 1880 - 7 Jul 1899

ALDERFER, ANGELINA G.
    wife of Lewis S. Alderfer
    first married to James A. Romig
    28 Aug 1859 - 21 Nov 1928

ROMIG, JAMES A.   33y 8m 3d
    7 Sep 1854 - 10 May 1888

GERHART, SUSAN   67y 7m 2d
    25 Nov 1853 - 28 Jun 1921

GERHART, MAHLON M.   41y 11m 26d
    7 Oct 1853 - 3 Oct 1895

SEIPLE, WILLIAM A.   1852 - 1935
    father

ALLEBACH, KATIE A.   1905 - 1935

ALLEBACH, ANNIE KRATZ
    11 Jul 1862 - 6 Jun 1939
ALLEBACH, JOHN
    22 Mar 1863 - 15 Jul 1945
    [above two on same stone]

SWARTZ, SARAH A.   1859 - 1940
SWARTZ, FRANK R.   1855 - 1945
    [above two on same stone]

GLICK, WILLIAM H.   1874 - 1944
GLICK, CARRIE E.   1874 - 1944
    [above two on same stone]

GANDORFER, FANNIE H.   1888 - 1967

Row 26

WEIKLE, HANNAH MARANDA   in 6th year
    daughter of Henry and Aramanda Weikle
    20 Dec 1867 - Aug 1873

ZETTLEMOYER, C. J.   1869 - 1914

ZETTLEMOYER, WILLIAM
    son of C. J. A. Zettlemoyer
    [no dates on stone]

ST. PETER'S UNION CEMETERY (Old Section)

Row 26 continued:

ZETTLEMOYER, ANNA ARNDT
    wife of C. J. Zettlemoyer
    [no dates on stone]

FRANKENFIELD, CHARLEY   5y 7m 14d
    son of [David?] and Sophia
    Frankenfield
    15 Aug 1872 - 28 May 1878

AIMS, SUSANNA   nee Beuller
    1 Dec 1842 - 29 Nov 1904

AIMS, RACHEL   1y 9m [13?]d
    18 Aug 1878 - 1 Feb 1880

AIM, PEIRIE   7m 2d
    27 Dec 1881 - 29 Jul 1882

SLIFER, SAM N.   68y 4m 4d
    7 Aug 1840 - 11 Dec 1908
    father

SLIFER, HENRY   9y 2m 23d
    son of Sam and Mary Ann Slifer
    4 Oct 1872 - 27 Dec 1881

SLIFER, MARY ANN   75y 4m 8d
    mother
    12 May 1850 - 20 Sep 1925

SCHABLE, ABRAHAM B.   1m [26?]d
    son of Abram G. and Magdaline
    Schable
    died 2 Aug 18[57?]

SCHNABLE, RAYMOND B.   1m 1d
    son of Abram G. and Magdalina
    died 8 Jan 18[25?]

SCHNABLE, FLORENCE W.   2m 3d
    daughter of Abram and Magdalena
    died 18[07?]

SCHNABLE, SABINA G.   9y 3m 7d
    daughter of Samuel and Lucy A.
    28 Mar 1876 - 15 Jul 1885

SCHNABLE, LUCYANNA   91y 9m 6d
    mother
    26 Mar 1834 - 3 Jan 1926

SCHNABLE, SAMMUEL   72y 5m 26d
    father
    16 Nov 1823 - 12 May 1896

SCHNABLE, TITUS E.
SCHNABLE, MORVAN E.
    sons of Samuel G. and L. Schnable
    born and died 4 Jan 1888

KERN, FLORA   28y 24d
    daughter of C. and Catharine Kern
    died 22 Dec 1903

KERN, AGNES   4y 4m 8d
    daughter of C. and Catharine Kern
    died 2 Apr 1888

KERN, PRISCILLA   16y 5m 28d
    daughter of C. and Catharine Kern
    died 8 Apr 1888

KERN, HIRAM   28y 4m 21d
    son of C. and Catharine Kern
    died 18 Nov 1898

NEWBOLD, RALPH W.   3m 9d
    son of B. I. and Mary W. Newbold
    died 3 Sep 1888

NEWBOLD, BERNHARD TOBIAS   7y 8m 21d
    son of B. F. and Mary W. Newbold
    17 Jun 1886 - 8 Mar 1894

NEWBOLD, BERNHARD F.   26y 9m 5d
    died 25 Apr 1889

KRAFT, ELIZ   aged [71?]y
    wife of Jacob Kraft
    died 24 Mar 1889

KRAFT, LIZZIE   1y 14d
    daughter of Jacob and Eliz Kraft
    died 27 Apr 1881

KOEING, MARGARET
    wife of Benjamin Koeing
    25 Apr 1831 - 8 Jan 1890

YOUNG, BENJAMIN
    [12?] Oct 1825 - [25|23?] Dec [1889?]

DETWEILER, EMMA E.   31y 8m 21d
    mother, wife of Frank G. Detweiler
    16 Feb 1860 - 7 Nov 1891

DEUSCHLE, CHRISTOPHER   76y 7m 10d
    father
    14 Feb 1817 - 24 Sep 1893

DEUSCHLE, BARBARA   72y 8m 4d
    mother
    18 Jul 1837 - 22 Mar 1910

Row 27

ZILL, INFANT SON
    son of John and Sarah Zill
    [no dates]

ZILL, INFANT
    son of John and Sarah Zill
    [no dates]

ZILL, JOHN   [1860?] - 1910
    father

Row 27 continued:

ZILL, SARAH   1849 - 1914
    mother

FREED, WILLIAM   2m
    son of Jesse and Hannah Freed
    28 Nov 1875 - 22 Feb 18 [26?]

DAUBER, JOHN GEORGE   1845 - 1900
DAUBER, WALBURGA   1850 - 1920
DAUBER -- four infants
DAUBER, FREDERICK brother [no dates]
    [above on same Dauber stone]

SMITH, ANNIE   12y 5m 7d
    daughter of Conrad and Dorothy Smith
    6 Dec 1879 - 17 May 1892

SMITH, JOHN   16m 13d
    son of Conart and Dorothy Smith
    22 Oct 1860 - 9 May 1862

SMITH, CONART   64y 2d
    father
    26 Mar 1837 - 24 Apr 1901

SMITH, DOROTHY   89y 2m 23d
    mother
    5 Dec 1839 - 28 Feb 1829

GERHART, CHARLES   [26?]y 2m 7d
    [17?] Oct 1868 - 23 May 1889

SINE, ELIZ F.   77y 5m 1d
    wife of John G. Sine
    30 Mar 1812 - 31 Aug 1896

SINE, JOHN G.   73y 4m 18d
    15 Jan 1817 - 3 Jun 1890

WHITE, ELEANOR   1876 - 1949

WEISS, ELIZ G.   66y 4m 1d
    mother
    15 Feb 1857 - 16 Jun 1923

WEISS, CHARLES H.   53y 11m 10d
    father
    31 Oct 1852 - 11 Oct 1906
    [above two on same stone]

NACE, ANNIE   1y 3m 20d
    daughter of Wm. H. and Hester Nace
    died 27 Jul 18[98?]

NACE, WILLIAM FRANKLIN   12d
    died 21 [Jan?] 18[93|95?]

NACE, WILLIAM D.   35y 2m 27d
    3 Apr 1869 - 30 Jun 1904
    [Flag P.O.S. of A. No. 225 PA]

LABOE, RUSSEL
    9 Apr 1896 - 9 Aug 1898

LARGE, DAVID L.
    20 Jan 1895 - 9 Apr 1897

DEATERLY, LUZYETTE   73y 8m 2y
    16 Nov 1835 - 18 Feb 1909

DEATERLY, IDA V.   25y 4m 15d
    daughter of Lewis and Luzyatte
    Deaterly
    1 Aug 1879 - 16 Dec 1904

DEATERLY, KATIE MINERVA   20y 2m 5d
    daughter of Lewis and Luzyatte
    Deaterly
    30 Nov 1873 - 5 Feb 1894

SNOVEL, RUSSELL
    son of Frank and Annie Snovel
    10 May 1890 - 22 Jul 1896

SNOVEL, ANNIE O.   24y 3m 20d
    wife of Frank Snovel
    9 Nov 1871 - 29 Jul 1891

Row 28

LARGE, WALTER
    20 Dec 1905 - 1906

SNOVEL, INFANT
    daughter of Frank and Mary Snovel
    29 Jul 189[6?] - or [1890?]

ASHGROFT, JOHN T.   father
    3 Jul 1833 - 17 Aug 1907

ASHGROFT, MARY B.   mother
    11 Aug 1841 - 15 Nov 1912
    [above two on same stone]

RAPPOLD, CORA   1y 17d
    daughter of John and Willinana
    Rappold
    12 Jul 1895 - 4 Sep 1898

M. B. A.

J. T. A.

ST. PETER'S UNION CEMETERY (Old Section)

The following section is the oldest portion of St. Peter's Union Cemetery. The stones in this part face east and west in rows more or less parallel. Row 29 is the first row which begins about the middle of the older section of the church. The stones were read beginning nearest the church or Hilltown Pike and reading toward the church parking lot.

Row 29

SHELLENBERGER, RACHER M.
    daughter of Henry and Sarah
    died 20 Oct 1906

[same size stone as above--face down]

SHELLENBERGER, SARAH   74y 1m 3d
    mother, wife of Henry Shellenberger
    [1?] May 1797 - 4 Jul 1871

SHELLENBERGER, MARY A.   Aged 70y
    daughter of Henry and Sarah
    died 3 Apr 1902

[Metal repaired stone -- cannot read]
    [?], JOHN   1y [10?]m 14d
    son of John U. and Anne [?]
    20 [Oct|Dec?] 18[?] - [?]180[7?]

Row 30

LEIDY, HENRICH   88y 10m 24d
    9 Oct 175[?] - 2 Sep 18[44|49?]
    [Rev War Veteran Flag]

LEIDY, MARY   59y 5m 6d
    wife of George Leidy
    16 Dec 1791 - 22 May 1841

LEYDE, ANNA BARBARA
    22 Sep 1762 - 23 [?] 1838

LEIDY, GEORGE   46y 11m 19d
    16 Oct 1784 - 5 Oct 1831

LEIDY, ELIAS
    son of Henry and Sarah Leidy
    27 Nov 1827 - 30 Jan 1838

LEIDY, THOMAS [E?]   [18y 6m 6d ?]
    son of John and Lydia Leidy
    14 Nov 1827 - 20 May 1846

LEIDY, HENRY   89y 10m 25d
    29 Nov 1791 - 28 Oct 1881

LEIDY, SARAH   62y 10m 25d
    wife of Henry Leidy
    24 Oct 1794 - 13 Sep 1857

BLOOM, OLIVER U.
    son of Sarah Bloom
    19 sep 1855 - 24 Jan 1957

BLOOM, MISSOURI H.   1y 10m 3d
    daughter of Wm. and Sarah Bloom
    5 Sep 1850 - 8 Jan 1852

BRUNER, SON
    son of Aaron and Sarah Ann Bruner
    [no dates on stone]

Between rows 30 and 31 - [upper end]

TRAUGER, AGNES   12y 10m 6d
    [?] 18[4?] - [? 1867?]

TRAUGER, MARY   8y 9m 18d
    daughter of Solomon and Sarah Trauger
    12 Sep 1852 - 10 Jun 186[?]

TRAUGER, ADALINE   4y 3m
    daughter of Solomon and Sarah Trauger
    9 Apr 1857 - 19 Jun 1861

TRAUGER, SOLOMON   79y 11m 1d
    husband
    6 Nov 1815 - 7 Oct 1895

TRAUGER, SARAH N.   74y 7m 9d
    7 Apr 1826 - 16 Nov 1900

Row 31a

[row 31 is in three sections which are laid at different angles]

HARTMAN, MIGHAEL   64y 5m 29d
    23 Dec 1757 - 22 Jun 1822

HARTMAN, MIGHAEL   28y 9m 2d
    son of Henry and Sarah Hartman
    died 30 Sep 1826

SCHEIBIN, LIDLA
    28 Nov 1822 - 16 Feb 1823

LEIDY, MARY   7m 10d
    daughter of Francis and Elizabeth
    13 Apr [1860?]- 2|3?] Jun 1861

LEIDY, ELIZABETH   31y 8m 18d
    wife of Francis D. Leidy
    9 Dec 1830 - 27 Aug 1862

[five spaces]

KLINE, JOHN   18y 10m 13d
    16 Jun 1791 - 29 Apr 1812

Row 31b

LEISTER,   aged 1 [rest illegible]

Row 31b continued:

LEISTER, NOAH   9m 5d
    son of Thomas and Elizabeth Leister
    12 Jul 1850 - 17 Oct 1851

LEISTER, ELIZABETH   90y 5m 9d
    wife of Thomas Leister
    died   23 Jan 1912

POLK, SUSANNAH P.   5y 8m 17d
    died 16 Jun 1836

Row 31c

KLINE, JOHN   47y 10m 17d
    16 Jun 1794 - 29 Apr 1812

KLINE, MARY   75y 5m 5d
    wife of John Kline
    died   14 Aug 1867

KLINE, CATRINA   28y
    6 Sep 1820 - 17 Dec 1848

KLINE, OLIVER   6y 6m 5d
    son of John and Mary Kline
    [10 ?   1832 ?]

SCHEID, LYDIA ANNA   4y
    22 Jul 1833 - 27 Jan 1838

LEISTER, PETER
    son of Jacob and Lydia Leister
    Dec 184[?] - 1849

LEIDY, JACOB   6m 24d
    son of Jacob and Lydia Leidy
    28 Mar 1853 - 19 Oct 1854

LEIDY, JACOB   [?y ?m 21d]
    son of Jacob and [?] Leidy
    21 Mar 18[?] - 18[31?]

LEISTER, MARIA   8y 17d
    daughter of Jacob and Lydia
    Leister
    21 Dec 18[4?]8 - 7 Jan 18[57?]

[six small illegible stones]

SAVACOOL, [HENRY?]   aged 20y
    died 26 May 1863

SAVACOOL, MAGDALENA
    died 8 Mar 1859

SAVACOOL, MARIA
    died 18 Mar 1859

SAVACOOL, FRANKLIN
    son of Mahlon and Eliza Ann Savacool
    1 [Nov?] 1864 - 28 Nov 1864

SAVACOOL, CATHARINE
    daughter of Mahlon and Eliza Ann
    21 Feb 1860 - 17 Feb 1868

SAVACOOL, HARRIET
    daughter of Mahlon and Eliza Ann
    18 Nov 18[68?] - 9 May 1870

Row 32

LEIDY, [ELIAS?]   15y 9m 12d
    died 16 Jun 1827

LEIDY, [SAMUEL?]   1826

LEIDY, LEVY   2m 24d
    died [8?] Apr 1821

LEIDY, [AMELIA?]   in 7th year
    [15 Apr?] 1820

[EERKART?], ALFRED   8m 7d
    [14 Apr 1818?]

SCHEIB, GEORG   aged 71y
    10 Aug 1744 - 10 Sep 1815

SCHEIB, ELIZABETH
    26 May 1747 - 19 Dec 18[31|34?]

SCHEIB, JOHANNES   47y 4m 1d
    24 Feb 1771 - 25 [Jun?] 1818

SCHEIB, CATHARINA   86y 7m 6d
    9 Jan 1774 - 16 Aug 1860

SCHEIB, GEORGE   39y 10m 18d
    27 Feb 1783 - 9 Jan 1823

SCHEIB, BARBARA   89y 12m 21d
    21 Sep 1782 - 12 May 1872

SCHELLENBERGER, JOHANNES   66y 7m 16d
    16 Feb 1756 - [21|24?] Oct 1822

[space]

HACKMAN, JAMES   aged 22y

COPE, ELIZABETH   41y [3|9?]m 18d
    Wife of Charles Cope
    died   22 Mar 18[53?]

COPE, MALINDA   20y 9m 23d
    Daughter of Charles and Elizabeth
    Cope   Died 28 [Jan|Mar?] 1860

COPE, CHARLES   [60|64?]y 4m [1|6?]d
    died 29 Feb 1884

[space]

BRUNER, ELIZABETH   11y 8m
    daughter of Henry Bruner
    died 22 Feb 1837

ST. PETER'S UNION CEMETERY (Old Section) 109

Row 32 continued:

BRUNER, SAMUEL C.
   20 Nov 1831 - 24 Nov 1862

BRUNER, HENRY   75y 9m 6d
   16 Nov 179[0?] - 22 Aug 1866

BRUNER, SARAH   [71|74?]y 11m 27d
   wife of Henry Brunner
   [?] Apr 17[83?] - [8?] mar 1868

KOBER, CATHARINA
   7 Jul 1777 - 17 Aug 1854

KOBER, PHILIP   20 Oct 1777 - 9 Aug 1846

SABELEUHL, MICHAEL
   16 Nov 1795 - 8 Nov 1869

SABELEUHL, [Margaret?]
   wife of Michael Sabeleuhl
   [1805?]

NACE, JAMES   26y 4m 25d
   [no dates on stone]

NACE, LAANNA   19y 3m 15d
   12 Sep 1841 - 27 Dec 1860

NACE, JOHN
   23 Jan 1807 - 1 May 1864

NACE, BARBARA   70y 2m 8d
   wife of John Nace
   10 Feb 1811 - 18 Apr 1881

Row 33a

[This row 33 has two parts at different angles.]

BODDER, NOAH   [?50y]11d
   23 Dec 1803 - 6 Jan 18[54?]
   [G.A.R. 1861 - 65 flag]

BODDER, JACOB   in 71st year
   died 22 Feb 1830
   [Rev. Flag]

BODDER, ELIZABETH   72y 11d
   8 Mar 1770 - 18 Mar 1843

BADER, JOHANNES   38y 10m 2d
   18 Feb 1768 - 3 Jan 1807

BADER, PETER   78y 2m 3d
   22 Jun 1727 - 25 Aug 1805

BADER, MARIA [VIRGINIA?]   73y 3d
   24 Dec 1735 - 3 Dec 1808

TROXEL, JOSEPH   42y 2m 6d
   8 Dec 1760 - 9 Feb 18[??]

TROXELL, ELIZABETH   in 84th year
   wife of Jacob Troxell
   died 2[9?] Jul 1844

TROXELL, JACOB   aged 31y
   died 26 Aug 1845

TROXEL, SARAH   aged 27y
   died 8 Jan 1827

Row 33b

MAYER, MARIA   aged 47y
   27 Apr 1785 - 30 Oct 1833

W. S.

SCHWENK, [SUSANA?]
   28 May 1819 - 1 May 1821

[space]

FUHRMAN, HENRY   63y 1m 16d
   son of Henry and Hannah Fuhrman
   14 Sep 182[1?] - 30 Oct 188[4?]

FUHRMAN, HEINRICH
   4 Sep 1782 - 2 Jul 1864

FUHRMANN, HANNAH
   [1|7?] Apr 1783 - 19 Jul 1812

[four spaces]

FUHRMAN, ELIZABETH
   [no dates]

OTT, AMANDA   9m 11d
   died 26 Mar 1833

OTT, SAMUEL H.   17y 3m 25d
   died 31 Feb 1826

OTT, ELIZABETH   89y 10m 3d
   wife of Samuel Ott
   daughter of Paul [Apple?]
   24 Aug 17[94|34?] - 27 Jun 18[81|62]

OTT, SILAS PAUL   44y 4m 3d
   son of Samuel H. and Elizabeth Ott
   3 Dec 1817 - 6 Apr 1862

OTT, SIMON
   11 Sep 1821 - 9 Mar 1893

SNYDER, JACOB   64y 7m 11d
   6 Jan 1796 - 17 Aug 1860

SNYDER, SUSANNAH
   wife of Jacob Snyder
   25 Mar 1802 - 5 May 189[5?]

SLICK, JACOB   3y 8m
SLICK, JOHN   4y 11m
   sons of John and Mary Slick
   both died 3 Jan 1857

Row 33

KERNS, JOHN   aged 69y
    died 16 Jul 1819

KERNS, MARY
    wife of John Kerns
    died 17 Oct 18[2?]3

BENNET, [MADALINE?]   40y 9m 29d
    12 Jan 18[29?]

[?], AMANDA   8m 14d
    daughter of John [?]
    died 1835

GRUNNER, PHILIP   84y 4m 23d
    died 28 May 1855

COPE, MARIA ELIZABETH
    [illegible]

COPE, ANDREW
    [illegible]

COPE, CHARLES
    [illegible]

E. S.

L. S.

SEIBEL, JOHN   86y 11m 15d
    14 Sep 1779 - 29 Aug 1855

SEIBEL, ELIZABETH   82y 2m 21d
    23 Dec 1780 - 17 Mar 1863
    [same style stone as John Seibel]

MILLER, ELIZABETH   11y 7m 20d
    17 Jun 1806 - 16 Feb 1818

MILLER, MARGARET   59y 24d
    wife of Josiah A. Miller
    10 Nov 1806 - 4 Dec 1865

BA[C?]E SOPHIA   29y [?]m 2d
    died 3 May 18[??]

Row 34

APPLE, ABRM   72y 2m 2d
    10 Oct 18[71|21?]

APPLE, MARY
    wife of Abraham Apple
    daughter of Phillip and Sussanna
    Shellenberger
    20 May 1789 - 13 Feb 1856
    [G.A.R. Flag]

KLEIN, JOHN   61y less 11d
    died 20 Oct 1822
    [Rev. War Flag]

KLEIN, HENRICK   30y 1m 3w 3d
    [15|13?] Sep 1787 - 6 [Nov?] 1817

STIERIN, CATHARINA   45y 5m 2w 2d
    "des Andreus Stiers eheliches..."
    8 Aug 1768 - 3 Feb 1814

STIERIN, [ELIZABETH?]   22y 2m 2d
    18 Jun 1791 - [20|29?] Jun 1813

MOYERIN, MAGDALENE   95y 10d
    April 1745 - 25 [? 18??]

MOYER, MICHAEL   78y 7m
    11 Nov 17[3?]9 - 10 May 1818

KLINE, MARY   84y 10m [24?]d
    wife of John Kline
    died [12|13?] Dec 1854

KLINE, [JOHANNY?]
    died 6 Jul 18[40?]

FISCHER, [CAROLUS?]   20y 2m 26d
    2[8?] Jan 1807 - 16 Apr 1827

FISCHER, [GEORG?]   4y 7m 2d
    died 11 Nov 1807

BRUNNER, [THOMAS?]
    died 10 [? 1813?]

BRUNNER, SAMUEL
    "lovely Child"   [no dates]

BRUNNER, [HIRAM?]
    died 11 Sep 1823

STEER, ANDREAS   69y 11m 25d
    16 Apr 1762 - 11 Apr 1832

[five spaces]

STIERIN, CHRISTINE   71y 3m 2w 6d
    26 Jul 1750 - 16 Nov 1821

[STINE?], ELIZABETH   30y 2m 4d
    wife of Philip [Stine?]
    16 Jul 1796 - 20 Sep 1826

STEED, MARY ANN   9y 3m 7d
    daughter of Sebastian and
    Elizabeth Steed
    1[2?] [?] 1846

STEED, ELIZABETH
    [illegible]

STEED, SEBASTIAN   33y [5|8m?1d?]
    10 Sep 1797 - 14 Mar 1831

KELLER, [MARIA?]   18[30|36?]- 1848

KELLER, [SAMUEL?]   31y 21d
    died 4 Jul 1831

KELLER, ELIZABETH   [dates buried]

ST. PETER'S UNION CEMETERY (Old Section) 111

Row 34 continued:

LAMBARH?WAR, GEORGE   67y 2m
    17 [?] 1778 - 27 May 1845

COPE, EDWIN   1y 3m 20d
    [no dates]

COPE, MARY   3m
    [no dates]

COPE, [?]
    [no dates]

COPE, EMALINE   [12|11?]m 4d
    [no dates]

COPE, SARAH ANN   18y 2m 25d
    daughter of Abraham and Mary Ann
    Cope
    1 Apr 180[9?] - 16 Jun 18[?]

[COPE?], ANNA MARIA   21d
    daughter of David and Catharine
    Cope   died 6 Apr 1852

Row 35

SMITH, JOHN   77y 11m 22d
    7 Jun 1788 - 23 [May?] 1866

SMITH, SUSAN   91y 2m 21d
    14 Jun 1787 - 4 Sep 1878

OPP, [LAVINIA?]   1y [?]m 16d
    1896 - 14 Jul 1899

OPP, [HURRUHINOU?]   82y 6m 15d
    born to Anna Catharine and
    Valentine Opp in Europe
    "del Valentine Opp Gu?word"
    5 Mar 17[??] - 20 Sep 1815

COPE, HANRECH   47y 10m 2d
    8 Nov 1762 - 23 Sep 1810

[DETTERO?], ZACHARIAS   aged 80y
[Lettero?]
[Settero?]
    1726 - 24 Oct 1806

"Zum Gedachunms von MARIA Gerirautha
Dederersie" [Dederer?]
    [dates on stone]   72y 10m 25d
    8 Mar 1744 - 31 Jan 1844

    [six spaces]

REPPERT, PETER   86y
    25 Dec 1717 - 12 Dec 1804

REPPERT, MARGARET   77y
    7 Aug 1835 - 16 Mar 1812

BRUNNER, JOHANN   65y 9d
    died 13 May 1810

BRUNNER, CATHARINE   in 59th year
    16 Mar 1812

COOPER, ANN MARGARET   85y
    [wife?] late of John Brunner
    died 7 Sep 1840

KELLER, MAGDALENA   49y 6m 1d
    17 Mar 1776 - 18 sep 1825

KELLER, HENRY   89y 9m 11d
    15 Feb 1760 - 26 Nov 1840

    [five spaces]

SELLERS, CATHARINE   82y 2m [?]d
    wife of Abraham Sellers
    died 15 Mar 1853

SELLERS, ABRAM   69y 8m 7d
    10 Jul 1808
    born [?] Oct 1786
    [as recorded]

SELLERS, ANN MARY
    daughter of Ephraim and Elizah
    Sellers
    5 Nov 1840 - 28 Aug 1844

SELLERS, JOHN
    son of Ephraim and Elizabeth
    Sellers
    4 Sep 1843 - 25 Jun 1844

SEIPLE, LOUISA   47y 9m 13d
    wife of Enos B. Seiple
    15 Jan 1811 - 28 Mar 1859

SEIPLE, ENOS B.   53y 1m 14d
    9 Feb 1805 - 23 Mar 1858

LEIDY, LEVI   54y 8m 28d
    4 Jan 1808 - 1 Oct 1862

LEIDY, MARIA   32y 11m 21d
    wife of Levi Leidy
    daughter of George & Barbara Shire
    21 Jul 1812 - 1 Jul 1844

Row 36

OPP, VALENTINE   aged 56y
    died 26 Aug 1855

OPP, CATHARINA   [49?]y [4?]m 10d
    wife of Valentine Opp
    [7?] Apr 177[?] - 6 Jun 18[33?]

OPP, MARY   58y
    sister   died 19 Dec 1858

OPP, PETER   [33?]y 11m 21d
    23 Sep 1827

[TRIEWIG?], [Andrew?]   57y [5?]m 10d
    30 [Dec?] 1766 - 9 Sep 1824

Row 36 continued:

[TRIEWIG?], CHRISTINA   81y 6m 21d
    widow of Andren [Triewig?]
    7 Aug 1765 - 2 Mar 1847

WASSER, JOHN   69y 4m 26d
    died 24 Jun 1821

WASSER, ANN MARIA   63y 9m 8d
    died 13 Dec 1829

[SION???], [CHRISTOPHER?] in 49th year
    [2?] Sep 1824

WASSER, ELIZABETH   11y 7m 24d
    daughter of John Wasser
    died 7 Sep 1814

STEINBACH, ELIZABETH   82y 4m [?]d
    17 Apr 1748 - 23 Aug 1829

STEINBACH, MICHAEL   In 68th year 5m
    [? Sep?] 1745 - 10 Mar 1814

[seven spaces]

SHAMAL, EMANUEL   86y 4m 8d
    19 Feb 1787 - 27 Jun 1873

SHAMAL, CONRAD   72y 5d
    died 12 Aug 1823

SCHEINELIN, NATALENA
    3 Mar 1758 - 8 Dec 1814

NEAVEL, MARGARET   [29?]y 20d
    wife of John Neavel
    died 18 Nov 1864

NEAVEL, JOHN   88y
    5 Mar 1781 - 5 Mar 1869

BRUNNER, ADELINE
    [no dates on stone]

MARTIN, ELIZAEBTH   62y 6m 13d
    wife of George Snyder
    [31?] Mar 1811 - [15?] Sep 1873

SNYDER, LYDIA   59y 6m 15d
    wife of George Snyder
    3 Jul 1807 - 18 Jan 1858

SNYDER, GEORGE   82y 2m 28d
    father [G.A.R. flag]
    12 Oct 1801 - 10 Jan 1884

SNYDER, MARY   aged 35y
    [wife?] of George Snyder
    1 Mar 1804 - 16 Nov 1837

SNYDER, ABRAM   10y 4m 12d
    20 Apr 1830 - 2 Sep 1840

SNYDER, EMALINE LUCINDA   [9y?]
    daughter of Jacob and Frany Snyder
    died 7 Sep 1852

SNYDER, Wm. HENRY   3d
    20 Nov - 23 Nov 1850

SNYDER, ELLA VIRGINIA   2y 3m 18d
    3 Mar 1864 - 21 Jun 1866

[twelve spaces]

SEHER, ANTON   83y [?]m 2d
    Veteran of 1812 - 1814 War
    12 Jun 17[79?] - [?] Oct 18[64?]

SHERER, MARIA MAGDALEN   100y 3m
    wife of Anton Sherer
    26 Oct 1785 - 26 Jan 1885

Row 37

SNYDER, MICHAEL   63y 6d
    died 29 Jan 1867

SNYDER, MARY   60y 5m 8d
    wife of Michael Snyder
    4 Jan 1804 - 12 Jun 1864

JACOBY, CATHARINE   92y 9m 11d
    wife of Philip Jacoby
    died Jul 1852

JACOBY, HANNAH   [99?]y 6m
    wife of Conrad Jacoby
    died 27 Nov 1828

JACOBY, PHILIP   71y 8m 21d
    died 24 Aug 1827

SCHNEIDER, [HANNA?]   32y 10m 1d
    12 Feb 1799 - 13 Dec 1831

SCHNEIDER, JACOB ADAM   57y 2m 2w 3d
    17 Oct 1765 - 3 Jan 1823

[REPPERT?], ELIZABETH   20y 16d
    3 Apr 1800 - 19 May 1820

SNYDER, ELIZABETH   93y 4m 16d
    wife of Jacob Adam Snyder
    13 Oct 1778 - 29 Feb 1872

[three spaces]

REPPERT, [CATHERINE?]   2y 28d
    daughter of John and Elizabeth
    Reppert   died [13|17?] Sep 1822

[?], JACOB
    [28? ?] 1806 - 29 [? 18_7?]

[three spaces]

ST. PETER'S UNION CEMETERY (Old Section) 113

Row 37 continued:

JACOBY, BABE [?HOBUCK?]
   18[11?]

JACOBY, SARAH ANN   [4?]y 3m
   daughter of [Benjamin?] and
   Elizabeth Jacoby
   died 9 Feb 1833

[four spaces]

ECKHART, MARY   71y 1m 10d
   died [8?] Apr 1848

ECKHART, CARL   83y
   [17 Feb?] 17?7 - 12 Jan 1830

[Frailz], MARIA
   17 [Sorning] 1766 - 15 Sep 1841

RUPPERT, MAGDALENA   70y 1m 10d
   died 12 Jun 1839

REPPERT, FREDERK   in 68th y
   died 10 Apr 1824

REPPERT, JOHN   52y 1d
   died [4?] Oct 1846

[three spaces]

BAKEL, JACOB   68y 6m 23d
   12 Oct 1770 - [4 Ma_?] 1839

BAKEL, HANNAH
   May 1858

BAKEL, ELIZABETH   15y 15d
   1819

KING, CATHRINA   84y
   wife of George Eckhart
   died 6 Jul 1869

ECKHART, GEORGE   78y 1m 4d
   12 Feb 1770 - 16 Mar 1848

ECKHART, JOHN   41y 10m 15d
   son of George and Catharine Eckhart
   28 Jun 1814 - 13 May 1856

ROSENBERGER, ELIZABETH
   mother, wife of John Eckhart
   later of Michael Snyder
   6 Mar 1816 - 17 Nov 1893

ECKHART, ANNE ELIZABETH   22y 11m 11d
   daughter of John and Eliz Eckhart
   died 4 Apr 1868

ECKHART, OLIVER P.
   son of John and Elizabeth Eckhart
   died 27 Feb 1870

WEISEL, GEORGE L.
   [illegible]

WEISEL, MARGARET   82y 11m 19d
   wife of George J. Weisel
   [8?] Jun 1775 - 27 May 1858

WEISEL, JOHN GEORGE
   son of Harry and Maria Weisel
   29 May 1850 - [23|18?] Feb 1853

WEISEL, MARY LUCINDA   10m 26d
   daughter of Harry and Maria Weisel
   26 Nov 1857 - 22 Oct 1858

[three small stones]

[three RICHLEY stones - no date]

REICHLEY, CHRISTIAN   47y 3m
   6 Jan 1825 - 6 Mar 1872

REICHLEY, MARGARET   86y 9m 19d
   wife of Christian Reichley
   21 Sep 1821 - 10 Jul 1908

LOUX, CHRISTIAN   82y 10m 8d
   11 May 1791 - 19 Mar 1874

LOUX, MAGDALENA   63y
   wife of C.S. Loux
   died 6 Dec 1857

FREDERICK, INFANT
   daughter of Isaac W. and Sarah
   Frederick   died [25?] Mar 1899

FREDERICK, INFANT
   child of Isaac W. and Sarah
   Frederick   died 10 Apr 18[95?]

FREDERICK, JOSEPH   [1?]y 2m 10d
   son of Samuel and Elizabeth
   Frederick   died 20 [Jan 1883?]

FREDERICK, SALLIE   2y 10m 16d
   daughter of Saml. and Elizabeth
   Frederick   died 27 Mar 1878

FREDERICK, WILLIAM   8y 5m 6d
   son of Samuel and Elizabeth
   Frederick   died 27 Dec 18[68?]

FREDERICK, ELIZABETH
   wife of Samuel Frederick
   11 Mar 1837 - 16 Nov 1912

FREDERICK, SAMUEL
   17 Aug 1827 - 7 Aug 1909
   A private of Co. 2
   174 Reg. of PA

Row 38

SUMMERS, EMMA   21y 4m 21d
    daughter of Enos and Lydia Summers
    died   12 May 1870

SUMMERS, LYDIA   79y 11m 19d
    daughter of Enos and Lydia Summers
    31 Dec 1850 - 19 Dec 1930

SUMMERS, ENOS   44y 11m
    13 May 1809 - 13 Apr 1857

SUMMERS, LYDIA   81y 1m 27d
    wife of Enos Summers
    17 Mar 1812 - 14 May 1893

SUMMERS, ISAAC   34y 8d
    died   6 Sep 1834

SUMMERS, NICHOLAS   86y 5m 3d
    died 27 Mar 18[31?]

SUMMERS, ANN   51y 3m 2d
    8 Nov 1776 - 10 Aug 1827

[three spaces]

MARTIN,[? German script] 60y 10m 3w 6d
    1755 - 8 Oct 1816
    [Rev. War flag]

GARNER, SAMUEL   5y 1m 8d
    died   21 Sep 1825

MOR[H?]IN, ELIZABETH   63y 6m 2d
    wife of George Mor[h?]
    8 Apr 1759 - 22 Oct 1822

ME[?]AROR, GEORGE   20y 9m 2d
    died   5 Jul 1852

[four spaces]

[illegible]   [2?]0y 6m 9d
    6 [?] 180[6?]

LEIDY, JACOB   56y 8m 2d
    died 10 Jun 1811
    [Rev. War Flag]

LEIDY, CATHARINE   in 79th year
    wife of Jacob leidy
    died   [1?] Jun 1836

[fifteen spaces]

[?], WILLIAM HENRY   2y [?]m 20d
    son of [illegible]

SNAVEL, WILLIAM   1y 4m 5d
    son of Henry and Maria Snavel
    19 May 1848 - 21 Sep 1849

WOLF, PIERSON   8y 4m 27d
    son of Samuel and Margaret Wolf
    12 Mar 1855 - 1 Aug 1862

TICE, ANNIE   17y 10m 5d
    daughter of Conrad and Magdalena Tice
    17 Dec 1862 - 22 Oct 1880

TICE, ELLA A.   11y [?]m 10d
    daughter of Conrad and Magdalena Tice
    died [?] 1880

TICE, CONRAD   76y
    father
    28 Apr 1819 - 28 Apr 1895

TICE, MAGDALENA   30y 6m 2d
    mother
    6 Jun 1832 - 8 Dec 1913

WIMMER, NANCY   41y 3m 25d
    wife of Joseph Wimmer
    30 Jul 1814 - 25 Nov 1855

WIMMER, JOSEPH   74y 4m 17d
    2 Dec 1815 - 19 Apr 1899

WIMMER, MARY   69y 7m 6d
    wife of Joseph Wimmer
    12 Jul 1830 - 6 Mar 1900

GERHART, ANNA MARIA
    died   9 Sep 1865

GERBER, LYDIA ANN
    daughter of F. and B. Gerber
    died   14 Nov 1857

GERHART, EDWIN S.   5y 8m 28d
    son of [?] and R. Gerhart
    16 Apr 186[?] - 14 Jan 1874

GERHART, FRANCIS   9m
    son of J. F. and A. C. Gerhart
    died   14 Feb 1889

BRYON, EMELINE   4y 10m 5d
    daughter of John and Mary Bryon
    23 Jul 185[4?] - 25 Jan 1859

BRYAN, JOHN   72y [?]
    Feb [?] - 18 Mar [?]

BRYAN, MARY   73y 1m 22d
    mother, wife of John Bryan
    1 Feb 1821 - 23 Mar 1894

BRYAN, MARY E.
    10 Apr 1861 - 17 Feb 1933

BRYAN, HENRY M.   50y 7m 12d
    husband
    21 Feb 1848 - 13 Oct 1896

WITTMAN, SOPHIA MATHILDA   11y 3m 15d
    daughter of John George and
    Margaret Wittman
    7 Sep 1861 - 22 Jan 1872

ST. PETER'S UNION CEMETERY (Old Section) 115

Row 39

SAVACOOL, LYDIA   89y 3m 26d
    wife of Jacob Savacool, mother
    22 Aug 1809 - 17 Dec 1898

SAVACOOL, JACOB   72y 3m 25d
    father
    11 Sep 1803 - 9 Jul 1876

SUMMERS, CHRISTIANNA   79y 7m 12d
    Wife of Noah Summers
    later of John Sheip
    died 7 Sep 1901

SUMMERS, NOAH   45y 9m
    died 11 Nov 18[89?]

RODEROCK, CATHERINE   42y 9m 17d
    wife of David Roderock
    10 Oct 1840

RODEROCK, DAVID   38y 5m 7d
    12 Jul 1831

    [twelve spaces]

AETMANS, BARBARA   89y 7m 6d
    1766 - 1846

[SCHALNEELER?], ADAM
    28 May 1760 - 19 Feb 1828

WAGNER, HANNAH   68y
    born in Germany
    died 8 Jun 1866

SNYDER, [M ?]   2y 8m
    6 Jan 18[34?]

FRIEDRICH, JACOB   1898

BONNAWITZ, CATHARINE   56y 12d
    wife of Joseph Bonnawitz
    20 Feb 183[8?] - 2 Mar 1891

    [four spaces]

MILLER, SARAH C.   72y 3m 15d
    wife of Tobias Miller
    1818 - 11 Apr 1891

MILLER, TOBIAS   48y 1m 11d
    23 Dec 1813 - 16 Apr 1862

MILLER [Manrow?]   [?]y 2m 4d
    died [4?] Jul 1851

MILLER, NOAH   5y 6m 19d
    died 2 Apr 1857

MILLER, JOHANNES   61y 8m 29d
    14 Mar 1787 - 13 Dec 1848

MILLER, TOBIAS   76y 1m 5d
    born in Germany 1753 - 11 Jan 1862

SHOLL [ADAM?]
    son of Simon and Hannah Sholl
    8 Jun - 8 Aug 1847

[buried stone]

SHOLL, WILLIAM HENRY   4m
    son of Simon and Hannah Sholl
    died 10 May 1855

SCHOOL, MARIA HANNAH   aged 5[?]y
    died 27 Oct 1837

SNYDER, EVE REPPERT   [42|72?]y 4m 20d
    10 Jan 1769 - 30 May 1811

SCHNEIDER, CATHARINA
    married Conrad Schneider
    on the 25 Oct 1803
    born 24 Jul 1781
    death [date buried]

SCHNEIDER, CONRAD   88y 4m 7d
    2 Feb 1771 - 9 Jun 1862
    [1812 - 1814 War Flag]

WOLF, ANNA ELIZABETH   2m 1d
    daughter of Saml. and Margaret Wolf
    14 Dec 1854 - 15 Feb 1854

WOLF, WILLIAM   1m 8d
    son of Saml. and Margaret Wolf
    12 Aug 1845 - 20 Sep 1845

WOLF, FRANKLIN   10m 6d
    son of Saml. and Margaret Wolf
    21 [?] 1846 - 27 Jul 1847

E. T.

E. T.

M. T.

J. T.

H. K.

KLETZING, AMANDA
    [11|10?] Jun 1847
    [other dates underground]

KLETZING, JEREMIAH
    son of Charles and Catharine
    Kletzing [rest underground]

KLETZING, CHARLES   56y 11m 22d
    27 Jan 1823 - 19 Jan 1880

KLETZING, CATHAEINE   70y 6m 4d
    wife of Chas. Kletzing
    7 Oct 1827 - 11 Apr 1898

    [four spaces]

Row 39 continued:

DELP, SARAH ANN   11y
   daughter of [?] and Catherine
   Delp   died   1 Jul 1865

[three spaces]

DELP, CATHARINE   mother
   3 Feb 1822 - 15 Aug 1896

SHAFFER, M. L.
   [G.A.R. Flag]

SHAFFER, H.

Row 40

SABELRHUHL, ELIAS   4y 8m 19d
   3 Dec 1857 - 22 Feb 1862

SABELHUHL, [MARIA ANNA?]   12y 2m 6d
   daughter of Enoch and Lydia Sabelhuhl
   12 May 1842 - 29 Jul 1854

SABELHUHL, WILHELMINA   11y 2m 20d
   daughter of Enoch and Lydia Sabelhuhl
   19 Feb 1840 - 9 May 1851

SABEHUHL, [? UIANNA   16y 3m 6d
   daughter of Enock and Lydia Sabehuhl
   4]?] 1835 - 10 [?] 1851

[illegible stone]

SABELHUHL, HENRICH
   15 Oct 1797 - 25 Feb 1830

SABELFUHL, ELISABETH   71y 10m 21d
   wife of Wilhelm Sabelfuhl
   died   27 Mar 1833

SABELFUHL, WILHELM   72y 21d
   died   16 Apr 1852

   [eighteen spaces]

[buried stone]

BEIDELMAN, MARY CATHARINE
   wife of John Beidelman
   [dates underground]

BEIDELMAN, JOHN   70y 10m 28d
   died 30 [?] 1852
   [two spaces]

[? , ?]
   son of Heinrich E. [?]
   [dates underground]

   [five spaces]

SNYDER, MICHAEL   46y 1m 22d
   9 Dec 1800 - 1 Feb 1847

SNYDER, ANNA   71y 2m 2d
   wife of Michael Snyder
   27 Dec 1802 - 1 Mar 1874

SNYDER, JACOB   11m
   son of [Francis?] and Mary Snyder
   7 Sep 1867 - 11 Apr 1868

SNYDER, LYDIA ANN   23d
   daughter of Francis and Mary Snyder
   [?] Sep 1867 - 20 Sep 1867

SNYDER, CAROLINE   9m 14d
   daughter of Francis and Mary Snyder
   died   9 Sep 1867

SNYDER, [?]   1y 8m 22d
   son of Francis and Mary Snyder
   died   25 [May?] 1860

SNYDER, EMELINE   8m 3d
   daughter of Francis and Mary Snyder
   died   3 Jan 1860

SNYDER, FRANCIS S.   1y 11m 4d
   11 Jun 1862 - 22 May 1864

KLEIN, MARY ELIZABETH   17d
   daughter of Jesse and Anna Kline
   Feb [1848?] - Feb 1851
   [as recorded]

KLINE, JESSE   31y 10m 12d
   died   17 Apr 1854

GRASS, ANNIE   34y 4m
   died   2 Mar 1905

Row 41

Row begins near red tombstone of Ruth
Frick, along Hilltown Pike.

SAVACOOL, SUSANNAH   [14|11?]d
   daughter of Enos and Hannah Savacool
   died   18[51|57?]

SCHOOL, HANNAH   30y 4m 2d
   wife of Simon School
   22 Jul 1846 - 24 Aug 1875

SCHOOL, SIMON   [19?]y [?]m [?]d
   9 Oct 18[?] - [10|16?] [Jan?] 1858

SCHOOL, INFANT
   daughter of J[?] and Sallie A.
   School   [no dates on stone]

SNYDER, SIMON   28y 10m 26d
   19 Feb 1809 - 14 Jan 1838

   [none spaces]

GIBSON, CATHERINE   23y 2m 1d
   died 27 Apr 1811

ST. PETER'S UNION CEMETERY (Old Section)

Row 41 continued:

KRONER, E. 88y [3|9?]m 8d
   [no date on stone]

[KRONER?], [?] 71y 4m 26d
   [14?] Sep 1785 - 10 Feb 1857

KRONER, SAMUEL 7y 1m 4d
   son of L. and E. Kroner
   died 25 Feb 180[3?]

[small gray stone - illegible]

[small gray stone - illegible]

[LEISTER?], SAMUEL 6y 11m 1[5?]d
   died 12 Feb 1844

LEISTER, ANN ELIZABETH 2y 6m 22d
   died [30?] Jan 1844

LEISTER, MICHAEL 77y
   died 23 Oct 1859

LEISTER, MARIA A. 39y 4m 26d
   wife of Michael Leister
   died 30 Jan 1844

[long space]

Row 42

TRIEWIG, JACOB 68y 2m 3d
   13 Dec 1791 - 10 Mar 1860

[LEIDY?], OLIVER [1?]y 10m 14d
   son of Mary and Jacob Leidy
   17 [?] 1827

LEIDY, MARY ANN 11y 1m 20d
   daughter of John and Mary Leidy
   died 30 Mar 18[38?]

LOUX, HANNAH 23y 3m [?]d
   wife of John A. Loux
   daughter of Leonard Jacoby
   5 Dec 1820 - 19 Mar 1844
   [G.A.R. Flag]

KROUT, ELIZABETH 79y 4m 11d
   died 5 May 1863

KROUT, PHILIP 82y 10m 15d
   died 4 Jan 1865

EEDMAN, JOST 66y 2m 19d
   Soldier of Revolutionary War
   20 Mar 1824 -

[nine spaces]

BERINGER, HANNAH 70y 11m 11d
   mother, widow of Henry Beringer
   19 Jun 1794 - 2 Jun 1865

BERINGER, HENRY 76y 2m 12d
   father
   3 Nov 1788 - 17 Jan 1835

BERINGER, JOHANNES 84y
   5 Jan 1759 - 4 Jan 1843

BERINGER, GEORGE 73y 6m 30d
   29 Jan 1791 - 28 Aug 1861

BERINGER, CATHARINA 70y 6m 27d
   wife of George Beringer
   24 Feb 1792 - 22 Sep 1862

BEITZ, [WENDEL?]
   born 30 Aug 1780
   married Magdalena 4 Mar 1806
   died [date buried]
BEITZ, MAGDALENA
   9 Jan 1788
   died [date buried]
   [above two on same stone]

HANM [HAUM?], ELIZABETH 71y
   wife of William Hanm
   daughter of John and Catharine
   Everhust [Everhart?]
   29 Aug 1784 - 2 May 1855

GEISEL, 1st Sgt. C. 25y 3m 23d
   4 Feb 1839
   died at Point Lookout 27 May 1864

[small stone -- illegible]

ZOLLER, JACOB 2y 2m 25d
   son of Henry and Caroline Soller
   8 Aug 1859 - 2 Nov 1861

LANDIS, ELLA VIOLA
   22 Sep 1870 - 31 Jul 1872

SHEPHERD, EMMA
LANDIS, PERMELIA
   21 Mar 1865
   3 Dec 1868
   [above two names and dates on same
    stone]

LANDIS, FRANKLIN PIERCE 1y 6m 15d
   son of [?] and Elizabeth Landis
   29 Jun 18[51|31?]

COPE, BENJAMIN FRANKLIN 24y 7m 10d
   son of Adam and Hannah Cope
   18 Apr 1850 - 28 Nov 1874
COPE, MARY MARGARET 16y 6m 2d
   daughter of Adam and Hannah Cope
   6 Jun 1853 - 13 Dec 1869

BUCKS COUNTY TOMBSTONE INSCRIPTIONS - HILLTOWN TOWNSHIP

Row 42 continued:

COPE, LEANNA   1y 2m 9d
    daughter of Adam and Hannah Cope
    6 Feb 1834 - 4 Apr 1852

COPE, HANNAH   1y 1m [?]d
    daughter of Adam and Hannah Cope
    3 Mar 1877 - 3 Sep 18[?]

KOHL, JOHN
    24 Feb 1798 - 28 Mar 1860

Row 43

H. W.

E. W.

WEIKLE, MARY   7y 9m 5d
    daughter of Peter and Hannah Weikel
    died   10 Apr 1855

WEIKEL, HANNAH   25y 5d
    wife of [?] Weikel
    181[?] - 1847

CROUTHAMEL, JACOB
    [no dates on stone]

[HAUS?]. ELIZABETH   67y
    7 May 1772 - 18 May 1839

SCHEIB, GEORGE   89y 1m 5d
    27 Dec 1797 - 2 Feb 1887

SCHEIB, ELIZABETH
    wife of George Scheib
    [dates illegible]

SCHEIB, ABIGAIL
    [dates illegible]

    [four spaces]

R. C. U.
    8 Apr 1847

PRIESTER, HENRY G.   51y 10m 2d
    11 Mar 1811 - 5 Feb 1866

[stone - illegible]

TREFFINGER, FRIETERICK   63y 15d
    16 May 1793 - 1 Jun 1856

HUBLER, SOPHIA   2y 10d
    daughter of [?] Hubler
    died   21 Jul 1836

    [five spaces]

T. K.

T. K.

T. K.

[KERNS?], EMMA C.   4y 9m 26d
    daughter of [?   Kerns?]
    7 Jul 1853 - 2 May 1858

Row 44

SLEIFER, GEORGE   61y 9m 6d
    15 Jun 1780 - 21 Mar 1852

SLEIFER, ELIZABETH   82y 9m 28d
    19 Nov 1781 - 17 Sep 1861

[KAUP?], JACOB   73y 3m 16d
    died   2 [?] 1847

KAUP, HANNA   74y 8m 18d
    died 22 Oct 1842
    [above two stones - same style]

E. J.

A. J.

JENKINS, AMANDA
    [dates illegible]

JENKINS, [?]
    [stone illegible]

JENKINS, ANNA C.
    [dates illegible]

JENKINS, Wm. S.   48y 11d
    18 [?] 18[5?|32?]

JENKINS, ANNA   73y 23d
    wife of W. S. Jenkins
    died   31 May 18[86?]

FRANTZ, PETER   47y 7m 3d
    4 Jul 1793 - 7 Feb 1841

FRANTZ, MARIAH   72y 6m 17d
    wife of Peter Frantz
    21 Jul 1793 - 8 Feb 1866

AIMS, HARVEY F.   1y 7m
    17 Dec 1875 - 17 Jul 1877

BEIDLER, [?   ]
    son of [?] and Mary Beidler
    [dates illegible]

BEIDLER, MARY E.   40y 7m
    wife of Nathan Beidler
    22 Oct 1850

DELP, CHRISTIANA   50y 17d
    wife of Isaac Delp
    died 3 Feb 1852

    [long space]

ST. PETER'S UNION CEMETERY (Old Section) 119

Row 45

FEUSNER, CHARLES -- his children:
   C. F.
   M. F.
   H. F.
   J. F.
[above appear on a square memorial]

[three spaces]

GRASS, ANTHONY   33y 1m 23d
   died 28 Jun 1905

GRASS, MARY ANN   44y 3m
   wife of Anthony Grass
   died 29 Apr 1859

GRASS, JOSEPH
   [dates underground]

[three spaces]

HEDRICK, PETER D.
   13 Apr 1775 - 4 Jul 1851

SLUTTER, SARAH   29y 8m [23?]d
   wife of Jacob Slutter
   25 Jun 1816 - 20 Mar 1846

HEDRICH, MARY   89y 6m 29d
   wife of Peter D. Hedrich
   31 Oct 1796 - 30 May 1886

[stone base -- top missing]

SLUTTER, JACOB   48y 6m 17d
   3 Feb 1810 - 20 [Jun?] 1858

[five spaces]

MOYER, JOHANNES   79y 1m 23d
   14 Mar 1772 - 7 May 1851

HEDRICH, ELIZABETH   65y
   2 Aug 1788 - 24 Aug 1853

BITTING, ABEL   79y 18m
   4 Jul 1774 - 22 Jul 1873

BITTING, CATHARINE   82y 5m 5d
   wife of Abel Bitting
   22 May 1774 - 27 Oct 1856

KEIL, LUCINDA   24y 9m 2d
   wife of Zeno S. Keil
   15 Oct 1832 - 17 Jul 1857

ROSENBERGER, LYDIA
   mother, wife of David D. Rosenberger
   25 Oct 1818 - 28 Dec 1894

ROSENBERGER, DAVID D.
   father
   21 Jun 1821 - 28 Apr 1876

Row 46

[eight spaces]

[BIRRIS?, CATHERINE?]   74th year
   died Sep 1866

[BIRCKS?] HENRICH   54y
   died 11 Nov 1842

[six spaces]

[GEGGUS?], LEWIS
   5 Apr 1807 - 13 Jan 1858

[two spaces]

SELLERS, MARY   72y 6m 6d
   wife of Francis Sellers
   daughter of Samuel and Elizabeth
   Musselman
   12 Jun 1835 - 18 Dec 1907

SELLERS, FRANCIS   84y 10m 20d
   28 Oct 1828 - 18 Sep 1913

SELLERS, [ELMINA?]   53y 11m 16d
   daughter of Francis and Elmina
   Sellers
   3 Feb 1830 - 19 Jan 1884

SELLERS, MARY ELEANOR   2y 7m 4d
   daughter of Francis and Elmina
   Sellers
   13 Feb 18[55?] - 10 Sep 1857

SELLERS, ISAIAH
   son of Francis and Elmina Sellers
   18 Oct 1869 - 27 Apr 1860

CARVER, MARY ANN   7y 6m 10d
   29 Oct 1840 - 8 Mar 1848

CARVER, HARVEY   4y 2m 17d
   16 Feb 1844 - 2 May 1818

CARVER, PETER   3y 22d
   16 Sep 1838 - 8 Sep 1840

Row 47

[five spaces]

LOFT [Toft?], CATHARINE L.[?6y 8m 2d?]
   daughter of Johannes and C. L. Beik
   married Isaac Loft [Toft?]
   26 Aug 1814 - 14 Mar 1837

[stone - illegible]

LOFT, [Toft?], ISAAC   36y 7m 12d
   4 [?] 1807 - 16 [?] 184[3?]

[six spaces]

Row 47 continued:

BAKER, HENRY   18y 2d
    son of Leidy and Elizabeth Baker
    died   28 Oct 1868

[stone, mostly underground]

BAKER, ELIZABETH   9m 21d
    daughter of Leidy and Elizabeth Baker
    died 17 Apr [1866?]

LUFT, MATILDA   27y 1m 21d
    14 Oct 1835 - 3 Dec 1863

H. L.

H. L.

H. L.

Row 48

    [twelve spaces]

[SELLER?], PHILA-ANN   35y 10m 3d
    wife of Reuben [Seller?]
    25 Nov 1818 - 28 Sep 1853

[broken stone - part missing]

[?], AMANDA
    daughter of Reuben and Phila [Seller?]
    [dates underground]

[SELLER?], CATHARINE
    daughter of Reuben and Phila
    [dates - underground]

[GIEP|GIEF?], LOURINE
    daughter of George and Anna [Giep?]
    25 Sep 1852 - 5 Sep 1861

Row 49

[G.A.R. Flag -- no stone]

    [six spaces]

[DERR?], HENRICH   71y 8m 20d
    died [? ?] 1861
    [G.A.R. Flag at stone of Elizabeth]

Row 48

[????] CHARLES   5y 6m 10d
    son of William and Sarah [????]
    26 Aug 184[?] - 3 Mar 1853

The following short rows are arranged perpendicular and adjacent to Hilltown Pike. Row A is closest the church. The stones are read from the roar toward the parking lot.

Row A

AHLUM, CLAUDE C.   1888 - 1962
AHLUM, ELIZABETH   1891 - 1929
AHLUM, WOODROW W.   son
    4 Feb 1913 - 9 Feb 1926

SCHNABLE, AMELIA J.   1866 - 1958
SCHNABLE, ABRAHAM G.   1861 - 1944
    mother and father [same stone]

Row B

THIEROLF, ADAM [G.A.R.] 1843 - 1922
THIEROLF, MARGARET wife   1846 - 1909

Row C

CROUTHAMEL, WARREN L.
    23 Nov 1877 - 22 Mar 1946

CROUTHAMEL, ELI O.   1838 - 1925
CROUTHAMEL, BARBARA wife 1843 - 1926

Row D

HEARING, IDA M.   mother
    6 Jan 1878 - 13 Dec 1920
HEARING, MILTON O.
    26 Feb 19[11?] - 2[?] Aug 19[?]1

Row E

RUTH, ELMER L. 18 Sep 1876 - 13 Feb 1948
RUTH, ANN MARY 26 Jun 1879 - 10 Dec 1924
RUTH, SAMUEL B. son of above
    15 Sep 1910 - 21 Feb 1911
RUTH, MARY   daughter of above
    28 Mar 1912

Row F

RUTH, JACOB R.   1890 - 1970
    Cpl. U.S. Marine Corps WWI
RUTH, CORA E.   1898 - 1950
RUTH, WILLIAM R.   1933
BEIHN, PETER   69y 8m 23d
    husband   died 23 Jun 1909

Row G

FRICK, EMMA K.   mother 1865 - 1914
FRICK, HENRY H. father 1862 - 1938

L. S.

Row H and I

VOCK, CHRISTIAN   1857 - 1936
VOCK, MAGDALENE   1866 - 1938
HAINES, MARY A.   1882 - 1970
HAINES, WARREN   1909 - 1915
HAINES, LINCOLN P.   1882 - 1947

121

ROW AND LOT MAP

FOR

ST. PETER'S UNION CEMETERY (NEW CEMETERY) SECTIONS

<--- to Line Lexington   HILLTOWN PIKE   to Hilltown ---->

ROW-1 2 3 4 5 6 7 8 road 9 10 11 12 13 14 15 16 17 18 19 20 21 22 23 24 road 25 26 27 28 29 30 31 32

| 57 | 49 | 41 | 33 | 25 | 17 | 9 | 1 |

(lot numbers)

SECTION A

SECTION B

SECTION C

SECTION D

SECTION H

SECTION G

SECTION F

SECTION E

SECTION I

SECTION K

SECTION L

SECTION M

SECTION Q

The newer section of St. Peter's Union Cemetery is across the Hilltown Pike and sligltly northeast of St. Peter's United Church of Christ and the older Hilltown Union Cemetery.

The rowas have been numbered starting with row one being along the dedge row nearest to the old cemetery. The stones were copied starting with those closest to Hilltown Pike and reading toward the picnic grove.

The Cemetery Association maps organize these rows in 13 sections, each measuring 92 feet by 116 feet, with paths to divide the lots. EAch lot has four burial spaces. In each section, lot #1 is closest to Hilltown Pike as you face that section from the driveways in the cemetery. (Every other section map is numbered in reverse order. A and I are missing and no section was assigned "J".)

ST. PETER'S UNION CEMETERY (New Section)

Row 1

This row was read starting at Hilltown Pike, next to the hedge row, nearest to St. Peter's United Church of Christ. The row is composed of lots 57 through 64 of the cemetery maps Sections A, H, I, and Q.

Section A

A-57   [No tombstone]

A-58   [No tombstone]

A-59
KOLLO, JOHN   76y 6m 1d
    15 Sep 1811 - 16 Mar 1891

KOLLO, ELIZABETH
    1 Jan 1813 - 15 Oct 1895

A-60
HEARING, MARY
    20 Jan 1851 - 1 Mar 1889
    wife of Frank Hearing

A-61 and 62
KOBER, JOHN C.   Father
    19 Jan 1844 - 5 Apr 1898

KOBER, LAVINIA R.   Mother
    10 Apr 1840 - 14 Jun 1917

KOBER, CLARA MAY
    died 23 Dec 1881 Aged 27 days
    daughter of John C. & Lavinia R.

KOBER, J. PENROSE
    9 Sep 1895 - 19 Feb 1922

KOBER, WILLIAM R.
    13 Aug 1871 - 6 Dec 1925

KOBER, MARY C.
    15 Aug 1872 - 6 May 1946

A-63
GRASS, CHARLES   36y 3m 17d
    8 Nov 1869 - 16 Dec 1888
[GRASS?], CHARLOTTE
    15 Oct 1877 - 20 Dec 1889
    Daughter of Charles & Sallie

A-64
CARVER, JAMES H.   Father
    25 Sep 1846 - 4 Dec 1908

CARVER, MARY   Mother
    21 Aug 1842 - 17 Feb 1917
CARVER, DELLA
    30 May 1882 - 10 Jun 1888

Section H

H-57 Rachael Weikle [owner]
WEIKEL, JOHN   2y 7m 19d
    24 Jan 1860 - 21 Sep 1862
    son of Peter and Rachel Weikle
WEIKLE, RACHEL   wife   70y 24d
    26 Oct 1824 - 20 Nov 1894
WEIKLE, PETER   62y 6m 17d
    25 Oct 1819 - 12 May 1882
H-58 Calven Bilger [owner]
BILGER, CLARENCE   1886 - 1887

H-59 Jacob Frank

ZELLWEGER, ANNA J.
    26 Feb 1866 - 5 Feb 1914

ZELLWEGER, JACOB
    18 Jul 1866 - 6 Aug 1913

H-60 Blair Eckharte

ECKHART, NORMAN   2m 24d
    4 Aug 1884 - 28 Oct 1884
    son of Blair and Emma Eckhart

ECKHART, ALVERDA   8 months
    17 Jan 1893 - 17 Sep 1893

ECKHART, BLAIR   1858 - 1936
ECKHART, EMMA S.   1857 - 1927
    [above two on same stone]

H-61 Horace Bloom
    [No tombstones in lot]

H-62 Edward Carver

KELLY, CHARLES P.   1862 - 1932
KELLY, LAVINA H.   1867 - 1954
CARVER, IVA   1890 - 1891
    [above three on same stone]

H-63 E. C. Hagey

HAGEY, STANLEY   12 days
    8 May 1888 - 20 May 1888
    son of Edward & Maggie Hagey

Row 1, Continued:

HAGEY, HOWARD
    27 Aug 1887 - 12 May 1898
    son of Edward and Maggie Hagey

H-64 Joseph Goder [lot map]
YODER, REBECCA E.
    18 Dec 1859 - 8 Sept 1896
YODER, JOSEPH D.
    6 Jan 1855 - 10 Sept 1934
YODER, CHARLES E.
    8 Jan 1887 - 1 Nov 1901
    14y 9m 22d
    son of Joseph D. & Rebecka Yoder
YODER, HOWARD E.
    14 Feb 1893 - 8 May 1895
    1y 10m ?d
    son of Joseph & Rebecka Yoder

SECTION I

I-57
BLOOM, KATIE S.   38y 24d
    25 Mar 1862 - 19 Apr 1900
    Wife of J. Madison Bloom
BLOOM, JAMES MADISON 76y 11m 12d
    25 Dec 184? - 7 Dec 1923
BLOOM, ARA S.
    3 Jul 18?0 - 20 Sept 1890 [?]

I-58
SAHM, MICHAEL   Father
    27 May 1847 - 19 Sept 1934
SAHM, ROSENA   Mother
    1 May 1848 - 29 Nov 1937

I-59
FUNK, DOROTHY K.
    6 Jan 1886 - 29 Nov 1941
FUNK, JESSE C.
    18 Oct 1885 - 27 Feb 1973

I-60

I 61 & 62
BISHOP, ALBERT B. Father 1854 - 1932
BISHOP, SALLIE T. Mother 1858 - 1945

BISHOP, HERMAN L.   1894 - [Blank]
BISHOP, MABEL R.   1896 - 1978
    [Above two on same stone]

BISHOP, NORMAN L.   1886 - 1947
BISHOP, HANNAH   1886 - 1957
    [Above two on same stone]

I-63
FORD, HENRY J.   1905 - 1978
FORD, MARY ANN   1913 - [Blank]

I-64
LOCKE, HOWARD F., Sr. 1918 - 1978
    SSGT US Army

SECTION Q

Q-57 Elmer Rosenberger
ROSENBERGER, ELMER W. 1882 - 1943
ROSENBERGER, LAURA M. 1883 - 1973
    [Above two on same stone]

Q-58 Norman Haines
HAINES, NORMAN K. 1890 - 1968
HAINES, AGNES Y. 1886 - 1964
HAINES, C. RAYMOND 1922 - 1961

Lots Q-59 through Q-64 do not have
    owners marked on the Section map.

ROW 2
SECTION A

A-49 & 50
    [Corner stone "S"]
GROSS, SUSAN
    died 23 Oct 1916
    Aunt of Archibald & Beatrice Olpp

SEIPLE, HENRY F., Rev.
    died 22 Oct 1908
SEIPLE, SALOME GROSS
    died 23 Feb 1913
SEIPLE, LILLIAN SALOME
    [No dates recorded]

MILDER, SAMUEL A.
    3 Dec 1919 - 9 Jun 1921
    Son of Samuel & Viola Milder

A-51 & 52
SCHEIP, TITUS A.
    3 Nov 1894 - 28 Aug 1926
SCHEIPP, GEORGE W.
    11 Mar 1856 - 18 Jun 1924
SCHEIPP, Lydia
    3 Nov 1856 - 22 Apr 1934
    [Above two on same stone]

SCHEIPP, CHARLOTTE
    b & d 15 Jul 1900
SCHEIPP, JOHN L.
    1 Feb 1893 - 6 Dec 1893
SCHEIPP, MARIA
    4 Apr 1879 - 22 Jan 1882
    [Above three on same stone]

A-53 & 54
HENLEY, SOPHIA
    Died 7 Jan 1894 Aged 77y 8m 29d

ST. PETER'S UNION CEMETERY (New Section)

Row 2, Continued:
HENLEY, ISAAC   71y 8m 15d
   9 Apr 1810 - 24 Dec 1881

BOORSE, ALICE   1873 - 1943

HEINLEY, SUSAN T.   1876 - 1951
HEINLEY, NORMAN H.   1877 - 1932
   [Above two on same stone]

HENLEY, CATHERINE   Mother
   Died 2 Nov 1902   aged 59y 26d
HENLEY, CORNELIUS L.   Father
   Died 2 Oct 1896   aged 55y 7m 12d

A-55
[Monument with low stone wall]
SMITH, ANTHONY GROSS
   6 Jul 1878 - 28 Oct 1878
   Son of J. & M. Smith
SMITH, JOHN F.   63y 5m 15d
   [No dates]
SMITH, MARY ANN   79y 0m 6d
   Wife of John F. Smith
   [No dates] [Above two on same stone]

A-56
RUTH, JOSEPH S.   Father
   24 Apr 1848 - 18 May 1921
   73y 23d
RUTH, SARAH A. -nee Leidy -Mother
   28 Feb 1851 - 11 May 1912
   61y 2m 14d
RUTH, MAGGIE
   8 Feb 1880 - 18 Apr 1881
   Daughter of Joseph & Sarah Ruth
RUTH, LIZZIE   3y 2m 23d
   23 Nov 1874 - 16 Feb 1878
   Daughter of Joseph & Sarah Ruth

SECTION H

H-49 John Bilger
BELGER, LEIDY
   Died 25 Nov 1870   aged 18y 19d
   Son of John H. & Elizabeth Belger
   [Stone is off its pedestal]
BELGER, JOHN H.   77y 11m 26d
   26 Oct 1829 - 22 Oct 1907
BELGER, ELIZABETH   82y 5m 21d
   31 Aug 1832 - 5 Mar 1915

H-50 Oliver Keller
KELLER, OLIVER S.   1855 - 1924
KELLER, ELLEN B.   1855 - 1929
KELLER, ANITA L.   1877 - 1879
KELLER, HANNAH M.   MOTHER
   4 Aug 1833 - 27 Sept 1910
KELLER, LEVI B.   FATHER
   14 Feb 1829 - 19 Feb 1903
   [Above five stones on same base]

H-51 John Ommeren
[a stone very difficult to read]

H-52 Israel Kramer
KRAMER, ISRAEL G.   1863 - 1907
KRAMER, MATILDA W.   1861 - 1944
KRAMER, SALLIE W.   1888 - 1888

H-53 & 54 H.L. Bishop
LEIDY, ELIZABETH, wife of Jonas
   10 Aug 1829 - 14 Sept 1904
   75y 1m 4d
LEIDY, JONAS   68y 11m 9d
   23 Oct 1824 - 2 Oct 1893

SEMPEY, HARVEY   1882 - 1962
SEMPEY, FLORA   1883 - 1919

H-55 & 56 Samuel Leidy
LEIDY, SAMUEL C.
   28 Nov 1832 - 7 Sept 1906
   Father   Aged 73y 9m 9d
LEIDY, SARAH ANN
   13 Apr 1840 - 7 May 1918
   Mother   Aged 78y 24d
LEIDY, H. FRANKLIN   63y 5m 22d
   24 Oct 1862 - 16 Apr 1926
LEIDY, LYDIA A.   80y 4m 23d
   18 Apr 1866 - 11 Sept 1946
   [Above four on same stone]

SECTION I

I-49
SCHEEBER, JOHN   1846 - 1916
SCHEEBER, LOVINA, wife of Christian
   11 Sept 1821 - 16 Oct 1899
   Aged 78y 1m 5d
SCHEEBER, CHRISTIAN   83y 4m 16d
   17 Nov 1843 - 3 Apr 1892 [?]
KOCH, ELIZABETH   85y 8m 5d
   24 Jul 1840 - 29 Mar 1896 [1810?]

I-50
BARNABY, MARY A.   32y 7m 25d
   6 Jun 1866 - 31 Jan 1899
   Wife of Wm. H. Barnaby

I-51
SLUTTER, SOPHIA F.   83y 2m 6d
   26 Oct 1833 - 2 Jan 1917
SLUTTER, HENRY T.   76y 3m 7d
   2 Mar 1846 - 9 Jun 1922
SLUTTER, JOHN A.
   20 Mar 1864 - 19 Mar 1944
   [Above three on sames stone]

I-52
NELSON, JAMES C.   1881 - 1938
NELSON, IDA E.   1892 - 1975

Row 2, Continued:
WILLIAMS, CORA J.
   21 Jan 1867 - 27 Sept 1939

I-53
BISHOP, VERNA
   10 Jul 1906 - 7 May 1928
BISHOP, WILSON L.   1880 - 1946
BISHOP, CARRIE E.   1876 - 1948
   [Above two onssamesstone]

I-54
BISHOP, ROBERT
   Shelly Funeral Home, Lansdale marker
   [Card illegible]

I-55
STEVER, ABRAHAM S.
   29 Mar 1868 - 25 Aug 1948
STEVER, VESTILLA
   18 Feb 1869 - 30 Jan 1953

I-56
KISTER, GEORGE
   11 Sept 1900 - 2 Jun 1960
KISTER, VESTILLA D.
   23 Jan 1902 - [Blank]

SECTION Q

Q-49 William Rosenberger
ROSENBERGER, LEIDY H.   1892 - 1952
ROSENBERGER, MILDRED D. 1895 - 1964

Q-50 No name on map
KRIEBEL, EDNA   1896 - 1978
KRIEBEL, EDWIN N.   1895 - 1970
   SGT HQ Co 32   ENG   WWI

Q-51 through Q56 have no owners

ROW 3

SECTION A

A-41
WEISEL, CATHERINE   85y 22d
   22 Aug 1802 - 11 Feb 1888
WEISEL, J. GEORGE   61y 3m 15d
   8 Nov 1790[?] - 23 Feb 1851
WEISEL, MARY ANN   ?y 4m 17d
   3 Oct 18__ - _ Feb 1875 [?]
WEISEL, MICHAEL   70y 1m 3d
   24 Feb 1802 - 27 Mar 1872 [?]

A-42
SOWER, WILMER   2m 19d
   20 Sept 1855 - 9 Dec 1855
   Son of Adam & Magdalena Sower

PETERS, EDITH S.   nee SOWER
   1889 - 1976
SOWERS, ADAM F.   1860 - 1898
SOWERS, MAGDALENA   1861 - 1934
   [Above two on same stone]

A-43
SNYDER, FRANCIS
   Died 13 May 1880   Aged 55y 3m
SNYDER, MARY S., wife of Francis
   8 Nov 1827 - 19 Nov 1892
   85y 11d

A-44
SNYDER, SARAH JANE   widow of Isaih S.
   Died 23 Sept 1881   Aged 23y 10m 21d
SNYDER, MIRIAM E.
   Died 31 Mar 1896   Aged 1y 3m 11d
SNYDER, RUTH D.   3y 2m 3d
   1 May 1877 - 4 Jul 1900
   [Above two daughters of ISAIAH and
    ANNA E. SNYDER]

A-45 & 46
SHEIP, JOHN
   10 May 1804 - 8 Apr 1883
SHEIP, HANNAH
   26 Nov 1804 - 14 Nov 1869
   [Above two on same stone]

SHEIP, J. STANLEY HARTZELL
   16 Nov 1891 - 20 Sept 1980
SHEIP, HANNAH B.
   12 Nov 1881 - Mar 1959

A-47
ALBRIGHT, CATHARINA
   Died 19 Oct 1900   Aged 79y 8m 5d
   Mother, wife of Henry Albright
ALBRIGHT, HENRY
   Died 24 Jun 1874   Aged 56y 6m 7d

A-48
COAR, JOHN W.
   15 Sept 1861 - 8 Apr 1918
COAR, CATHARINE E.
   31 Mar 1862 - 3 Dec 1930

SECTION H

H-41 John Bilger
LINDAMAN, MARY   Mother
   2 Nov 1865 - 24 Aug 1918
LINDAMAN, J.O., Rev.   Father
   31 May 1856 - 30 Jan 1925

H-42 Abraham Gerhart
GERHART, BARBARA   Mother
   Died 26 May 1897   Aged 69y? 8m 6d

ST. PETER'S UNION CEMETERY (New Section)

Row 3, Continued:

GERHART, FRANCIS   Father
    Died 8 Apr 1898 Aged 74y 11m 16d

H-43 Harvey Kremer
KREMER, HARVEY H.   1860 - 1930
KREMER, ELIZABETH B. 1856 - 1936
    [Above two on same stone]

H-44 Mathias Musselman
MUSSELMAN, LOVINA   Mother
    Died 25 Jun 1915 Aged 81y 6m
MUSSELMAN, MATHIAS   Father
    Died 8 Feb 1911 Aged 77y 2m 3d

H-45 Aaron Kramer
KRAMER, AARON   1858 - 1927
KRAMER, HANNAH   1858 - 1936
    [Above two on same stone]
    [Their three children follow]
KRAMER, ANNA LAURA   4y 2m 8d
    31 Dec 1891 - 9 Mar 1896
KRAMER, MARY ELLEN   6y 11m 16d
    24 Mar 1889 - 10 Mar 1896
KRAMER, JOSEPH HOWARD 3y 4m
    29 Jan 1887 - 29 May 1890

H-46 Alida VanOmmeren
OMMEREN, ALIDA, wife of J.V. Ommeren
    1 Sept 1827 - 23 Nov 1898
OMMEREN, J.V.   Father
    21 Feb 1825 - 13 Jan 1891
    Alida 71y 2m 22d -- J.V. 65y 10m 22d

H-47 Adam Smith
SMITH, MATILDA   72y 17d
    29 May 1835 - 16 Jun 1907
    Wife of Adam Smith - Mother
SMITH, ADAM Father 64y 1m 2d
    20 Aug 1828 - 22 Sept 1892

H-48 Harry Richenback
RICHENBACH, HARRY M. 1861 - 1911
RICHENBACH, MATILDA   1863 - 1935

VIDT, VALERIA S.   Died 6 Oct 1926

SECTION I

I-41
PRESS, INFANT DAUGHTER
    of John & Eliza Press
    Died 30 Jun 1900
PRESS, ELIZA RUTH   Daughter
    Died 2 Jul 1899   1m 28d
PRESS, MARY EDNA   Daughter
    26 Sept 1892 - 30 Jan 1893 4m 4d
PRESS, MATILDA ELLA   Daughter
    18 Mar 1888 - 14 Apr 1894 6y 26d

I-42
SMITH, CLIFFORD E.
    14 Jun 1907 - 27 Apr 1932

SMITH, ELLEN JANE
    27 Mar 1874 - 21 Jun 1956
SMITH, ADAM G.
    21 Dec 1872 - 5 Nov 1944
    [Above two on same stone]

I-43 & 44
APPLE [See Row 4 I-33 & 34 for names]

I-45
    [No stones]

I-46
    [Two spaces]
RUTH, LEIDY L.   1880 - 1938
RUTH, MARY E.   1884 - 1965
    [Above two on same stone]

I-47
HARTZEL, ABRAM L.   1899 - 1952
HARTZEL, AMANDA S.   1908 - [Blank]

I-48
    [No stones in lot]

SECTION Q

Q-41 Wilmer Kline
KLINE, WILMER Z.   1892 - 1970
KLINE, GLADYS B.   1890 - 1977
    [Above two on same stone]

Q-42 through Q-48 have no owners marked on Section map.

ROW 4

SECTION A

A-33
ROSENBERGER, FLORA ESTELLA
    Dau. of Isaac R. & Harriet
    Born in Hilltown, Bucks County
    4 Jun 1871 - 20 Jun 1876 5y 16d
ROSENBERGER, MARY ALICE
    Dau. of Isaac R. & Harriet
    12 Apr 1868 - 29 Sept 1881
    13y 5m 17d
ROSENBERGER, HARRIET 1848 - 1913
ROSENBERGER, ISAAC R. 1846 - 1908

A-34
SELLERS, DANIEL W.   Father
    1847 - 1902
SELLERS, ELIZABETH C. Mother
    1845 - 1936
SELLERS, H. LINFORD   1885 - 1902
SELLERS, LAURA E.   1876 - 1877
    [Above four on same monument]

A-35 & 36
HARTZEL, FRANCIS D. 1824 - 1888
    Father
HARTZEL, CATHARINE A. 1828 - 1913
    Mother

Row 4, Continued:
HARTZEL, LEIDY S.   1853 - 1912
    Brother
    [Above three on same stone]

A-37
WEISS, CATHARINE,   76y 3m 7d
    25 Nov 1816 - 2 May 1893
    Wife of Charles Weiss
WEISS, CHARLES   83y 1m 28d
    23 Feb 1815 - 21 Apr 1900
LEISTER, SAMUEL S.
    21 Jul 1854 - 5 Jan 1923

A-38
FRETZ, FRANCIS HENRY   1870 - 1871
    Son of Elias & Anna B. Fretz
FRETZ, ANNA B   Mother
    21 Dec 1830 - 13 Mar 1897
FRETZ, ELIAS C.   Father
    11 Aug 1839 - 21 Jan 1903
    [G.A.R. Flag]

A-39
SHAW, CATHARINE   78y 5m 21d
    28 Aug 1797 - 19 Feb 1876
    Wife of Robert Shaw
SHAW, ROBERT   91y 3m 23d
    14 Apr 1801 - 7 Aug 1892
SHAW, SARAH W.   46y 11m 17d
    15 Mar 1829 - 2 Mar 1876
    Daughter of Robert & Catharine Shaw

A-40
COAR, ARTHUR
    Died 13 Jul 1824   Aged 6m
    Son of John & [illegible] Coar
COAR, VIOLETTA
    Died 20 Mar 1884   Aged 24y 4m 20d
    Daughter of Thomas & Margaret Coar
COAR, VALERIA
    Died 14 Jan 1872   Aged 11 m
    Daughter of Thomas & Margaret Coar
COAR, MARGARET
    Died 8 Aug 1871   Aged 35y 10m 27d
    Wife of Thomas Coar
COAR, THOMAS
    Died 11 Aug 1898   Aged 71y 6m 2d

SECTION H

H-33 No owner on map
DAUBERT, SUSANNA
    Died [Illegible 187_]
    Aged 1y ?m 14d
    Daughter of Henry & Elizabeth

DAUBERT, ELIZABETH   44y 2m 13d
    15 Jan 1841 - 2 Mar 1875
    Wife of Henry Daubert
    Daughter of ------M and A------?
    Swartley

H-34 Samuel Repparte
REPPERT, EVE   Wife of Samuel
    30 Apr 1801 - 25 Sept 1885
REPPERT, SAMUEL   95y 6m 14d
    6 May 1800 - 20 Nov 1895

H-35 Lewis Philips
PHILIPS, [Illegible]   5m 7d
    20 May 1887 - 27 Oct 1887
    Son of Lewis R. & Fanney B. Philips
PHILLIPS, LEWIS R.   1860 - 1932
PHILLIPS, FANNIE E.   1864 - 1938

H-36 Sarah Cressman
BEISEL, ELSIE P.
    25 Dec 1888 - 25 May 1889
    Daughter of Elmer J. & Angeline
BEISEL, ELMER J.   21y 9d
    20 Sept 1868 - 29 Sept 1889
BEISEL, ERWIN G.   1874 - 1934
BEISEL, SARAH A.   1872 - 1956
    [Above two on same stone]

H-37 Amanda Snyder
HARGRAVES, PEARL M.   nee Bilger
    27 Aug 1896   (No other date)
SNYDER, FRANKLIN P.   1860 - 1890
SNYDER, AMANDA B.   1863 - 1947

H-38 Emma Booz
    [Two spaces]
BARNER, ELIZABETH
    Died 29 Apr 1908   Aged 77y 21d
    Wife of John Barner
BARHER, JOHN
    Died 5 Nov 1890   Aged 69y 11m 26d

H-39 Sallie Leister
GODSHALK, ABRAM   1855 - 1931
GODSHALK, SARAH A. wife   1861 - 1935
LEISTER, ALLEN T.   30y 7m 19d
    12 Aug 1861 - 1 Apr 1892

H-40 James Mumbour
MUMBAURER, ALLEN   2y 3m 21d
    15 May 1894 - 6 Sept 1896
    Son of James & Margaret Mumbaurer
MUMBAUER, JAMES M.   1858 - 1938
MUMBAUER, MARGARET W.   1863 - 1928

ST PETER'S UNION CEMETERY (New Section)   129

SECTION I

I-33
REIFF, MARY M.   69y 9m 2d
    29 Mar 1835 - 31 Dec 1904
    Wife of Abraham R. Reiff
REIFF, ABRAHAM R.   62y 2m 29d

I-34
KLINE, JAMES M.   1852 - 1904
KLINE, SARAH E.   1856 - 1948
    [Above two on same stone]
    [POS of A Flag]

BRUNER, SARAR   73y 4m 26d
    8 Dec 1824 - 4 May 1898
    Wife of Aaron Bruner
BRUNER, AARON C [G?]   76y 3m 5d
    19 May 1822 - 24 Jan 1900

I-35 & 36
    [APPLE monuments between rosw 3 & 4]
APPLE, LEWIS W.
    19 Sept 1864 - 15 Apr 1904
APPLE, LEWIS
    15 Aug 1808 - 19 Dec 1873
APPLE, MATILDA
    23 Mar 1826 - 1 Aug 1897
APPLE, PRESTON R.
    17 Nov 1844 - 2 Dec 1897
APPLE, IDA M.
    27 Sep 1860 - 3 Aug 1897
APPLE, RODMAN H.   1854 - 1933
APPLE, M. IDA   1858 - 1940
    [There are seven small stones
     marked:] Rodman H., M. Ida
    PRA IMA LA MA LWA

I-37
ALDERFER, HORACE L.   1889 - 1969
ALDERFER, DORA L. wife   1889 - 1929
    [above two on same stone]
ALDERFER, MARION RUTH   1818

WARREN, JOSEPH C.   6 Sept 1970
    [Between Rows 4 & 5]

I-38
    [No tombstones]

I-39
DIEHL, CHRISTIAN   1879 - 1962
DIEHL, ANNIE W.   1881 - 1956

I-40
DIEHL, LEIDY S.   1907 - [Blank]
DIEHL, SADIE A.   1909 - 1979

SECTION Q

Q-33 Leidy Nickle
KNECHEL, LEIDY S.   1902 - [Blank]

KNECHEL, MARY W.   1903 - 1972
    [Previous two on same stone]

Q-34 Vincent Gallagher
    [No tombstones]
Q-35 through Q-40 No owners on map

ROW 5

SECTION A

A-25
BRUNER, SARAH   87y 3m 2d
    Died 30 Oct 1914
BRUNER, WILLIAM   65y 8m
    Died 12 Nov 1885
BRUNER, HIRAM C.   1852 - 1940
BRUNER, ELLA   1859 - 19__

A-26
    [Four spaces]
BURDETT, LINNEAUS   3m 7d
    12 Feb 1880 - 19 May 1880

A-27
    [four spaces]

A-28
BLOOM, WILLIAM   Brother
    24 Feb 1860 - 1 Nov 1928
BLOOM, CALVIN H.
    20 Apr 1864 - 15 May 1912
BLOOM, SARAH
    22 Mar 1827 - 29 Dec 1904
BLOOM, WILLIAM
    26 Aug 1825 - 15 Jan 1909
    [Above two on same stone]

A-29 SHEIP
SHEIP, MARY ANN   75y 9m 6d
    3 Aug 1829 - 9 May 1905
    Wife of Noah Sheip
SHEIP, NOAH S.   90y 4m 2d
    1 Sept 1826 - 3 Jan 1917

A-30
GODSHALK, LEON S.   5 years
    Died 12 Mar 1880
GODSHALK, SARAH G.
    Died 5 Aug 1882   Aged 48 years
    Wife of Oliver R. Godshalk
GODSHALK, OLIVER R.
    Died 23 Nov 1878   Aged 44 years
A-31
JOHNSON, SUSANNA   60y
    6 Aug 1833 - 6 Aug 1893
    Wife of L.H. Johnson
JOHNSON, L.H.   36 years
    20 Sept - 1833 - 26 Nov 1869

Row 5 Continued:

JOHNSON, HARRY ANDREW   10y 1m 9d
   22 Oct 18[?] - 1 Mar 18?6
   Son of Levi & Susanna Johnson

A-32
SNYDER, JOHN W   1838 - 1926
SNYDER, HANNAH   1837 - 1877
SNYDER, SUSAN   1871 - 1872
SNYDER, HARVEY   1869 - 1883

SECTION H

H-25 Jacob Smith
SMITH, ROBERT S.
SMITH, THOMAS S.

SMITH, JACOB H.

SMITH, BERTHA L.
   19 Dec 1848 - 31 Dec 1935

H-26 Charles Priester
   [No tombstones]

H-27 & 28 John G. Barndt
TANNER, MARGARET   71y 11m [23d?]
   23 Feb 1829 - 10 Feb 1890
   Wife of George Tanner
TANNER, GEORGE   77y 1m 14d
   21 Sept 1819 - 5 Nov 1896

STEVENS, AMANDA A.
   Died 16 Apr 1914   Aged 63y 11m 11d
   Wife of John R. Stevens
STEVENS, JOHN R.   Father
   Died 12 Apr 1916   Aged 70y 16d
   [Three spaces]
BEISEL, WILLIAM   1833 - 1927
BEISEL, ELLEN MARY   1840 - 1924

H-29 No owner on map
H-30 Jonas Hinkel
HINCKEL, JONAS HARRISON
   24 Nov 1888 - 11 Feb 1889
   Son of John & Mary E. Leister
LEISTER, EMMA M.   68y 6m 15d
   26 May 1890 - 11 Jan 1959
LEISTER, MARY E.   90y 3m 8d
   4 Oct 1861 - 12 Jan 1952
   Wife of John S. Leister

LEISTER, JOHN S.   50y 8m 9d
   1 Jan 1861 - 10 Sept 1911
E.C.H.
J.H.H.

H-31 George Knipe
KNIPE, GEORGE C.   1868 - 1944
KNIPE, EMMA G.   1872 - 1951
KNIPE, LLOYD H.   1890 - 1891
KNIPE, GLADYS M.   1910 - 1912

H-32 Ross Beisell
BEISEL, WM. ROSS   1866 - 1949
BEISEL, ALICE H.   1874 - 1960
BEISEL, A. ROY   1891 - 1892

SECTION I

I-25
   [No tombstones]

I-26
ROSENBERGER, MONROE S.
   22 Feb 1902 - 19 Sept 1924
ROSENBERGER, WILSON S.
   13 Nov 1892 - 18 Oct 1918
   "Died in France in the Service of
   His Country."
ROSENBERGER, MELVIN S.   1897 - 1901
   Son of Abraham G. & Bertha
ROSENBERGER, INFANT SON
   12 Aug 1900
   Son of Abraham G. & Bertha

I-27
BARNDT, JOHN G.   1839 - 1929
BARNDT, ANNIE M.   1844 - 1914

I-28
TREICHLER, VAN J.   1829 - 1915

I-29
FRICK, EMMA V.
   5 Nov 1885 - 25 Jan 1919

FRICK, JOHN HOWARD   1886 - 1952

I-30
   [No tombstones]

I-31
ROSENBERGER, ABRAM G.   1870 - 1935
ROSENBERGER, BERTHA S. 1872 - 1936
ROSENBERGER, FLORA   1894 - 1964

I-32
SCHNEIDER, JOSEPH, Sr.   1909 - 1972
SCHNEIDER, BERTHA R.   1905 - [Blank]

SECTION Q

Q-25 Thomas Griffiths
   [No stones]

Q-26 Ray Kendra
KENDRA, ANNA   1900 - 1981
   [Funeral parlor marker]

Q-27 through Q-32 No owners on map

ST. PETER'S UNION CEMETERY (New Section)

ROW 6

SECTION A

A-17
SNYDER, LEVI S.   1854 - 1927
SNYDER, SARAH J.   1853 - 1886
SNYDER, LETITIA M.   1854 - 1917
    [Above three on sames stone]

A-18
SNYDER, FRANCIS K.   1879 - 1962
SNYDER, IDA S.   1882 - 1911
SNYDER, EMMA L.   1876 - 1962

A-19
KILE, ARTHUR FRANCIS
    Died 23 Feb 1860   Aged 6m 15d
    Son of Francis & Catharine Kile
KILE, HAMILTON M.
    23 Apr 1861 - 31 Oct 1911
KILE, CATHERINE HELLER   81y 9m 5d
    28 Jul 1818 - 2 May 1900
    Wife of Francis Kile
KILE, FRANCIS   Father   74y 10m 9d
    12 Jun 1818 - 21 Apr 1893

A-20
KUSTER, CHARLES   Son   71y 3m
    28 Sept 1865 - 28 Dec 1936
KUSTER, SARAH   80y 9m 20d
    8 Oct 1823 - 28 Jul 1904
    Wife of Casper Kuster
KUSTER, CASPER   Father   83y 10m 13d
    7 Jul 1815 - 20 May 1839

A-21
SHEIP, FLORENCE ELIZABETH
    14 Jan 1876 - 30 Apr 1876
SHEIP, CHARLES PIERCE
    26 Jun 1880 - 11 May 1885
SHEIP, BEULAH LEE
    30 Jul 1884 - 11 Jul 1885
SHEIP, ELLEN M.
    17 Nov 1855 - 15 Oct 1926
SHEIP, FRANKLIN P.
    8 Jun 1853 - 12 Apr 1930

A-22
TAYLOR, IRENE   2 days
    11 Mar 1884 - 13 Mar 1884
    Daughter of Maidell & Anna Taylor
    [Three spaces]

A-23
SOWERS, SAMUEL   1844 - 1912
SOWERS, CATH   1845 - 1939
SOWERS, HARVEY F.   1875 - 1943
SOWERS, MARY JANE   1875 - 1875

A-24
FUHRMAN, CATHARINE   57y 3m 11d
    26 Dec 1812 - 9 Apr 1870

FUHRMAN, MICHAEL   87y 23d
    26 Jun 1803 - 19 Jul 1896
    Husband of Catharine Fuhrman

SECTION H

H-17 Joel Weand
WEAND JOEL   [38 years ?]
    8 Apr 1829 - 28 Jan 1882
    [Three spaces]

H-18 Leonard Douhle
DOPPEL, LEONARD
    12 Apr 1841 - 19 Dec 1912

H-19 & 20 John G. Barndt
KRATZ, ARTHUR W.   10m 19d
    6 Aug 1893 - 25 Jun 1894
    Son of Henry & Emma A. Kratz
TREFFINGER, LEWIS F.
    6 Dec 1857 - 23 Aug 1926
TREFFINGER, HARRIET   nee Barner
    4 Jan 1854 - 9 Jan 1925
                                    ?
HALBERT, ANNIE   [23y 11m 19d]
    3 Sept 1865 - 22 Aug [1930 ?]
    Wife of Harry C. Halbert

H-21 Emeline Strong
    [No tombstones]

H-22 John Piercey
    [Monument PIERCEY - HINCKEL]
PIERCEY, JOHN
    11 Aug 1836 - 19 Apr 1909
PIERCEY, ANNA   Wife of John Piercey
    10 Nov 1839 - 9 Jul 1901
HINCKEL, ELIZA C. wife of Jonas H.
    24 Apr 1839 - 3 Apr 1896
HINCKEL, JONAS H.
    12 Aug 1849 - 28 Feb 1913

H-23 Catharine King
KING, CATHARINE   Mother
    25 Mar 1836 - 12 Apr 1910
KING, CHARLES E.   Father
    25 Jul 1825 - 12 Apr 1892
WILLAUER, MARY A.   Mother
    22 May 1856 - 12 Jun 1913
WILLAUER, GEO. J.   Father
    19 Apr 1840 - 12 Apr 1916
    [GAR 1861 - 1865 Flag]

H-24 Henry Hangy
HANGEY, HENRY H.
    3 Aug 1877 - 5 Jun 1948
HANGEY, MARGARET S.
    22 Aug 1881 - 12 Jun 1955

BUCKS COUNTY TOMBSTONE INSCRIPTIONS - HILLTOWN TOWNSHIP

Row 6, Continued:

SECTION I

I-17 & 18
MARTIN, WALTER S.   1889 - 1911
MARTIN, ADAM   1853 - 1939
MARTIN, ABIGAIL R.   1853 - 1940
MARTIN, EDWARD   1892 - 1892
  [Above four on same stone]

I-19 & 20
BARNDT, J. HARVEY 28 Jan 1870 - 8 Nov 1944
BARNDT, VIOLA N.   5 Nov 1870 - 12 May 1942
BARNDT, BERTHA T.   1878 - 1957

BARNDT, CHARLES F.   1876 - 1939
BARNDT, MARY VALERIA   1866 - 1931

I-21
FRICK, IDA MATILDA
  11 Jan 1864 - 20 Aug 1941
FRICK, FRANCIS J.
  23 Oct 1859 - 23 Dec 1931

BANNISTER, JENNIE
  2 Jun 1897 - 9 Oct 1944

I-22
  [Four spaces]

I-23
PLEISS, MAGDALENA   1876 - 1971
PLEISS, CHARLES F.   1866 - 1937

I-24
  [Four spaces]

SECTION Q

Q-12 & 18   Christian Kummerle
KUMMERLE, CHRISTIAN   1898 - [Blank]
KUMMERLE, HELEN   1903 - 1975

Q-19 through Q-24 [No owners on map]

ROW 7

A-9 & 10   Bloom
BLOOM, ELIZABETH   9   17d
BLOOM, MARIA

BLOOM, AMANDA   10y 8m 2d
  Died 9 Oct 1892
  Daughter of Henry & Mary Bloom
  [Two spaces]
MOORE, WILLIAM H. Jr.   1897 - 1963
  CPL 59th Pioneer Inf. WWI

BLOOM, WILHELMINA   54y 7m 1d
  21 Jul 1861 - 22 Feb 1916

BLOOM, MARY G.   61y 2m 13d
  25 Oct 1836 - 8 Jan 1898
  Wife of Henry Bloom
BLOOM, HENRY H.   63y 3m 7d
  11 Sept 1832 - 21 Dec 1895

A-11 & 12   Snyder
SNYDER, ELIZABETH   Mother
  19 Nov 1806 - 4 Jul 1901
  94y 7m 15d
  Wife of Enos Snyder
SNYDER, ENOS   Father   82y 6m 29d
  26 Jul 1806 - 25 Feb 1889

DEILY, PHILENA   Mother   78y 5m 21d
  8 Oct 1837 - 29 Mar 1916

CROUTHAMEL, CATHARINE   1840 - 1932
[SNYDER, CATHARINE CROUTHAMEL ?]

SNYDER, JAMES ERWIN
  Died 29 Jan 1872   Aged 1y 6m 1d
  Son of Elias & Catharine Snyder
SNYDER, ELIAS   38y 3m 25d
  25 Jul 1840 - 20 May 1879

A-13
SMITH, IDA G.   1859 - 1948
SMITH, HENRY F.   1855 - 1934
  [Above two on same stone]

A-14
VARWIG, GEORGE B.   1878 - 1939
VARWIG, EDNA S.   1879 - 1944
  [Above two on same stone]

SHEIP, ELIZABETH born SCHNEIDER
  11 Oct 1807 - 3 Aug 1876
  Wife of Noah Sheip
SHEIP, NOAH   82y 9m 4d
  4 Jan 1808 - 8 Oct 1890

A-15 & 16
WEISS, JACOB   Father   78y 5m 20d
  29 Feb 1828 - 19 Aug 1906
WEISS, MARY   Mother   80y 11m 18d
  22 Jan 1836 - 8 Jan 1916
  [Above two on same stone]

WEISS, HARRISON F.   1868 - 1954
WEISS, LAURA M.   1875 - 1946
  [Above two on same stone]

KING, HELEN MYRTLE   1909 - 1980
  [Metal funeral parlor marker]

WEISS, Wm. E.S.   31y 4m 28d
  9 Feb 1861 - 7 Jul 1892

ST. PETER'S UNION CEMETERY (New Section)   133

Row 7, Continued

SECTION H

H-9 Mathias Hartman
HARTMAN, CATHARINE
   26 Sept 1837 - 2 Jun 1915
HARTMAN, MATHIAS   1817 - 1921

H-10 Washington Crouthamel
CROUTHAMEL, ANNA CAROLINE
   1m 10d [No Date]
   Daughter of W.O. & Mary A.
CROUTHAMEL, Ma ? MAY
   Daughter of W.O. & MARY A.
CROUTHAMEL, MARY A.   1850 - 1908
   Mother
CROUTHAMEL, WASHINGTON O.
   Father   1848 - 1926

H-11 & 12 Wm. Swartly
SWARTLEY, BERTHA A.
   8 Dec 1887 - 15 Apr 1971
SWARTLEY, ALMA A.
   13 Feb 1895 - [Blank]
SWARTLEY, HOWARD A.
   9 May 1886 - 15 Dec 1923
SWARTLEY, SALLIE J.
   2 Jan 1861 - 3 Nov 1933
SWARTLEY, WILLIAM R.
   4 Oct 1854 - 17 Feb 1922
SWARTLEY, MELVIN A.
   Died 21 Aug 1891 Aged 24d
   Son of Wm. R. & Sallie J. Swartley
SWARTLEY, MABEL   5m 18d
   Daughter of Wm. R. & Sallie J.
   [No date recorded]

H-13 & 14 Wm. Sherm
SHERM, NERI B.
   26 Feb 1872 - 6 Dec 1889

OVERPECK, AARON S.   1864 - 1959
OVERPECK, ALICE B.   1969 - 1933
OVERPECK, BLANCH S. 1902 - 1908
OVERPECK, ELIZABETH S. 1896 - 1961

H-15 Eli Crouthamel [No stones]
CROUTHAMEL, OSCAR W. 1865 - 1930
   Father
CROUTHAMEL, IDA G.   1868 - 1947
   Mother
CROUTHAMEL, INFANTS 3 Jun 1892
   Twins of Oscar W. & Ida Crouthamel

H-16 Oscar Crouthamel [See above]

SECTION I

I-9
FRICK, JOHN C.
   10 Nov 1879 - 25 Apr 1951

FRICK, LAURA V.
   30 Oct 1878 - 21 Jan 1966
FRICK, ELSIE M. 30 Apr 1918

I-10
FRICK, J.
   [Three spaces]

I-11
AKER, SALLIE   84y 4m 17d
   26 Feb 1826 - 13 Jul 1913
   Wife of William Aker
AKER, WILLIAM   78y 11m 5d
   9 Jan 1823 - 24 Dec 1901
KRATZ, MENAN   Father
   11 Oct 1850 - 6 Aug 1916
KRATZ, CATHARINE   Mother
   5 Nov 1851 - 4 Oct 1931

I-12
   [Four spaces]

I-13 & 14
   [No stones in these lots]

I-15
BUHNER, DOROTHEA   Mother
   23 Apr 1856 - 16 Jul 1936
HANG, GERTRUDE   1903 - [Blank]
HOLZMANN, KATHARINA
   25 Jul 1878 - 7 Jan 1944

I-16
   [Two spaces]
KLINK, GOTTLOB   1890 - 1979
KLINK, ANNA   1894 - [Blank]

SECTION Q

Q-9 Vanhook
VAN HOOK, VERNA M. 1897 - 1981
   [Metal funeral parlor marker)
VAN HOOK, PETER   1894 - 1979

Q-10 Reese

Q-11 through Q-16 [No names on map]

ROW 8

SECTION A

A-1
VAN OMMEREN, ANNA ELIZABETH 70y ?m
   10 Dec 186[?] - [? Jun   ?]
   Wife of R. Van Ommeren

FLUCK, EMMA H.   13y 4m 17d
   14 Nov 1889 - 1 Apr 1903
   Dau. of Lee M. & Sarah Fluck

Row 8, Continued:
FLUCK, LEE M.
   22 Nov 1842 - 6 Apr 1919
FLUCK, SARAH
   17 Aug 1860 - 26 Sept 1930

A-2
   [Two spaces]
KELLER, OLIVER
   28 Sept 1853 - 10 May 1895
KELLER, ANNA M.
   14 May 1865 - 28 Mar 1946
   [Above two on same stone]

A-3 & 4
NEAVEL, CATHARINE A.   69y 10m
   19 Jan 1817 - 26 Nov 1896
NEAVEL, HENRY
   20 Dec 1818 - 16 Jul 1878
NEAVEL, JANE   Wife of Henry
   1? Feb 1824 - 5 May 1882
NEAVEL, MARY   Dau. Of Henry & Jane
   14 Dec 1853 - 2 Apr 1877
NEAVEL, ANNA   Dau. of Henry & Jane
   19 Dec 1856 - 5 Aug 1876
   [Above four on same stone]

A-5
SCHEETZ, AARON   64y 8m 17d
   Died 2 Sept 1888
SCHEETZ, EMELINE M.   75y 2m 16d
   Died 14 [?] 1907   [Dec.?]

A-6
GRAVEN, HOWARD A.
   20 Apr 1852 - 15 Dec 1902
GRAVEN, MARY ALICE
   18 Apr 1855 - 20 Jan 1945
   [Space]
LONG, CATHARINE   69y 8m 14d
   Died 29 Dec 1891

A-7
LICEY, ENOS H.   Husband
   20 Feb 1852 - 20 Feb 1894
[LICEY, EMMA M.]
GRUVER, EMMA M.   Wife
   21 Jan 1856 - 9 Feb 1927
   [Above two on same stone]

A-8
KEARNS, WILLIAM
   Died 21 Feb 1878   Aged 10y 7m
KERNS, ELIZABETH PROCTOR
   Died 20 Oct 1899   Aged 71y 4m 12d
KERNS, THOMAS C.
   Died 13 May 1902   Aged 75y 8m 4d

SECTION H

H-1   Henry Shelly
Maggie, Daughter of Rebecca [rest
   is illegible]
[Three spaces]

H-2   Rebecca Derr
SMITH, NORA J.   16y 8m 8d
   Died 6 Jul 1885
DERR, REUBEN   64y 1m 10d
   Died 17 Apr 1891
DERR, REBECCA   56y 16d
   Died 27 Feb 1886

H-3 & 4   Wm. Swartley
   [No stones]

H-5 & 6   Wm. Sherm
SHERM, WILLIAM H.   1839 - 1909
   Aged 69y 9m 3d
SHERM, ELIZABETH L.   1847 -1920
   Wife of William Sherm 72y 25d
   [Above two on same stone]

HARTZEL, FRANK S.   1893 - 1960
HARTZEL, JEAN F.   1892 - 1942
   [Above two on same stone]

HARTZELL, FRANK S.   1866 - 1932
HARTZELL, MARGARET B.   1867 - 1942
   [Above two on same stone]

H-7   John B. Sherm
SHERM, CAROLINE   Mother
   13 Apr 1847 - 3 Feb 1916
   68y 9m 20d   Wife of John B. Sherm
SHERM, JOHN B.   Father
   2 Sept 1844 - 26 Oct 1914
   90y 1m 24d
   [Above two on same stone]

SHERM, E. ELIZABETH
   22 Jan 1881 - 30 Jun 1922

MOLL, MARTHA   20y 8m 26d
   7 Jul 1875 - 3 Apr 1896
   Wife of George A. Moll

H-8   Samuel Campbell
CAMPBELL, SAMUEL   1864 - 1931
CAMPBELL, WILHELMINA   1868 - 1943
CAMPBELL, IRENE   1888 - 1932
   [These three on same stone]

CAMPBELL, CLARENCE   Son
   18 Sept 1943 [?]

ST. PETER'S UNION CEMETERY (New Section)

Row 8, Continued:

SECTION I

I-1 & 2
HARTZEL, ELSIE MAY   Daughter
   15 Sept 1882 - 22 May 1959
HARTZELL, BLANCHE E.   Daughter
   of James M. & Isabella J. Hartzell
   23 Jun 1891 - 24 Dec 1891
HARTZEL, ISABELLA J.   Mother
   30 Dec 1855 - 25 Aug 1935
HARTZEL, JAMES M.   Father
   23 Aug 1851 - 29 Oct 1930

I-3 & 4
   [Curve in driveway]

I-5 & 6
   [Curve in driveway]

I-7
[Two spaces]
WHINNEY, CHARLES B.   1892 - 1966
WHINNEY, ISABELLA M.   1895 - 1932

I-8
   [four spaces]

SECTION Q

Q-1   No name on map
   [Note that the stones for Q-9
     appear in lot Q-1]
VAN HOOK, VERNA M.   1897 - 1981
VAN HOOK, PETER   1894 - 1979
   [These two on same stone]

Q-2   No name on map
   [Note the stone for Q-10
     appear in lot Q-2]
REESE, JOHN H.   1925 - [Blank]
REESE, ANNA MARY   1928 - [Blank]
REESE, T. SCOTT   1958 - 1980

Q-3 through Q-6   No owners on map

Q-7 & 8   Irene Consaley
CONSALEY, EUGENE A.   1883 - 1962
CONSALEY, IRENE L.   1894 - [Blank]

Between Rows 8 and 9 is a driveway into the cemetery which leads to a circle. There are evergreens planted in this circle which is located in Lots I-3,4,5,6 and Lots K-3,4,5,and 6.

BUCKS COUNTY TOMBSTONE INSCRIPTIONS - HILLTOWN TOWNSHIP

ROW 9   This row is on the left of driveway nearest St. Peter's U.C.C. building.   SECTION B

B-1 Lee Fluck
FLUCK, MARY CATHARINE
    14 Jun 1840 -- 24 Apr 1883
    42y 10m 10d
    wife of Lee M. Fluck
    dau. of John & Elizabeth Eckhart

FLUCK, H. MARCO
    2 Mar 1869 - 20 May 1892
    23y 2m 18d
    son of L.M. & M.C. Fluck

FLUCK, HIRAM E.
    1 Oct 1867 - 25 Jun 1892
    24y 8m 24d
    My husband, son of
    L.M. & M.C. Fluck

FETTEROLF, Emma K.
    1872 - 1933,   Mother

B-2 Noah Steer
STEER, JOHN ANDREW
    7 Nov 1876 -   2 m 19d
    son of Noah & Annie Steer

STEER, ANNIE
    2 Jul 1844 - 3 May 1909
    wife of Noah Steer

STEER, NOAH
    28 Jul 1831 - 9 Jul 1900

B-3 Adam Adleman [lot map]
[monument contains information in
 German, including town]
EDELMAN, CHRISTIANA
    born 18 ?   1815 in
    [?   ] Wurtenberg
    died 29 Dec 1880 65y 2m 11d
EDELMAN, ADAM
    born in 1818 - 11 Apr 1890
    died in 72 year

B-4 Lizzie Ruth
RUTH, CHARLES
    12 Jan 1809 - 10 Feb 1855
    46y 28d

RUTH, MARY   wife of Charles Ruth
    24 Feb 1816 - 13 Jan 1859
    [¿62y 10m 19d?]

RUTH, MARY   1839 - 1929

B-5&6 Henry Weisell [lot map]
TYSON, MARTIN A.
    9 Sept 1873 - 12 Oct 1909
    36y 1m 3d

TYSON, HENRY A.
    20 Apr 1872 - 6 Sep 1911
    39y 4m 16d

TYSON, HANNAH ALBRIGHT
    12 Oct 1848 - 6 Feb 1914
    65y 3m 24d, Mother

TYSON, WILLIAM
    15 Sept 1841 - 6 Oct 1904
    63y 21d,   Father

(Space)
WEISEL, MARIA L.
    2 Nov 1816 - 5 Dec 1897
    81y 1m 3d, Mother

WEISEL, HENRY
    21 Sept 1823 - 3 Jun 1885
    61y 8m 12d,   Father

B-7 Henry Funk
FUNK, LYDIA ANN,   Mother
    13 Jul 1852 - 11 Mar 1879

FUNK, HANNAH A.,   Mother
    23 Sept 1855 - 16 Feb 1914

FUNK, HENRY G.,   Father
    27 Apr 1848 - 21 May 1822

B-8 Allen Kerns
KERNS, ALLEN P.   1851 - 1926
KERNS, ELIZA G.   1856 - 1875

SECTION G, Row 9

G-1 Thomas Landis
LANDIS, WILLIAM MICHAEL
    7 Jun 18[35?] - 18 Jul 1874

LANDIS, ELIZABETH S.,   Mother
    8 Jun 1832 - 18 Sep 1904

LANDIS, THOMAS Y.,   Father
    10 Sept 1827 - 19 Jul 1884

G-2 William Hamm
HAMM, WILLIAM B.
    4 Aug 1832 - 23 May 1911

HAMM, FRANCES,   wife of James A.
    born in 1813 - 24 Apr 1893

HAMM, JAMES A. [stone broken]
    10 Jul 1808 - [? Nov 1887 ?]

ST. PETER'S UNION CEMETERY (New Section)

Row 9 continued:

G-3 James Hamm
CARTER, EMMA, wife of William
   Carter, daughter of James A. &
   Frances Hamm
   16 Aug 1842 - 2 Aug 1895

HAMM, JAMES P.
   16 Nov 1844 - 13 May 1921

G-4 Susan Cope
COPE, JAMES
   22 Jun 1857 - 13 Nov 1897

COPE, SUSAN
   25 Jan 1829 - 14 May 1907

COPE, ISAAC
   5 May 1815 - 16 Feb 1895

G-5 & 6 Jacoby Ott
   OTT, MONROE   1897 - 1947
   OTT, ALBERTA M. 1902 - 1941
   WWI flag [Above two same stone]

OTT, HARVEY S.
   12 Jul 1862 - 12 Jan 1928
OTT, ELIZABETH H., wife
   25 Jan 1869 - 4 Aug 1938
   [above two on same stone]

OTT, AMANDA
   dau. of Jacoby & Maria Ott
   27 Jul 1861 - 18 Oct 1897
   36y 2m 21d

OTT, MARIA, Mother
   12 Jan 1832 - 9 Aug 1903
   71y 6m 27d

OTT, JACOBY, Father
   18 Aug 1827 - 24 Jan 1902
   74y 5m 8d

G-7, Charles Kletzing
KLETZING, CHARLES S.   1855 - 1941
KLETZING, SARAH E.   1859 - 1921
   [above two on same stone]

KLETZING, SAMUEL, Brother
   10 Dec 1852 - 3 Jan 1916

G-8 Grier Shearer
SHEARER, INFANTS,
   children of Grier & Ellen SHearer
   d. 25 Mar 1892
   d. 10 Aug 1894

SHEARER, B. ELLEN   1865 - 1914
SHEARER, GRIER M.   1861 - 1915
   [Above two on same stone]

SECTION K of Row 9

K-1 William Price
[large stone-monument between rows 9
and 10 PRICE--MUSSER with stones:]
PRICE, MARY ANN, Mother
   1843 - 1893

PRICE, WILLIAM H., Father
   1837 - 1910

PRICE, JOANTHAN, Brother
   1826 - 1901

K-2 Edwin Musselman
MUSSELMAN, MARY JANE, Mother
   1861 - 1944

MUSSELMAN, EDWIN R., Father
   1862 - 1940

K-3 Chauncey Buckley
[no stones]

K-4, 5, 6 [no owners, The circle
for the driveway is in this area.]

K-7 Ralph Lengel, also owns K-8.
LENGEL, ADAM H.   1897 - 1954
LENGEL, S. RALPH   1920 - 1972
   [above two on same stone]
   [two spaces]

LENGEL, GRACE W., wife of Ralph
   born 8 Sept 1923 - [blank]

LENGEL, SAMUEL R.   1920 - 1972
   T/SGT. U.S. MARINE CORPS-WWII

ROW 10   Section B

B-9 Franklin Snyder
[at the end, between rows 9 and 10
is an illegible stone 2y 8m 16d]

BOOZ, JACOB S.   1824 - 1903
BOOZ, EMMA D.   1846 - 1936
   [above two on same stone]

   [two spaces]

B-10 John Leidy
LEIDY, LYDIA, wife of John Leidy
   4 Jun 1793 -- 14 Sept 1881
   88y 3m 11d

LEIDY, JOHN
   22 Feb 1795 - 7 Nov 1883
   88y 8m 15d

Row 10, continued:
B-11 Joel Leidy
LEIDY, ANNA MARIA
    20 Sept 1833 - 28 Dec 1881
    wife of Joel R. Leidy

LEIDY, JOEL R.
    28 Sept 1833 - 14 Jan 1914

[3 spaces]

B-12 George Frick
FRICK, GEORGE   1836 - 1890
FRICK, MATILDA   1834 - 1897
    [above two on same stone]

FRICK, WELLINGTON 1891 - 1923
FRICK, ELLA   1862 - [blank]
    [above two on same stone]

B-13 & 14   Samuel Weisell
REIFF, CALVIN C. 1861 - 1929
REIFF, SARAH J.   1862 - 1942
REIFF, CLARA H.   1885 - [blank]
    [above three on same stone]

SNYDER, IDA C.   1866 - 1941
SNYDER, LEIDY F. 1867 - 1954
    [above two on same stone, before
     path, in Lot B-14]

B-15 William Snyder
SNYDER, SIMON LANDIS
    d. 22 Sept 1872   2y ?m 12d
    son of Emile L. & Wm. B. Snyder

"Our little Haysie & Susie"
SNYDER, FLORA MAY
    d. Sept 14, 1879   4m 10d
    dau of William R. & Emily L.
    Snyder
SNYDER, SUSIE IDESSA
    d. 15 Sept 1879   9m 10d
    daughter of Wm. R. & Emily L. Snyder

SNYDER, EMILY L.,   Mother
    17 May 1848 - 22 Jan 1901
    wife of William R. Snyder

SNYDER, WILLIAM R.,   Father
    2 Feb 1836 - 27 Dec 1908
    Member Co. D 104th Reg. Pa. Vol. L

B-16 Joseph Landis
LANDIS, ANNIE,   My wife
    d. 25 Dec 1872   aged 45y 8m 19d
    wife of Joseph K. Landis

LANDIS, JOSEPH K.
    21 Jan 1826 - 12 Apr 1901
    75y 2m 22d

LANDIS, LYDIA L.
    10 Oct 1843 - 5 Jul 1904
    60y 8m 25d
    widow of Joseph K. Landis

SECTION G of row 10
G-9 Addie Cope
COPE, ANNA
    23 Jan 1815 - 26 Apr 1870
    wife of Addi M. Cope

COPE, ISABELLA
    20 Apr 1845 - 19 May 1896

[two spaces]

G-10 Albert Hamm
HAMM, SARAH J.
    23 Dec 1842 - 25 Dec 1915

HAMM, ALBERT
    3 May 1835 - 3 Oct 1904

G-11 Mahlon Cope
COPE, MAHLON L.   1862 - 1939
COPE, MARY A.   1860 - 1938
    [above two on same stone]

WELDER, JULIANN GROSS
    9 Sep 1830 - 5 Aug 1912
    81y 10m 27d

G-12 Abraham Cope
COPE, ELIZABETH L.
    7 Dec 1852 - 1 Jun 1918
    65y 5m 24d

COPE, MARY ANN, wife of Abraham K.
    19 Feb 1833 - 3 Jan 1894
    60y 10m 14d

COPE, ABRAHAM K.
    19 Mar 1826 - 5 Oct 1903
    77y 6m 16d

G-13 & 14 Jacoby Ott
VANOMMEREN, EMMA 1887 - 1889
VANOMMEREN, Maria 1892 - 1893
VANOMMEREN, FRANK 1896 - 1897
VANOMMEREN, ADA   1902 - 1902
    [above four on same stone]

VANOMMEREN, PETER
    12 dec 1860 - 6 Jun 1925
OTT, MALINDA, his wife
    16 Apr 1865 - 20 Mar 1947
    [above two on same stone]

VANOMMEREN, AMANDA 1890 - 1959

OTT, JACOB S.   1869 - 1955
OTT, BERTHA R.   1873 - 1935

ST. PETER'S UNION CEMETERY (New Section) 139

Row 10 continued:
OTT, RAYMOND O.   1899 - 1900
   [above three on same stone, with
    a POS of A flag]

G-15 Charles Slifer
SLIFER, CATHARINE M.
   9 Nov 1873 - 29 Dec 1894
   21y 1m 29d
   wife of Chars. B. Slifer
SLIFER, CHARLES B.
   5 May 1875 - 30 Jul 1907
   32y 2m 25d
SLIFER, JULIANN
   25 Mar 1875 - 16 Feb 1962
   wife of Chars. B. Slifer
SLIFER, INFANT
   died 8 Nov 1902
   [above four on same stone]

G-16 Maggie Springer
SPRINGER, MARGARET, Mother
   21 Jun 1862 - 3 Jan 1925
SPRINGER, CHARLES H.,   Father
   22 Sept 1851 - 3 Oct 1897
   [above two on same stone]

SECTION K of Row 10
K-9 Simon Frantz
FRANTZ, MARY
   24 Oct 1808 - 11 Jul 1897
   wife of John Frantz

FRANTZ, MARY,   Mother
   5 Apr 1835 - 30 Jul 1898
   63y 3m 25d
   wife of Simon B. Frantz

FRANTZ, SIMON B.
   16 Feb 1837 - 25 A r 1899
   61y 2m 9d

K-10 Oliver Frantz
FRANTZ, OLIVER   1862 - 1940
FRANTZ, MARY J.   1863 - 1947
   his wife [same stone]

K-11 & 12 Chauncey Buckley
BUCKLEY, STERRETT K.
   38 May 1858 - 25 June [1899 ?]
   son of C.J. & S.R. Buckley

K-13 & 14 [no owners]

K-15 Adam Lengel
   [no stones]

K-16 Raymond Williams
   [no stones]

ROW 11   Section B
B-17 & 18 Jacob Bachman
BACHMAN, AMANDA
   28 Dec [1852?] - 18 Oct 1854
   aged 2y 10m
   dau. of Jacob & Caroline Bachman
BACHMAN, CAROLINE
   5 Aug 1823 - 12 Sept [1858?]
   aged 35 years ?m 5d
   wife of Jacob Bachman
   dau. of John & Lydia Leidy
BACHMAN, JACOB
   2 May 1822 - 23 Dec 1891
   69y 7m 21d
BAGHMAN, ELIZABETH
   30 Sept 1825 - 12 May 1875
   49y 7m 11d
   wife of Jacob Baghman
   dau. of John & Lydia Leidy

   [space]

BURTON, WALLACE B.
   21 Dec 1880 - 22 Feb 1889
   son of Chas. H. & Lydia A. Burton
BURTON, LYDIA ANN
   15 Apr 1856 - 7 Jun 1938
BURTON, CHARLES HENRY
   17 Oct 1847 - 17 Feb 18___
   [above on same stone]

B-19 & 20 Michael Beck
BECK, ELIZABETH
   20 Apr 1798 - 10 Jun 1881
   83y 1m 20d
   wife of Michael Beck
BECK, MICHAEL
   27 May 1802 - 19 Jun 1881
   79y 22d
BECK, HENRY
   10 Dec 1883 - 4 July 1903
   69y 6m 24d [information recorded]
BECK, ANNA
   7 Aug 1912 [died] aged 74y 3m 18d
BECK, MARIA
   7 Jul 1928 [died] aged 86 years

B-21 & 22 Henry Maurer
MAURER, EMMA H.   1862 - 1933
MAURER, FRANK P.   1853 - 1934
MAURER, ELIZABETH, Mother
   20 Sept 1812 - 24 Aug 1876
   aged 63y 11m 4d
MAURER, EVA PEARL, daughter
   died 12 June 1910

Row 11 Continued:
MAURER, HENRY, Father
    22 Aug 1812 - [16?] Aug 1891
    aged 78 years

CLEVELAND, HENRY
    born ?

    [above Maurer information on
    same monument]

B-23 Simon Snyder
SNYDER, LYDIA
    9 Jun 1829 - 9 Sept 1891
    62y 3 months

SNYDER, SIMON
    12 Feb 1831 - 19 Mar 1908
    77y 1m 7d

B-24 Milton Snyder
MYERS, CLARENCE S.
    30 Apr 1892 - 4 Sept 1973

SNYDER, MILTON H.   1859 - 1916
SNYDER, OLIVIA   1864 - 1944
    [above two on same stone]

SNYDER, BERTHA T.
    11 Mar 1889 -- 6 Oct 1889

SECTION G of Row 11
G-17 George Gehaman [on lot map]
GEHMANN, CHRISTIANA
    10 May 1812 - 30 Apr 1882
    69y 11m 20d
    wife of Georg Gehmann
GEHMANN, GEORG
    22 Jan 1812 - 4 May 1901
    89y 3m 13d

G-18 Allen Treffinger
TREFFINGER, CLAYTON S.
    born 17 Feb 1895 died 9 days
    son of [Mary L. & Allen?] Treffinger

YODER, MARY L.

    wife of Joseph D. Yoder
    former wife of Allen G. Treffinger

TREFFINGER, ALLEN
    27 Mar 1872 - 18 Oct 1895
    23y 5m 22d

G-19 Isaac Krout
KROUT, ADALINE S.
    27 Aug 1848 - 8 Jan 1923
KROUT, ISAAC
    11 Sept 1841 - 8 Jan 1917
    [above two on same stone]

KROUT, FRANCIS D.   1859 - 1940
KROUT, LEANNA M.   1855 - 1938
    [above two on same stone]

KROUT, AMOS K.
    21 Jun 1840 - 6 Aug 1917

G- 21 & 22 Leidy Scheip
[SEE row 12 G-29 & 30 for names
 and dates] footstones:
    S.E.S.,   L. S.,   E.M.S.J., R.S.J.,
    E.T.J.

G-23 & 24 Ward Heckler
HECKLER, SAMUEL H.
    died 1 Mar 1899, aged 1 day
    son of Ward M. & Kate Heckler
    [marker between rows 11 & 12]

HECKLER, GRACE H.
    died 11 Sept 1895, aged 1 day
    dau. of Ward M. & Kate Heckler

HECKLER, ESTHER H.   1906 - 1926

HECKLER, KATE R.   1874 - 1956
HECKLER, WARD M.   1875 - 1952
    [above two on same stone]

HECKLER, STANLEY H. 1896 - 1958

    [space]

VETCH, EVA H. (nee Heckler)
    1901 - 1963
VETCH, HUGH A.   1896 - 1977
    [above two on same stone]

SECTION K of row 11
K-17 Ruben Fry
FRY, A. RUBERTA   1908 - [blank]
FRY, CHARLES A.   1905 - 1967
    [above two on same stone]

K-18 Robert Addleton, Sr.
ADDLETON, ELIZABETH
    1 May 1840 - 2 Feb 1902
    wife of Robt. Addleton
    dau. of James A. & Francis Hamm

ADDLETON, ROBERT
    11 Dec 1839 - 17 Jan 1914

K-19 & 20 Clinton Kramer
KRAMER, OSCAR H.
    22 Jun 1892 - 22 Mar 1900
KRAMER, LIZZIE R.
    12 Aug 1870 - 1 Mar 1936
KRAMER, CLINTON G.
    24 Jan 1869 - 12 Mar 1946
    [above three on same stone]
    [a stone removed]

ST. PETER'S UNION CEMETERY (New Section)

Row 11 continued:
QUINTRELL, ANNA KRAMER, Mother
   1896 - 1969

   [two spaces]

K-21 Andrew Flommer
FLAMMER, ANDREW [HAMMER?]
   3 Mar 1848 - 23 Aug 1937
   Pvt. Co. G 197th PA Vol. INFT.
   Civil War

K-22 Julia Race
RACE, M. LEWIS   1884 - 1952
RACE, JULIA A.   1891 - 1953

K-23 William Fickert
FICKERT, PAUL R. 1939 - 1955
FICKERT, CLARA O. 1903 - [blank]
FICKERT, WILLIAM L.
   1895 - 1975
   In memory - from the Sophomore
   Class 1955 North Penn School
   [2nd World War marker & flag]
   [above three on same stone]

K-24 William Fickert
   [no stones]

ROW 12   Section B
B-25 & 26 Jacob Bachman
BACHMAN, JACOB HOWARD
   [?] 1872 - Feb 10 [?]
   son of Frances & Mary Bachman
BACHMAN, CHARLES PARKER
   3 Sept 1875 - 30 Jan 1877
   son of Frances M. and Mary Bachman

BACHMAN, MARY M.
   16 Aug [1850?] - 16 Apr 1886
   85y 8m
   wife of Frances Bachman

BACHMAN, FRANK M., Father
   22 Jan 1847 - 5 Jun 1928

   [two spaces]

CRESSMAN, MARY E.
   9 Sept 1864 - 16 Feb 1939
CRESSMAN, EDWIN C.
   27 Jul 1856 - 15 Jan 1908
   [above two on same stone]

   [three spaces]

B-27 & 28   Michael Beck
BECK, MICHAEL PAUL MILLER
   10 Jan 1873 - 20 Feb 1887
   aged 14y 1m 18d
   son of Samuel S. & Angeline Beck

BECK, ANGELINE
   died 28 Jan 1902, aged 66y 10m 24d

BECK, SAMUEL S., Brother
   22 Sept 1843 - 12 Sept 1893

   [one space]

BECK, ISAAC
   died 6 Jan 1913, 77y 1m 11d

   [one space]

BECK, DAVID
   died 8 Mar 1915, 88y 7m 10d

B-29 Wm. H. Myers
ROSENBERGER, MARIA
   20 Oct 1836 - 31 May 1903
   66y 7m 11d
   wife of Wm. H. Rosenberger

ROSENBERGER, WILLIAM H., Father
   2 Nov 1837 - 24 Oct 1906
   68y 11m 22d

   [three spaces]

B-30 Peter Kline
KLINE, PETER A.
   20 May 1869 - 7 Apr 1900
   30y 9m 17d

YOUNG, CARRIE KLINE
   14 Apr 1872 - 20 Nov 1949
   77y 7m 6d
   wife of Peter A. Kline

KLINE, INFANT daughter of
   Peter & Carrie Kline

B-31 Dr. A.B. Meyers
MYERS, MARIAN S.   1898 - 1936

MYERS, WILHELMINA S. 1864 - 1946
MYERS, ANTHONY, F. MD
   1856 - 1948
   [above two on same stone]

B-32 Simon Snyder, Jr.
SNYDER, HELEN M., daughter
   24 Oct 1901 - 8 Sept 1923

SNYDER, ELLA R., Mother
   15 Mar 1861 - 5 May 1918
SNYDER, SIMON S., Father
   28 Jun 1862 - 18 Mar 1933
   [above two on same stone]

Row 12 continued:
SNYDER, CHARLES CLINTON
    3 Aug 1897 - 9 Nov 1900
    3y ?m 3d
    son of Simon S. and Ella R. Snyder

SECTION G of row 12
G-25 & 26 Harrison Kerns
KERN, CLARENCE L.
    died 20 Apr 1896 aged 1y 27d
    son of Harrison & Anna Kern

KERN, HOWARD E.
    died 4 Feb 1899
    4m 4d
    son of Harrison & Anna Kern

KERN, ANNA, Mother
    9 Aug 1870 - 6 Dec 1904
    24y 3m 27d
    wife of Harrison Y. Kern
    dau. of Frederick & Lo[?] Steep

KERN, HARRISON Y., Father
    10 Jun 1866 - 4 May 1923
    56y 10m 24d

KERN, NORMAN E.
    16 Apr 1897 - 8 Jun 1952

KERN, LOUISE E.
    1904 - [blank]

    [three spaces]

G-27 Henry & May Krout
KROUT, HENRY
    27 Apr 1814 - 12 May 1896

KROUT, LYDIA
    26 Aug 1814 - 22 Apr 1895
    [above two on same stone]

PRICE, MARY D.
    31 Mar 1837 - 9 Jul 1929

G-28 Levi Krout
KROUT, SAMUEL K.
    16 Oct 1880 - 5 May 1951

KROUT, MARY E.
    21 Sept 1892 - [blank]
    [above two on same stone]

KROUT, ROSALINDA, Mother
    6 Apr 1852 - 17 Nov 1926

KROUT, LEVI D., Father
    29, Sept 1842 - 15 Feb 1927

G-29 Marget Moyer
G-30 Marcella Moyer

[information for G-29 & 30 is on the same monument with two footstones marked M S M and I M M]
MOYER, IRWIN M.
    2 May 1881 - 26 Aug 1971

MOYER, MARGARET S.
    25 May 1888 - 30 Mar 1948

SCHEIP, SUSANNA E.
    5 Apr 1838 - 20 Oct 1896

JOHNSON, E. MARTHA S.
    26 Apr 1863 - 6 Nov 1896

JOHNSON, RAYMOND S.
    23 Aug 1891 - 25 Nov 1898

SCHEIP, LEIDY
    25 Mar 1836 - 12 Jun 1920

JOHNSON, Dr. Erwin T.
    18 Jun 1857 - 17 Jan 1926

G-31 Melvin Atkinson
[no tombstones]

G-32 H.H. Hedrick
HEDRICK, ANNA S.
    22 Sept 1849 - 18 Apr 1946

HEDRICK, HENRY H.
    6 Aug 1846 - 3 Aug 1902

SECTION K of row 12
K-25 Abraham Leatherman
LEATHERMAN, LAURA F. 1873 - 1950
LEATHERMAN, ABRAHAM L. 1876 - 1967
    [above two on same stone]
    [five spaces]

K-26 Robert Addleton, Jr.
ADDLETON, ROBERT, JR.
    29 Jul 1877 - 28 Apr 1933
    56 years

K-27 George Hedrick
HEDRICK, GEORGE L.
    died 29 May 1902   1m 17d
    son of George R. & Rosie M. Hedrick

HEDRICK, INFANT DAUGHTER
    b/d 21 Nov 1908
    dau. of George R. & Rosie M. Hedrick

HEDRICK, WILSON L.
    died 12 Sept 1903 1y 5m 10d
    son of George R. & Rosie Hedrick

ST. PETER'S UNION CEMETERY (New Section)

Row 12 continued:
K-27 continued:
HEDRICK, GEORGE R.   1877 - 1942
HEDRICK, ELLA J.   1882 - 19[blank]
   [above two on same stone]
   [five spaces]

K-28 Charles Jenkins
JENKINS, CHARLES   1898 - 1963
   PVT. Amer. Sal. Shops   WWI
   [four spaces]

K-29 Artemus Bishop
BISHOP, ARTEMAS M.   1887 - 1937
BISHOP, ELVA A.   1887 - 1966
BISHOP, EDWIN M.   1918 - 1932
   [above three on same stone]

K-30 Elva Schive
   [no tombstones on lot]

K-31 & 32 Joseph Holdcroft
HOLDCRAFT, JOSEPH R.
   1898 - 1968
HOLDCRAFT, CATHERINE V.
   1901 - [blank]

   [three spaces]

JUDD, VIRGINIA J.   1938 - 1972
   Nee Holdcroft

   [four spaces]

ROW 13   Section B

B-33 & 34 Charles Bruner
BRUNER, MARY,   Mother
   died 4 Nov 1880 aged 53y 13d

BRUNER, CHARLES,   Father
   died 30 Jun 1894 aged 72y 8m 5d

   [two spaces]

BRUNER, CHARLES
   22 May 1877 - 17 Apr 1887
   9y 10m 16d
   son of Leidy S. & Emaline Bruner

BRUNER, LEIDY S.
   22 Aug 1849 - 15 Feb 1920

BRUNER, EMALINE
   19 Aug 1849 - 23 Apr 1930
   [above two on same stone]

B-35 & 36 Fredrick Geisell
GEISEL, FREDRICKA
   16 Aug 1812 - 20 Mar 1867
   54y 7m 4d
   wife of Frederick Geisel

GEISEL, FREDERICK
   25 Nov 1813 - 7 Jul 1888
   75y 7m 12d

ULMER, ANNA M.
   12 Nov 1876 - 18 Jun 1882
   5y 7m 6d
   dau. of Jacob S. and Hannah Ulmer

ULMER, HANNAH,   Mother
   17 Aug 1842 - 26 Jul 1899
   59y 11m 9d
   wife of Jacob Ulmer

ULMER, JACOB,   Father
   15 May 1833 - 18 Jan 1906
   72y 8m 3d

SWALLOW, GEORGE W.   1851 - 1873
SWALLOW, ANNIE   1843 - 1912
   [above two on same stone]

B-37 & 38 Charles Feisinger
FEUSNER, CHARLES,   Father
   27 Sept 1829 - 18 Nov 1906
   77y 1m 21d

FEUSNER, MARY,   Mother
   23 Aug 1836 - 10 Feb 1904
   67y 5m 17d
   wife of Charles Feusner
   [four spaces]
   [above monument between rows 13-14]

B-39 Jonas Schloffer
SCHLOSSER, JONAS F. 1855 - 1945
SCHLOSSER, LIZZIE M. 1861 - 1955
SCHLOSSER, GRACE   1900 - 1900
   [above three on same stone]

BERGEY, WILLARD K.   1901 - 1971
BERGEY, GRACE B.   1902 - 1979
BERGEY, PATRICIA ANN   1935
   [above three on same stone]

B-40 BISHOP, ERWIN
BISHOP, ERWIN H.   1874 - 1954
BISHOP, EMMA T.   1872 - 1965
   [above two on same stone]

SECTION G of Row 13

G-33 Lewis Knoll
KNOLL, HANNAH
    5 Feb 1832 - 4 Nov 1893
    60y 8m 29d
    wife of Lewis Knoll

KNOLL, LEWIS
    23 Feb 1829 - 10 Mar 1911
    82y 15d
    G.A.R. flag next to stone

KNOLL, FREDERICK
    3 Nov 1856 - 28 Mar 1859
    2y 4m 24d

FRITZ, MARY M.
    7 Apr 1848 - 18 Mar 1926

G-34 John Knectle
[two spaces]
KNECHEL, ANNIE
    1871 - 1950
KNECHEL, JOHN
    1871 - 1948
    [above two on same stone]

G-35&36 Irwin Detwiler
[two spaces]
DETWEILER, ANNA MARY   Mother
    31 Aug 1875-- 30 May 1934

DETWEILER, IRVIN S.   Father
    5 Mar 1872 - 18 Oct 1923

DETWEILER, WALTER S.   Our Son
    14 Jul 1899 - 21 Dec 1916

DETWEILER, BERTHA S.
    24 Nov 1896 - 19 Mar 1897

DETWEILER, EARL S.
    23 Dec 1897 - 20 May 1898

G-37 Ira Crouthamel

G-38 Charles King
KING, CHARLES H.
    1905 - 1951

KING, CHARLES S.
    1869 - 1945
KING, MARY M.
    1871 - 1943
    [above two on same stone]
    [three spaces]

KING, ROSIE
    1902 - 1980
KING, ALBERT R.
    1900-1967
    [above two on same stone]

G-39 & 40 Hartman Dungan
DUNGAN, CATHARINE   Sister
    wife of Peter Jenkins
    died 15 Jan 1901   aged 53y 9m 1d

[4 spaces]

DUNGAN, HARTMAN   Brother
    died 10 Apr 1916   aged 65y 3m 10d
    [broken and very worn stone
     lying flat on ground]

DUNGAN, CAROLINE   Mother
    died 8 May 1912   93y 3m 19d

SECTION K or row 13

K-33 & 34 Samuel Swartz
SWARTZ, KATHERINE
    1 Jan 1858 - 6 May 1904
    wife of William Swartz
    [one space]
SWARTZ, WILLIAM
    1875 - 1940
SWARTZ, MARGARET
    1876 - 1939
    [above two on same stone]

SWARTZ, SARAH
    Mother, nee Ruth
    5 Jun 1835 - 17 Mar 1914
    78y 9m 12d
SWARTZ, SAMUEL   Father
    28 Aug 1837 - 5 Jul 1911
    73y 10m 7d
    [above two on same stone]

K-35 Reuben Opdyke

OPDYKE, LILLIAN MAE
    daughter of Reuben & Laura Opdyke
    died 28 Aug 1906   aged 23days

OPDYKE, LAURA M.
    1887 - 1966
OPDYKE, REUBEN
    1881 - 1922
STEELEY, SUSAN N.
    1865 - 1954
    [above three on same stone]

K-36 David Cope
[four spaces]

K-37 Elmer Ott
OTT, SALLIE A.
    1897 - 1959
OTT, ELMER H.
    1892 - 1952
    [above two on same stone]
[six spaces]

ST. PETER'S UNION CEMETERY (New Section)

Row 13 continued:

K-38 Raymond Ott

K-39 & 40 Annie Smith
SMITH, ANNIE B.
   1905 - [blank]
SMITH, LeROY E.
   1903 - 1960
   [above two on same stone]

BEANS, MATILDA S.
   1879 - 1966
BEANS, FRANK E.
   1882 - 1963
   [above two on same stone]

SMITH, EDWARD L.
   1928 - 1972
   257-655 Engineman
   2nd Class U.S.C.G.
   [Korean War flag]

ROW 14   SECTION B

B-41 & 42 Charles Bruner
BRUNER, MILTON H.
   1851 - 1927
   [one space]

BRUNER, EMMA E.
   24 Feb 1889 - 24 Feb 1976
BRUNER, J. NORMAN
   30 Sept 1874 - 11 Oct 1954
   [above two on same stone]

BRUNER, ANNA BELLA
   2 Jan 1892 - 14 Jul 1952
BRUNER, WILLARD LYNN
   25 Jul 1882 - 29 Jul 1961
   [above two on same stone]

B-43 & 44 Frederick Geisell
EBINGER, LOUISA
   died 1 Dec 1903
   aged 56y 2m 28d

   [one Space]

ASURE, EDWARD
   1840 - 1925
ASURE, AMANDA
   1846 - 1921
   [above two on same stone]
   [two spaces]

GEISEL, FREDERICK
   1852 - 1924

B-45 & 46 Charles Feisenger
BERINGER, SOPHIA F.
   1868 - 1940

BERINGER, AMOS S.
   1868 - 1935
   [previous two on same stone]
   [one space]

KRAMER, ELLEN S.
   wife of Henry C. Kramer
   7 Sept 1871 - 10 Aug 1901
   29y 11m 3d

KRAMER, IRWIN B.
   10 Mar 1890[?] - 4 Sept 1893
   3y 5m 24d
   son of Henry & Ellen Kramer

B-47 Nathan Coar
COAR, NATHAN B.
   1867 - 1946
COAR, WILBUR G.
   1897 - 1980
COAR, AGNES L.
   1893 - 1977
   [above three onsame stone]
   [space]

B-48 Ida Coar
COAR, WILLIAM S.
   1865 - 1898
COAR, IDA C.
   1865 - 1948
COAR, RELLA P.
   1895 - 1918
   [above three on same stone]

SECTION G

G-41 Milton Haines
HAINES, SARAH
   28 Aug 1825 - 10 Jul 1912

HAINES, GEORGE
   20 Jul 1824 - 7 May 1901

HAINES, E. AMANDA
   25 Jan 1860 - 6 Feb 1943
HAINES, MILTON
   2 Jun 1851 - 13 Oct 1929
   [above two on same stone]
   [one space]

G-42   John S. Barndt
BARNDT, MARY A.   Mother
   6 May 1858 - 15 May 1942

BARNDT, JOHN S.   Father
   13 Oct 1863 - 16 Jan 1924
   [above two on same stone]

BARNDT, MARY A.
   6 May 1857 - 11 Jun 1920
   63y 1m 5d

146   BUCKS COUNTY TOMBSTONE INSCRIPTIONS - HILLTOWN TOWNSHIP

Row 14 Section G Continued:

G-43 John Hedrick
HEDRICK, JOHN
   1874 - 1931
HEDRICK, HARRIET, his wife
   1874 - 1920
HEDRICK, FLORENCE
   1896 - 1898
HEDRICK, CATHERINE S.
   1898 - 1909
   [above four on same stone]

G-44 Henry Gerhart
GERHART, HENRY C.
   1845 - 1910
GERHART, EMMA E.
   1852 - 1928
GERHART, EMMA J.
   1876 - 1952
   [above three on same stone]

G-45 Charles King
[Note this stone should be in G-37, error on map of lots?]

CROUTHAMEL, LAURA B.
   1897 - 1967
CROUTHAMEL, IRA S.
   1894 - 1954
CROUTHAMEL, MARION
   1917 - 1918
   [above three on same stone]

G-46 Doris Beared
   [no stones]

G-47 Christina Sherm
SHERM, JOHN G.   1895 - 1961
SHERM, CHRISTIANNA 1872 - 1902
SHERM, JACOB   1871 - 1902
   [two spaces]

G-48 Charles Strmer
BOKUM, MARIA
   8 Oct 1841 - 21 Mar 1902
   Beloved wife of George Bokum
   [two spaces]

SECTION K of row 14

K-41 & 42   E.S. Althouse
ALTHOUSE, EDWIN S. 1872 - 1937
ALTHOUSE, SOPHIA S. 1872 - 1936
ALTHOUSE, HARRIE S. 1889 - 1904
ALTHOUSE, AGNES S. 1903 - 1904
   [above four on same stone]
   [three spaces]
ALIFF, EDITH PAULINE
   26 Dec 1922 - 26 Apr 1923

K-43   Joseph Krout
RENNER, MARY A.
   23 Aug 1865 - 6 Dec 1933
RENNER, Emanuel A.
   26 Mar 1862 - 15 Mar 1943
   [above two on same stone]
   [two spaces]

K-44 Harvey Pearson
REARSON, ANNIE
   22 Feb 1887 - 29 Mar 1913
PEARSON, HARVEY   1881 - 1931
PEARSON, JENNIE   1907 - 1919

K-45 Wayne Grubb
GRUBB, WAYNE S.   1903 - 1966
GRUBB, EVA O.   1907 - 1937
GRUBB, RAE DELLA H.
   1906 - 1963
   [above three on same stone]
   [three spaces]

K-46 Titus Ott
OTT, TITUS H.   1890 - 1943
OTT, VERNA R.   1869 - 1953

K-47 Mercedes Ortiz
ORTIZ, MARION L. 1931 - 1971
ORTIZ, MERCEDES 1933 - [blank]

K-48 Frank Ott

ROW 15

B-49 & 50   Leidy Aker
[Large monument between rows 15 & 16 contains the following, in addition to these foot stones: LLA CR EMA CHT and SHA]

AKER, LEIDY L.   1862 - 1953
AKER, EMMA M.   1861 - 1942

ROSENBERGER, Carrie
   11 Jul 1860 - 20 Apr 1951

HENDRICKS, AMANDA C.
   3 Mar 1840 - 3 Feb 1908

SCHOLL, JACOB C.   1848 - 1917
SCHOLL, SARAH M.   1854 - 1929
SCHOLL, PHARES M. 1842 - 1911
SCHOLL, LAVINA   1846 - 1911

AKER, SALLIE H.
   19 Jul 1896 - 9 Feb 1897

TAYLOR, GRACE H.
   31 Jan 1891 - 1 Dec 1925

ST. PETER'S UNION CEMETERY (New Section)

Row 15, Section B, continued:
B-51 Jacob Snyder
B-52 Henry Snyder
[Monument between rows 15 & 16]
H.H.S. [corner stone in row 15]
E.R.S.
Father
Mother
F.Y.S.
J.B.S.
J.B.S [corner stone in row 15]

SNYDER, HENRY H.   1842 - 1918
SNYDER, AMANDA R. 1842 - 1926
SNYDER, ELMER R., M.D.   31y 6m 25d
   21 Aug 1866 - 16 Mar 1888
SNYDER, JACOB B.
   27 Apr 1827 - 9 Jun 1902
   75y 1m 12d
SNYDER, FRANEY YOST
   25 Dec 1826 - 10 May 1903
   76y 4m 15d
FAGELY, GRACE AMANDA
   28 Jan 1897 - 25 May 1897

B-53 Franklin Snyder
LEISTER, LYDIA, wife of Jacob Y.
   30 Oct 1821 - 9 Aug 1900
   78y 9m 10d

LEISTER, JACOB Y.
   19 Nov 1819 - 23 Aug 1904
   84y 9m 4d
   Camp D 171 Reg [flag]

SNYDER, FRANKLIN B.
   8 Jul 1848 - 7 Apr 1922

SNYDER, HANNAH
   16 Mar 1851 - 31 Mar 1936

B-54 Kate Hartzell
HARTZELL, OLIVER S. 1854 - 1914
HARTZELL, CHARLES W. 1886 - 1938

BENNER, CATHERINE HARTZELL
   1858 - 1944

B-55 & 56 as well as
B-63 & 64 of row 16 are owned by:
Frank Bloom.   Row 15 contains:
B corner stone
[two spaces]
E.H.
H.S.B. [flag]
A.B.   [flag]
F.P.B.   and B [corner stone]

[Between row 15 and 16 is a monument:]

BLOOM, FRANK P.
   14 Nov 1852 - 20 Apr 1921
BLOOM, ADDIE
   19 Aug 1860 - 26 Aug 1931
BLOOM, HARRY S.
   3 Feb 1885 - 25 Apr 1943
SMITH, HENRY   Father
   14 May 1806 - 9 Jan 1862
SMITH, BARBARA   Mother
   20 Aug 1816 - 1 Jan 1901
SMITH, EMALINE   Sister
   20 Dec 1844 - 31 Jan 1863
SMITH, LIZZIE
   8 Sept 1862 - 26 Oct 1931
BLOOM, FRANK S.
   8 Jun 1899 - [blank]
BLOOM, NAOMI
   15 Apr 1803 - 19 Aug 1953
     [?]1893
BLOOM, BLANCH
   23 Apr 1890 - 14 Jan 1948
BLOOM, CLEVELAND
   17 Jan 1893 - 5 Nov 1977

SECTION G

G-49 & 50 John Wagner Jr. & Sr.
WAGNER, KATIE B. 1877 - 1951
WAGNER, JOHN N. 1874 - 1964
[above two on same stone]
[two spaces]

MUMBAUER, ANNA MARY
   26 Jan 1892 - 24 Apr 1950

WAGNER, MARIA   Mother
   30 Jun 1836 - 23 Nov 1910

WAGNER, JOHN   Father
   26 Jul 1831 - 6 Jun 1900

G-51 & 52 George Meyers
KINDIG, JOHN
   12 Aug 1869 - 1 Oct 1939
KINDIG, ORVILLA   His Wife
   5 Jul 1871 - 5 Aug 1924
[above two on same stone]

   [space]

MYERS, RICHARD GLENN
   13 Sep 1924 - 18 Dec 1924
[two spaces]

MYERS, GEORGE W.
   21 Oct 1876 - 2 Jan 1947
MYERS, EPHIA   His Wife
   died 24 Dec 1918
   41y 5m 10d [above two same stone]

BUCKS COUNTY TOMBSTONE INSCRIPTIONS - HILLTOWN TOWNSHIP

Row 15 continued:
KELLER, STEPHEN
    14 May 1832 - 25 Oct 1910
KELLER, SARAH   His wife
    20 Feb 1836 - 15 Mar 1928
    [above two on same stone]

G-53 Harvey Sampey
CROUTHAMEL, IRMA MAY
    18 Aug 1888 - 16 Jun 1900
    11y 9m 28d
    daughter of Elvey & Maria Crouthamel
CROUTHAMEL, ELVY   1863 - 1924
CROUTHAMEL, MARIA   1864 - 1943
    [above two on same stone]

SAMPEY, ETTA C.
    21 Aug 1886 - 5 Jan 1964
    [space]

G-54 Marcia Crouthamel
CROUTHAMEL, LAURA A.
    28 Sept 1900 - 10 Mar 1901

CROUTHAMEL, LAURA
    17 Apr 1888 - 24 Apr 1904
    wife of Irwin L. Crouthamel

CROUTHAMEL, IRWIN L.
    17 Dec 1865 - 29 Mar 1902

G-55 & 56 Michael Renner
DIMMICK, LIZZIE   1871 - 1902
    Mother
    [six spaces]

RENNER, ALBERTA
    18 Mar 1900 - 20 Dec 1904
    4y 8m 2d
    daughter of Michael & Catherine Renner
RENNER, CATHERINE   Mother
    1871 - 1951

RENNER, MICHAEL A.   1867 - 1937

Section K

K-49 John Byers
BYERS, JOHN O.   1876 - 1947
BYERS, PHOEBE M.   1883 - 1948
    [three spaces]

K-50 Henry Hittle
HITTLE, OSCAR C.
    son of Henry & Catharine Hittle
    8 Sept 1884 - 29 Nov 1906
    22y 2m 21d

HITTLE, KATHRYN   1850 - 1924
HITTLE, HENRY   1845 - 1910

K-51 & 52 Frank Moll, Jr.
    [four spaces]
MOLL, FRANK C.   1920 - 1964

    [two spaces]

MOLL, ALICE M.   1885 - 1948
MOLL, FRANK   1880 - 1957
    [four spaces]

K-53 Alvin Overholtzer
OVERHOLTZER, ELIZABETH
    1903 - 1960
OVERHOLTZER, ALVIN D.
    1900 - 1970
    [four spaces]

K-54 Thomas Frick
    FRICK, S. PRESTON   Son
    4 May 1912 - 4 Jan 1938
    FRICK, ELLA G.   Mother
    20 Jul 1888 - 5 Mar 1954
    FRICK, THOMAS F.   Father
    30 Jul 1880 - 6 Apr 1952

K-55 Donald Smith

K-56 Stanley Smith

ROW 16

B-57 & 58 Jacob Scholl &
    Lovina Scholl
A.C.H.   G.F.H.
[two spaces]   J.C.S.
P.C.S.   C.C.S.
L.S.   W.O.F.
S.M.S.   S. near Smith
J.C.S.   Monument
[See monument listed in Row 15 for
B-49 & 50 for names between rows]

B-59 Charles Snyder
SNYDER, SALLIE E.
    19 Nov 1867 - 29 Sept 1924
SNYDER, CHARLES C., REV.   Husband
    23 Oct 1866 - 14 Oct 1943
[See Snyder monument listed for
B-51 & 52 in row 15--between rows]

B-60 William Fegely
    [See monument in row 15 for B-52]

B-61 Paul Crouthamel
CROUTHAMEL, ANTIONETTE M.
    12 Nov 1928 -
CROUTHAMEL, PAUL S.
    5 May 1918 -
    [three spaces]

B-62 Chepus Crouthamel
CROUTHAMEL, ELLA MAE
   18 Jan 1888 - 23 Mar 1978
CROUTHAMEL, CEPHAS K.
   9 Apr 1887 - 2 Jul 1972

B-63 & 64 Frank Bloom
   N.B.
   L.S.
   E.S.
   B.S.
   H.S.
   [See monument between rows
    listed in Row 15 B-55 & 56]

Section G

G-57 Sylvester Hedrick
HEDRICK, WILLIAM RAYMOND   son
   16 Apr 1891 - 6 Jan 1916

HEDRICK, LLOYD
   27 Mar 1913 - 28 Mar 1929

HEDRICK, SYLVESTER S.
   1865 - 1935
   [five spaces]

G-58 Allen Knipe
KNIPE, ALLEN   1865 - 1941
KNIPE, KATE   1866 - 1905
   [above two on same stone]

G-59 & 60 Frank Detwiler
"Family of Franklin G. & Louisa B.
 Detwiler"   No dates on stone.

G-61 & 62 Philip Haring
HERING, PHILIP S.   1852 - 1931
HERING, CATHARINE A. 1848 - 1930
   [above two on same stone]
SHEARER, CLAYTON   1882 - 1958
SHEARER, ANNIE L.   1880 - 1935
   [Above two on same stone]

SHEARER, J. THEODORE
   15 May 1907 - 19 May 1946
   [two spaces]

G-63 Charles Constanger
CONSTANZER, CHARLES   1873 - 1951
CONSTANZER, BARBARA ALICE
   1874 - 1928
CONSTANZER, INFANT   1903
CONSTANZER, WALBUROA 1907 - 1918
   [above on same stone]

G-64 Jesse Bissey
BISSEY, MARY E.   Mother
   26 Apr 1844 - 12 Feb 1904
   59y 9m 16d
BISSEY, JESSE T.   Father
   5 Nov 1838 - 31 Oct 1915
   76y 11m 26d
   [above two on same stone]

BISSEY, LEVI A.   1871 - 1958

SECTION K

K-57 Noah Miller
MILLER, CATHARINE   Mother
   25 Jul 1846 - 17 Feb 1905
   58y 6m 22d
   wife of Noah Miller
   daughter of Sam & Mary Sine

MILLER, NOAH F.   Father
   6 Nov 1846 - 16 Jan 1913
   64y 2m 10d

MILLER, NOAH S.   1881 - 1952
MILLER, ELIMY M.   1876 - 1962
   [above two on same stone]

K-58 Emanuel Kerns

K-59 Walter Meyers
MYERS, WALTER W.   1898 - [blank]
MYERS, BERTHA K.   1899 - 1977
MYERS, W. ALBERT   1927 - 1928
   [above three on same stone]
K-60 Alfred Meyers
MYERS, ALBERT H.   1860 - 1934
MYERS, EMMA H.   1866 - 1950
   [above two on same stone]
K-61 Mont Graham
GRAHAM, MONT L.   1887 - 1972
GRAHAM, EVA M.   1892 - [blank]
   [above two on same stone]
K-62 Willard Constanzer

K-63 Christian Eurich
EURICH, GERALDINE B. 1906 - [blank]
EURICH, CHRISTIAN J. 1904 - 1963

K-64 Elmer Ott
OTT, ELMER, JR.   1926 - 1969
   CPL. HQ. CO. 648th Eng BN
   US Army WWII   [Flag]

ROW 17   (on other side of trail)

C-57 George Snyder
C-58, 50 & 49 also owned byssame
[a large monument between rows 17
and 18--part listed here]

SNYDER, GEORGE S.   1855 - 1911
SNYDER, CLARA J.   1860 - 1947

FRANTZ, LUCY ANN   1832 - 1914
FRANTZ, SAMUEL F.   1829 - 1910
   [above four onsame stone]
C-59 Leidy Snyder

C-60 Mirriam Myers
MYERS, LORENZO R., Jr.
   27 Jan 1895 - 9 Aug 1924
   [3 spaces]

150   BUCKS COUNTY TOMBSTONE INSCRIPTIONS - HILLTOWN TOWNSHIP

Row 17 continued:
MYERS, CRAIG A.
    12 Aug to 27 Sept 1953

MYERS, ELIZABETH M.
    20 Aug 1858 - 18 Oct 1924
MYERS, WILLIAM S.
    30 Aug 1854 - 14 Oct 1934
    [above two on same stone]

C-61 & 62 James Detwiler
DETWILER, HOWARD
    died 17 Sept 1904 13y 11m 27d
    son of James R. & Louisa S.
    Detwiler

DETWILER, GEORGE K.
    died 4 Mar 1915 15y 10m 25d
    Son of James R. & Louisa Detwiler

DETWILER, JAMES R.   1863 - 1933
DETWILER, LOUISA   1862 - 1945
    [above two on same stone]

C-63 Charles Pleiss
PLEISS, KATIE MAGDALENA   Daughter
    28 Dec 1898 - 2 Jan 1899 26ds

PLEISS, ROSIE M.   Daughter
    died 1905   aged 1y 2m 26d

PLEISS, JOHN F.   Son
    29 Nov 1894 - 15 Oct 1918
    30th Recruit Co. C.S. 1
    Fort Thomas KY
    died in service of his Country

PLEISS, WARREN C.
    8 Apr 1913 - 13 Aug 1935

C-64 Frank Reaser
REASER, KATE E.   wife of Frank H.
    12 Jan 1857 - 1 Feb 1905

BARBER, SIBYL C. wife of Rev. W. Barber
    6 Apr 1824 - 20 Jan 1910
REASER, FRANK H.
    5 May 1853 - 14 Jan 1908
    [above three on same stone]

SECTION F
F-57 Henry Ekert, also owns F-58
    [large marker between rows]
    ECKERT, HENRY   1829 - 1905
    ECKERT, EMMALINE   1841 - 1926
    ECKERT, ANNIE E.   1874 - 1958
    ECKERT, DONALD F. 1877 - 1960
    ECKERT, MARY J.   1873 - 1967

F-59 Reuben Fellman
    FELLMAN, REUBEN N.   1858 - 1939
    FELLMAN, RACHEL R.   1865 - 1937
    FELLMAN, LLOYD C.   1900 - 1900
    FELLMAN, ETHEL C.   1906 - 1906

F-60 Isac Stout

F-61 Wm. Renner
RENNER, ALAN C.
    5 Feb 1906 - 13 Jul 1909
    son of Wm. & Ida L. Renner
    [three spaces]

F-62 Wm. Renner
RENNER, Herbert B.
    6 Jul 1895 - 5 Nov 1945
    PA Cpl 110 INF 28 DIV WWII

RENNER, IDA L.
    13 Jun 1872 - 18 Apr 1934
RENNER, Wm. A.
    5 Aug 1868 - 8 Jan 1924
    [above two on same stone]

F-63 no owner

F-64 Allen Detwiler
DETWILER, ALLEN C.   1865 - 1918
DETWILER, SARAH C.   1873 - 1968
    [above two on same stone]

WAYNE, LILLIAN M.   1892 - 19__
WAYNE, THOMAS S.   1894 - 1969
    [above two on same stone]

SECTION L

L-57 & 58 Edward Bloom
BLOOM, EDWARD H.   1862 - 1946
BLOOM, Carrie M.   1874 - 1927
BLOOM, MILDRED I.   1905 - 1907
    [above three on same stone]

BLOOM, EDWARD   1908 - 1974
    PFC 109th Av. Eng. BN WWII

L59 & 60 Emma Moll
MULL, EMMA E.   1865 - 1935
MULL, HENRY E.   1865 - 1926
    [above two on same stone]

MULL, LINFORD LUTHER
    4 Jan 1932 - 26 Jul 1952
    A2C 492 AF BOMB SQ - Korean War
MULL, LUTHER LDS OM USNRF WWI
    4 Oct 1896 - 16 Mar 1964

L-61-62 Wellington Hedrick [no stone]
L-63 Hildegard Gilbert

L-64 Albert Cooper

ROW 18

C-49 & 50 George S. Snyder
HECKLER, STELLA F.   1888 - 1951
HECKLER, HOWARD E.   1873 - 1933

C-51 Leidy Snyder

C-52 Allison Rickert

ST. PETER'S UNION CEMETERY (New Section)

Row 18 continued:
C-52 continued
RICKER, J. ALLISON   1883 - 1950
RICKER, FLORENCE M.   1883 - 1964

C-53 Paul Bensing
BENSING, CATHERINE T.   1876 - 1941
BENSING, PAUL D.   1879 - 1944

C-54 Eugene & Abraham Tyson
TYSON, MAY A.   1876 - 1960
TYSON, EUGENE A.   1875 - 1949

C-55 Wm. H. Curtis
CURTIS, ANNA ELIZABETH
    3 Oct 1839 - 7 Mar 1922
    82y 5m 64d
CURTIS, Wm. H.
    3 Sept 1841 - 31 Dec 1906
    65y 3m 28d

FRANKENFIELD, SOPHIA   MOTHER
    22 Apr 1842 - 16 Nov 1922
    [Is this stone in C-55 or C-56?]

C-56 Frank Reaser
    [four speces]

SECTION F
F-49 Henry Albright
ALBRIGHT, SUSAN M.
    14 Nov 1854 - 13 Oct 1905
ALBRIGHT, HENRY   1850 - 1918

F-50 Ben Mumbauer
M.W.M. [little stone sunk in ground]
MUMBAUER, MARY WILHELMINA
    11 Mar 1855 - 16 Nov 1905
    wife of Benjamin Mumbauer
    50y 8m 4d

F-51 & 52 Wm. Seidel
SEIDEL, WILLIAM M.
    9 Dec 1908 - 5 Jun 1910
    son of Wm. M. & Katie M. Seidel

SEIDEL, CHARLES
    17 Feb 1911 - 7 Mar 1911
    son of Wm. M. & Katie M. Seidel

F-53 [no owner on lot map]
RUTH, CHRISTIAN   1866 - 1941
RUTH, MARY   1887 - 1964
RUTH, RUDOLPH   1915 - 1916
RUTH, EDWARD   1918 - 1919
RUTH, THOMAS   1921 - 1930
    [above five on same stone]
F-54 Samuel Cassel
CASSEL, MARION   1922 - 1922
CASSEL, IDA L.   1905 - [blank]
CASSEL, SAMUEL G.   1900 - 1961
    [above three on same stone]

F-55 Henry Moyer
MOYER, LEILA
    16 Nov 1885 - 11 Nov 1933
MOYER, HENRY D.
    15 Apr 1887 - 2 Nov 1951
    [above two on same stone]
    [three spaces]

F-56 Ira Hartzel
HARTZELL, IRA F.   1888 - 1952
HARTZEL, LEVI M.   1859 - 1922
HARTZEL, CHRISTIANNA F. 1863 - 1928
    [above two on same stone]

SECTION L

L-49 Ella King
KING, FREDRICK W.   1869 - 1926
KING, ELLA S.   1869 - 1944
    [above two on same stone]

SMITH, FRANK
    21 Nov 1875 - 20 Mar 1948

L-50 Joseph Fonda
FONDA, JOSEPH   1867 - 1938
FONDA, BARBARA   1870 - 1928
    [above two on same stone]

L-51 Joseph Darner

L-52 Freeman Weks
DIMMICK, BENJAMIN
    died 24 Mar 1941

WEEKS, LAURA C. DIMMICK
    1878 - 1957
    Laura C. Dimmick, wife of
    J. Freeman Weeks

L-53 Russell L. Weiss
L-54   "   "   "
WEISS, RUSSELL C.   1904 - 1976
WEISS, RUTH C.   1904 - 1978
WEISS, RICHARD D.   1930 - 1943
    [four spaces]

L-55 Anna Hahn
HAHN,   Father & Mother
    [no names nor dates on marker]
    [three spaces]

L-56 Marie Nace
NACE, ROBERT C.   1919 - 1970

ROW 19

C-41 & 42 Margret Haldeman
HALDEMAN, ABEL C.   Father
    7 Apr 1858 - 3 Oct 1908

Row 19, Section C continued:
HALDEMAN, MARGARET R.   Mother
    7 Mar 1861 - 1 Nov 1915
    [no others in Lot]

C-43 Irwin Erney
ERNEY, IRVIN F.   1870 - 1947
ERNEY, ELIZABETH   1878 - 1962
ERNEY, RUSSELL S.   1906 - 1907
    [all of above are on same stone]

C-44 Tom Frick
CONSTANZER, THOMAS J.   Father
    1876 - 1940
CONSTANZER, CATHERINE L. Mother
    1881 - 1976

C-45 & 46 William Curtis
    [six spaces]
CURTIS, THE REV. WILLIAM FRANKLIN
    12 Feb 1873 - 5 May 1941
    President of Cedar Crest College
    1908 to 1941
CURTIS, ANNA DELINGER
    20 Dec 1878 - 19 Mar 1970
    [above two on same stone]

C-47 Elizabeth Erich
EHRIG, CONRAD E.
    24 Mar 1836 - 6 Aug 1909
EHRIG, ELIZABETH M.
    4 Jul 1847 - 3 Jun 1938
    [above two on same stone]

C-48 Allen Curtis
CURTIS, ELLA K.   Mother
    28 Aug 1871 - 15 Dec 1944
CURTIS, ALBANUS M.   Father
    21 Mar 1869 - 9 May 1933

SECTION F

F-41 Horace Fellman
FELLMAN, LAURA D.   1888 - 1949
FELLMAN, HORACE C.   1886 - 1954
FELLMAN, GOLDIE   1907 - 1908
FELLMAN, VIOLET   1911 - 1911
    [above four on same stone]

F-42 Levi Grasse
    [four spaces]

F-43 Lot owner Walter Fellman
F-44 No owner on map [check deeds]
SLIFER, IRWIN C.
    11 Nov 1870 - 3 Dec 1910
SLIFER, ELMER C.
    8 Nov 1876 - 23 Oct 1927
KELLER, Wm. H.
    23 May 1877 - 14 Apr 1960
KELLER, BERTHA C.
    23 Oct 1866 - 30 Jan 1967

FELLMAN, WALTER C.   1884 - 1967
FELLMAN, CATHARINE S.   1882 - 1961
    [above two on same stone]

FELLMAN, RACHEL ANN
    14 Jan 1903 - 9 Feb 1927

F-45 Warren Tyson
TYSON, CLAYTON M.   1917 - 1917
TYSON, MARY M.   1884 - 1969
TYSON, WARREN M.   1886 - 1956
    [above three on same stone]

MAGEE, MARY J.   Mother
    1848 - 1931
COLE, JOHN   1977 - 1977
    Great-grandson

F-46 Mahlon Landis
LANDIS, PAUL C.   1924 - 1924
LANDIS, SCOTT K.   1948 - 1948
LANDIS, LIZZIE F.   1902 - [blank]
LANDIS, MAHLON L.   1900 - 1964
    [above four on same stone]

F-47 Frank Alderfer
[cement base with the top missing]
ALDERFER, EVELYN FERYL
    18 Sept 1922 - 23 Mar 1924
ALDERFER, BARBARA C.
    5 Oct 1898 - [blank]
ALDERFER, FRANK R.
    3 Feb 1895 - 6 Oct 1973
    WWI flag
    [above three on same stone]

F-48 Arthur Brey
BREY, ARTHUR H.   1895 - 1953
BREY, KATIE C.   1895 - 1961
SECTION L
L-41 & 42 S.G. Moyer
MOYER, GRACE H.
    23 Apr 1914 - 24 Mar 1927

MOYER, CHARLOTTE S.   1873 - 1935
MOYER, SYLVANUS G.   1871 - 1963
    [above two on same stone]
MOYER, VERNON H.   1897 - 1956

L-43 & 44 Margaret Handschin
HANDSCHIN, JOHN   1901 - 1979
    Brother
HANDSCHIN, ELIZABETH C. Sister
    1899 - 1979
    [above two on same stone]

HANDSCHIN, MARY F.   1903 - 1955

HANDSCHIN, DANIEL K.   1873 - 1941
HANDSCHIN, MARGARET C. 1871 - 1946
    [above two on same stone with
    a POS of A 6 flag]

ST. PETER'S UNION CEMETERY (New Section)

Row 19, Section L Continued:
L-45 Stanley Detwiler

L-46 Merret Felman

L-47 & 48 Eileen Garatt
   [six spaces]

GARRETT, WILLIAM E.   1938 - 1969

ROW 20

C-33 & 34 Margaret Haldeman
   [Stone listed on Row 19 between rows]

C-35 & 36 Henry Zoller
ZOLLER, HENRY   Father   1834 - 1917
ZOLLER, CAROLINE G.   1835 - 1911
   Mother
ZOLLER, ELMER   1868 - 1955
ZOLLER, HANNAH   1864 - 1954
ZOLLER, CAROLINE   1873 - 1960
ZOLLER, ELIZABETH   1877 - 1958
ZOLLER, GEORGE H.   1857 - 1934
SWARTLEY, ANNIE L.   1861 - 1937
   [these two on same stone]
   [Zoller monument with no names]

C-37 Herman Cressman
C-38 Henry Caney

SZYMANSKI, MARTHA S.   1902 - [blank]
SZYMANSKI, MATTHEW A.   1908 - 1970
   [space] [above two on same stone]
GARNER, ETHEL U.   1911 - [blank]
GARNER, WILLIAM S.   1909 - 1969
   [above two on same stone]
UMSTEAD, EVERARD R.   1876 - 1932
UMSTEAD, ESTELLA A.   1880 - 1942
   [above two on same stone]
C-39 James Constanzer
C-40   "   "
CONSTANZER, ANNA MARGARET
   17 Mar 1917 - 17 Oct 1918
   daughter of Jas. A. & Eliz. Constanzer
   [three spaces]

CONSTANZER, ELIZABETH E.
   22 Dec 1895 - 21 Jul 1953
CONSTANZER, JAMES A.
   31 Jul 1895 - 2 Apr 1942

SECTION F

F-33 Joseph Grasse
GRASSE, JOSEPH   1849 - 1936
GRASSE, MARY   1854 - 1917
   [above two on same stone]

GRASSE, LEVI H.
   8 Oct 1866 - 22 Jan 1942
   [three spaces]

F-34 Horace Fellman
KULP, SARAH S.   1912 - [blank]
KULP, LEROY A.   flag   1913 - 1971
   1941 - 1945 Eagle flag

K-35 & 36 George Seitz
SEITZ, GEORGE M.   1866 - 1949
SEITZ, ANNA C.   1867 - 1931
SEITZ, GEORGE SEEBERGER 1914 - 1949
   [above three on same stone]

ARMON, MARGARET S.
   4 Sept 1888 - 27 Jun 1913
   wife of A. Harry Armon

F-37 & 38 Wesley Albright
ALBRIGHT, WESLEY F.   1885 - 1948
ALBRIGHT, A. MARY   1890 - 1972
   [above two on same stone]
ALBRIGHT, CAMERON   1909 - 1952
   Father
ALBRIGHT, AMANDA   1840 - 1921
ALBRIGHT, HIRAM Y.   1859 - 1920

F-   & 40 Raymond Detweiler
DETWEILER, WILLARD
   29 Oct 1925 - 31 Oct 1925
   son of Raymond & Anna Detweiler

DETWEILER, ANNA MAE
   25 Mar 1906 - 12 Jul 1940
[Raymond Detweiler]
   22 Aug 1902 - 27 Jan 1972
   [the above record should be
   checked, some confusion]

SECTION L

L-33 & 34 S.G. Moyer
VOGEL, EDNA H.   1905 - [blank]
VOGEL, RUSSELL C.   1901 - 1970
   [above on same stone]
LUKENS, CLARA H.   1899 - [blank]
LUKENS, H. ELMER, Sr.   1896 - 1980
   [four spaces] [above on same stone]

L-35 Author Thieroff
THIEROFF, DALTON R.   1944 - 1946
THIREOFF, Stillborn   1948

L-36 Augusta Handschin
HANDSCHIN, DANIEL   1906 - 1945
HANDSCHIN, AUGUSTA   1918 - 1980
[Augusta Handschin Kosiw ?]

L-37 & 38 Norman Ott
KRATZ, LAMAR R.   1948 - [blank]
KRATZ, Baby girl   1971
KRATZ, GLORIA J. OTT   1946 - 1971
   [space]

Row 20, Section L Continued:
OTT, NORMAN L.   1919 - [blank]
OTT, EVA E.   1920 - [blank
   [above two on same stone]

L-39 Herbert Miller
MILLER, HERBERT M.   1912 - 1978
MILLER, MARY T.   1912 - 1971
   [above two on same stone]

L-40 Ronald Ott

ROW 21

C-25 Glenwood Eckert
ECKHART, FLORENCE MAY 1885 - 1918
   [space]
CRESSMAN, FLORENCE   1893 - 1940
CRESSMAN, HIRAM R.   1892 - 1944
   [above two on same stone]

C-26 [no owner]

C-27 & 28 William Snyder
   [monument between rows 21 & 22]
SNYDER, WILLIAM D.   Father
   2 Feb 1862 - 4 Oct 1918

SNYDER, ELLA F.
   4 Oct 1887 - 28 Jun 1933

SNYDER, RALPH M.
   20 Apr 1895 - 16 Oct 1908

SNYDER, SARAH
   26 Sep 1890 - 11 May 1938

SCHOLL, WILLIAM H.   1883 - 1966
SCHOLL, EDITH S.   1887 - 1971
SCHOLL, ANNIE   1914 - 1923
   [Three School names on the op-
   posite side of Snyder monument.]

C-29 & 30 Nelson Lapp
LAPP, IDA MAY   1882 - 1909
LAPP, NELSON S.   1880 - 1948
   [Large monument marked LAPP]

C-31 Hettie Snyder
SNYDER, WESLEY A.   1881 - 1928
SNYDER, HARRIET L.   1872 - 1950
SNYDER, MARION H.   1886 - 1951
   [These on same stone]

C-32 Frank Sherm
SHERM, JOHN CLAUDE
   [child--stone is buried]
SHERM, ANNIE M.   1877 - 1939
SHERM, FRANKLIN   1878 - 1942
   [Above two on same stone]

SECTION F

F-25 & 26 [No owners on map]
FEUSNER, GEORGE L.   1909 - 1910
FEUSNER, SARAH L.   1874 - 1965

FEUSNER, GEORGE M.   1868 -1958
   [above three on same stone]
   [three spaces]

F-27 Samuel Frick
FRICK, SAMUEL F.   1857 - 1913
FRICK, ANNA E.   1868 - 1958
   [above two on same stone]

WORTHINGTON, WILLIAM H. 1876 - 1920
WORTHINGTON, SALLIE C. 1880 - 1946
   [above two on same stone]

F-28 Sebatia Leaper
LECHER, SEBASTOAN   1859 - 1914
LECHER, MARY   1861 - 1947
   [above two on same stone]

F-29 Price Greulich
GREULICH, BARBARA   Sister
   2 Oct 1907 - 6 Aug 1951
GREULICH, PIUS   Father
   30 Apr 1879 - 17 Dec 1972

F-30 William Koehler

F-31 & 32 George & Liz Nessler
NESSLER, LORENZ   1839 - 1933
NESSLER, BARBARA   1849 - 1926
NESSLER, GEORGE   1874 - 1954
NESSLER, ELIZABETH B. 1876 - 1955
NESSLER, JOSEPHINE   1878 - 1967
NESSLER, EMILY   1883 - 1959
   [above all on same monument]

SECTION L

L-25 & 26 Harvey Kratz
KRATZ, HARVEY G.   1874 - 1948
KRATZ, ANNA S.   1875 - 1936
KRATZ, HAROLD S.   1903 - 1966
BARGER, EDNA K.   1899 - 1936
   [above on same monument]
   [three spaces]

L-27 & 28 Everett Garrett
GARRETT, ROBERT E.   1942 - 1948
GARRETT, EDWARD H.   1886 - 1950
GARRETT, EVERETT N. 1911 - 1977
   [above on same monument]

L-29 & 30 Guy Ruch
RUCH, ROBERT ALLEN
   10 Jul 1938 - 17 Apr 1949

RUCH, GUY A. P.   1906 - 1966

L-31 Wilmer Smith

L-32 Leidy Lewis
LEWIS, LEIDY H.   1907 - 1979
LEWIS, MARY S.   1907 - [blank]
   [above two on same stone]

ST. PETER'S UNION CEMETERY (New Section) 155

Row 22

C-17 James Dunfer
DUNFEE, CHARLES H.
    [Metal marker--no dates]

C-18 Jacob Snyder
SNYDER, JACOB R.   1868 - 1942
SNYDER, IDA F.   1869 - 1953
    [Above two on same stone]

C-19 & 20 Wm. Scholl
    [See Marker between rows 21 & 22
     recorded in C-27 & 28, in Row 21]

DETTERLINE, FLORENCE S.   1909 - 1942

C-21 Moses Old and Walter Soliday
OLD, SALLIE
    15 Dec 1890 - 22 Dec 1910
    Daughter of Moses & Annie L. Old
    aged 20y 7 days
    [Two spaces]

C-22 Elmer Swartley
SWARTLEY, ELMER A.   1877 - 1915
SWARTLEY, ROSELLA   1879 - 1951
SWARTLEY, M. ELIZABETH   1912
    [Above on same stone]

C-23 Morris Clymer
CLYMER, CAROLINE
    Died 4 Dec 1912 Aged 57y
    Wife of Morris A. Clymer
    [Two spaces]

C-24 Clinton Ott
OTT, HAROLD EUGENE
    23 June - 27 June 1916
    son of Mr. & Mrs. Clinton Ott
OTT, BERTHA MAE
    23 May 1921 - 5 Feb 1964

SECTION F

Section 17 & 18 [No owners lister]
FROST, PAUL
    30 Aug 1934 - 13 Aug 1938

    [Four spaces]

F-19 & 20 George Frick
FRICK, GEORGE H.   1867 - 1932
FRICK, LOUISA C.   1867 - 1916
    his wife

FRICK, EDWARD F.   1890 - 1942
FRICK, LOTTIE N.   1892 - 1956
FRICK, BABY   1932 - 1932
    [Above three on same stone]

F-21 Stephen Vogel
VOGEL, CHRISTIAN
VOGEL, PETER
    Sons of Steven and Magdalena Vogel
    [No dates on stone]

F-22 Charles Reinstick
    [No stones]

F-23 & 24 Thomas Wynne
SCOTT, LUELLA J.   1913 - [blank]
SCOTT, LAIRD B.   1913 - 1977
SCOTT, AGNES W.   1885 - 1970
    [Above on same stone]

HANSON, EDWARD L.   1905 - 1964
HANSON, SARA C.   1907 - [Blank]
    [Above two on same stone]

SECTION L

L-17 & 18 Adam W. Crouthamel
CROUTHAMEL, LAURA N.   1892 - 1940
CROUTHAMEL, ADAM W., SR. 1893 - 1960
    [Three spaces] [Above same stone]

CROUTHAMEL, ADAM   1923 - 1974
    PFC 915 F.A. US Army WW II
CROUTHAMEL, CONNIE LEE
    15 Mar - 28 Mar 1955

L-19 George Schmidt
SCHMIDT, WINNIE M.   1874 - 1948
SCHMIDT, GEORGE C.   1874 - 1951
    [Above two on same stone]

L-20 William Hatcock
HITCHCOCK, LORA   1872 - 1948
HITCHCOCK, LOTTIE   1894 - [blank]
HITCHCOCK, WILBUR K.   1871 - 1950
    [Above three on same stone]

L-21 Edwart Crouthamel
CROUTHAMEL, EDWARD M.   1885 - 1954
CROUTHAMEL, LAURA J.   1884 - 1952
    [Above two on same stone]

L-22 Helen Gulick
GULICK, MERARI   1876 - 1956
GULICK, SALLIE S.   1877 - 1958
    [Above two on same stone]

L-23 Marrian Snyder

L-24 John Smith
    [Above lots are vacant]

Row 23

C-9 & 10 Wil Ritter
RITTER, WILHELMINA S.   1864 - 1927
RITTER, FREDERICK WM. MD 1867 - 1920
    [Large monument on Row 23 & 24]

C-11 & 12 Isiah F. Snyder
SNYDER, ANNA E.   1863 - 1924
SNYDER, ISIAH S.   1857 - 1919

Row 23, continued:
C-11 & 12 continued:
SNYDER, PENROSE D.
   17 Sept 1888 - __ Jul 1959
SNYDER, MARY R.
   14 Oct 1884 - 28 Jul 1970

C-13 Frank Springer
SPRINGER, HANNAH
   26 Jul 1854 - 27 Jun 1926
SPRINGER, FRANK
   31 Jan 1849 - 22 Jul 1911
   [Two spaces]

C-14 Morris Smith
SMITH, MAURICE   1882 - 1963
SMITH, CLARA S.   1882 - 1969
SMITH, EVELYN S.   1909 - 1971

C-15 Minerva Hedrick
SHERM, WILLIAM S.
   19 Aug 1886 - 21 Nov 1958

HEDRICK, MINERVA
   16 Sept 1856 - 22 Mar 1920

HEDRICK, HENRY F.
   7 Mar 1866 - 5 Mar 1913

C-16 Dilmon Heckler
HECKLER, HERMAN K.
   21 MAr 1916 - 22 Jun 1929
   Our son
HECKLER, FLORA K.
   24 Apr 1883 - 18 Feb 1933
HECKLER, DILLMAN H.
   3 Jun 1876 - 4 Jul 1968
   [Above three on same stone]

SECTION F

F-9 & 10 Damon Meyers

ALDERFER, ROBERT KENNETH
   7 May 1926
   Son of Noble & Anna Alderfer
ALDERFER, ANNA W.   1898 - 1951
ALDERFER, NOBLE R.   1899 - 1964
   [Above two on same stone]
   [Three spaces]

MYERS, EMMA J.   1870 - 1945
MYERS, DAMON M.   1868 - 1933
   [Above two on same stone]

F-11 Eli Frankenfield
FRANKENFIELD, ELIM.
   10 Aug 1861 - 28 Jun 1917
FRANKENFIELD, MARY E.
   18 Dec 1861 - 4 Jan 1945
   [Above two on same stone]

FRANKENFIELD, CLARA   1894 - 1975

F-12 Deed #397
HUSTON, GEORGE Father   1842 - 1918
HUSTON, DORA   Mother   1872 - 1962

F-13 Clifford Bergey
   [Space]
F-14 Charles Tice
TICE, CHARLES W.   1877 - 1931
TICE, EMMA B.   1880 - 1949
TICE, NORMAN W.   1913 - 1920
   [Space]
TICE, WILMER B.   1900 - 1978
   [Space]

F-15 Jacob Seitz
SEITZ, KATIE
   7 Aug 1866 - 8 Apr 1929
SEITZ, JACOB
   14 Dec 1864 - 18 Feb 1943

F-16 Norman Stever
TAYLOR, BERTHA W.   Mother
   10 Jun 1883 - 20 May 1950
   [one space]
STEVER, NORMAN F.
   17 Dec 1906 - 12 Jan 1972

SECTION L

L-9 & 10 Wilmer Gehman
   [Four spaces]
GEHMAN, MARY JEAN
   24 Jan 1932 - 4 May 1945
   [Two spaces]

L-11 Charles Conrad
CONRAD, CHARLES W.
   17 Feb 1909 -
CONRAD, ALICE
   17 Oct 1908 -
   [above two on same stone]
L-12 Nicholas Dybiak
   [No Stones]

L-13 & 14 Howard Rappold
WORTHINGTON, MELVIN H. 1899 - 1974
WORTHINGTON, HELEN C.   1901 - 1971
   [Above two on same stone]

RAPPOLD, HOWARD J.   1896 - 1973
RAPPOLD, ALICE W.   1898 - 1979
   [Above two on same stone]
   [Two spaces]

L-15 & 16 Dick Ott
OTT, RICHARD T.   1938 - [Blank]
OTT, MARY LOU   1940 - [blank]
OTT, INFANT SON   18 Feb 1973
   [Four spaces]

ST. PETER'S UNION CEMETERY (New Section)

Row 24

Section C

C-1 & 2 Wil Ritter
   [See Stone in Row 23]

C-3 & 4 Isaik F. Snyder
SNYDER, BLANCHE A.   1896 - 1979
SNYDER, ENOS D.   1892 - 1918

SNYDER Monument [No first names]

LAPP, WALTER S.   1893 - 1971
LAPP, MYRTLE S.   1899 - [blank]

SNYDER, GEORGE D.   1890 - 1961
SNYDER, ANNA M.   1892 - 1954

C-5 & 6 George Tice, Jr.
TICE, IDA G.
   7 Jan 1877 - 27 Mar 1952
TICE, GEORGE M.
   28 Nov 1873 - 9 Feb 1955
   [Two spaces]
TICE, GEORGE, JR.   1911 - 1974
TICE, IDA C.   1913 - [Blank]
   WWII Flag

C-7 James Moyer
MOYER, MARY K.   Mother
   23 Sept 1870 - 14 Dec 1913
   wife of James E. Moyer
MOYER, JAMES E.   1869 - 1951
MOYER, IDA H.   1871 - 1941
   [Above two on same stone]

MOYER, WAYNE W.   Son
   22 Feb 1897 - 7 Oct 1918
   Flag 1941 - 1945 [Should be WWI!]

C-8 Frank Klopfer
KLOEPFER, FRANK
   20 Nov 1868 - 14 May 1954
KLOEPFER, CHARLES
   17 Mar 1880 - 12 Jul 1943
KLOEPFER, ADAM
   31 Dec 1864 - 9 Aug 1935

SECTION F

F-1 Robert Werman[?]
   [No stones]

F-2 Elmer Clemmer
CLEMMER, INFANT
   25 Jul 1917
   Daughter of C.H. & Florence M. Clemmer

CLEMMER, ELMER B.   1891 - 1971
CLEMER, FLORENCE M.   1898 - 1959

F-3 Henry Schlosser
SCHLOSSER, HENRY F.
   18 May 1854 - 16 Sept 1922
SCHLOSSER, ANNIE F.
   18 Sept 1864 - 21 Jan 1917

F-4 Jessie Swartley
SWARTLEY, MARY A.   wife
   30 Nov 1859 - 19 Jan 1918
   58y 1m 29d
SWARTLEY, JESSE K.   Husband
   2 Oct 1855 - 9 Mar 1922
   66y 5m 7d

F-5 John Swartley
SWARTLEY, JOHN K.
   2 Aug 1860 - 22 Jul 1918
   57y 11m 20d
   Husband of Sarah Swartley

SWARTLEY, SARAH   Mother
   9 Mar 1869 - 9 Sept 1941
   72y 6m

F-6 Nicholas Michels
MICHELS, NICHOLAS A.   1891 - 1969
MICHELS, MARTHA A.   1896 - 1939
MICHELS, HILDA D.   1897 - [Blank]
   [above two on same stone]
F-7 Francis Kile
KILE, FRANCIS B.   1859 - 1936
KILE, ELIZABETH K.   1853 - 1925
   [above two on same stone]
F-8 Sallie Kile
KILE, HENRY H.   1861 - 1943
KILE, SARAH M.   1866 - 1939
KILE, IRMA M.   1888 - 1966
   [above two on same stone]
SECTION L

L-1 William Kerber
KERBER, GERTRUDE C.
   13 Jan 1898 - 30 Jun 1980
KERBER, WILLIAM J., Jr. 1894 - 1959
   P.F.C. 312 MGB Co. D WWI

L-2 Earnest Kile
KILE, ERNEST A.   1897 - 1977
KILE, ANNA R.   1901 - [Blank]
   [above two on same stone]
L-3 & 4 George Wilson
WILSON, GEORGE W.   1882 - 1954
WILSON, LENA H.   1882 - 1948
   [Above two on same stone]
   [Four spaces]

L-5 & 6 Joseph Ruth
RUTH, JOSEPH B.   1903 - 1956
RUTH, MARGARET N.   1903 - [Blank]
L-7 Floyd Alderfer [no stones]
L-8 Wm. Lewis [No stones]

Sections D, E and M contain the rows on the easterly side of the second drive through the cemetery, fartherest from the church (St. Peter's U.C.C.) These rows are numbered 25 through 32. In this part the Section numbers 1, 17, 25, 33, 41, 49 and 57 are closest to Hilltown Pike.

Row 25

Section D

D-1 [No owner recorded]

D-2 Wm. Bidding
BITTING, MATILDA J.   1856 - 1937
BITTING, WILLIAM G.   1847 - 1935
BITTING, LAURA E. Sister 1869 - 1939
   [above two on same stone]
D-3 & 4 Wm. Moll
MOLL, MARIE E.   1886 - 1919
MOLL, MARY MATILDA   1855 - 1932
MOLL, WILLIAM H.   1847 - 1933
   [above two on same stone]
D-5 John Fry
FREY, WARREN D.
   20 Nov 1891 - 2 Oct 1918
FREY, JOHN H.   1859 - 1935
FREY, EMMA S.   1866 - 1936
   [Above two on same stone]

D-6 [No owner listed]
SENSINGER, HOWARD S.
   14 Apr 1860 - 3 May 1937
SENSINGER, ELIZABETH J.
   21 Sept 1866 - 10 Jun 1959
SENSINGER, STANLEY
   6 Oct 1898 - 16 Jan 1969
SENSINGER, STEWARD
   10 Jul 1895 - 27 Oct 1918

D-7 & 8 Adam Lengel
LENGEL, SAMUEL R.   1859 - 1921
LENGEL, MARY A.   1857 - 1934
   [Above two on same stone]

LENGEL, MAUDE D.
   17 Jan 1931 - 7 Jun 1944
   Daughter of Adam H. & Naomi Lengel

LENGEL, MELVIN DEWEY
   28 Nov 1923 - 4 Jun 1926
   Son of Adam H. & Naomi Lengel

LENGEL, MARY ELIZABETH
   6 Mar 1919 - 6 May 1920
   Daughter of Adam H. & Naomi Lengel
LENGEL, E. NAOMI DEWEY
   24 Nov 1896 - 9 Aug 1972
   Wife of Adam H. Lengel

SECTION E

E-1 & 2 Fred Void
COPE, ELIZABETH   84y 6m 6d
   2 Dec 1818 - 8 Jun 1898
   Wife of Charles Cope
VOID, MARY A.
   10 Jan 1861 - 6 Apr 1915
VOID, FREDRICK R.
   15 Apr 1856 - 28 Jul 1923
VOID, ELSIE C.   1885 - 1950
VOID, EDITH C.   1888 - 1955
   [above two on same stone]
E-3 John Rappold
RAPPOLD, WILHELMINA
   15 Jul 1863 - 18 Apr 1948
RAPPOLD, JOHN A.
   30 Jul 1858 - 8 May 1940
RAPPOLD, HENRY   Son   1888 - 1961

BLACKWELL, SON
   10 Feb 1942 - 12 Feb 1942
   son of Mr. & Mrs. M.H. Blackwell

E-4 [No owner on map]
BROWN, VERA   1899 - 1938

E-5 Paul Holl
HOLL, PAUL T.   1879 - 1939
HOLL, MARGARET   1889 - 1954
HOLL, PAUL E.   1911 - 1931
   [Above three on same stone]
   [Shelly Funeral Home Marker]

E-6 Eugene Schlopsna
SCHLOPSNA, JULIA G.   1884 - 1934
SCHLOPSNA, EUGENE E.   1881 - 1951
   [above two on same stone]
E-7 Margaret Kile
KILE, MARGARET H.   1904 - 1978
KILE, RAYMOND T.   1900 - 1941
   [above two on same stone]
E-8 Harvey Kile
KILE, EDITH I.   1901 - 1957
KILE, HARRY L.   1893 - 1979
   [above two on same stone]
SECTION M

M-1 John Godshall
GODSHALL, ANNA W.
   born 20 Jun 1908
GODSHALL, JOHN K.
   born 21 Jun 1899
   [above two on same stone]
M-2 Frank Ryzner
RYZNER, FRANK V.   1889 - 1951

M-3 Paul Mattern
MATTERN, JOSEPH M.   1900 - 1958

M-4 Margaret Kramer
KRAMER, MABEL M.   1888 - [Blank]
KRAMER, WARREN S.   1894 - 1965
   [above two on same stone]

ST. PETER'S UNION CEMETERY (New Section)

Row 25 Continued:
M-5 & 6 Gladys Kling
KLING, FRANK   1903 - 1979

M- 7 & 8 No owners on map

Row 26

SECTION D

D-9 Anne Sheip and Titus Roberts
   [no stones]

D-10 Merton Kline
KLINE, HERBERT S.
   17 Nov 1901 - 11 Mar 1921
KLINE, ERWIN B.   1876 - 1965
KLINE, SALLIE B.   1882 - 1978
   [Above two on same stone]

KLINE, MARGARET S.   1924 - [blank]
KLINE, MERTON E.   1920 -   "
SNYDER, MARY E.   1906 - 1979
   [Above three on same stone]

D-11 & 12 George Moll
VanOMMEREN, SUSANNAH   Mother
   17 Jan 1859 - 21 Mar 1922

VanOMMEREN, YOST   Father
   29 Sept 1859 - 29 Jan 1921

VanOMMEREN, EMMA ROSE   Sister
   20 Dec 1894 - 30 Dec 1923
   [Two spaces]

D-13 & 14 Robert Snovel
   [Four spaces]
SNOVEL, LILLIAN M.   1892 - 1980
SNOVEL, ROBERT   1890 - 1968
   [Above two on same stone]

SNOVEL, MARY Y.   1865 - 1939
SNOVEL, ISAIAH A.   1863 - 1945
   [Above two on same stone]

D-15 & 16 M.H. Lengel
LENGEL, MARGARET A.   1889 - 1967
LENGEL, MELVIN H.   1890 - 1955
   [Above two on same stone]
   [Six spaces]

SECTION E
E-9 Jacob Shilling
SHILLING, JACOB M.   1856 - 1924
SHILLING, ANNIE   1855 - 1922
   [above two on same stone]
E-10 W.D. Gabel
GABEL, ORPHA S.   1885 - 1973
GABEL, WILSON D.   1880 - 1968
   [Above two on same stone]

GABEL, LILLIAN H.   1909 - 1957
GABEL, RUSSELL S.   1908 -
GABEL, VERA G.   1908 -
   [Above three on same stone]

E-11 Orpha Bergey
BERGEY, ORPHA M.
   21 May 1873 - 24 Dec 1952
BERGEY, WILSON S.
   11 May 1872 - 10 Mar 1938
   [Above two on same stone]

E-12 Wm. Gum
GUM, OLIVE B.
   27 Jan 1899 - 7 Dec 1972
GUM, WILLIAM A. III
   3 Jul 1898 - [blank]
   [above two on same stone]
E-13 Clifford Bergey
BERGEY, RUTH M.   1897 - 1977
BERGEY, CLIFFORD C.   1894 - 1958
   [Above two on same stone]

E-14 Robert Hinkle
HINKLE, MARIAN KEZIA   1916 - [Blank]
HINKLE, ROBERT LAPP   1911 - 1972
HINKLE, INFANT   28 Aug 1924
   [above three on same stone]
E-15 Harold Leatherman
LEATHERMAN, MARGARET S. 1906 - [Blank]
LEATHERMAN, HAROLD S.   1906 - 1976
   [Above two on same stone]
   [Six spaces]

E-16 Russell Leatherman
   [No stones]

SECTION M

M-9 Earl Clemmer
   [No stones]

M-10 Harriet Carver
CARVER, HARRIET B.   1881 - 1968

CARVER, MILTON D.   1878 - 1953
   Sgt 69th Co. C.A.C.
   Spanish American War

M-11 & 12 Ruth & Ken Knapp
   [No stones]

M-13 Vanthuyme
   [No stones]

M-14 Kulp
   [No stones]

M-15 & 16 No owners on map

Row 27

SECTION D

D-17 No owner on map

D-18 Anna Scheip
ROBERTS, CATHERINE SCHEIP
   8 Jun 1889 - 7 Jun 1936
ROBERTS, TITUS A.
   SC2 USNR WWII

159

Row 27 continued:
Roberts, Titus A. Continued:
   29 Aug 1912 - 30 Aug 1960
SCHEIP, ANNA ALBRIGHT
   born 22 Nov 1890 -
SCHEIP, WILLIAM F.   1877 - 1934
SCHEIP, ANNA M.   1879 - 1969
[[Note: D-9 owners are probably
   the ones who own D-17!]

Lot D-19 Blanche Taylor
   [Note that Lot D-19 & D-20 owners
   are probably switched on map!]
LACKNER, ALEXANDER   1853 - 1923
LACKNER, CAROLINA   1854 - 1924
LACKNER, HENRY   1886 - 1950
   [Above three on same stone]
   [Two spaces]

Lot D-20 Henry Lackner [see above]
TAYLOR, BLANCH ROSENBERGER
   4 Mar 1875 - 23 Aug 1946

D-21 No owner on map
   [Is this turned around with D-22?]
SENSINGER, EVELYN
   11 Feb 1918 - 12 Jan 1922
SENSINGER, LILLIAN H.   1892 - [Blank]
SENSINGER, TRUMAN E.   1889 - 1955
   [above two on same stone]
D-22 Stan & Sherwood Sensinger
   [See note above]
   [Three spaces]

D-23 Edgar Steir
STYER, ELLA M.   1881 - 1952
STYER, GEORGE R.   1919 - 1921
STYER, EDGAR E.   1877 - [Blank]
   [Above three on same stone]

D-24 George E. Moll
MOLL, GEORGE   1903 - 1963
MOLL, IRENE R.   1910 - [Blank]
   [above two on same stone]
SECTION E

E-17 & 18 Harvey Reiff
REIFF, HANNAH B.
   16 Mar 1854 - 29 Jan 1931
   76y 10m 18d
REIFF, DAVID Z.   67y 5m 16d
   12 Sept 1953 - 28 Feb 1921

REIFF, MARTHA A.   1883 - 1955
REIFF, HARVEY CLINTON 1880 - 1956
   [Above two on same stone]
   [Two spaces]

E-19 & 20 Anne Eurich
   [Three spaces]
EURICH, ANNA S.
   3 Feb 1876 - 29 Jul 1956

EURICH, CHRISTIAN J.
   23 Aug 1869 - 2 May 1939
   [previous two on same stone]
E-21 & 22 Clarence Kramer
KRAMER, JEMIMA F.   1886 - 1976
KRAMER, LEIDY S.   1883 - 1967
   [Above two on same stone]
   [Two spaces]
KRAMER, RONALD LEE
   16 May 1939 - 31 May 1939
KRAMER, EDNA M.   1912 - [Blank]
KRAMER, A. CLARENCE 1910 - 1980
   [above two on same stone]
E-23 William Moser
MOSER, CLARA M.   1896 - 1966
MOSER, WILLIAM C.   1905 - 1955
   [Above two on same stone]

E-24 Lillian Young
YOUNG, LILLIAN   1898 - 1973
YOUNG, THOMAS A.   1893 - 1956
   PVT Motor Trans. Corps 791 WWI .

SECTION M

M-17 Leroy Boehner
BOEHNER, CHRISTINE
   Born 26 Dec 1890 -
BOEHNER, LEROY
   19 Jul 1891 - 13 Oct 1959
   [Above two on same stone]

M-18 Henry Stout
STOUT, ANNA M.   1892 - 1977
STOUT, HENRY M.   1893 - 1974
   [above two on same stone]
M-19 Margaret Karczmar
KARCZMAR, MARGARET E. 1917 - [Blank]
KARCZMAR, JOHN R.   1912 - 1967
   [Above two on same stone]

M-20 Robert Frohnapel
FROHNAPFEL, BABY
   4 Dec 1970

M-21 Felix
   [No stones in lot]

M-22 Wert
WERT, ROBERT W., SR.   1926 - 1981

M-23 & 24 No owners on map

Row 28

SECTION D

D-25 Bessie Carlen
CARLIN, BESSIE H.   1881 - 1974
   [3 spaces]

D-26 Frank Lewis
   [No stones in this lot]

ST. PETER'S UNION CEMETERY (New Section)

Row 28, Continued:

D-27 Allen Moyer
MOYER, ALLEN M.   1868 - 1944
MOYER, L. HORTENSE   1871 - 1953
GIERSE, OLGA MOYER   1900 - 1941
   [Above three on same stone]

D-28 Allen Moyer
   [No stones in this lot]

D-29 George Moyer
MOYER, GEORGE E.   1894 - 1956
MOYER, CLARA   1892 - 1942
MOYER, GOERGE A.   1922 - 1922
   [Above three on same stone]

D-30 Samuel Myers
   [No stones in this lot]

D-31 & 32 Joe Renner
RENNER, ELIZABETH mother 1847 - 1935
RENNER, JOSEPH H. father 1845 - 1927
   [Above two on same stone]

RENNER, JOSEPH L.   1878 - 1954
RENNER, LAURA D.   1884 - 1976
RENNER, OLIVER D.   1884 - 1963
   [Above three on same stone]

SECTION E

E-25 Grace Landis
LANDIS, HORACE
   4 Feb 1866 - 14 Oct 194?
   [R.A. Benner Funeral Home marker]

E-26 C. H. Moore
MOORE, CLARENCE H.   1893 - 1959
MOORE, GRACE L.   1894 - 1978
   [above two on same stone]

E-27 & 28 Mame Landis
LANDIS, HENRY S.   1885 - 1940
LANDIS, MAME   1886 - 1944
   [Above two on same stone]
   [Two spaces]
LANDIS, RACHEL   1920 - [Blank]

BEVAN, PHILIP   1902 - 1962
BEVAN, MARTHA   1907 - 1970
   [above two on same stone]

E-29 Ida Miller
MILLER, IDA L.
   23 Jan 1864 - 9 Aug 1953
MILLER, HENRY A.
   21 Nov 1860 - 29 May 1945
   [above two on same stone]

E-30 Michel Muller
MÜLLER, PAULINE
   19 May 1888 - 4 Apr 1947
MÜLLER, MICHAEL
   8 Sept 1884 - 19 Apr 1956
   [above two on same stone]

E-31 Arthur Muller
MULLER, REGINA M.   1916 - 1957
MULLER, ARTHUR C.   1913 - [Blank]
   [Above two on same stone]
   [Five spaces]

E-32 Margaret Fissel
KISSEL, MAX C.   1904 - 1957
   First Lt. 42 - Inf. USA WWII
   Phillipine Army

SECTION M

M-25 Paul Kober
   [No stones in this lot]

M-26 Helen Roth
ROTH, NORMAN T.   1910 - 1961

M-27 & 28 Terdinand [Ferdinand]
[Two spaces]
NACE, KAY F.   1947 - 1978
   married 20 April 1968
NACE, ROBERT C.   1942 - [Blank]
   [above two on same stone]
FERDINAND, IRENE B.   1907 - 1978
FERDINAND, WILLIAM J.   1903 - 1973
   WWI 1917 - 1918

M-29 Moyer

M-30 Detwiler

M-31 & 32 No owner on map

ROW 29

SECTION D

D-33 & 34 Maria Schwartz
SWARTZ, MARY
   20 Jun 1876 - 7 Aug 1942
SWARTZ, NICHOLAS
   29 Dec 1873 - 13 Mar 1937
   [Above two on same stone]

SCHWARTZ, JOSEPH   son   1915 - 1973
SCHWARTZ, ANTHONY son   1911 - 1964
SCHWARTZ NICHOLAS   1913 - 1980

D-35 & 36 Enos Detwiler
DETWEILER, MARY ELLEN   1877 - 1963
DETWEILER, ENOS R.   1873 - 1931
DETWEILER, RICHARD K.   1929 - 1980
   [Above three on same stone]
   [Four spaces]

D-37 Frank Tice
TICE, CARL R.   1924 - 1924
TICE, MAY   1900 - [Blank]
TICE, FRANK S.   1897 - 1957
   [Above three on same stone]

161

162   BUCKS COUNTY TOMBSTONE INSCRIPTIONS - HILLTOWN TOWNSHIP

Row 29, Continued:

D-38 No name on map
   [Two spaces]
MYERS, EMMA E.   1872 - 1947
MYERS, S. ALLEN   1869 - 1948

D-39 & 40 Martin Hartman
HARTMAN, MARTIN   1873 - 1959
HARTMAN, ANNA M.   1869 - 1924
   [Above two on same stone]
   [Five spaces]

SECTION E

E-33 & 34 Otto Market
MARKERT, RICHARD
MARKERT, WILHELMINA
   [Three Spaces--No dates on above]
MARKERT, OTTO A.   1894 - 1967

E-35 Harold Crouthamel
CROUTHAMEL, HAROLD S.   1895 - [Blank]
CROUTHAMEL, GRACE C.   1896 - 1957
   [Above two on same stone]

CROUTHAMEL, ELMER E.   1869 - 1951
CROUTHAMEL, RACHEL   1869 - 1953
   [above two on same stone]

E-36 John Keck
   [Two spaces]
KECK, JOHN G.   1900 - 1974
KECK, GRACE C.   1898 - 1976

E-37 Mary Oremusz
   [Two spaces]
OREMUSZ, JOHN   1896 - 1957
   49th AERO SQN USA WWI

E-38 Kathern Harrow
HARROW, KATHRYN M.   1909 - [Blank]
HARROW, ALEXANDER W.   1895 - 1977
   [Above two on same stone]

HARROW, ALICE
   28 Jun 1875 - 9 Aug 1966
HARROW, ALEXANDER
   3 Jun 1874 - 13 Apr 1958
   [above two on same stone]

E-39 William Undercoffer
UNDERCOFFLER, MARY M.   1913 - 1961
UNDERCOFFLER, WILMER   1912 - [Blank]
   [Above two on same stone]
   [Two spaces]

E-40 Cliff & Lill Branchild
   [Two spaces]
BRANCHIDE, LILLIAM M.   1910 - [Blank]
BRANCHIDE, CLIFFORD H. 1901 - 1962
   [above two on same stone]

SECTION M

M-33 Wesley Landis
LANDIS, CLARA U.   1904 - [Blank]
LANDIS, G. WESLEY   1905 - 1974
   [above two on same stone]
M-34 Ralston Mellon
   [No stones in this lot]

M-35 Schaffer
   [Two spaces]
SCHAFFER, SADIE M.   1905 - [Blank]
SCHAFFER, SAMUEL J.   1902 - 1974
   [above two on same stone]
M-36 May Hinkle
   [Three spaces]
HINKLE, MAY D.   1900 - [Blank]
HINKLE, JOHN L.   1869 - 1975
   [above two on same stone]
M-37, 38, 39, & 40 have no owners
   [There are no stones on these lots]

ROW 30

SECTION D

D-41 No owner on map
BARTL, NICK   1880 - 1933

SCHMIDT, JOHN P.   Husband
   9 Jul 1899 - 14 Apr 1957

D-42 Harold Detwiler
DETWILER, BARRY W.   20 May 1948
   Son of Harold C. & Alice H.
   Detwiler

DETWILER, HAROLD C., Jr.
   28 May 1922 - 10 Jan 1976
   Tec 5 US Army WWII

D-43 & 44 Enos Detwiler
DETWILER, INFANT SON of R.C. &
   Anna F. Detwiler
   27 Dec 1922

DETWILER, ANNA (Nee HERBER)
   4 Nov 1900 - 6 May 1927
DETWILER, ROOSEVELT
   9 Sept 1900 - 30 May 1935
DETWILER, ANNA W.
   19 Dec 1896 - 14 Oct 1969
DETWILER, HAROLD C.
   7 Jun 1897 - 19 Sept 1951

D-45 & 46 Christian Zehner
ZEHNER, CHRISTOPHER   1850 - 1924
ZEHNER, MINNIE   1850 - 1928
ZEHNER, CHRISTIAN M.   1898 - 19__
ZEHNER, MINNIE M.   1904 - 19__
   [Four spaces] [above on same stone]

ST. PETER'S UNION CEMETERY (New Section)   163

Row 30, Continued:

D-47 Wilson Stock
STOCK, WILSON A.   1908 - 1979
STOCK, HILDA   1910 - [Blank]
ELLISON, ANNIE   1885 - 1939
    [Above three on same stone]
STOCK, WILSON A.   1908 - 1978

D-48 Hugo Wessman
WESSMAN, HUGO C.   1879 - 1950

SECTION E

E-41 John Johnson
JOHNSON, ELIZABETH   1900 - 1938
JOHNSON, JOHN   1893 - 1962
    [Above two on same stone] [2 spaces]

E-42 Wm. Frick
    [Two spaces]
FRICK, WM. H.   1903 - 1965
FRICK, RUTH E.   1902 - 1981
    [above two on same stone]
E-43 Elmer Tice   [Two Spaces]
TICE, LAURA E.   1902 - [Blank]
TICE, ELMER S.   1897 - 1953
    [above two on same stone]
E-44 Monroe Crouthamell
CROUTHAMEL, ABBIE   1889 - 1956
CROUTHAMEL, MONROE   1900 - 1973
    [Above two on same stone]

CROUTHAMEL, CHRISTINE   1906
    27 Oct 1906 - 7 Jun 1967

E-45 John Bergey
    [No stones in this lot]

E-46 Anna Nolting   [Two spaces]
NOLTING, KARL
    Oct 1882 - Nov 1962
NOLTING, ANNA
    Feb 1889 - Jan 1966
    [above two on same stone]
E-47 Joseph Mallis
MALLIS, MARIE
MALLIS, JOSEPH   1906 - 1970
    [Two spaces]

E-48 Christian Wurster
    [No stones in this lot]

SECTION M

M-41 Umstead
    [No stones in this lot]

M-42 Roland Kratz
    [Two spaces]
KRATZ, SARAH K.   1918 - 1976
KRATZ, ROLAND W.   1916 - [Blank]
    [above two on same stone]

M-43 Wack [No stones in this lot]

Lots M-44 through M-48 have no owners
marked onnSection map.
[These lots have no stones]

ROW 31

SECTION D

D-49 Karoline Frederick
FREDERICK, CAROLINE   1885 - 1967
FREDERICK, JACOB   1873 - 1933
    [Two spaces]

D-50 Cathrine Erdman
ERDMANN, JOHN   1873 - 1933
ERDMANN, KATHARINA   1874 - 1951
    [Above two on same stone] [Space]

D-51 & 52 Paul and Charles Wack
WACK, CHARLES C.
    28 Nov 1866 - 17 Feb 1942
WACK, ELLEMINA
    28 Aug 1878 - 21 Jan 1925
    [Above two on same stone]

WACK, ELIZABETH B.   1906 - 1969
WACK, PAUL M.   1902 - 1966
    [Above two on same stone]

D-53 & 54 Albert Stock
STOCK, ALBERT C.   1876 - 1955
STOCK, SUSAN E.   1876 - 1941
STOCK, ALBERT D.   1914 - 1938
    [Above three on same stone]
    [Four spaces]

D-55 Raymond Frankenfield
FRANKFIELD, ELIZABETH M. 1865 - 1939

D-56 John Rockel
ROCKEL, JOAN LEE   1946 - 1951
    [Space]

SECTION E

E-49 Monroe Snyder [Two spaces]
SNYDER, LAURA CATHERINE 1921 - 1943
    [Snyder & Koons on same stone]

E-50 Harry Koons
KOONS, MARY GRASS   1895 - 1978
KOONS, HARRY M. Our Pal 1892 - 1961
    [above two on same stone]
E-51 Raymond Johnson
JOHNSON, RAYMOND F.   1934 - [Blank]
JOHNSON, JANE   1935 - [Blank]
JOHNSON, BREND JOAN   1960 b&d

E-52 Clara Shelly
SHELLY, LIZZIE F.   1889 - 1971
SHELLY, CLARA E.   1911 - [Blank]
    [above two on same stone]
    [space]

Row 31, Continued:

E-53 Chas. Trout
TROUT, CHARLES H.   1890 - [Blank]
TROUT, PHOEBE S.   1891 - 1980
ARANGO, FLORENCE S.   1915 - 1966
   [Above three on same stone]
   [Two spaces]

E-54 Arnold Chencinski
CHENCINSKI, KURT   1948 - 1970
CHENCINSKI, ERNA   1929 - [Blank]
CHENCINSKI, ARNOLD   1900 - 1974
   [Above three on same stone]

E-55 William Foelker [Two spaces]
FOELKER, WILLIAM R.   1908 - 1972

E- 56 Robert M. Moyer [Space]
HECKLER, FLORENCE   1920 - 1974

   [Metal Funeral Parlor marker
    burnt by son - illegible]

SECTION M

M-49 Price Nice
NICE, PRICE P.   1894 - 1979
   PFC US Army WWI
NICE, BEATRICE A.   1904 - 1978
NICE, EMMA daughter   died 1925
   [Above three on same stone]

M-50 Hoffman
HOFFMAN, ROSANN M.   born 1933
HOFFMAN, FREDERICK C.   1917 - 1977
   [above two on same stone]
M-51 Senter Holl
M-52 Senter Holl
   [No stones on these lots]

M-61 through M-64 have no owners
   listed on the section map.

ROW 32

SECTION D

D-57 Anne Mack
MACK, JOHN   Husband
   5 Jan 1907 - 31 Mar 1936
FORD, JOSEPH   1904 - 1981
   [Jay C. Kriebel Funeral Home marker]

D-58 Joseph Dixon
   [No stones in this lot]

D-59 Donald Wack
   [This owner probably should be
    changed with D-60]
RUTH, EMMA B.   1904 - [Blank]
RUTH, ERNEST B.   1905 - 1936
   [above two on same stone]

D-60 Emma Ruth
   [No burials in this lot--probably
    ownes lot D-59]

D-61 & 62 Peter Darde
DARDE, STEVEN J.   1966 - 1980
   [Funeral parlor metal marker]
   [Two spaces]

DARDE, SUSAN P.   1906 - [Blank]
DARDE, PETER, Sr.   1904 - 1979
   [Above two on same stone]

DARDE, ELIZABETH   1885 - 1954
DARDE, JOSEPH   1884 - 1965
   [Above two on same stone]

D-63 Edwin Hedrick
HEDRICK, SALLIE T.
   15 Dec 1867 - 30 Sept 1961
HEDRICK, EDWIN S.
   26 Jun 1868 - 17 Nov 1942
   [Above two on same stone]

HEDRICK, EDWIN D.
   27 Dec 1902 - 3 Sept 1964

D-64   Paul Hunsicker
   [four spaces]

SECTION E

E-57 Elmer Knipe
KNIPE, ELMER K.   1880 - 1952
KNIPE, EMMA   1885 - 1973
   [Above two on same stone]
   [Two spaces]

E-58 Samuel Landis
LANDIS, EMMA L.
   15 Jan 1899 - 28 Nov 1953
LANDIS, CLARA K.   1893 - 1965
LANDIS, SAMUEL L.   1892 - 1966
   [Above two on same stone]

E-59 Dorothy Hayden
   [Rhodedendron Bush]
HAYDEN, JULIUS A.   1908 - 1964
HAYDEN, DORTHY H.   1909 - 1972

E-60   Florence Brey
   [Two spaces]
BREY, RAYMOND
   23 Dec 1906 - 16 Apr 1966
BREY, FLORENCE
   [Dates blank]

E-61 Elsia Esslinger
ESSLINGER, ELSIE R.   1901 - [Blank]
ESSLINGER, ADOLPH   1888 - 1971
   [Two spaces]

Row 32, Continued:

E-62 Allen Fellman
   [No stones in this lot]

E-63 Marion Clemens
CLEMENS, MARIAN H.   1913 - [Blank]
CLEMENS, RUSSELL M.   1914 - 1974
   [Base of stone--no marker]

M-64 U__ocheck [Urbanchuk]
   [No stones in this lot]

SECTION M

M-57 Harry Moore
MOORE, HARRIET L.   1925 - 1979

M-58 No owner--no stone

M-59 No owner on map
KRAMER, PAUL K.   1913 - 1980
   TEC 4 US Army WWII

M-60 Mattern

M-61 through M-64

   [No owners recorded on cemetery map and no tombstones in this part]

SILVERDALE BRETHREN IN CHRIST CEMETERY

The Silverdale Brethren in Christ congregation was formed about 1825. It first met at the Wismer farm and later built a church building along Route 113 in Silverdale.

The cemetery is located behind the church and its parking lot along the westerly side of Route 113. Row 1 is located at the corner of the parking lot fartherest from the church. The stones in rows 1 through 6 face southwest, while the ones in rows 7 through 13 face northeast. The rows were read beginning with the ones closest to the parking lot and church and reading toward the field. They were transcribed during the summer of 1982.

Row 1

    [four spaces]

HUBER, JAMES P.   25y 9m 15d
    19 Jul 1800 - 1 May 1886
    [as recorded on stone]

LANDIS, REED F.
    13 Dec 1888 - 30 Mar 1946

    [space]

LANDIS, ALBERT Y.   36y 19d
    1 May 1850 - 20 May 1880

LANDIS, MARY D.   71y 6m 8d
    wife of Albert Landis
    late wife of Henry Keeler
    12 Dec 18[51|61?] - 20 Jun 19[28|23?]

BENNER, MILTON ERNEST
    15 Dec 1884 - 21 Aug 1969

    [two spaces]

HAYES, JOHN M.   1876 - 1935
HAYES, LYDIA B.   1873 - 1950
    [above two on same stone]

    [space]

HAYES, JOHN W.   Infant son
    14 Mar 1940 - 15 Mar 1940

    [five spaces]

RUPERT, PETER H.   1896 - 1939
    brother

Row 2

    [four spaces]

FELLMAN, KATE
    2 Nov 1817 - 22 Mar 1909

FELLMAN, ISAAC   70y 5m 16d
    10 Jun 1813 - 26 Nov 1883

STROHM, PETER R.
    15 Oct 1838 - 23 Mar 1908

STROHM, ELIZABETH
    26 Jun 1836 - 10 Feb 1932

STROHM, NOAH F.
    7 Jun 1863 - 3 Jul 1926

BENNER, MIRIAM K.
    8 Aug 1893 - 14 Jan 1981

BENNER, MILTON B.   1857 - 1947
BENNER, MARY   1855 - 1900
BENNER, ANNA M.   1863 - 1941
    [same stone]
BENNER, ELIZABETH
    daughter of Milton and Mary Benner
    born and died 14 Mar 1904

BENNER, MARY H.   1905 - 1952
BENNER, GEORGE K.   1898 - 19--
    [above two on same stone]

MARSHALL, HARRY, Jr.   1909 - 1979
    [burial records 3/2/79]
MARSHALL, ANNA T.   1929 -
    [above two on same stone]

    [three spaces]

BENNER, MARVIN H.
    son of [? and ?] Benner
    died 10 Feb 19[??]
    aged 1[?]y [1?]m 20d
    [James Renner 1922- 1923?]

    [two spaces]

H. L. H.

Row 3

    [two spaces]

LANDIS, HENRY L.   1896 - 1951

167

Row 3 continued:

LANDIS, ORPHA M.   1891 - 1963
    [above two on same stone]

LANDIS, JOHN H.   father   70y 5m 19d
    4 Feb 1840 - 23 Jul 1916

LANDIS, REBECCA   73y 2m 15d
    mother
    23 May 1814 - 8 Aug 1917

LANDIS, ALBERT   1y 2m [?]d
    son of John and Rebecca Landis
    18 Apr 18[80?] - 1 Jul 1881

LANDIS, SARAH D.   36y 4m 25d
    daughter of John and Rebecca Landis
    24 Nov 1879 - 18 Apr 1916

LANDIS, JOSEPH D.   76y 26d
    2 Sep 1867 - 28 Sep 1943

ROSENBERGER, MARY
    wife of Samuel Rosenberger
    2 May 1876 - 13 Mar 1901

ROSENBERGER, INFANT
    son of Samuel and Mary Rosenberger
    born and died 18 Mar 1901
    [note mother died in childbirth--
    was it the 13 or 18 ?]

ROSENBERGER, SILRONUS   aged 5 weeks
    son of Samuel and Mary Rosenberger
    17 Feb 1897 - 14 Mar 1897

ROSENBERGER, EVA L.   1y 3m 5d
    daughter of Samuel and Mary
    21 May 1898 - 26 Aug 1899

ROSENBERGER, LIZZIE   10m 10d
    daughter of Samuel and Mary
    22 Nov 1899 - 1 Oct 1900

ROSENBERGER, ISAIAH D.   65y 10m 1d
    father
    26 Feb 1878 - 27 Dec 1943

LANDIS, CASSANDRA D.   77y 6m 28d
    mother
    19 May 1875 - 17 Dec 1852

LANDIS, ANNIE S.   2m 2d
    daughter of Isaiah and Katie
    19 Aug 1900 - 21 Oct 1900

LANDIS, PAUL S.
    son of Isaiah and Katie Landis
    stillborn 27 Jan 1908

    [space]

RAWN, EDWARD M.   1918 - 1966

RAWN, ELLEN L.   1917 -

HABORLE, CHARLES   54y 4m 5d
    father
    6 Jan 1868 - 11 May 1922

HABORLE, REBECCA D. (WISSLER)
    mother   83y 7m 23d
    29 May 1872 - 22 Jan 1956

    [space]

HABERLE, HARMON L.   9m 3d
    Twin son of Charles B. and Rebecca
    24 Dec 1907 - 27 Sep 1908

LEATHERMAN, ABNER L.   1898 - 1974

LANDIS, RUFUS   1899 - 1978

LANDIS, KATHRYN   1911 -
    [above two on same stone]

KERR, RACHEL L.   1931 - 1980
KERR, WILMER L.   1928 -
    [above two on same stone]

Row 4

CASSEL, RUTH S.   1903 - 1972

CASSEL, CHARLES S.   1893 - 1977

STOUT, SARAH M.   1870 - 1949

STOUT, HOWARD B.   1864 - 1938

STOUT, RAYMOND A.   16y 4m 25d
    son of Howard and Sallie M. Stout
    17 nov 1889 - 12 Apr 1906

STOUT, INFANT DAUGHTER   1901
    of H. B. and S. M. Stout

FRAVEL, CHRISTINA   86y 22d
    30 Sep 1798 - 22 Oct 1884

ROTH, ANNA   58y 11m 17d
    wife of Elias R. Roth
    27 Jan 1826 - 11 Jan 1881

ROTH, ELIAS R.   73y 6m 8d
    died 25 Mar 1899

LEISTER, SALOME
    1 Jun 1849 - 1 Dec 1936

    [space]

FREDERICK, MARY M.
    31 May 1875 - 9 Apr 1954
FREDERICK, ALLEN G.
    9 Mar 1874 - 19 Dec 1958

    [two spaces]

Row 4 continued:

LANDIS, KATHRYN M.   mother
    27 Mar 1912 - 22 May 1975
LANDIS, ELMER S.   father
    2 May 1906 - 24 Sep 1974
    [above two on same stone]

A. M. A.

LANDIS, BERTHA L.   1897 - 1966
LANDIS, HOWARD F.   1898 -
    [above two on same stone]
    [ten spaces]

Row 5

WALLIS, EDNA A.   1901 - 1971

ZIEGLER, DANIEL F.   1871 - 1961
ZIEGLER, EMMA M.   1868 - 1939

ANGLEMOYER, HENRY F.   77y 10m 26d
    28 Mar 1831 - 24 Feb 1909
ANGLEMOYER, ANNA M.   71y 4m 22d
    21 Jan 1837 - 13 Jun 1908

ANGLEMOYER, ANNIE M.   13y 5m 26d
    daughter of Henry and Annie
    Anglemoyer
    18 Jan 1873 - 14 Jul 1886

ANGLEMOYER, SAMUEL M.   32y 2m 15d
    28 Jun 1866 - 13 Sep 1898

LANDIS, MARTHA ANGLEMOYER 74y 7m 9d
    5 Aug 1866 - 14 Mar 1941

    [two spaces]

ANGLEMOYER, MARTIN   74y 8m 8d
    father
    4 Jul 1821 - 12 Mar 1896

ANGLEMOYER, ELIZABETH   85y 9m 10d
    wife of Martin Anglemoyer
    20 Oct 1823 - 30 Jul 1909

HENDRICKS, MARY   78y 9m 12d
    1 Oct 1830 - 13 Jul 1909

LANDIS, JOHN K.   father
    2 Mar 1862 - 21 Apr 1827
    aged 65y 1m 19d

LANDIS, EMMA D.   44y 5m 8d
    mother, wife of John K. Landis
    24 Nov 1865 - 2 May 1910

LANDIS, PAUL L.   5m 17d
    son of John K. and Emma Landis
    11 Jan 1900 - 28 Jun 1900

LANDIS, INFANT
    daughter of John K. and Emma Landis
    born and died 27 Jun 1901

LANDIS, JOHN L.   10y 1m 11d
    son of John K. and Emma Landis
    16 Feb 1893 - 27 Mar 1903

LANDIS, EMMA L.   16d
    daughter of John K. and Emma Landis
    29 Jan 1905 - 11 Feb 1905

LANDIS, ELMER L.   7w 6d
    son of John K. and Emma Landis
    29 Jan 1905 - 25 Mar 1905

HENDRICKS, RAYMOND A.   1891 - 1973
HENDRICKS, MARY L.   1894 - 1978
HENDRICKS, KATHRYN L.   1913 -
HENDRICKS, MERRILL L.   1924 - 1925
    [above four on same stone]

GARIS, EILMER D., Sr.   1913 - 1982
    [Anders Funeral Home]

Row 6

    [three spaces]

WISMER, CHRISTIAN   85y 1m 8d
    13 Apr 1817 - 21 May 1902

WISMER, MARY   89y 1m 12d
    wife of Christian Wismer
    24 Apr 1814 - 6 Jun 1903

WISMER, SARAH   84y 7m 6d
    daughter of Christian and Mary
    Wismer
    25 Jun 1841 - 1 Feb 1926

    [space]

WISMER, JOEL H.   85y 6m 27d
    7 Jan 1853 - 4 Aug 1938

WISMER, MARY S.   65y 1m 13d
    wife of Joel Wismer
    21 Nov 1856 - 3 Jan 1922

WISMER, CHRISTIAN   11m 25d
    son of Joel H. and Mary Wismer
    6 Nov 1887 - 1 Nov 1888

WISMER, ANNA MARY   3y 8m 12d
    daughter of Joel H. and Mary Wismer
    17 Jan 1889 - 4 Dec 1892

WISMER, EVA S.   1y 23d
    daughter of Joel and Mary Wismer
    1 Jan 1893 - 24 Jan 1895

Row 6 continued:

WISMER, MARTHA S.   18d
    daughter of Joel and Mary Wismer
    14 Feb 1896

KAUFMAN, HARRIE A.   65y 5m 28d
    16 Nov 1845 - 14 May 1911

KAUFMAN, MARTHA   59y 2m 5d
    wife of Harrie A. Kaufman
    20 Dec 1848 - 25 Feb 1907

[space]

ROSENBERGER, INFANT SON   1910
ROSENBERGER, JENNIE L.   1881 - 1910
ROSENBERGER, HENRY F.   1877 - 1975
    [above three on same stone]

ROSENBERGER, KATIE L.   1906 -
ROSENBERGER, MARTHA L.   1908 -
    [above two on same stone]

[space]

MOYER, MARTHA S.   1886 - 1950
MOYER, MENNO H.   1884 - 1947
    [above two on same stone]

[space]

DETWEILER, MARIA G.   1883 - 1964
DETWEILER, ISAAC S.   1875 - 1953
    [above two on same stone]

Row 7

DETWEILER, HENRY S.   89y 7m 11d
    9 Feb 1874 - 20 Sep 1963

DETWEILER, ALICE H.   61y 9m 3d
    14 Jun 1880 - 17 Mar 1942

DETWEILER, LILLIE F.   30y 4m
    19 Oct 1901 - 19 Feb 1932

DETWEILER, JOSEPH B.
    18 Feb 1848 - 16 Jan 1915

DETWEILER, SARAH D.
    2 Aug 1850 - 22 Mar 1929

DETWEILER, JOSEPH S.
    27 Jun 1884 - 30 Nov 1902

DETWEILER, LIZZIE S.
    23 Feb 1898 - 26 Apr 1928
    [three spaces]

GARIS, FRANK D.   1867 - 1948
GARIS, IDA S.   1870 - 1948
    [above two on same stone]

GARIS, AMANDA D.   1864 - 1930
GARIS, JOSEPH D.   1875 - 1921
GARIS, RACHEL S.   1880 - 1964
    [above two on same stone]

GARIS, FRIEDA D.   10y 1m 2d
    daughter of Joseph D. and Rachel Garis
    4 Jan 1910 - 6 Feb 1920

GARIS, PAUL   16y 1m 10d
    son of Joseph and Rachel Garis
    17 Jan 1907 - 27 Feb 1823

BAUER, ROSA P.   28y 9m 12d
    wife of Chas. Traber
    25 Oct 1874 - 7 Jul 1903

TRABER, CARL B.   1y 16d
    son of Chas. and Rosa Traber
    died 28 Jul 1900

ERB, SAMUEL C.   1897 - 1956
ERB, MARTHA D.   1899 - 1975
    [above two on same stone]

ERB, BERNICE
    son of Samuel and Martha Erb
    31 May - 1 Jun 1917

[three spaces]

ROSENBERGER, EMMA L.   1907 -

Row 8

[two spaces]

PRINGLE, DOUGLAS R.
    husband and father
    18 May 1842 - 25 Nov 1973

[two spaces]

PRINGLE, DONALD RAY   baby
    29 Jul 1964 - 1 Dec 1964

SHELLY, ABRAHAM D.   66y 1m 20d
    father
    24 Apr 1827 - 13 Jun 1893

SHELLY, MATILDA   89y 1m 6d
    mother
    4 Oct 1832 - 10 Nov 1921

HUNSICKER, HARRY C.
    4 Jun 1872 - 25 Nov 1942
HUNSICKER, MARTHA B.
    21 Nov 1875 - 14 Dec 1929
    [above two on same stone]

ERB, CLARENCE W.   1894 - 1967

Row 8 continued:

ERB, ELLA MAY H.   1895 - 1964
   [previous two on same stone]

KEELY, WILLIAM P.
   22 Aug 1871 - 14 Mar 1945
KEELY, MINA K.
   13 Aug 1872 - 14 Apr 1924
   [above to on same stone]

KEELY, INFANT DAUGHTER
   of W. P. and M. K. Keely
   [no dates on stone]

KEELY, JOHN L.   2y 21d
   son of W. P. and M. K. Keely
   27 Dec 1901 - 12 Nov 1902

KAUTZ, ESTELLA L.
   7 Apr 1899 - 15 Oct 1919

ROSENBERGER, RALPH B.   1912 - 1980
ROSENBERGER, ROGER B.   1919 - 1919

ROSENBERGER, RODGER
   son of [? and ?] Rosenberger
   born and died [?] Sep 1919

   [space]

ROSENBERGER, MAYME   1889 - 1938
   wife of Elder Edwin C. Rosenberger

   [two spaces]

ESHLEMAN, HENRY L.   1907 - 1970
ESHLEMAN, FLORENCE G.   1903 -
   [above two on same stone]

[?], SARAH G.   1933
   [Church register]

Row 9

   [four spaces]

MOLL, CHARLES W.   1849 - 1935
MOLL, EMMA L.   1860 - 1948
   [above two on same stone]

LANDIS, JOSEPH A.   66y 4, 16d
   father
   23 Aug 1828 - 9 Jan 1895

LANDIS, RACHEL R.   91y 8m 3d
   mother
   28 Jul 1835 - 31 Mar 1927

LANDIS, MARY A.   36y 6m 21d
   daughter of Joseph A. and Rachel
   30 Oct 1862 - 21 May 1899

SEMMERN, CHARLES   1869 - 1941
SEMMERN, ELLA   1866 - 1947
   [above two on same stone]

[Illegible stone]

[illegible stone]

[illegible stone]

I. L.

   [three spaces]

GARIS, VIRGINIA
   mother, wife of Earl D. Garis
   31 Aug 1902 - 3 May 1929

GARIS, WARREN DALE
   22 May 1923 - 23 May 1923

GARIS, EARL D.   1900 - 1953

MOLL, OSWIN D.   1871 - 1937
MOLL, IDA L.   1875 - 1931

   [space]

MOLL, RAYMOND L.   1899 - 1981
MOLL, EMMA W.   1895 - 1959
   nee Derstine
MOLL, OSWIN R.   son   1926 -
   [above three on same stone]

   [three spaces]

MOLL, WILLIAM C.   1905 - 1959
   Pvt. 1318 Ser. Unit World War II

Row 10

MILLER, JAMES S.
   9 Feb 1869 - 5 Dec 1932
MILLER, KATIE G.
   4 Feb 1872 - 10 Jul 1961
   [above two on same stone]

   [space]

KRATZ, ALBERT P.   1853 - 1930

KRATZ, MALINDA B.   1867 - 1938

KRATZ, PEARL   1y 9m [19?]d
   daughter of Albert and Malinda Kratz
   11 Dec 1892 - 29 Aug 1893

KRATZ, JACOB HAROLD   5m 15d
   son of Albert and Malinda Kartz
   [2?] Sep 1897 - 22 Feb 1898

KRATZ, LUTHER B.   1889 - 1918

   [two spaces]

BUCKS COUNTY TOMBSTONE INSCRIPTIONS - HILLTOWN TOWNSHIP

Row 10 continued:

GULICK, JONATHAN   72y 10m 7d
    20 Mar 1848 - 27 Jan 1921

GULICK, ELIZABETH   51y 11m 12d
    mother, wife of Jonathan Gulick
    5 Feb 1851 - 17 Jan 1903

MOYER, CATHARINE
    widow of Abraham Moyer
    19 Oct 1835 - 29 Apr 1929

FELLMAN, MAGGIE B.   47y 6m 2d
    daughter of Henry P. and Catharine Fellman
    31 Aug 1866 - 12 Mar 1914

PETERSON, LOREN   27y 1m 12d
    1869 - 2 Nov 1896

FREED, ALLEN L.   husband
    29 May 1888 - 12 Feb 1948

FREED, KATIE
    [on church register]

RICHMAN, FRANCIS
    1882 - 1967
    [church register]

BOWERS, FRED K., Rev.
    5 Oct 1872 - 2 Feb 1967

BOWERS, SALLIE S.
    23 Jul 1872 - 3 Mar 1949

Row 11

    [three spaces]

BISHOP, HARRY S.   1890 - 1976
BISHOP, REBECCA C.   1894 - 1964
BISHOP, MOSES G.   father   1833 - 1909
BISHOP, MARY ANN   mother   1842 - 1927
    [above four on same stone]

    [three spaces]

YODER, WILLIAM M.   22y 2m
    29 Jun 1893 - 28 Sep 1915

BENNER, REBECCA W.   mother
    8 Aug 1864 - 25 Dec 1925

RHIMER, WILSON B.   son
    7 Feb 1892 - 28 Apr 1912

SMITH, J. MATTHEW   1908 -
SMITH, LIZZIE MAE   1908 - 1972
    [these two on same stone]

SMITH, MERRIE   1937 - 1938

SMITH, JOHN ALLEN   1946

FREED, LLOYD F.
    3 Nov 1913 - 23 Oct 1973

FREED, KATIE F.
    7 Nov 1885 - 10 Nov 1950

HECKLER, ABRAHAM S.   1878 - 1974
HECKLER, HANNAH S.   1882 - 1982
    [above two on same stone]

Row 12

    [two spaces]

CRIDER, KENT RICHARD
    11 Jun 1963 - 31 Oct 1963

    [space]

ROSENBERGER, SAMUEL H.   82y 10m 5d
    father, Elder
    12 Feb 1836 - 17 Dec 1918

ROSENBERGER, AMANDA L.   69y 1m 9d
    mother
    20 Apr 1858 - 20 May 1927

    [three spaces]

SMITH, WALTER P.   father
    19 May 1859 - 16 May 1945

SMITH, ANNIE C.   mother
    1871 - 1931

SMITH, BERNARD D.
    4 Sep 1910 - 13 Nov 1931

SMITH, JOSEPH M.   1901 - 1932
SMITH, JOSEPH M.   1927 - 1928

LONG, LEROY
    son of Charles and Katie Long
    stillborn   1 Jul 1920

    [four spaces]

LEHMAN, LOUS ANNA   1927 - 1960
LEHMAN, KIMBERLY ANN   1927 - 1960
    [above two on same stone]

Row 13

[TERTERSY?], DENNIS PAUL
    buried 1952
    [church register]
    [three spaces]

STONE, JAMES S.   74y 12d
    1 Jan 1840 - 13 Jan 1914

STONE, ELIZA
    wife of James Stone
    3 May 1843 - [1924?]

Row 13 continued:

   [space]

CONLEY, WILLIAM F.   1895 - 1966
CONLEY, MARY AGNES   1897 - 1952
   [above two on same stone]

   [space]

DETWEILER, RAYMOND H.   1906 - 1978
DETWEILER, CARRIE O.   1908 - 1973
   [above two on same stone]

   [two spaces]

WITMER, LEVI B.   1877 - 1929

WITMER, KATHERINE M.   1884 - 1978

LIGHT, CARL S.   1916 - 1979
LIGHT, LUCY K.   1921 -
   [above two on same stone]

Additional information obtained from the Church cemetery records:

Row 1

BECKLEY, [Buckler?]   died 1941

Row 2

LANDIS, ETHAN   1929 - 1969
HEBERLE, KATHERINE F.   1907 - 1944
   wife of Herbert Heberle

HEBERLE, INFANT DAUGHTER 1944

Row 4

LANDER, SAMUEL HENRY   1850 - 1916

Row 8

ESHLEMAN, SARAH G.   1933

Row 10

PATTERSON, LORNG   1869 - 1896

FREED, KATIE   1885 - 1950

RICHMAN, FRANCIS   1882 - 1967

   The Cemetery lot map was dated 17 Jul 1953 by Surveyor, Stanley Moyer. The map and cemetery records are in the care of Walter H. Berger of Souderton.

TRINITY EVANGELICAL CEMETERY

The Trinity Evangelical Cemetery located on Green Street north of the Hilltown Pike in Hilltown Twp. is the cemetery belonging to the church which once stood on the adjoining property. The church was known by several names including: Trinity Evangelical, Leidytown Methodist Episcopal, and Methodist Evangelical. The church building was moved to Lansdale.

The church and cemetery were part of the Albright family farm.

The rows were recorded beginning with the stones nearest Green Street and reading toward the opposite direction.

Row 1

FRETZ, SALLIE   22y 1m 25d
    wife of Lewis Fretz
    3 Jul 1863 - 3 Dec 1885

STAHR, GEORGE   76y 11m 14d
    29 Nov 1824 - 12 Nov 1891

STAHR, JOHN C.   aged 62y
    son
    20 Aug 1867 - 25 Nov 1919

Row 2

HACKMAN, ABIGAIL   aged 40
    wife of Allen Hackman
    13 Dec 1815 - 8 Jun 1856

REED, MARY   73y 8m 29d
    wife of Andrew Reed
    4 Oct 1788 - 3 Jun 1862

REED, ANDREW   88y 27d
    16 May 1781 - 10 Jun 1869

[ZIEGEN?], JOHN   aged 17d
    son of Andrew and Mary Ann [Ziegen?]
    died 7 Dec 1857

GERHART, ISAIAH   12y 1m 2d
    son of Sybil and Samuel Gerhart
    12 Aug 1856 - 11 Dec 1868

MOLL, MARY ELMIRA   7y 5m 8d
    daughter of Michael and Mary Ann Moll
    25 Jun 1853 - 3 Dec 1860

MOLL, JOHN HENRY   1y 10m 18d
    son of Michael and Mary Ann Moll
    21 Jan 1859 - 18 Dec 1860

Row 3

FRETZ, JEREMIAH
    son of John and Elizabeth Fretz
    [stone is partly buried]

FRETZ, AMANDA LOUISA   aged 8y
    daughter of John and Elizabeth Fretz
    8 May 1852 - 19 Jan 1861

FRETZ, ELIZABETH   23y 6m 18d
    daughter of John and Elizabeth Fretz
    15 Jul 1843 - 2 Feb 1867

CUFFEL, MARIA
    wife of John Cuffel
    25 Nov 1819 - 27 Oct 1868

CUFFEL, JOHN
    son of John and Maria Cuffel
    2 Oct 1817 - 8 Dec 1867

CROUTHAMEL, MARY MALINDA
    daughter of Francis and Elizabeth Crouthamel
    12 Sep 1858 - 2 Apr 1861

CUFFEL, LYDIA ANN
    daughter of John and Maria Cuffel
    11 May 1850 - 1 Aug 1851

Row 4

SWINK, WILLIAM   aged 89y
    22 May 1778 - 2 Oct 1859

SWINK, MARY   62y 11m 18d
    died 31 Mar 1847

SWINK, JACOB   45y 2m 14d
    14 Apr 1806 - 18 [?] 1851

Row 4 continued:

SWINK, FANNY　　　　　　　77y 6m 15d
　　wife of Jacob Swink
　　19 Feb 1812 - 4 Sep 1889

SWINK, ELVIA A. G.　　　　26y 8m
　　daughter of Jacob and Fanny Swink
　　16 Oct 1861

SWINK, SARAH E. F.　　　　27y 5m 29d
　　daughter of Jacob and Fanny Swink
　　1 Nov 1847 - 30 Apr 1875

RUMER, HANNAH H.　　　　　37y 12d
　　wife of Sam. H. Rumer
　　died　29 Jul 1871

RUMER, AMANDA　　　　　　　77y 6d
　　22 Jan 1827 - 28 Jan 1914

FLUCK, MARY E.　　　　　　18y 3m
　　6 Jun 1845 - 2 Oct 1863

MYERS, JOHN L.

MYERS, HANNAH　　　　　　　1y 7m 28d
　　daughter of John L. Myers
　　died　22 Mar 18[62?]

[T　? BERT], MARY A.　　aged 31y
　　wife of Henry [T　?　bert
　　died 5 Mar 1865

Row 5

GOODMAN, HANNAH ELIZABETH
　　21 Sep 1858 - 10 Jan 1864

GOODMAN, WILLIAM　　　　　aged 30y
　　died　2 Jul 1854

[　　?　　], AUGUSTUS　　31y 1m 28d
　　11 Aug 18[?] - 8 Oct 1870

[　　?　　], JOSEPH
　　son of [illegible]

MAGARGAL, LOVINIA　　　　23y 11m 21d
　　1 Jun 1837 - 28 Apr 1861

COPE, THOMAS HENRY
　　9 Aug 1807 - 2 Dec 18[?]

COPE, LYDIA
　　1 Mar 1804 -　　?

Row 6　　F. K.

KLETZING, CORA P.　　　　 2y 8m 16d
　　daughter of Frederick and Katie
　　Kletzing
　　16 Sep 1902 - 2 Jun 1906

KLETZING, FERDINAND　　　86y 3m 12d
　　18 Oct 1829 - 30 Jan 1916

KLETZING, MAGDALEN　　　　67y 3m 21d
　　wife of Ferdinand Kletzing
　　1 Dec 1823 - 22 Mar 1891

[　　?　　], ELIZABETH
　　[illegible]

[　　?　　], Wilhemina
　　wife of Levi [　　?　　]
　　[illegible]

RACE, ANTHONY E.　　　　　1y 1m 14d
　　son of Levi and Wilhemina Race
　　17 Jul 1867 - 31 Aug 1868

BERGER, MARY　　　　　　　84y 2m 4d
　　wife of William Berger
　　23 Jan 1831 - 27 Sep 1913

Row 7

SHELLY, JOHN
　　son of Jonas and Susan Shelly
　　[21|24?] Dec 1863 - 18 Feb 1864

ALBRIGHT, JOHN H.
　　son of [Henry?] and C. Albright
　　19 Mar 1844 - 12 Apr 1845

ALBRIGHT, MARIAH M.　　　2y 6m
　　daughter of Henry and C. Albright
　　20 Sep 1842 - 16 Apr 1845

SMITH, PAUL L.　　　　　　2y 4m
　　[no date on stone]

SMITH, MARY M.　　　　　　?4y 9m 16d
　　wife of Samuel Smith
　　12 Dec 18[18?] - 28 Sep 1853

MARIA M. BUQ [RIARIA M. BUIG ?]
　　[How should this name read?]
　　15 Nov 1797 - 11 Nov 1850

BERGER, JOHN WESLEY　　　9y 11m 11d
　　son of [Wm.?] and Mary Berger
　　14 Aug 1862

BERGER, CATHARINE　　　　3y 9m 12d
　　daughter of [Wm.?] and Mary Berger
　　died　22 Aug 1862

BERGER, AMELIA E.　　　　15y 10m 28d
　　daughter of Wm. and Mary Berger
　　died 15 Nov 18[72 or 79?]

TRINITY EVANGELICAL CEMETERY

Row 8

ALBRIGHT, DANIEL   87y 1m 13d
    6 Jan 1791 - 19 Feb 1878

ALBRIGHT, MARGARET   67y 10m 26d
    19 Mar 1807 - 14 Feb 1875

ALBRIGHT, JOHN   80y 9m 17d
    died 24 Apr 1902

ALBRIGHT, MARY   53y 11m 10d
    wife of John Albright
    26 Feb 1823 - 6 Feb 1877

ALBRIGHT, EDWIN   2y 2m 17d
    son of John and Mary Albright
    5 Jan 1850 - 22 Mar 1852

ALBRIGHT, WARREN F.   3y 1m 18d
    son of John and Amanda Albright
    8 Jan 1883 - 26 Feb 1886

LEVERS, GEORGE W.   60y 1m 5d
    7 Apr 1841 - 12 May 1901

LEVERS, HAROLD
    son of William A. and Laura Levers
    died May 1917

LEVERS, MINERVA   18y 10d
    daughter of George and [Kate?] Levers
    8 Aug 18[78?] - 18 Aug 18[88?]

LEVERS, MAHLON   1y ?m [14?]d
    son of George and Kate Levers
    27 [?]18[76?]

LEVERS, CLARA
    daughter of George and Kate Lever
    died 16 Sep 187[?]
    [stone is chipped]

ALBRIGHT, JOHN   1y 5m 15d
    son of [Pharis?] and Matilda Albright
    died 10 Apr 1883

KOL   [young]

Row 9

HECKLER, ELIAS R.   71y 7m 17d
    2 Sep 1828 - 19 Apr 1900

HECKLER, REBECCA M.   70y 8m 10d
    nee Gerhart
    25 Mar 1837 - 5 Dec 1907

GERHART, ABRM M.   50y 7m 9d
    1 Nov 1839 - 10 jun 1890

GERHART ABRAHAM   79y 5m 12d
    8 Apr 1800 - 20 Sep 1879

GERHART, ELIZABETH   89y 1m 4d
    wife of Abm. Gerhart
    9 Mar 1810 - 13 Apr 1899

[ZIEGENIN?], MARY A.   38y [4?]m 23d
    wife of Rev. A. [Ziegenin?]
    19 Dec 1830 - 11 May 1869

SMITH, SAMUEL   68y 9m 4d
    died 20 Nov 1883

SMITH, FRANCES   78y 3m 27d
    wife of Samuel Smith
    17 Apr 1816 - 10 Aug 1894

ECKHART, GEORGE
    10 Jul 1835 - 10 Jul 1895
    Private in Co. B. 104 Regt. PA Vol.
    in the late Rebellion

ECKERT, MARY   aged 98y
    wife of John Eckhart
    died 26 Mar 1894

ECKHART, JOHN   75y 19d
    13 Mar 1802 - 2 Apr 1877

ECKHART, MARY E.   2y 1m 24d
    31 May 1867 - 24 Jul 1869

WIREMAN, HENRY S.   1869 - 1944

Row 10

SLIFER, MARY   84y 10m 22d
    daughter
    3 Mar 1848 - 25 Jan 1933

SLIFER, HANNAH   81y 9m 17d
    wife of Christian Slifer
    11 May 1817 - 28 Feb 1899

SLIFER, CHRISTIAN   81y 3m 27d
    11 Jun 1820 - 8 Oct 1901

ECKEL, SARAH ANN
    wife of Samuel Eckel
    21 Feb 1813 - 14 Sep 1899

ALBRIGHT, ELLA G.   24y 5m 8d
    wife of John . lbright
    23 May 1855 - 31 Oct 1879

MYERS, FREDRICKA D.   80y 1m 20d
    1 Feb 1824 - 21 Mar 1904

SWARTZ, MARY   55y 5m 22d
    mother, wife of John Swartz
    7 Dec 1843 - 29 May 1899

SCHILLING, ARTHUR   1885 - 1885
SCHILLING, MAMIE   1883 - 1898
    [above two on same stone]

THOMAS, LILLIE S.   1879 - 1903

Row 10 continued:
GRAHAM, A. BRITTAIN   1849 - 1910
GRAHAM, A. ESTELLA   1859 - 1953
    [above two on same stone]

Row 11

FRETZ, JOHN   83y 4m 5d
    died 7 Jan 1888

FRETZ, ELIZABETH   85y 1m 10d
    nee Kline
    wife of John Fretz
    16 Jun 1811 - 26 Jul 1896

GEHMAN, EMMA   [22?]y 8m 10d
    died 29 Dec 18[81?]

SWINK, AMOS   79y 6m
    9 Feb 1839 - 9 Aug 1918

HUNSBERGER, ELLA MABEL   11y 3d
    daughter of Joseph and Anna
    Hunsberger
    27 Sep 1889 - 30 Sep 1900

[stone missing]

HUNSBERGER, ERVIN   3y 2m 2d
    son of Joseph and Anna Hunsberger
    4 Jun 1879 - 6 Aug 1882

HUNSBERGER, ANNA ADA   4y 6m 8d
    daughter of Joseph and Anna
    Hunsberger
    18 Feb 1895 - 26 Aug 1899

HUNSBERGER, ANNA
    4 Jul 1857 - 27 Jun 1928

HUNSBERGER, JOSEPH
    19 Mar 1847 - 7 Jan 1937

HUNSBERGER, HOWARD   [?1891]- 1859

Row 12

SWINK, DAVID   79y 7m 19d
    20 Aug 1821 - 2 Apr 1900

BENSON, MARY ANN   56y 10m 25d
    5 Feb 1833 - 30 Dec 1889

WILLIAMS, ELIZA
    1 Aug 1814 - 19 Apr 1882

BUCKS COUNTY TOMBSTONE INSCRIPTIONS -- HILLTOWN TOWNSHIP
INDEX

A.
   A. M., 169
   D. S., 32

AARON
   [CYII?], 58
   Amelia, 57
   Belinda, 57
   Caroline, 58(2)
   Derostus, 58(3)
   Harriet, 58
   Horation B., 58
   Hughes, 58
   John, 58
   John P., 74(2)
   Juliet Rowland, 74(2)
   Martha Caroline, 74
   Millie, 58
   Obed, 58
   Obed Hughes, 58
   Owen, 58
   Robert, 58
   Samuel, 57
   Sarah, 58

ACKERMAN
   George L., 89

ADDLETON
   Elizabeth, 140
   Robert, 140
   Robert, Jr., 140(2)
   Robert, Sr., 140

ADELMAN, see Edelman

AETMAN/AETMANS
   Barbara, 115

AHLUM
   Claude C., 120
   Elizabeth, 120
   Woodrow W., 120

AIM, see Eim
   Peirie, 105

AIMS
   Harvey F., 118
   Rachel, 105
   Susanna Beuller, 105

AKER
   Emma M., 146
   Leidy, 146
   Leidy L., 146
   Sallie, 133
   Sallie H., 146
   William, 133(2)

ALBRIGHT
   A., Mary, 153
   Alta M., 12, 53
   Amanda, 153, 177
   C., 176(2)
   Cameron, 153
   Catharine, 126
   Charles Milton, 77
   Christina, 12
   Daniel, 177
   Edwin, 177
   Ella G., 177
   Flora Courter, 77
   Henry, 126(2), 151, 176(2)
   Hiram Y., 153
   Infants, 12, 72
   John, 177(5)
   John B., 177
   John H., 176

ALBRIGHT
   Lizzie, 72
   Margaret, 177
   Mariah, 176
   Mary, 177(2)
   Matilda, 177
   Pharis, 177
   Reuben, 12(2)
   Susan M., 151
   T. A., Dr., 72
   Walter, 12
   Walter H., 53
   Warren F., 177
   Wesley F., 153(2)

ALDERFER
   Angelina G., 104
   Anna, 8
   Anna W., 156
   Arthur L., 8
   Barbara C., 152
   Catherine, 49
   David Alan, 53
   Dora L., 129
   Evelyn Feryl, 152
   Floyd, 157
   Frank R., 152(2)
   Franklin, 11(2); L., 8, 11
   Horace L., 129
   Ida D., 7
   Katie, 11
   Katie L., 11
   Katie R., 11
   Lewis S., 104
   Linford L., 11
   Lizzie P., 6, 11
   Maria B., 8
   Marion Ruth, 129
   Noble R., 156
   Preston S., 6
   Robert Kenneth, 156
   William L., 7

ALEXANDER
   BARNDT E., 89
   Mark W., 89

ALIFF
   Edith Pauline, 146

ALFF
   Mary Louise, 86

ALLEBACH, ALLABOUGH
   Annie Kratz, 104
   Hannah, 24
   Harvey K., 14
   Henry B., 24(2)
   John, 41, 104
   Katie A., 104
   Mabel G., 8
   Mamie D., 8
   Norman L., 14
   Rose L., 14
   W. Ernest, 8
   Wilson G., 8

ALLEN
   James Henry, 91
   Susan Ruth, 91

ALTHOUSE
   Agnes A., 146
   Edwin S., 146
   Harrie S., 146
   Sophia S., 146

ALVAREZ
   C. Lino, 91

ANGLEMOYER, Angelmeyer,
   Angelmäuer, Angelmeier
   Angelmoyer
   Anna, 41, 42
   Anna M., 169
   Annie, 169
   Annie H., 13
   Annie M., 169
   Catharina, 43
   Elizabeth, 41, 169
   Emma, 41
   Hannah, 26
   Heinrich, Henry, 41(3),
     42, 169
   Henry F., 169
   Henry O., Rev., 13
   Henry S., 93
   J., 43
   James, 41
   Jacob M., 41
   John H., 13(2)
   Joseph, 43
   Leanna M., 13
   Lizzie M., 42
   Lucy Ann, 13, 26
   Maria, 41
   Maria Anna, 43
   Martha, 169
   Martin, 169(2)
   Mary, 93
   Samuel, 13, 26
   Samuel M., 169

ANDERSON
   Frances, 84

ANDREWS
   Aaron, 44
   Barbara, 26
   Elias H., 26(2)

ANGENY, ANGENEY
   Catharine, 41(3)
   Catharine S., 42
   Cathryn F., 43
   David S., 41
   Infant, 41
   J. K., 41(3)
   Jacob K., 43(2)

ANGSTADT
   Anna M., 6
   J. Raymond, 6

APPLE
   ------, 127
   Abraham, 110(2)
   Elizabeth, 109
   Ida M., 129
   Lewis, 129
   Lewis W., 129
   M. Ida, 129
   Mary, 110
   Matilda, 129
   Paul, 109
   Preston R., 120
   Rodman H., 129

APPENZELLER
   Jacob, 94
   Susanna, 94

ARANGO
   Florence S., 164

ARMON
   A. Harry, 153
   Margaret S., 153

ARTMAN/AETMAN
    Barbara, 115

ASHGROFT
    John T., 106
    Mary B., 106

ASURE
    Amanda, 145
    Edward, 145

ATKINSON
    Melvin, 142

B.
    B., 93
    H. H., 97
    I., 41
    J., 31
    M. C., 97

BACE
    Sophia, 10

BACHURSKI
    Anna, 88
    Louise M., 86
    John, 88
    Joseph G., 86
    Mary Ethel, 84
    Mary Pieuski, 84

BACHMAN, BAGHMAN
    Amanda, 139
    Caroline, 139(2)
    Charles Parker, 141
    Elizabeth, 139
    Frances M., 141
    Jacob, 95, 139(5), 141
    Jacob Howard, 141
    Mary, 141(2)
    Mary M., 141

BADER
    See Bodder
    Johannes, 109
    Maria Virginia, 109
    Peter, 109

BAKEL
    Elizabeth, 113
    Hanna, 113
    Jacob, 113

BAKER
    Anna, 79
    Catherine, 101(2)
    Eliz Ziegler, 101(2)
    Elizabeth, 120(3)
    Frank, 101
    Henry, 101(2), 120
    Leidy, 101(3), 120(2)
    Wilhelmina, 101

BANNISTER
    Jennie, 132

BARBER
    Sibyl C., 150
    W., Rev., 150

BARGER
    Edna K., 154

BARINGER, BEHRINGER
    See Beringer
    Bella, 17(2)
    Christian F., 98(2)
    Ellamae, 17
    Frederick, 98
    Isabella M., 17
    Julian, 98(2)
    Mildred M., 17
    W. B., 17(2)
    W. Paul, 17

BARNABY
    Anna Mary, 97
    Catherine, 97
    Erwin, 97
    Frances, 97
    Julianna, 98
    Lydia, 39
    Margaret, 97(2)
    Mary A., 125
    Samuel, Sammuel, 97(3)
    William, 39
    William H., 125

BARNDT
    Annie M., 130
    Bertha T., 132
    Charles F., 132
    J. Harvey, 132
    John G., 130, 131
    John S., 145(2)
    Mary A., 145(2)
    Maria Valeria, 132
    Viola N., 132

BARNER, BARHER
    Elizabeth, 128
    John, 128
    Harriet, 121

BARNED
    -------, 62
    Elsie, 62
    John H., 62
    Laura M., 62

BARTHOLOMEW
    Albert R., 71
    Mary Martha, 71(2)
    Samuel, 71(2)

BARTL
    Nick, 162

BARTLES
    Christian, 98

BASGIL
    Angela M., 88

BAUER
    Rosa P., 170

BAUM
    Abraham, 33
    Abraham B., 30(2)
    Alice M., 33
    Anna, 33(2)
    Anna H., 33
    Annie, 30
    Arthur M., 32(2)
    Henry H., 30, 33
    Laura H., 33
    Lillie F., 32
    Sarah, 33
    Sarah G., 30

BEAN
    David B., 28(2)
    Elizabeth C., 28
    Mary G., 28
    William B., 28, 29

BEANS
    Frank E., 145
    Matilda S., 80

BEARED
    Doris, 146

BECHTEL
    Enos, 38
    Jacob, 41
    John, 41
    Joshua Aaron, 53
    M., 38
    Martin, 38, 42(2)

BECHTEL, continued:
    Nophiah, 48

BECK
    Angeline, 141(2)
    Anna, 139
    Annie M., 26
    Aquillas, 26
    Catharina, 47
    David, 141
    Elizabeth, 139
    Henry, 139
    Isaac, 47, 141
    John P., 20
    Maria, 132
    Michael, 139(3), 149
    Michael Paul Miller, 149
    Rudolph, 26
    Sallie S., 20
    Samuel S., 141(2)
    Susanna, 47
    Willis B., 20

BECKLEY
    -------, 173

BEDNARZEWSKI
    John, 89
    Karol, 86
    Mary Anna, 86

BEER
    Elizabeth, 61
    John, 61

BEIDELMAN
    John, 116(2)
    Mary Catharine, 116

BEIDLER, BEYDLER
    --------, 118
    Henry, 27
    Henry D., 4
    Jacob, 16, 27(2)
    Mary E., 118
    Mary L., 4
    Nathan, 118
    Nathan G., 4
    Samuel D., 4

BEIHN
    Peter, 120

BEIK
    C. L., 119
    Catharine, 119
    Johannes, 119

BEISEL, BEISELL
    A. Roy, 130
    Alice H., 130
    Angeline, 128
    Ellen Mary, 130
    Elmer J., 128
    Elsie P., 128
    Erwin G., 128
    Sarah A., 128
    William, 130
    William Ross, 130(2)

BEITZ
    Magdalena, 117(2)
    Wendel, 117

BELGER
    Elizabeth, 125(2)
    John H., 125(2)
    Leidy, 125

BENNER
    A. R., Dr., 23(5)
    Anna M., 167
    Bessie Eva, 23
    Catharine, 37
    Catherine Hartzell, 147
    Elizabeth, 40, 167

BENNER, continued:
    Ethel, 91
    George K., 167
    Howard, 23
    Infant daughter, 91
    James, 167
    Katie S., Kate S., 23(4)
    Madaline, 110
    Marvin H., 167
    Mary, 167
    Mary H., 167
    Milton B., 167
    Milton Ernest, 167
    Miriam K., 167
    Nellie Viola, 23
    Norman, 91
    Norman B., 91
    Oscar Abner, 23
    Rebecca W., 172
    Rosa May, 23
    Steven Kirk, 91

BENSING
    Catherine T., 151
    Paul D., 151

BENSON
    Mary Ann, 178

BERGER
    Amelia A., 176
    Catharine, 176
    John Wesley, 176
    Mary, 176(4)
    William, 176(2)

BERGEY, BERGE
    Barbara, 40
    Catharina, 49
    Clifford, 156, 159
    Clifford C., 195
    Elizabeth, 44(2), 49
    Grace B., 143
    Isaac, 50(3)
    Jacob, 22, 23
    John, 163
    Joseph, 49(2)
    Mary Ann, 50
    Mary Magdalena, 44
    Minerva, 50
    Nathan, 44(2)
    Orpha M., 159
    Patricia Ann, 143
    Ruth M., 159
    Sophia, 22
    Susanna, 49
    Willard K., 143
    Wilson S., 159

BERINGER
    See Baringer
    Amos, 93(3)
    Amos S., 145
    Barbara, 93
    Catharina, 117
    Ephraim A., 93
    George, 117(2)
    Hannah, 117
    Henry, 117(2)
    Johannes, 117
    Mary Ann, 93
    Sophia, 93
    Sophia F., 145

BERNOTAS
    Anna H., 88
    Anthony T., 87
    Cecelia, 87
    Edward, Jr., 88
    Edward, Sr., 88
    Frederick W., 87
    Gregory, 88

BETANCOURT
    Beatrice, 86

BEULLER
    Susanna Aims, 105

BEVAN
    Martha, 161
    Philip, 161

BEYER
    Kenneth L., 13

BIBIGHAUS
    Anna B., 33

BILGER
    Anna, 11
    Anna M., 11
    Bessie M., 11
    Calven, 123
    Clarence, 123
    John, 125, 126
    John H., 104(2)
    Levi H., 104
    Mary, 104
    Mary Jane, 104
    Pearl M., 104
    Samuel, 11
    Samuel B., 11
    Sarah F., 101

BIRCKS/BIRRIS
    Catherine, 119
    Henrich, 119

BISHOP
    Abm., 26
    Albert B., 124
    Amy, 24
    Annie, 21, 27
    Artemus M., 143(2)
    Carrie E., 126
    Carroll, 64
    Clara G., 5
    Claud, 16
    Claude B., 5(2)
    Clayton A., 15
    Cora Lee, 21
    Craig, 5
    Edna Earl, 21
    Edwin, 14(2)
    Edwin M., 143
    Elva A., 143
    Elizabeth, 16, 27, 43
    Emma, 19
    Emma T., 143
    Enos, 50(2)
    Erwin H., 143
    Erwin Thomas, 26
    Esther, 13
    Evelyn, 5
    Evelyn G., 5
    Florence M., 15
    Floyd A., 16
    Garwood, 4
    Gertrude May, 8
    Gordon Lynn, 5
    H. L., 125
    Hannah, 124
    Harry S., 173
    Harvey, 21
    Henry A., 6
    Herman L., 124
    Howard, 19
    Howard D., 19
    Ida H., 37(2)
    Infants, 13, 64
    Jacob, 5, 24, 42, 43
    Jacob B., 3
    Jacob H., 5
    Jacob M., 13(2)
    Jacob Ray, 5
    James H., 64(3)
    Joseph D., 26
    Katie K., 3
    Leon M., 20(2)
    Lester, 21
    Lillie M., 20

BISHOP, continued:
    Lillie S., 4
    Linford M., 20
    Lizzie H., 20(2)
    Lloyd, 8
    Lorie, 8
    Lucinda, 14
    Mabel R., 124
    Margaret D., 5(2)
    Margareth, 7
    Marie, 8, 15
    Martha H., 20
    Marvin L., 20
    Mary Ann, 50, 172
    Mary M., 19
    Melvin A., 7
    Merle, 21
    Michael B., 19
    Moses G., 172
    Nicole Michal, 8
    Norman L., 124
    Pauline, 16
    Pearl M., 64
    Pearson M., 8
    Rebecca C., 172
    Robert, 126
    Ruth C., 19
    Sallie, Sally, 19(2), 26
    Sallie M., 13
    Sallie T., 126
    Stanley, 21
    Susanna, 26
    Verna, 126
    W. D., 26
    Walter H., 20
    Warren A., 37(2)
    Willard H., 37
    William, 13
    William B., 13
    William D., 26
    Wilson, 126

BISSEY
    Jesse, 149
    Jesse T., 149
    Levi A., 149
    Mary E., 149

BISSING
    see Bitting
    Mary Jane, 100
    Mary, 100(3)
    Simon, 100(3)
    Theodore, 100
    Wihlamma, 100

BITTING, BIDDING, BISTING
    see Bissing
    Abel, 119(2)
    Alfred, 71
    Catharine, 119
    Eddie, 100
    Edna, 100
    Eleazer, 71
    Jack E., 58
    Josephine, 58
    Laura E., 158
    Mary, 71
    Matilda J., 158
    Michael M., 158
    Rachel, 103
    Sophia, 103
    Thomas R., 71
    William G., 158

BITTNER
    Annie E., 102
    Winfield S., 102

BLACKWELL
    M. H. (Mr. & Mrs.), 158
    son, 158

BLAHUT
    Mary, 63

BLOOM
    ------, 132
    Addie, 147
    Amanda, 132
    Ara S., 124
    Blanch, 147
    Calvin H., 129
    Carrie M., 150
    Catherine, 97
    Christina, 97
    Cleveland, 147
    Edward, 150(2)
    Edward H., 150
    Elizabeth, 132
    Frank, 147, 149
    Frank P., 147
    Frank S., 147
    Harry S., 147
    Harvey, 97
    Henry H., 132(3)
    Horace, 123
    James Madison, 124(2)
    Katie S., 124
    Maria, 132
    Mary G., 132(2)
    Mildred I., 150
    Missouri H., 107
    Naomi, 147
    Oliver U., 107
    Peter, 97(3)
    Sarah, 107, 129
    Wilhelmina, 132
    William, 107, 129(2)

BODDER
    see Bader
    Elizabeth, 109
    Jacob, 109
    Noah, 109

BOEHNER
    Christianna L., 101
    Christine, 160
    Emma, 101
    Gilbert, 101
    Henry, 101(4)
    John, 101
    Leroy, 160(2)
    Maddelene, 101
    May, 101
    Sarah, 101

BOKUM
    George & Maria, 146(2)

BOLD
    Jacob Kirsch, 83
    Magdalena, 83
    Nicholas, 83

BOLIG
    Lois Arlene, 56
    Pauling G., 56

BONGART, Helen A., 83

BONNAWITZ
    Catharine, 115
    Joseph, 115

BOORSE
    Alice, 125

BOOZ
    Emma, 128
    Emma D., 137
    Jacob S., 137

BOWERS
    Fred K., 172
    Sallie E., 172

BRAND
    John, 79

BRANCHIDE, BRANDHILD
    Clifford H., 162(2)
    Lillia M., 162

BRANDENBERGER
    Betty S., 53
    Ezra J., 53

BRADFORD
    Harvey Derr, 53
    Katharine, 53
    Sara R., 53
    Theodore W., 53

BRAQUEHAIS
    Cecile U., 88
    Louis A., 88

BRENNAN
    Thomas J., 89

BREY
    Arthur, 152
    Arthur H., 152
    Florence, 164(2)
    Katie C., 152
    Raymond, 164

BROOM
    John J., 95
    Lydia Ann, 95

BROWN
    Vera, 158

BRUNER, BRUNNER
    Aaron, 107, 129
    Aaron C. or G., 129
    Adeline, 112
    Ann Margaret, 111
    Anna Bella, 145
    Barbara, 37
    Catharine, 11
    Charles, 143(3), 145
    Elizabeth, 108
    Ella, 129
    Emaline, 143
    Emma E., 145
    Henry, 109(2)
    Hiram, 110
    Hiram C., 129
    Isaiah S., 37
    J. Norman, 145
    John, Johann, 111(2)
    Leidy S., 143
    Mary, 143
    Milton H., 145
    Samuel, 110
    Samuel C., 109
    Sarah, Sarar, 109, 129(2)
    Sarah Ann, 107
    Son of Aaron, 107
    Thomas, 110
    Willard Lynn, 145
    William, 129

BRYAN, BRYON
    David K. 22(2)
    Elizabeth, 22
    Emeline, 114
    Henry M., 114
    John, 114(3)
    Mary, 114(2)
    Mary E., 114

BUCKLEY
    C. J., 139
    Chauncey, 137, 139
    S. R., 139
    Sterrett K., 139

BUEHNER, BUHNER
    Antonia, 87
    Dorothea, 133
    Joseph, 87

BUIG/BUQ
    Maria M., 176

BURDETT
    Linneaus, 129

BURKHART
    Anthony, 98
    Laura Ginna, 98
    Mary, 98

BURTON
    Charles Henry, 139(2)
    Lydia Ann, 139
    Wallace B., 139

BUSSEL
    Jenina, 59
    Thomas, 59

BUSWELL
    Della Rowland, 74

BUTLER
    Martha P., 63

BUTTON
    Elizabeth, 25(2), 43
    Heinrich, 43
    Jacob, 25(2)
    John, 25(2), 43
    Mary Ann, 43

BYERS
    John, 148
    John O., 148
    Phoebe M., 148

CAHILL
    ALma E., 87
    Theresa M., 87

CAMPBELL
    Clarence, 134
    Irene, 134
    Mary Ellen, 84
    Samuel, 134(2)
    Wilhelmina, 134

CANEY
    Henry, 153

CARLIN
    Bessie H., 160

CARTER
    Emma, 137
    William, 137

CARTER
    A. S., 80
    Alfred S., 59(2)
    Della, 123
    Edward, 123
    Harriet B., 159(2)
    Harvey, 119
    Iva, 123
    James H., 123
    Maria, 80
    Mary, 59
    Mary Ann, 119
    Milton D., 159
    Peter, 119
    Terressa, 80
    Wilhelmina, 59

CASSEL, CASSELL
    Allen, 46
    Alvin, 46
    Catharine, 25
    Charles S., 3, 168
    Christianna, 96(2)
    Elizabeth, 46(8)
    Elizabeth H., 3
    Emma, 96
    George, 96
    Howard, 72

CASSEL, continued:
   Ida L., 151
   Infant, 96(4)
   Isaac, 25, 96(6)
   J.K., 22
   J.M., 72
   Joseph, 46, 72
   K. A., 22
   Karen Theresa, 88
   Lauressa, 72
   Magdalen, 96(3)
   Marion, 151
   Mary Ann, 46
   Ruth S., 168
   Samuel G., 151
   Samuel K., 46(8)
   Ulysses Grant, 22
   Wilemina, 46

CHARLES
   Oliver H., 44

CHENCINSKI
   Arnold, 164(2)
   Erna, 164
   Kurt, 164

CHESNUS, CHESNES
   David P., 89
   Elizabeth, 86
   George, 86

CHOROMANSKI
   Marianna, 87

CHRISTINE
   John S., Rev., 76

CIMORELLI
   Raymond A., 84

CLARK
   Vernon M., 59
   Viva L., 59

CLEMENTS
   George T., 83

CLEVELEND
   Henry, 140

CLEMENS
   Marion H., 165
   Russell M., 165

CLEMMER
   Earl, 159
   Elmer, 157
   Elmer R., 157
   Florence M., 157
   Infant, 157

CLIFFORD
   Anna M., 85
   Robert J., 85

CLIME
   Kevin Michael, 88
   Thomas E., 86

CLOAK
   Catherine E., 85
   Joseph E., 85

CLYMER
   Caroline, 55
   Infant, 21
   Levi R., 95(2)
   Lizzie, 21(2)
   Lovina Ott, 95
   Morris A., 155(2)
   Samuel, 21
   Samuel B., 21

COAR
   Agnes L., 145
   Arthur, 128
   Ida, 145

COAR, continued:
   Ida C., 145
   John, 128
   John W., 126
   Margaret, 128(3)
   Nathan, 145
   Nathan B., 145
   Rella P., 145
   Thomas, 128(4)
   Valeria, 128
   Violetta, 128
   William S., 145
   Wilbur G., 145

COLE
   John, 152
   Shirley R., 91
   Viola R., 91

CONDICT, Cora H., 56
   David, 77
   May Hinkle, 77
   Newton Parsons, 77

CONLEY
   Mary Agnes, 173
   William F., 173

CONNELY
   Catherine A., 84
   Herbert, 84
   Marie, 84
   Samuel, 84

CONRAD
   Alice, 156
   Charles W., 156(2)

CONSTANZER
   Anna Margaret, 153
   Barbara Alice, 149
   Catherine L., 152
   Charles, 149(2)
   Elizabeth E., 153
   Infant, 149
   James, 153
   James A., 153
   Thomas J., 152
   Walburoa, 149
   Willard, 149

CONTE
   Joseph, 88

COONEY
   Adelia M., 87
   Richard T., 87

COOPER
   Albert, 150
   Ann Margaret, 111

COPE
   -------, 111
   Abraham, 111
   Abraham K., 138(2)
   Adam, 117(2), 118(2)
   Addie, 138
   Addi M., 138
   Andrew, 110
   Anna, 138
   Anna Maria, 111
   Benjamin Franklin, 117
   Catherine, 111
   Charles, 108(3), 110
   David, 111, 144
   Edwin, 111
   Elizabeth, 108(2), ~~156~~ 158
   Elizabeth L., 138
   Emaline, 111
   Hannah, 117(2), 118(3)
   Hanrech, 111
   Isaac, 137
   Isabella, 138
   James, 137
   Leanna, 118
   Lydia, 176

COPE, continued:
   Mahlon L., 138
   Malinda, 108
   Maria Elizabeth, 110
   Mary, 111
   Mary A., 138
   Mary Ann, 111, 138
   Mary Margaret, 117
   Sarah Ann, 111
   Susan, 137(2)
   Thomas Henry, 176

COURSEY
   Brian J., 88

COURTER
   Bertha W., 74
   Clara W., 74
   Emma L., 74(2)
   Emma May, 76
   Emma S., 77
   Flora May, 77
   Gaynor, 76
   Gaynor R., 74
   George, Rev., 74(2)
   George H., 76
   George W., 74
   Jacob, 76(2)
   Jacob H., 77
   Lewis C., 77(2)
   Mariah A., 74
   Mary, 77
   Minerva, 74
   Norman C., 74
   Peter L., 76(6)
   Raymond Norman, 74
   Rebecca M., 76(5)
   Sallie Elinda, 76
   Sarah E., 77
   Sarah Jane, 74
   Susanna K., 77
   Uriah D., 74(2)
   William Calvin, 76
   William W., 77

COX, Joseph, 74
   S. L., Rev. 75
   Sarah D., 74, 75

CRAIG
   Joseph V. & Julia V. 84

CRAWFORD
   Alfred E., 55
   Deborah Chester, 55

CRESSMAN
   Edwin C., 141
   Florence, 154
   Herman, 153
   Hiriam R., 154
   Katie, 41
   Mary E., 141
   Paul, 41
   Sarah, 128
   William H., 41

CRIDER
   Kent Richard, 172

CROSS
   Joseph M., Rev., 14(2)
   Maria, 14

CROUTHAMEL
   Abbe Bertha, 97
   Abbie, 163
   Adam, 91
   Adam W., Sr., 91(2)
   Anna Caroline, 133
   Antionette M., 148
   Barbara, 120
   Catharine, 133
   Cephas K., 149(2)
   Christine, 163
   Connie Lee, 155
   Edward M., 155
   Eli, 133
   Eli O., 120

CROUTHAMEL, continued:
  Eliz, Elizabeth, 101, 175
  Ella Mae, 149
  Elmer E., 162
  Elvy, 148
  Emily M., 77
  Francis, 175
  Grace C., 162
  Harold S., 162
  Harvey, 101
  Henry A., 77
  Ida G., 133(2)
  Infant, 133
  Ira, 144
  Ira S., 146
  Irma May, 148
  Irwin L. 148(2)
  Isaac O., 101(4)
  Israel G., 25
  Jacob, 118
  Laura, 148
  Laura A., 148
  Laura B., 146
  Laura J., 155
  Ma? May, 133
  Marcia, 148
  Maria, 148
  Marion, 146
  Mary A., 133(3)
  Mary Ann, 25
  Mary Malinda, 175
  Monroe, 163(2)
  Oscar, 133
  Oscar W., 133(2)
  Paul, 148
  Paul S., 148
  Rachel, 162
  Sarah, 101(2)
  Warren L., 120
  Washington O., 133(3)

CROWELL
  Andrew J., 77(2)
  Esther L., 77
  Flora R., 77(2)
  Frank, 77
  Margaret, 77
  Thomas, 77(2)

CUFFEL
  John, 175(4)
  Lydia Ann, 175
  Maria, 175(3)

CUGEL
  Johann, 98

CURLIE
  Jesse Elmer, 101
  Lizzie, 101
  William, 101

CURTIS
  Albanus M., 152
  Allen, 152
  Anna Delinger, 152
  Anna Elizabeth, 151
  Ella K., 152
  William, 152
  William Franklin, Rev., 152
  William H., 151(2)

D.
  A., 38
  E., 46
  I., 42
  J., 38
  M., 38
  S., 29

DAMM
  Edward J., 85
  Madeline D., 85

DANNENHOWER, DANENHOWER
  Abraham, 94(2)
  Abraham T., 94

DANNENHOWER, continued:
  Barbara, 94
  Elizabeth H., 59
  Euphemia, 59
  Euphemiana, 59(2)
  Hannah, 94
  John, 59(4)
  Joseph, 59
  Philip, 59(2)
  Wilson, 59

DARDE
  Elizabeth, 164
  Joseph, 164
  Peter, 164
  Peter, Sr., 164
  Steven J., 164
  Susan P., 164

DARNER
  Joseph, 151

DARRAR
  Amelia F., 83
  Harry A., 83

DAUBER
  Frederick, 106
  Infants, 106(4)
  John George, 106
  Walburga, 106

DAUBERT
  Elizabeth, 128
  Henry, 128
  Susanna, 128

DAVIS
  John, 102
  Sophia, 102

DEATERLY
  Ida V., 106
  Katie Minerva, 106
  Lewis, 106
  Luzyette, 106(3)

DEFRATIS
  Francis, 80

DEILY
  Philena, 132

DELP
  Amanda, 50
  Catherine, 116(2)
  Christiana, 118
  George, 49
  Isaac, 118
  Jacob Alan, 91
  Samuel G., 50(2)
  Sarah, 50
  Sarah Ann, 116

DEMBROWSKY
  Arthur W., 84
  Margaret, 84
  Susanne R., 84
  Walter J., 84

DePHILLIPO
  Catherine V. & William J. 84(2)

DERBYSHIRE
  Anna M. & Louisa, 56(2)

DERR
  Elizabeth, 120
  Henrich, 120
  Rebecca, 134(2)
  Reuben, 134

DERSTINE, DIRSTEIN, DIRSTINE
  Amanda, 47
  Catherine, 50
  Claude, 5
  Elizabeth, 48
  Ester, 34
  Granville Lewis, 37

DERSTINE, continued
  Hannah W. Moyer, 26
  Henry, 37(2), 147
  Henry F., 49
  Henry G., 50
  Infant, 5
  Joseph H., 16
  Miriam K., 5
  Sophia, 16
  Susan, 37(2)

DETTERER
  Amelia Aaron, 57, 58
  Charles, 57, 58
  Infant, 58

DETTERLINE
  Florence S., 155

DETTERO, DEDERERSIE
  Maria Gerirautha, 111
  Zacharias, 111

DETWEILER, DETWILER
  -------, 161
  A. Frank, 4
  Abraham H., 18(2)
  Addie M., 3, 33
  Alice H., 170
  Allen, 150
  Allen C., 150
  Anna Herber, 162
  Anna F., 162
  Anna L., 4
  Anna Mae, 153
  Anna Mary, 144
  Anna W., 162
  Annie, 40(3)
  Annie A., 40
  Barbara, 40
  Barry E., 162
  Bertha S., 144
  Carrie O., 173
  Charles, 4
  Charles B., 4, 18
  Clifford, 16
  Cora M., 4
  Daniel, 34, 40
  David A., 15(5)
  David R., 44
  Dianna, 35
  Earl S., 144
  Eli H., 13
  Elizabeth B., 11
  Ella A., 19
  Ellen M., 18(2)
  Elmer, 33
  Elmer B., 3
  Elmer M., 91
  Emma E., 105
  Emma M., 7, 21
  Enos, 161, 162
  Enos R., 161
  Ephraim, 16
  Florence, 16
  Frank G., 3, 105, 149
  Franklin G., 149
  Garwood, 21
  George K., 150
  Gladys, 54
  Hannah, 35(2)
  Hannah H., 19
  Harold, 162
  Harold C., 162
  Harold C., Jr., 162
  Harvey H., 15
  Henry, 40(3)
  Henry K., 40
  Henry S., 170
  Howard, 150
  Howard G., 19
  Ida K., 15(4)
  Infant, 162
  Ira B., 7
  Irene H., 15
  Irvin, 8, 144
  Irvin S., 144

DETWEILER, continued:
  Isaac F., 54
  Isaac S., 170
  Jacob, 11, 40(2)
  Jacob A., 19(2), 35(2)
  Jacob L., 11
  James R., 150(3)
  Jean F., 4
  John A., 11(2)
  Joseph, 47, 48(2)
  Joseph A., 47(2)
  Joseph B., 170
  Joseph S., 170
  Katie, 35
  L. Edna, 8
  Laura G., 18
  Lilliah C., 91
  Lillie F., 170
  Linford R., 33
  Lizzie, 40
  Lizzie S., 170
  Louisa, 150(2)
  Louisa B., 149
  Louisa S., 150
  Maria, 11
  Maria G., 170
  Mary, 15, 40
  Mary E., 18
  Mary Ellen, 161
  Mary M., 3
  Minerva H., 12
  Paul C., 18
  R. C., 162
  Raymond, 15, 153(3)
  Raymond H., 173
  Regina, 4
  Richard K., 161
  Roosevelt, 162
  Sadie, 44
  Samuel, 40
  Sarah, 47(2)
  Sarah C., 150
  Sarah D., 170
  Sarah M., 7
  Stanley, 153
  Stella A., 13
  Terry Brian, 4
  Valentine R., 21
  Walter S., 144
  Willard, 153
  William G., 4
  William Henry, 47
  Wilson C., 12

DEUSCHLE
  Barbara, 105
  Christopher, 105
  Juliana Regena, 98

DIEHL
  Annie W., 129
  Christian, 129
  Leidy S., 129
  Sadie A., 129

DIETERICH
  John F., 95(2)
  Mary, 95

DIMMICK, DIMMIG
  Aaron, 102(2)
  Benjamin, 151
  Jacob, 93
  Jeffrey Lynn, 54
  Kate, 102
  Laura C., 151
  Lizzie C., 148
  Mary A., 93

DINGEE
  Howard C., 77

DIXON
  Joseph, 164

DONIS
  Anne E., 85
  Nicholas, Sr., 85

DOPPEL, DOUHLE
  Leonard, 131(2)

DORSANEO
  Maria F., 87

DUCKLOE
  Aaron S., 65
  Catharine, 65
  Elizabeth, 65
  Fred S., 65
  Grace M., 65
  Jacob B., 65
  Martha J., 65
  William, 65

DUNFEE, DUNFER
  Charles H., 155
  James, 155

DUNGAN
  Caroline, 144
  Catharine, 144
  Hartman, 144

DUNN
  Mary B., 73

DURSA
  George, 87
  Mary, 87

DYBIAK
  Nicholas, 156

EARLEY
  Ellen Jane, 93

EBERSOLE
  Hilda A., 91

EBINGER
  Louisa, 145

ECKEL
  Carrie M., 72
  Horace V., 72(2)
  J. Leidy, 72(2)
  Mary, 72
  Mary L., 72
  Robert, 72
  Samuel, 177
  Sarah Ann, 177
  William Leidy, 72

ECKERT, ECKHART, ECKHARTE
  Alfred, 108
  Alverda, 123
  Anne Elizabeth, 113
  Annie E., 150
  Blair, 123(3)
  Carl, 113
  Catharine, 113
  Cathrina King, 113
  Daniel L., 59
  Donald F., 150
  Ellen, 59(2)
  Elizzie, 59
  Elizabeth, 113, 136
  Emma S., 123(2)
  Emmaline, 150
  Florence May, 154
  George, 113(3), 177
  Glenwood, 154
  Henry 150(2)
  Henry L., 59(4), 76
  Isaac, 94
  Jesse, 59(2)
  John, 113(4), 136, 177(2)
  Joseph, 98
  Maria, 94
  Mary, 113, 177
  Mary E., 177
  Mary J., 150
  Norman, 123
  Oliver P., 113
  Ruth L., 59(3)
  Ruthetta, 76
  Warren L., 59
  William L., 59

EDELMAN, ADELMAN
  Adam, 136(2)
  Christiana, 136

EDWARDS
  Robert M., 56
  Susanne, 60

EEDMAN, see Erdman

EHRIG, ERICH
  see Ehrig and Eurich
  Conrad E., 152
  Elizabeth M., 152

EIM
  see Aim
  Eliza, 100

EISENBERGER
  Raymond, 20
  Veronica, 20

ELLENBERGER
  Henry, 93
  Infant, 93(2), 94
  J. Martin, 93(5)
  James, 95
  John, 103
  Martin, 95(2)
  Mary Ann, 93, 95(2)
  Matilda, 103
  Susanna, 95

ELLISON
  Annie, 163

ELTHAM
  Thomas, 71

ERB
  Bernice, 170
  Clarence W., 170
  Ella May H., 171
  Martha D., 170(2)
  Samuel C., 170(2)

ERDMAN, ERDMANN, EEDMAN
  Cathrine, 163
  John, 163
  Jost, 117
  Katharina, 163

ERICH
  see Ehrig and Eurich
  Elizabeth, 152

ERMLER
  John J., 85

ERNEY, ERNY
  Anna Elizabeth, 97
  Elizabeth, 152
  Irvin F., 152
  Irwin, 152
  Joseph, 97(2)
  Margaret, 97
  Mary, 97
  Russell S., 152

ERWIN
  Emaline, 75
  James, 75
  John B., 75
  Mary J., 75
  William B., 75(3)

ESHLEMAN
  Florence G., 171
  Henry L., 171
  Sarah G., 173

ESPOSITO
  Gloria, 84

ESSLINGER
  Adolph, 164
  Elsie R., 164

EURICH
  see Ehrig and Erich
  Anna S., 160
  Anne, 160
  Christian, 149
  Christian J., 149, 160
  Geraldine B., 149

EVANS
    Emily Rowland, 72
    Mary, 72
    Susan, 72
    Susanna, 72
    Robert, 72(2)
    T. R., Rev., 72

EVERHART, EVERHUST
    Catherine, 117
    Elizabeth, 117
    John, 117

F.
    E., 21, 32
    J. H., 33
    M., 32, 60
    M. B., 49
    S., 60

FAGELY, FEGELY
    Grace Amanda, 147
    William, 148

FEASTER
    Christian, 51

FEISENGER
    see Feusner
    Charles, 143, 145

FELIX
    -------, 160
    Samuel, 58

FELL
    Susanna S., 57

FELLMAN
    Abraham, 96(2)
    Allen, 165
    Annie B., 18
    Beada, Reata, 96(2)
    Catharine, 172
    Catharine S., 152
    Ethel C., 150
    Goldie, 152
    Henry P., 172
    Hester, 96
    Horace, 153
    Horace C., 152
    Isaac, 167
    Jacob, 98
    Kate, 167
    Laura D., 18, 152
    Leidy B., 18
    Lloyd C., 150
    Lydia S., 98
    Maggie B., 172
    Merret, 153
    Rachel Ann, 152
    Rachel R., 150
    Reuben N., 150(2)
    Violet, 152
    Walter, 152
    Walter C., 152

FERDINAND
    Irene B., 161
    William J., 161

FETTEROLF
    Emma K., 136

FEUSNER, FEUSNERS
    see Feisinger
    Charles, 119, 143(2)
    Children: C., M., H., J.,
        119(4)
    George L., 154
    George M., 154
    Mary, 143
    Sarah L., 154

FICKERT
    Clara O., 141
    Paul R., 141
    William, 141
    William L., 76

FISHER, FISCHER
    Abraham, 38(2)
    Bernard, 104(2)
    Carolus, 110
    Christina, 104
    George, 110
    H., 31
    Mary, 38(2)
    Samuel D., 38

FISSEL
    See Kissel
    Margaret, 161

FLAMMER, FLOMMER
    Andrew, 141(2)

FLORKOWSKI
    Naomi, 83
    Stanley, 83
    Stanley Francis, Jr., 83

FLUCK
    Arlo, 47
    Cath, 95(4)
    Emma H., 133
    Emmanuel, 95
    Enos G., 47
    H. Marco, 136
    Hiram, 47
    Hiram E., 136
    John, 95(3)
    Lee M., 133, 134, 136(4)
    Leidy, 95
    Lydia M., 47
    Mary, 94
    Mary Ann., 4
    Mary Catharine, 136
    Mary E., 176
    Philip, 94
    Sarah, 133, 134

FLY
    Annie Elizabeth, 65
    Artis M., 60
    Frank W., 64
    Frank Wesley, 65
    Harvey K., 65
    Henry K., 65
    Katie E., 64(2)
    Juliette E. Renoux, 65
    Mattie E., 64(2)
    Mary, 60(2)
    Mary G., 64
    Mary Gibson, 64
    Samuel, 60(2)
    Samuel Irvin, 65
    Seth W., 64(2)

FOELKER
    William, 164
    William R., 164

FONDA
    Barbara, 151
    Joseph, 151

FORD
    Henry J., 124
    Joseph, 164
    Mary Ann, 124

FOUNDS
    John R., 91

FRANCIS
    George, 87
    Rose, 87

FRANK
    Jacob, 123

FRANKENFIELD, FRANKFIELD
    Charley, 105
    Clara, 156
    David, 105
    Eli, 105
    Elim., 156
    Elizabeth M., 163
    Mary E., 156
    Raymond, 163
    Sophia, 105, 151

FRANTZ
    John, 139
    Lucy Ann, 149
    Mariah, 118
    Mary, 139
    Mary J., 139
    Oliver, 139(2)
    Peter, 118(2)
    Samuel F., 149
    Simon B., 139(3)

FRAVEL
    Christina, 168

FRAY
    Martha, 83
    William, 83

FREDERICK, FRIEDRICH
    Allen G., 168
    Caroline, Karoline, 163(3)
    Infant, 113(3)
    Isaac W., 113(2)
    Jacob, 115, 163
    Joseph, 113
    Mary M., 168
    Sallie, 113
    Samuel, 113(5)
    Sarah, 113(2)
    William, 113

FREED
    Abram H., 14(2)
    Allen L., 172
    Emma, 14
    Emma Jane, 16
    Hannah, 106
    Infant, 53
    Jesse, 106
    Katie, 172, 173
    Katie F., 172
    Lloyd F., 172
    Mary C., 14
    William, 106

FRETZ
    Abraham, 39
    Abraham M., 18
    Allen C., 42
    Amanda Louise, 175
    Anna, 32(2)
    Anna B., 128
    Catharine, 37
    Christian, 23, 42(2)
    Christian, Sr., 42
    David L., 28(2)
    E. Clarence, 5
    Eli, 46
    Elias C., 128
    Elizabeth, 23, 42, 45, 46,
        175(4), 178
    Ella Amanda, 5
    Emma Jane, 37
    Ernest Y., 45
    Esther, 37(2)
    Francis Henry, 128
    H. L., 75
    Hannah, 45
    Hannah M., 45, 50
    Heinrich, 37
    Henry D., 6
    Infant, 75
    Irene K., 6
    Jacob, 46
    Jacob M., 42
    Jeremiah, 175
    Johannes, 31

FRETZ, continued:
    John, 175(3), 178(2)
    Joseph, 37(3)
    Kathryn Fretz, 5
    Katie D., 5
    Leah, 32
    Levi, 28(2)
    Levi L., 28(2)
    Lewis, 175
    Lizzie, 42
    Lizzie D., 50
    Maria, 31, 42, 48
    Marietta, 28(2)
    Martin, 31, 32(2)
    Mary, 28(2), 47, 48, 50
    Mary E., 48
    Noah, 48(2), 50
    Paul H., 18
    Paul Y., 45
    Sallie, 175
    Sarah Ann, 18
    Sarah Elizabeth, 28
    Susanna H., 39, 46
    Wilbur Y., 45
    Wilhelmina, 75
    William D., 45(2), 50
    William H., 48
    William M., 47

FREY
    Emma S., 158
    Florence K., 102
    John H., 158
    Susanna, 96
    Warren D., 158
    William, 96(2)

FRICK
    Anna E., 154
    Edward F., 155
    Ella, 138
    Ella G., 148
    Elsie M., 133
    Emma K., 120
    Emma V., 130
    Francis J., 132
    George, 138(2), 155
    George H., 155
    Henry H., 120
    Ida Matilda, 132
    Infant, 155
    J., 133
    John C., 133
    John Howard, 130
    Laura V., 133
    Louisa C., 155
    Lottie N., 155
    Matilda, 138
    Ruth E., 163
    S. Preston, 148
    Samuel, 154
    Samuel F., 150
    Thomas F., 148(2)
    Tom, 152
    Wellington, 138
    William H., 163(2)

FRITZ
    Mary M., 144

FROHNAPEL, FROHNAPFEL
    Infant, 160
    Robert, 160

FROIO
    Frank P., 84

FROST
    Paul, 155

FRY
    A. Ruberta, 140
    Charles A., 140
    Joseph, 59
    Reuben, 140
    Susanne, 59

FUHRMAN, FUHRMANN
    Catharine, 131(2)
    Elizabeth, 109
    Hannah, 109(2)
    Heinrich, Henry, 109(3)
    Michael, 131

FULGINITI
    Clara T., 87

FULMER
    Catharina, 22
    Florence D., 5
    Jacob, 93
    Jacob G., 93
    John M., 17
    Kathryn H., 6
    Leidy K., 5
    Marvin D., 6
    Mary, 93
    Mary J., 17
    Mary Y., 22
    Ruth Ann, 6
    Ruth D., 5
    Sassaman, 22(2)

FULTON
    Anna, 62
    Benjamin, 62(2)
    Elizabeth, 62(2)

FU[?]STON
    Jos., Sgt., 58

FUNK, FUNCK, FUNCH
    Christian, 24
    Dorothy K., 124
    Edith, 46
    Hannah A., 136
    Henry, 136
    Henry G., 136
    Jesse C., 124
    Johannes, 23
    John, 46
    Lydia Ann, 136
    Mary, 46
    Samuel, 46(2)
    Susanna, 46

GABEL
    Lillian H., 159
    Orpha S., 159
    Russell, 159
    Vera G., 159
    Wilson D., 159

GAGAS
    Agnes, 88
    Frank, 88
    Sylvia, 88

GALLAGHER
    Vincent, 129

GANDORFER
    Fannie H., 104

GARGES
    Harry L., 56

GARIS, see Geris
    Amanda D., 170
    Earl D., 171(2)
    Eilmer D., Sr., 169
    Frank D., 170
    Frieda D., 170
    Ida S., 170
    Infant, 4
    Joseph D., 170(3)
    Paul, 170
    Rachel S., 170(3)
    Shirley M., 4
    Warren Dale, 171
    Willard, 4
    Virginia, 171

GARNER
    Emma C., 76

GARNER, continued:
    Ethel U., 153
    Jacob F., 76
    Mary C., 76
    Samuel, 114
    Sheldon, 76
    William S., 153

GARRETT, GARATT
    Edward H., 154
    Eileen, 153
    Everett N., 154
    Robert E., 154
    William E., 153

GEBHART
    Anna Maria, 114

GEBYS, GEEYS, GERYS
    see Geris
    Emmanual, 99
    John & Sophia, 99(2)

GEESAMAN
    Beverly K., 56

GEGGUS, see Gaggus
    Lewis, 119

GEHMAN, GEHMANN, GEHAMAN
    -------, 17
    Abrah B., 17
    Christiana, 140
    Della M., 17
    Emma, 178
    Emma H., 16
    Ephraim D., 19
    George, Georg, 140(3)
    Hannah, 48(2)
    Maria M., 16
    Mary Ann, 48
    Mary Jean, 156
    Samuel D., 48(3)
    Tobias R., 16(2)
    Valeria Y., 19
    Wilmer, 156

GEIL
    -------, 65

GEIP, GEIF
    Anna, 121

GEISEL, GEISELL
    C., Sgt., 117
    Christian, 101
    Frederick, Fredrick, 143, 145
    Fredricka, 143

GEORGE
    Jacob, 45
    Mary, 47
    Martin, 47(2)
    Sophia, 45
    Susanna, 45

GERBAR
    B., 114
    F., 114
    Lydia Ann, 114

GERBER
    Maria, 22

GERHART, GEARHART
    A. C., 114
    Abraham, 126, 177
    Abrm M., 177(2)
    Anna Maria, 114
    Barbara, 126
    Charles, 106
    Edwin S., 114
    Elizabeth, 42, 177
    Emma E., 146
    Emma J., 146
    Francis, 114, 127
    Henry, 146
    Henry C., 146

GERHART, continued:
    Isaiah, 175
    J. F., 114
    James, 49
    James M., 49
    Mahlon M., 104
    Mary Ann, 49
    R., 114
    Rebecca M., 177
    Samuel, 175
    Susan, 104
    Sybil, 175

GERIS, GERYS
    see Gebys
    see Garis
    Johannes, 98

GERRARD
    Stephen William, 53

GIBSON
    Catherine, 116

GIEP, GEIF
    see Geip
    Anna, 120
    George, 120
    Lourine, 120

GIERSE
    Olga Moyer, 161

GILBERT
    Hildegard, 150

GLICK
    Carrie E., 104
    Gwendolyn M., 86
    Henry A., 86
    Joseph F., 86
    Margaret M., 86
    William H., 104

GODER
    Joseph, 59

GODOWN
    Cora, 77
    Henry N., 77

GODSHALK, see GODSHALL
    Abram, 128
    Leon S., 129
    Oliver R., 129(2)
    Sarah A., 128
    Sarah G., 129

GODSHALL, GODSCHALL
    see Godshalk
    A. M., 35
    Aaron, 48(3)
    Allen M., 5
    Alvin, 32
    Amanda, 32
    Anna W., 158
    Elizabeth, 16, 49
    Elizabeth Aaron, 74
    Harvey M., 18
    Howard, 74
    Infant, 5
    Isaac M., 18
    John, 49, 158
    John K., 158
    Maimie, 3
    Maria, 48
    Maria H., 18
    Marion B., 35
    Mary, 48
    Reuben, 48
    Ruth, 5
    Sallie M., 5, 35
    Samuel, 49
    Samuel L., 18
    Shirley M., 3
    Warren, 5
    Wilmer, 3

GOOD
    Fannie, 91

GOODMAN
    Hannah Elizabeth, 176
    William, 176

GORCZYCA
    Józef K., 87
    Klara, 87

GOTWALS
    Barbara, 35

GRABOWSKI
    Helena, 87
    Julian, 87

GRAHAM
    A. Brittain, 178
    A. Estella, 178
    Eva M., 149
    Madilla, Matilda, 32
    Mont, 149
    Mont L., 149

GRANAN
    Christopher John, 88

GRASSE, GRASS
    Annie, 116
    Annie E., 62(2)
    Anthony, 119(2)
    Anthony B., 62(2)
    Anthony M., 15(2)
    Blanche L., 63
    Charles, 123
    Charlotte, 123
    Grace M., 65
    Hannah, 63
    Infant, 15
    Ira W., 62
    John M., 63
    Joseph, 119, 153(2)
    Leidy, 62
    Leidy R., 62
    Levi, 153
    Leidy H., 153
    Lillian L., 15(2)
    Martha J., 62
    Mary, 153
    Mary Ann, 119
    Oliver H., 63
    Rosetta L., 62
    Sallie, 123
    Walter N., 65

GRASSO
    Edward K., 85
    Jane M., 85

GRAVEN
    Howard A., 134
    Mary Alice, 134

GREGG
    Robert G., 87(2)

GREEN
    Mary S., 78
    Thomas J., 78

GREENWOOD
    Grace, 74
    Margaret R., 74
    Peter F., 74
    William F., 74

GREULICH
    Barbara, 154
    Price, Pius, 154(2)

GRIFFITHS
    Thomas, 130

GRIMEIGER
    Catharina, 27

GROSS
    A. B., 97
    A. E., 97
    Catharine B., 7
    Claude M., 19
    Clayton O., 8
    Ellen A., 19
    Elmer M., 19
    Hannah A., 6
    Harry or Harvey, 97
    Henry O., 8
    Hiram, 54
    J. Franklin, 4
    J. Paul, 7
    John C., 4
    Kathryn U., 4
    Lydia K., 8
    Marion B., 8
    Mary, 54
    Robert D., 6
    Susan, 124

GROTH
    Harold & Nettie M., 55

GRUBB
    Earlene R., 89; El[?], 89
    Edward C., 89(2)
    Eva O., 146
    Kathlene L., 89
    Margaret F., 89
    Michael G., 89
    Rae Della H., 146
    Wayne, 146
    Wayne S., 146

GRUNNER
    Philip, 110

GRUVER
    Emma M., 134

GULICK, Elizabeth, 172
    Helen, 155
    Jonathan, 172(2)
    Merari, 155
    Sallie S., 155

GUM
    Olive B., 159
    William A., III, 159

GUTHERMAN
    George A., 88
    Jennie F., 88

H.
    D., 30
    E. C., 130
    H. L., 167
    I., 24, 49
    J. H., 130
    J. S., 79
    M., 57

HABORLE HABERLE
    see HEBERLE
    Charles B., 168(2)
    Harmon L., 168
    Martha H., 104
    Rebecca D., 168

HACKER
    Augustine, 98
    Caroline, 98
    Henrietta, 98

HACKMAN
    Abigail, 175
    Allen, 175
    Arthur M., 80
    Catherine, 80
    Isabella, 79
    James, 108
    John, 79
    Maggie D., 80
    Mary, 79(2)
    Mary Lucinda, 80

HACKMAN, continued:
    Samuel, 79(2)
    Valentine, 80

HAENN
    Eva, 74
    Frederick G., 74

HAFFEY
    Anne M., 89
    Francis P., 89

HAGEY
    E. C., 123
    Edward, 123, 124
    Elizabeth Gerhart, 42
    Howard, 124, 124
    Jacob, 42
    Maggie, 123, 124
    Stanley, 123

HAHN
    Anna, 151
    Father & Mother, 151

HAINES
    Agnes Y., 124
    C. Raymond, 124
    E. Amanda, 145
    George, 145
    John F., 49
    Lincoln P., 120
    Mary A., 120
    Matilda, 49
    Milton, 145(2)
    Norman, 124
    Norman K., 124
    Sarah, 145
    Warren, 120

HALBERT
    Annie, 131
    Harry C., 131

HALDEMAN
    Abel C., 151
    Abraham, 41
    Daniel A., 41
    Hiram A., 41
    Margaret, 153
    Margaret R., 151, 152
    William A., 41
    Winfield S., 41

HALEY
    William G., 84

HAMM
    Albert, 138(2)
    Emma, 137
    Frances, 136, 137
    Francis, 140
    James, 137
    James A., 136, 137, 140
    James P., 137
    Sarah J., 138
    William, 136
    William B., 136

HANDSCHIN
    see Hansdin
    Augusta, 153(2)
    Daniel, 153
    Daniel K., 152
    Elizabeth C., 152
    John, 152
    Margaret, 152
    Margaret C., 152
    Mary F., 152

HANDSDIN
    see Handschin
    Catharine A., 84
    Herbert, 84
    Marie, 84
    Samuel, 84

HANG
    Gertrude, 133

HANGEY, HANGY, HENGEY
    Allen H., 36
    Elizabeth, 36(4)
    Enos, 35, 36(3)
    Enos C., 36
    Enos L., 36
    Harvey H., 35
    Henry, 131
    Henry H., 131
    John A., 36
    Margaret S., 131
    William H., 36

HANM, HAUM
    Elizabeth, 117
    William, 117

HANSON
    Edward L., 155
    Sara C., 155

HARBER
    Irene L., 86
    Leonard J., 86

HARDING
    Elizabeth, 69
    William, 69

HARGRAVES
    Pearl M. Bilger, 128

HARR
    Charles E., 75
    George C., 73
    Ida, 75(2)
    J. Harry, 75(3)
    John, 75(2)
    Lizzie, 75
    Margaret, 75
    Margaret J., 75
    William M., 75

HARROW
    Alexander, 162
    Alexander W., 162
    Alice, 162
    Kathryn M., 162(2)

HARTMAN
    Anna M., 162
    Catharine, 133
    Henry, 107
    Martin, 162(2)
    Mathias, 133(2)
    Mighael, 107(2)
    Sarah, 107

HARTZEL, HARTZELL
    Abram L., 127
    Amanda S., 127
    Blanche E., 170
    Catharine A., 127
    Charles W., 147
    Christianna F., 151
    Elsie May, 135
    Francis D., 127
    Frank S., 134(2)
    Gertrude, 26
    Ira F., 151(2)
    Isabella J., 135(2)
    James M., 135(2)
    Jean F., 134
    Kate, 147
    Leidy S., 128
    Levi M., 151
    Margaret B., 134
    Oliver S., 147

HARWICK
    Amanda, 47
    Henry, 47
    Susan, 47

HATCOCK
    see Hitchcock

HATTON
    John J., 85
    Sophia, 85

HAUFMAN
    C., 43
    J., 43
    Johannes, 41(2)
    Susanna, 41(2)

HAUM, HANM
    Elizabeth, 117

HAUS
    Elizabeth, 118

HAYDEN
    Dorothy, 164
    Dorothy H., 164
    Julius A., 164

HAYES
    John M., 167
    John w., 167
    Lydia B., 167

HEACOCK
    Aaron, 21(2)
    Elizabeth, 21
    Lovina K., 20
    Richard, 70
    Sally, 70
    Tobias S., 22

HEARING
    Frank, 123
    Ida M., 120
    Mary, 123
    Milton O., 120

HEASTAND
    David, 98
    Eliz, 98
    see Histand

HEATON
    E., 58
    E. R., 58
    Edmund R., 58
    Jane F., 58
    Jennie, 57
    Jonathan, 59
    Malachi, 57(2)
    Mary, 57, 58
    Matilda, 57(2)
    Owen, 58(3)
    Peninnah, 58(2)
    Robert, 58
    Zilah, 70

HEBERLE
    see Haborle
    Herbert, 173
    Infant, 173
    Katherine F., 173

HECKLER
    Abraham S., 172
    C. Albert, 77
    Dillman H., 156(2)
    Elias E., 177
    Ester H., 140
    Eva H., 140
    Flora K., 156
    Florence, 77, 164
    Grace H., 140
    Hannah S., 172
    Herman K., 156
    Howard E., 150
    Irwin S., 77(2)
    Kate R., 140(3)
    Rebecca M., 177
    Samuel H., 140

HECKLER, continued:
    Sarah B., 77
    Stanley H., 140
    Stella F., 150
    Ward M., 140(3)

HEDRICK, HEDRICH
    Catharine Anna, 97
    Catherine S., 146
    Edwin, 164
    Edwin D., 164
    Edwin S., 164
    Elizabeth, 119
    Ella J., 143
    Elmer, 76
    Elmira, 95
    Florence, 146
    George, 142
    George L., 142
    George R., 142(3), 144
    Hannah, 98
    Harriet, 146
    Harvey, 76
    Henry F., 156
    Henry H., 142(2)
    Infant, 142
    Jacob, 95(4)
    John, 146(3)
    Josephine W., 76
    Lloyd, 149
    Lycurcus L., 76(3)
    Mary, Maria, 76, 95(3), 119
    Mary A., 97
    Mary E., 76
    Minerva, 156(2)
    Peter, 97(2), 98
    Peter D., 97, 119(2)
    Rosie M., 142(3)
    Sallie T., 164
    Samuel, 76
    Sarah, 76
    Sylvester S., 149(2)
    Wellington, 86
    William H., 76
    William Henry, 95
    William Raymond, 149
    Wilson L., 142

HEINLEY
    see Henley

HELERICH
    Lizzie, 18

HELLERMAN
    Ida A., 63

HELVESTON
    Charles H., 89
    Edna M., 89

HENDRICKS, HENDRICH
    Aaron F., 19
    Abraham 29, 37
    Abraham A., 16, 25
    Abraham S., 37, 38, 41(2)
    Abram H., 20(2)
    Amanda C., 146
    Anna, 45
    Barbara, 37
    Benjamin, 29(3)
    Benjamin D., 27, 45(2)
    Catharine, 37(3), 38
    Catharina A., 38
    Catharine D., 41
    Charles, 69
    Clarence, 20; Dorothy M., 55
    Eliza, 17
    Elizabeth, 27, 29(4), 39, 45
    Ella D., 20
    Ella G., 20
    Fanny T., 18
    H., 38
    Hannah, 45
    Henry R., 35
    J. A., 26(2)
    J. O., 33

HENDRICKS, continued:
    Jacob, 29(3), 45
    Jacob A., 45
    John, 45
    John F., 27
    Joseph, 18, 39
    Joseph H., 29
    Kate C., 13
    Kathryn L., 169
    Lydia, 25
    Magdalina, 35
    Maria, 29, 39, 45
    Martha, 20
    Mary, 26, 169
    Mary H., 35
    Mary L., 169
    Merrill L., 169; Paul C., 55
    R. G., 33
    Raymond A., 169
    Ruth S., 20
    Samuel, 20
    Samuel H. or R., 29
    Sarah, 29
    Sophia, 38
    Susanna, 39(2)
    William F., 29

HENLEY, HENLEY
    Catherine, 125
    Cornelius L., 125
    Isaac, 125
    Norman H., 125
    Sophia, 124
    Susan T., 125

HENNESSY
    Amelia A., 89
    Clifford J., 89
    Edward F., 89

HERING
    Catharine A., 149
    Christianna, 102
    Harrison, 102
    Philip, 149
    Philip S., 102, 149

HERTZLER
    Aldus, 7
    Infant, 7
    Ruth, 7

HESS, HESSE
    Anna, 48
    Christianna, 96
    Daniel, 96(2)
    Eliz, 96(2)
    George, 96
    Infant, 96
    John, 96

HEUSCHER
    Sara M., 21

HEVERLY
    Terence S., 88

HIEGER
    Josephine S., 86

HILDEBRANDT
    Albert, 51
    Annie, 51
    William B., 50

HILL
    John A., 50
    Martha R., 50

HILLWICK
    Anna, 99
    Frederick, 99, 101
    Sarah, 99

HINCKEL
    see Hinkle
    Eliza C., 131

HINCKEL, continued:
    Jonas H., 131(2)
    Jonas Harrison, 130

HINES
    Hervey, 67
    Isaac, 67(2)
    Margaret, 67
    Miller, 67

HINKLE, HINKEL, see Hinckel
    Anna Lapp, 77
    Chrissie W., 56
    Edward Thomas, 77
    Infant, 159
    John L., 162
    Jonas, 130; Joseph L., 56
    Lester 77
    Marian Kezia, 159
    Mary Elizabeth, 77
    May D., 162(2)
    Robert Lapp, 159(2)

HIGH
    see HOCK

HISTAND
    see Heastand
    Arlene A., 6
    Claude H., 6
    Ronald Eugene, 6

HITCHCOCK
    Lora, 155
    Lottie, 155
    Wilbur K., 155
    William, 155

HITTLE
    Catharine, 148
    Henry, 148
    Kathryn, 148
    Oscar C., 148

HOCK, HICG, HOCH, HOCHIN, HUCH
    Addison, 47
    Allen M., 14
    Anna, 24, 29, 30, 43(2)
    Barbara, 30(2)
    Carolinn, 40
    Catharina, 27
    Catharine W., 46
    David, 30
    David K., 49
    Elizabeth, 30, 47
    Elmer H., 8
    Henry, Henrich, 24(2)
    Henry Y., 15(2)
    Howard H., 15
    Infant, 14(2)
    Jacob, 27, 41, 43, 46
    Jacob H., 43(2)
    Johannes, 27, 30
    John, 40(2), 47
    Lizzie G., 8
    Maimie E., 15
    Maria, 36, 40
    Mary, 15
    Mary B., 15
    Mary H., 14
    Philip, 29(2), 36
    Sammuel, 47

HOBART
    Chester W., 88
    Josephine A., 88

HOCKMAN
    Alice S., 17
    Amanda M., 14
    Christian M., 14
    Elizabeth, 14(2)
    Ella Mae, 17(2)
    Elmer, 91
    Eva M., 91
    George L., 91
    Gertrude, 5(2)

HOCKMAN, continued:
    Harold, 5(2)
    Harvey K., 17(2)
    Infant, 5, 17
    John K., 14
    John Landis, 19(2)
    John M., 14(3)
    Jonas, 17
    Jonas G., 17
    Kevin M., 8
    Laverne W., 8
    Leidy K., 14
    Mame, 17(2)
    Mary, 19
    Mary F., 19
    Paul F., 19(2)
    Samuel F., 5
    Sara, 91
    William, 19(2)
    William K., 19

HOFF, HAUFF
    Alice S., 49
    Amanda, 48
    Clarence S., 48
    Fannie S., 48
    Henry, 48

HOFFMAN
    see Haufman
    Frederick C., 164
    Hannah, 95
    John, 95
    Lydia Ann, 95
    Rosann M., 164

HOFFORD
    John & Orpha B., 64

HOIROCKS
    Isabel L. & Warren E., 55(2)

HOLCINGER
    Anna Rechner, 83

HOLDCRAFT, HOLDCROFT
    Catherine V., 143
    Joseph, 143
    Joseph R., 143
    Virginia J., 143

HOLL
    Margaret, 158
    Paul, 158
    Paul E., 158
    Paul T., 158
    Senter, 164(2)

HOLZMANN
    Katharina, 133

HOLTZEL
    Catherine, 101
    Joseph, 101(2)

HUBER
    James P., 167

HUBLER
    Sophia, 118

HUNSBERGER, HUNSPERGIN
HUNSPERGERIN
    --------, 48
    A. E., 48
    Abraham, 42, 45, 49, 51, 75
    Abraham M., 40
    Abrm F., 42(2)
    Abrm, Abram K., 40, 45
    Alvah R., 50
    Anna, 25, 32, 39, 42(3), 178(4)
    Anna Ada, 178
    Anna Mary, 40
    Arlin, 6
    Barbara, 25(2), 38, 39, 40(3)
    Barbara M., 24
    Barbara W., 42
    Catharine, 25, 30, 49
    Catharine H., 42
    Catharine S., 42

HUNSBERGER, continued:
    Dorothy M., 21
    Earl H., 4
    Eliz, 45(2)
    Elizabeth, 36, 40(2), 51
    Elizabeth H., 45
    Ella Mabel, 178
    Elmer E., 39
    Enos, 40(3)
    Emma, 40
    Ervin, 178
    Estella M., 4
    Ester, 42
    H., Russel, 75
    Henry, Henery, 18, 32, 42
    Henry, bishop, 30
    Henry B., 25
    Henry L., 19, 91
    Henry M., 42
    Henry W., 49(2)
    Hilda A., 91
    Horace H., 5
    Howard M., 50
    Isaac, 25, 31
    Isaac F., 34
    Isaac S., 41
    Isaiah M., 41
    J. B., 48
    Jacob, 35, 38(2), 42(2), 43(2)
    Jacob A., 42
    Jacob R., 25
    John, 40(3), 41, 45
    John H., 31
    John M., 39(2)
    Jonas S., 21
    Joseph, 25(2), 178(3)
    Joseph B., 24
    Joseph M., 39
    Kathryn H., 21
    Katie, 25
    Lydia A., 39
    Magdalena, 30
    Mahlon M., 40
    Maria, 42, 43
    Martin, 42
    Mary, 35, 40(2), 75
    Mary Emma, 32
    Mary Jane, 40
    Mary M., 50, 79
    Milton M., 45
    Naomi, 6
    Rachel D., 5
    Remandes, 42
    Roger Lee, 6
    S. M., 48
    Samuel, 31
    Sarah, 45
    Simeon, 45(2), 46
    Sophia, 18
    Steven Ray, 6
    Susan, 36, 45
    Susana, 29
    Vera M., 50
    Veronica, 39
    William, 31

HUNSICKER, HÜNSICKER
    A. M., 12(2)
    Abraham, Abram, 25, 26(5)
    Allen, 33
    Alvin M., 17
    Anna, 12, 49
    Barbara, 33
    Betty, 49
    Catharine, 25, 26, 30
    Della M., 17
    Elizabeth, 34
    Harry, 79
    Harry C., 170
    Henry, 30
    Infant, 26(2)
    Isaac, 33(5), 34, 49
    Isaac M., 17, 79
    Jacob, 33(2), 34, 49
    Jacob O., 26
    John S., 79
    Lea, 39
    Leanna, 39

HUNSICKER, continued:
    Leidy D., 17
    Lydia, 34, 39
    Maria, 49
    Martha B., 170
    Mary D., 17
    Paul, 164
    Sallie, 49
    Sarah, 33
    Sarah C., 33
    Sarah L., 33
    Susanna, 33
    Wilson, 33

HUSTON
    Dora, 156
    George, 156

J.
    A., 118
    E., 118

JACOBY
    Babe Hobuck, 113
    Benjamin, 113
    Catharine, 112
    Conrad, 112
    Elizabeth, 113
    Hannah, 112, 117
    Leonard, 117
    Philip, 112(2)
    Sarah Ann, 113

JAMES
    Abel N., 58
    Ann?, 60
    Catherine, 58
    Gainor, 67
    John, 67
    Owen, 58

JAVORKA
    Eliz, 83
    Paul, 83

JAWORSKI
    Anastasia, 88
    John F., 88

JENKINS
    --------, 118
    Amanda, 118
    Anna, 118
    Anna C., 118
    Catharine Hungan, 144
    Charles, 143
    Peter, 144
    William S., 118(2)

JOHNSON
    Abraham, 43
    Brend Joan, 163
    E. Martha S., 142
    Edwin T., Dr. 142
    Elizabeth, 163
    Harry Andrew, 130
    Heinrich, 43
    Jane, 163
    John, 163(2)
    L. H., 129(2)
    Levi, 130
    Max, 65
    Raymond F., 163(2)
    Raymond S., 142
    Salome, 43
    Susanna, 129, 130

JONCZYK
    Mary E., 84
    Stanley, 84
    Stanley P., 84

JONES
    Aaron, 58(2)
    Abel, 64(2), 68(3)
    Alice, 64
    Amos, 61(3)
    Andrew J., 68

JONES, continued:
   Ashbel, 62
   Clarence, 63
   Catharine, 64
   David, 68
   Edward, 58, 68(2)
   Eliza, 68
   Elizabeth, 64(2)
   Frances, 61(2)
   Griffith, 64
   Frances, 61(2)
   Griffith, 64
   Ha[?]y, 61
   James, 61(4), 63
   Jane, 61
   John, 68
   John J., 62
   John M., 64
   Jonathan, 61
   Joseph, 64
   Margaret, 58
   Margaret B., 61
   Mary, 61(2), 64, 68
   Rachel, 61, 68(3)
   Rebecca, 68(2)
   Sallie S., 63
   Sarah, 58
   Susana, Susannah, 61, 62
   Theodore, 63(2)
   Thomas, 61(5), 62
   William, 61

JORDAN
   Mildred I., 89
   Steven Michael, 53

JUDD
   Virginia J. Holdvraft, 143

JURIN
   Anna S., 86
   Edward A., 86
   Ivan G., 86

K.
   B., 39
   C., 99
   C. A., 99
   H., 115
   I., 29
   I. H. - Froenik, 27
   J. M., 63
   M., 40
   M. A., 99
   P., 41
   T., 118(3)

KAHLE
   Margaret M., 84
   William F., Sr., 84

KALMAR
   Antal, 89

KARCZMAR
   John R., 160
   Margaret E., 160

KAUFFMAN
   Harrie A., 170(2)
   Martha, 170

KAUNAS
   Edmund, 87
   Mary, 87

KAUP
   Hanna, 118
   Jacob, 118

KAUTZ
   Estella L., 171

KAZLER
   Anna K., 83
   Peter, 83

KECK
   Grace C., 162
   John, 162
   John C., 162

KEELER
   Catharine, 27
   Elizabeth, 27
   Elizabeth J., 25
   Henry, 167
   Martin, 27
   Mary C., 27
   Mary D., 167
   Susan, 27
   William H., 25

KEELY
   Infant, 171
   John L., 171
   Mina K., 171(3)
   William P., 171(3)

KEIL
   Lucinda, 119
   Zeno S., 119

KELL
   Charles, 99
   Lydia K., 99

KELLER
   Abraham, 72
   Anita L., 124
   Anna M., 134
   Bertha C., 152
   Catharine Elizabeth, 99
   Charles, 99(2)
   Charles E., 86
   Ellen B., 125
   Elizabeth, 110
   Frank, 44
   Hannah, 125
   Henry, 111
   Levi B., 125
   Lydia, 99(2)
   Magdalena, 110, 111
   Maria, 110
   Maria G., 44
   Mary Amanda, 99
   Oliver, 125, 135
   Oliver S., 125
   Sallie, 72
   Samuel, 110
   Sarah, 148
   Stephen, 148
   William H., 152

KELLY, KELLEY
   -------y., 60
   Amos, 60
   Amos J., 60(2)
   Charles P., 123
   Christian Kneass, 60
   Eleanor, 60
   Erasmus, 60(9)
   Erasmus D., 60
   Hannah, 60
   Hannah Ann, 60
   Jane, 60 (3)
   Jane J., 60
   Janira, 60
   John, 60
   John E., 93
   Lavina H., Lovina H., 93, 123
   Lydia A., 60(2)
   Lydia May, 60
   Rachel, 60
   Thomas, 60

KEMMER
   Ray Ronald, 53

KENDRA
   Anna, 130
   Ray, 130

KENEDY
   James, 59
   Rachel, 59

KERBER
   Gertrude C., 157
   William, 157
   William J., Jr., 157

KERN
   see Kerns
   Agnes, 105
   Anna, 142
   C., 105(4)
   Casper, 103
   Catharine, 102, 105(4)
   Christian, 102
   Clarence L., 142
   Flora, 105
   Harrison Y., 142(4)
   Hiram, 105
   Hiram E., 75
   Howard E., 142
   Howard Wilmer, 102
   Infant, 102
   Jacob, 75(2)
   John, 102
   Louise E., 142
   Lydia Davis, 102(2)
   Norman E., 142
   Priscilla, 105
   Susannah Hill, 75

KERNER
   Phoebe I, 55

KERNS
   Allen P., 136
   Casper & Catharine E., 103(2)
   Eliza G., 136
   Elizabeth Proctor, 134
   Emanuel, 149
   Emma C., 118
   John, 110(2)
   Mary, 110
   Thomas C., 134
   William, 134

KERR
   Rachel L., 168
   Wilmer L., 168

KIESTER
   Carl A., 89
   see Kister and Kuster

KILE
   see Keil
   Anna R., 157
   Arthur Francis, 131
   Catherine Heller, 131 (2)
   Edith I., 158
   Elizabeth K., 157
   Emaline, 97(2)
   Ernest A., 157
   Francis, 131(3), 157
   Francis B., 157
   Hamilton M., 131
   Harry L., 158
   Harvey, 158
   Henry, 97
   Henry H., 157
   Infant, 97(2)
   Irma M., 157
   Margaret H., 158(2)
   Raymond T., 158
   Sallie, 157
   Sarah M., 157

KINDIG
   John, 147
   Orvilla, 147

KING
   Albert R., 144
   Catharine, 131(2)
   Cathrina, 113
   Charles, 144, 146
   Charles E., 131
   Charles H., 144
   Charles S., 144
   Content, 22
   Ella S., 151(2)

KING, continued:
    Fredrick W., 151
    George, 98
    Helen Myrtle, 132
    Mary, 98
    Mary M., 144
    Rosie, 144
    Samuel, 22

KISSEL
    Max C., 161

KISTER
    see Kiester, Kuster
    George, 126
    Vestilla D., 126

KLEIN
    see Kline

KLETZING
    Amanda, 115
    Catharine, 115(2)
    Charles, 115(2), 137
    Charles S., 137
    Cora P., 176
    Ferdinand, 176(2)
    Frederick, 176
    Jeremiah, 115
    Katie, 176
    Magdalen, 176
    Samuel, 137
    Sarah E., 137

KLINE, KLEIN
    Anna, 116
    Caroline, 49
    Carrie, 141(2)
    Catrina, 108
    Charles A., 75
    Clinton, 91
    David, 102
    Elizabeth, 178
    Emma J., 75
    Florence M., 75
    Erwin B., 159
    Gladys B., 127
    Henrich, 110
    Henry A., 95
    Herbert S., 159
    Herman, 49
    Infant, 141
    Ira, 95
    James M., 129
    Jesse, 116
    Johanny, 110
    John, 107, 108(3), 110(2)
    John F., 75
    Lucy Ann, 95(2). 96
    Lydia, 75
    Mamie, 91
    Margaret S., 159
    Mary, 108(2), 110
    Mary Elizabeth, 116
    Merton E., 159(2)
    Oliver, 108
    Peter, 141, 2
    Peter A., 141(2)
    Rachel, 102
    Sallie B., 159
    Sarah E., 129
    Simon P., 95(2), 96
    Wilmer, 127
    Wilmer Z., 127

KLING
    Frank, 159
    Gladys, 159

KLINK
    Anna, 133
    Gottlob, 133

KLOPFER, KLOEPFER
    Adam, 157
    Anna, 99
    Charles, 157
    Frank, 157(2)

KLOPFER, continued
    George, 99(7)
    Henry, 99
    Magdalena, 99(5)
    Philip, 99
    Samual, 99

KNAELY
    Amanda, 96
    Catherine, 96(2)
    Franklin, 96
    John, 96(2)

KNAPP
    infant, 53
    Ken, 159
    Ruth, 159

KNECHEL, KNECHTLE, NICKLE
    Annie, 144
    John, 144
    Leidy S., 129
    Mary W., 129

KNEULE
    Catharine A. Rohr, 104
    John, 104(2)

KNIPE
    Allen, 149(2)
    Elmer K., 154(2)
    Emma, 164
    Emma G., 130
    George, 130
    George C., 130
    Gladys M., 130
    Kate, 149
    Lloyd H., 149

KNOLL
    Frederick, 144
    Hannah, 144
    Lewis, 144

KOBER, KOVER
    Catharina, 109
    Clara May, 123
    Elizabeth C. 94
    J. Penrose, 123
    John C., 123(2)
    John M., 94(3)
    Lavinia R., 123(2)
    Mary, 94(2)
    Mary C., 123
    Paul, 161
    Philip, 109
    Sarah C., 94
    William R., 123

KOCH
    Balzathers M., 35
    Balzer, 35
    Barbara S., 35(2)
    Caroline, 80
    Elizabeth, 125
    Henry H., 39
    Laura Etta, 80
    Lewis, 80
    William, 35

KOEHLER
    William, 154

KOEING
    Benjamin, 105
    Margaret, 105

KOHL, KOL
    ------, 177
    John, 118

KOLLO
    Elizabeth, 123
    John, 123

KONSOWITZ
    Stephen J., 84

KOOKER
    Catharine, 24
    Jacob, 24
    Jacob B., 24

KOONS
    Harry, 163
    Harry M., 163
    Mary Grass, 163

KORMANSKI
    Marie C., 89

KOSOW
    Augusta Handchin, 153

KOVER
    see Kober

KOWALCZUK
    John, 87
    Mary, 87

KRABEHL, see Kriebel
    Catharine, 48(2)
    Hannah, 48
    Henry, 48
    John, 48
    Margaret, 48
    Mary, 48
    Philip, 48(2)

KRAINIAK
    Michael, 91

KRAFT
    Eliz, 105(2)
    Jacob, 105(2)
    Lizzie, 105

KRAMER, KREMER
    A. CLarence, 160(2)
    Aaron, 127(2)
    Abraham, 57(2)
    Anna, 141
    Anna Laura, 127
    Anna Maria, 98
    Blanche, 77
    Clinton G., 140(2)
    Edna M., 160
    Elizabeth, 57
    Elizabeth B., 127
    Ellen S., 145(2)
    Enos, 95(2)
    Gertrude, 86
    Hannah, 95, 127
    Harvey H., 127(2)
    Henry, 22
    Henry C., 145(2)
    Irwin B., 145
    Israel G., 125(2)
    Jemima F., 160
    John, 86
    Joseph Howard, 127
    Leidy S., 160
    Mabel M., 158
    Margaret, 158
    Mary Ellen, 127
    Mathias W., 98
    Matilda W., 125
    Oscar H., 140
    Paul K., 165
    Ronald Lee, 160
    Sallie W., 125
    Warren S., 158
    William M., 77

KRATZ, KRAZ
    A., 27
    Abraham, 13, 33
    Abraham D., 13
    Abraham Linford, 12
    Abraham O., 13
    Albert P., 171(3)
    Amanda, 27
    Anna, 33
    Anna Laura, 5
    Anna S., 154

KRATZ, continued:
    Arthur W., 131
    B., 39
    Barbara, 22
    Catherine, -arine, 43, 133
    Clayton H., 18
    Elizabeth, 18(2), 33
    Elizabeth H., 33
    Emely E., 64
    Emma E., 50
    Enos, 25
    Enos M., 25(2)
    Gerald D., 4
    Gloria J., Ott, 153
    Hannah, 25
    Hannah G., 25
    Harold S., 154
    Harvey G., 154(2)
    Henry, 27
    Henry M., 4
    Hilda S., 4(2)
    Isaac B., 102
    Isaiah, 37
    J. M., 63
    James M., 63
    Jacob, 22, 39
    Jacob Harold, 171
    John L., 27
    Joseph J., 64
    K., 50(3)
    Katy, 25
    Lamar R., 153
    Lizzie, 25
    Luther B., 171
    Lydia E., 13
    M. Emma, 4
    Malinda B., 171(3)
    Maria, 39
    Martha I., 64(4)
    Mary Ann, 50
    Menan, 133
    Oliver B., 5
    Pearl, 171
    Rowland W., 163(2)
    S., 39, 50(3)
    Sarah, 13, 50(2)
    Sarah A., 102
    Sarah Ann, 13
    Sarah K., 163
    Simeon, 43(2)
    Sophia L., 4
    Susanna, 49
    T., 50
    V., 39
    Valentine, 33(2), 50(2)
    W. A., 50
    Walter, 4
    Walter M., 4
    William, 39
    William H., 18, 63, 64(5)
    William M., 18(2)
    William P., 39

KRIEBEL, see Krabehl
    Edna & Edwin N., 126(2)

KREISHER
    Arthur W. & Edith E., 55(2)

KRONER
    E., 177(2)
    L., 117
    Samuel, 117

KRONMAIER
    Henry, 21
    Ida, 21

KROUT
    Adaline S., 140
    Amos K., 140
    Barbara, 44
    Elizabeth, 117
    Francis D., 140
    Henry, 142(2)
    Issac, 140(2)
    Joseph, 146
    Leanna M.,1 40
    Levi, 142

KROUT, continued:
    Levi D., 142
    Lydia, 142
    Mary E., 142
    May, 142
    Philip, 117
    Rosalinda, 142
    Samuel K., 142
    Susan, 32

KRUK
    James L., 88

KRUPP
    Gerald M., 15
    Harold M., 15
    Harvey H., 15
    Kenneth M., 15
    Mabel B., 15

KUCIKAS
    Edward R., 85
    Joseph J., 85
    Petronella, 85

KUHN
    James, 91

KULP, KOLB
    -------, 159
    Aaron, 38
    Abraham K., 15
    Anna, 36
    Annie, 36
    Barbara, 36
    Catharina, -ine, 23(2), 37
    Catharine B., 23
    Christian, 43
    Clifford T., 91
    Elizabeth, 37, 42
    Elizabeth A., 38
    Elizabeth H., 37
    Elizabeth R., 12
    Ella L., 15
    Enos, 43
    Fannie, 38(3)
    Franica, 36; Harold, 56
    Helen Lorraine, 3
    Henry, Heinrich, 36, 38(4)
    Henry L., 37(2)
    Henry M., 38, 43(2)
    Ida, 91
    Isaac, 36, 42(3)
    Isaac H., 33
    J., Harvey, 15
    Jacob, 31, 36
    Jacob K., 15
    John, 23, 38
    John H., 23(2)
    John K., 17
    John M., 14
    Joseph, 37(2)
    Joseph A., 91
    Joseph F., 15; Laura, 56
    Leroy A., 153
    Lizzie, 3
    Lloyd D., 17
    Maria, 23, 31, 36, 42(2)
    Mary, 38
    Mary Ann, 43
    Mary K., 33
    Moses, 31(2), 38
    Philip S., 26
    Sarah A., 15
    Sarah J., 14
    Sarah S., 153
    Sherry Lynn, 8
    Sophia D., 26
    Susanna, 38
    Warren, 3
    Willis F., 15

KUMMERLE
    Christian, 132(2)
    Helen, 132

KUNFARDIN
    Elizabeth, 24

KUNZ
    Anna M., 76

KURIAN
    Anna M., 86
    Frank G., 86

KUSTER
    see Kiester, Kister
    Casper, 131(2)
    Charles, 131
    Sarah, 131

KUTLER
    Loretta, 84

L.
    B., 48
    E., 33
    H., 45, 120(2)

LABOE
    Russel, 106

LACKNER
    Alexander, 160
    Carolina, 160
    Henry, 160

LAKE
    Azariah M., Capt., 61(2)
    George W. III,55; Jane, 61

LANDER
    Samuel Henry, 173

LANDIS, LANDES
    B., 48
    E., 33
    H., 45
    J., 171
    Abraham, 41
    Abraham L., 20
    Abram B., 20
    Albert, 167, 168
    Albert Y., 167
    Alice F., 6
    Allen, 24
    Alma, 54
    Alvin M., 7
    Anna, 49
    Anna L., 54
    Annie, 138
    Annie S., 168
    Barbara, 46
    Barbara C., 15
    Bertha H., 15
    Bertha L., 169
    Blanche A., 53
    Cassandra D., 168
    Catharine, 38(3)
    Clara K., 164
    Clara U., 162
    D. M., Dr., 19(2), 31
    Daniel M., Dr., 19
    Daniel O., 21
    Deborah, 19
    Deborah A., 22
    Edward M., 41
    Elizabeth, 3, 19, 117
    Elizabeth M., 41
    Elizabeth S., 136
    Ella Viola, 117
    Ellis, 54
    Elmer L., 169
    Elmer S., 169
    Emma D., 169(6)
    Emma L., 169
    Ephraim, 38(4)
    Ephraim M., 5
    Estella B., 7
    Esther Ann, 14
    Ethan, 173
    Eva G., 15(2)
    Franklin Pierce, 117
    G. Wesley, 162
    Grace, 161

LANDIS, LANDES, continued:
  George M., 22(2)
  George R., 15
  Hannah B., 51
  Hannah M., 15
  Harry T., 53
  Henry, 38
  Henry L., 167
  Henry M., 3(2)
  Henry S., 161
  Horace, 161
  Howard F., 169
  Howard M., 6
  Ida, 22
  Infant, 11(2), 12(2), 169
  Isaiah, 168(2)
  Jacob, 24, 46
  Jacob R., 14
  Jacob S., 46
  John, 168(2)
  John H., 168
  John K., 169(7)
  John L., 169
  John M., 15
  John R., 22(2), 38
  John T., 51
  Joseph A., 171
  Joseph D., 168
  Joseph K., 138(3)
  Joycelyn, 31
  Kathryn, 168
  Kathryn M., 169
  Katie, 168(2)
  Levina, Lavina, 24(2)
  Lizzie, 3, 31
  Lizzie F., 152
  Lizzie M., 11
  Lydia L., 138
  Mahlon L., 152(2)
  Mame, 161
  Mamie B., 5
  Maria, 22
  Martha Angelmoyer, 169
  Mary, 22, 24(2)
  Mary A., 169
  Mary Ann, 22(2)
  Mary C., 3
  Mary D., 167
  Orpha M., 168
  Paul C., 152
  Paul L., 169
  Paul S., 168
  Permelia, 117
  Rachel, 161, 169
  Rachel R., 169
  Rebecca, 168(3)
  Reed F., 167
  Reuben, 12(3)
  Reuben M., 11, 12
  Reuben R., 11
  Rufus, 168
  Samuel, 22, 164
  Samuel B., 22(2)
  Samuel H., 22
  Samuel L., 22
  Samuel M., 15(2)
  Sarah D., 168
  Sarah M., 21
  Scott K., 152
  Simeon, 24(2)
  Simeon C., 24(2)
  Thomas, 136
  Thomas Y., 136
  Wesley, 162
  Wesley M., 54
  William, 22
  William Michael, 136

LAPP
  Amanda M., 20
  Anna, 65, 77
  Deborah, 65; Edith M., 56
  Emma, 65; Howard S., 56
  Ida, 65
  Ida May, 154
  Nelson S., 154(2)

LAPP, continued:
  Mabel W., 91
  Myrtle S., 157
  Stanley W., 91
  Walter S., 157
  William L., 20

LARGE
  David L., 106
  Walter, 106

LEATHERMAN
  Abner L., 168
  Abraham, 142
  Abraham L., 142
  Clara W., 91
  Ellen M., 6
  Harold S., 159(2)
  Jacob S., 3
  John S., 6
  Laura F., 142
  Margaret S., 159
  Russell, 159
  Sallie G., 3
  Walter H., 91

LECHER, LEAPER
  Mary, 154
  Sebastian, 154

LEDERACH
  Edward G., 53
  Maria, 53

LEHMAN
  Kimberly Ann, 172
  Lous Anna, 172

LEIDY, LEYDE
  Amelia, 108
  Anna Barbara, 107
  Anna Maria, 138
  Catharine, 114
  Elias, 107, 108
  Elizabeth, 107(2), 125
  Francis D., 107(2)
  George, 107(2)
  H. Franklin, 125
  Henry, Henrich, 107(4)
  Jacob, 108(6), 114(2), 117
  Joel R., 138(2)
  John, 107, 117, 137(3)
  Jonas, 125(2)
  Levi, Levy, 108, 111(2)
  Lydia, 107, 108(2), 137
  Lydia A., 125
  Maria, 111
  Mary, 107(2), 117
  Mary Ann, 117
  Oliver, 117
  Samuel, 108
  Samuel C., 125
  Sarah, 107
  Sarah Ann, 125(2)
  Thomas E., 107

LEISTER
  ------, 107
  Allen T., 128
  Ann Elizabeth, 117
  Elizabeth, 108(2)
  Emma M., 130
  Jacob, 108(2)
  Jacob Y., 147(2)
  John S., 130(3)
  Lydia, 108(2), 147
  Maria, 108
  Maria A., 117
  Mary E., 130(2)
  Michael, 117(2)
  Noah, 108
  Peter, 108
  Sallie, 128
  Salome, 168
  Samuel, 117
  Samuel S., 128

LEISTER, continued:
  Thomas, 108(2)

LENGEL
  Adam, 139, 158
  Adam H., 137, 158(4)
  E. Naomi Dewey, 158
  Grace W., 137
  Isaac M., 25
  Margaret A., 159
  Mary A., 25, 158
  Mary Elizabeth, 158
  Maude D., 158
  Melvin Dewey, 158
  Melvin H., 159(2)
  Naomi, 158(3)
  Ralph, 137
  S. Ralph, 137
  Samuel R., 25, 137, 158

LEO
  Theresa Jo, 88

LESH
  Elizabeth, 86
  Elizabeth M., 86
  Frank P., 86; Theresa, 84

LEUZ
  Christopher, 55
  Ella E., 55
  Laura E., 65

LEVERS
  Clara, 177
  George, 177(3)
  George W., 177
  Harold, 177
  Kate, 177(2)
  Laura, 177
  Mahlon, 177
  Minerva, 177
  William A., 177

LEWIS
  Anna C., 76(2)
  Anna Eckhart, 75
  Caroline, 68(2), 76(2)
  Carrie, 76
  Elizabeth, 68, 77
  Elizabeth A., 75
  Emma, 65
  Frank, 160
  Gertrude E., 76
  Hannah, 76
  Harvey W., 77(2)
  Henry, 68(5)
  Isaac, 68, 75(2)
  James, 68
  John, 68
  John E., 76
  Leidy, 154
  Leidy H., 154
  Lizzie, 77(2)
  Lot, 76
  M., 65
  Magdalena B., 77
  Margaret, 65, 68(4)
  Margaret R., 76
  Mary, 68(3), 75
  Mary E., 75
  Mary S., 154
  Minerva H., 77
  Morris A., 76
  Morris P., 76(4)
  Nancy, 68
  Rachel, 68
  T., Dr., 65(2)
  Thomas Jefferson, 76(3), 68(2)
  Thomas W., 75
  Uriah, 75(3)
  Uriah D., 68
  Viola A., 6
  William, 68, 72(2), 157
  William H., 6, 77(2)
  William Henry, 68
  Zillah, 72

LEY
    Tobias, 100

LICEY, LEICY, LEISE, LEICE
    Abraham, 22(2)
    Anna, 22
    Anna B., 33
    Christian, 33
    E., 33
    Emma M., 134
    Enos H., 134
    Henry, 33, 48

LIGHT
    Carl S., 173
    Lucy K., 173

LINDAMAN
    Mary & Rev. J.O., 126

LOCKE
    Anna T., 55
    Howard F., Sr., 124
    Paul G., 55

LOFT, LUFT
    Catharina L., 119
    Isaac, 119(2)
    Matilda, 120

LONG
    Catharine, 134
    Charles, 172
    David C., 23
    Harry S., 86
    Katie, 172
    Leroy, 172
    Sarah, 23
    Sophia B., 86

LORIS
    Florence R., 85
    Frank N., 85
    Joseph, 85
    Katie, 85
    Margaret, 85

LOUX
    -------, 35
    Abraham F., 44
    Agnes, 35
    Alfred H., 44
    Anna, 35(4)
    Annie, 20
    C. S., 113
    Catharine B., 35(2)
    Christian, 113
    Claray, 20
    Eliza H., 29
    Emmeline, Emaline, 20(3)
    Enos B., 34, 35(7)
    H. Monroe, 56
    Hannah, 117; Henry E., 44
    Howard Pearson, 56(2)
    Isaac, 40; J., 40
    John A., 117
    Jacob, 40(3)
    Jacob B., 20(3)
    Katharine A., 80
    Leah Y., 35
    Levi, 44
    Levi Y., 35
    Magdalena, 113
    Mahlon B., 80
    Maria, 40
    Marietta Y., 35
    Martin, 35
    Oliver S., 44
    Paul H., 35
    Peter, 35
    Peter B., bishop, 29(2)
    R., 40(2)
    Rachael, 40(2)
    Samuel, 40
    Samuel F., 40
    Siles, 35
    Susanna, 34
    William M., 44

LUCAS
    Clinton H., 77

LUECKE
    Charles H., 83
    Elizabeth, 83
    Jennie Davern, 83

LUFT
    see Loft

LUKENS
    Clara H., 153
    H. Elmer, Sr., 153

LUKESCH
    Apolonie, 83
    Edward, 83
    Frank, 83
    Rose, 83

LUNN
    Alice, 61
    Amy, 61(2)
    Elisha, 61(2)
    Eury, 61
    Leah, 61
    Lewis, 61
    Joseph, 61
    Josiah, 61
    Sidney, 61
    Zillah, 61

LUTKAVAGE
    Joseph A., 88
    Stella, 88

LUTZ
    Carolina, 22
    John K., 22

Mc CARTHY
    Joseph G., 85
    Margaret J., 85
    Richard F., Jr., 85

McCAUSLAND
    William V., 89

McCRORY
    John, 80

McCURLEY
    Lansing C., 84

McGARTH
    Emma M., 89
    Louis J., Jr., 89

McINTYRE
    Catherine, 80
    Catrina, 80
    James, 80

McKENZIE
    John D., 56

McKNIGHT
    John H., 85

McLAUGHLIN
    Rev. & Tacy 65(2)
M.
    B., 33
    C., 27
    C. A., 33
    D., 28
    E., 27
    E. M., 41
    I. H., 19
    J., 33
    J. K., 24
    M., 28, 69
    S., 27

MACK
    Anne, 164
    John, 164

MAGARGAL
    Laura, 75
    Laura L., 75
    Lovinia, 176
    Samuel H., 75
    Sheldon G., 75

MAGEE
    Mary J., 152

MALACH
    Frank A., 88

MALLIS
    Joseph, 163(2)
    Marie, 163

MANNINO
    Cathrine Marie, 88

MARKERT
    Otto A., 162(2)
    Richard, 162
    Wilhelmina, 162

MARSHALL
    Anna T., 167
    Harry, Jr., 167

MARTIN
    ----, 114
    Abigail R., 132
    Adam, 102, 132
    Amanda, 103
    Anna F., 103
    Edward, 132
    Elizabeth Snyder, 112
    George, 102(3)
    Infant, 102
    Magail, 102
    Ronald, 91
    Ruth, 91
    Theresa, 102(2)
    Verna E. Stover, 16
    Walter S., 132

MARTS
    Catrina, 51
    Margaret, 51
    Nicholas, 51

MATHIAS
    Abel, 70, 72(2)
    Alice, 67(2)
    Amanda Malvina, 73
    Amos G., M.D., 67
    Ann, 68(2), 73
    Anna, 67, 68, 70(2)
    Ashbel, 67, 70
    Benjamin, 73
    Benjamin, Jr., 69
    Charles, 67
    Dinah, 73(4)
    Eleanor, 68
    Elizabeth, 67, 68
    Ella, 73
    Ellen, 73
    Emily R., 73
    Enoch, 67
    Fanny, 73
    Infant, 73
    J., 67
    Jane, 72
    Jane Mason, 72
    Jared M., 70
    John, 67, 68(4), 72, 87
    John H., 72(2)
    John N., 73(8)
    Joseph, 73(4)
    Joseph, Rev., 73(3)
    Lydianna, 73
    M. Ida, 73
    Maria, 68
    Margaret, 67
    Maria, 87
    Mary, 67
    Morgan, 67
    Peninah, 67

MATHIAS, continued:
    Rachel M., 73
    Rowland, 67(3)
    Sarah, 72
    Thomas, 67(2), 68, 70(2)
    Thomas, M.D., 73
    Thomas, Jr., 67
    Thomas, Sr., 68

MATTERN
    -------, 165
    Joseph M., 158
    Paul, 158

MATTSON
    Anna M., 87
    Nicholas J., 87
    Walter, Jr., 87

MAUGER
    Frank J., 86
    Gertrude, 86

MAURER, MAUERER
    ELizabeth, 139
    Emma H., 139
    Eva Pearl, 139
    Frank P., 139
    Henry, 139, 140
    Johann, 100
    John, 99

MAY
    Margaret, 84
    Samuel J., 84

MAYER
    see Moyer

ME[?]AROR
    see Morhin

MEANS
    Levi, 59
    Wilhelmina, 59

MELLOR
    John W., 74
    Marion, 74
    Ralston, 162

MERRILLS
    Boah Lee, 91

MICH
    David Leo, 86
    Isabella, 86
    Kenneth, 86

MICHELS
    Hilda D., 157
    Martha A., 157
    Nicholas A., 157

MIKETTA
    Ignatius, 88
    Northburga, 88

MILDER
    Samuel A., 124

MILL
    William, 100

MILLER
    -------, 63
    Ammanda Elizabeth, 99
    Anna Laurea, 99
    Benjamin W., 7
    Catharina, -arine, -erine,
        98, 99(4), 149
    Donna K., 7
    Elimy M., 149
    Elizabeth, 109
    Ephraim F., 98(2)
    Fietta, 97
    George, 102(2)

MILLER, continued:
    Grace, 99
    Henry A., 161
    Henry L., 63
    Herbert M., 154
    Ida L., 161
    Isaac, 69
    James H., 63
    James S., 171
    Jennie Eva, 99
    Johannes, 115
    John Henry, 98
    Josiah A., 109
    Katie G., 171
    Lydia A. J., 63
    Manrow, 115
    Margaret, 97, 109
    Mary T., 154
    Noah, 99(4), 115, 149(2)
    Noah F., 149
    Noah S., 149
    Olga, 53
    Philip, 63
    Sam, 103
    Sarah C., 115
    Serbia, 102
    Tobias, 115(3)
    Walter L., 53
    Washington, 63

MITNIK
    Blanche C., 88
    Charles J., 88
    Catherine, 87
    David E., 88
    Mary, 87

MOFFETT
    Florence, 77
    Joseph, 77

MOHN
    Albert W., 91(2)
    Kenneth W., 91
    Mella S., 91

MOLL
    Alice, 28
    Alice M., 148
    Charles W., 171
    Emma L., 171
    Emma W., 171
    Frank, 148
    Frank C., 148
    Frank, Jr., 148
    George, 159, 160
    George A., 134
    George E., 160
    Ida L., 171
    Infant, 28
    Irene R., 160
    James, 28
    James D., 30
    John Henry, 175
    Lizzie, 28
    Lizzie C., Moyer, 30
    Mamie E., 158
    Martha, 134
    Mary Ann, 175(2)
    Mary Elmira, 175
    Mary Matilda, 158
    Michael, 175(2)
    Oswin D., 171
    Oswin R., 171
    Raymond L., 171
    William C., 171
    William H., 158(2)

MOOD
    Enos F., 11
    Sarah M., 11

MOORE
    Clarence H., 161(2)
    Grace L., 161
    Harriet L., 165
    Harry, 165

MOORE, continued:
    Henry H., 7
    Mary Ellen, 7
    Mary S., 7
    William H., Jr., 132

MOOREHEAR
    Adelaide M., 56

MORHIN
    Elizabeth & George, 114(2)

MORGAN
    Allen D., 80
    David D., 80
    George, 75
    Maggie, 75
    Samuel G., 75
    Terressia, 80

MORRIS
    -------, 69
    Abner, 69
    Allison M., 75
    Arthur S., 75
    Barbara, 44
    Benjamin, 72(2)
    Burgiss A., 69(2)
    Catharine, 72
    Charles M., 75
    Eliza, 69
    Elizabeth, 69
    Gwentley Thomis, 69
    Hannah, 69
    Isaac, 69(2)
    John, 72
    John D., 69, 75
    Julia F., 75
    Justus, 69
    Mary, 69, 72
    Mathias, 69
    Mathias, Esq., 69
    Morris, 69(2)
    Oliver, 69
    Oliver G., 69
    Rachel, 69
    Samuel T., 44
    Sarah, 70
    Seneca C., 70
    Susanna S., 75
    Wilhemina, 69
    William, 69
    William I., 69
    William Thomas, Rev., 69

MOSER
    Arvilla H., 96
    Clara M., 160
    William, 160
    William C., 160

MOYER, MEYER, MEYERN, MEIER
MAYER, MIRER, MOYERIN
    A. M., 17
    Aaron S., 8
    Abraham, 30(3), 31(2),
        32(2), 172
    Abraham A., 18
    Abraham C., 17, 23, 20(3),
        44
    Abraham Elmer, 28
    Abraham F., Rev., 31(2)
    Abraham H., 39
    Abraham L., 31
    Abram B., 14
    Abram C., 31
    Abram M., 16(2), 17
    Abram R., 4
    Ada, 49
    Addison, 11
    Alda M., 31
    Allen, 161(2)
    Allen M., 161
    Alice A., 13
    Alice K., 7
    Allen K., 31
    Allen M., 17
    Alma F., 20(2)

MOYER, continued:
  Andrew, 22
  Ann, 98
  Anna, 23(2), 31(4)
  Anna D., 31
  Anna Martha, 19
  Anna Mary, 35
  Anna May, 19
  Anna Y., 22
  Annie, 44
  Annie B., 19
  Annie S., 3
  Annie W., 30
  Amanda, 17, 33
  Amanda G., 17
  Arthur, 49
  Azalia, 28
  Barbara, 24(3), 27, 30, 32, 34, 39, 98(2)
  Benjamin M., 20(2)
  Bessie C., 12
  Bessie S., 16
  Beulah E., 14
  Blanch M., 6
  Caroline H., 58
  Catharine, -arina, 29, 32, 34, 35, 172
  Catharine R., 15
  Charles K., 18
  Charles R., 8
  Charlotte S., 152
  Christian, 3, 17, 32, 39
  Christian C., 31
  Christian F., 24(2), 34
  Christian S., 38(2)
  Christine C., 12
  Clara, 19(2), 161
  Clara B., 19
  Clara G., 14
  Clarence, 4
  Clarence L., 50
  Clyde, M., 7
  Cordan, 27
  D. Laraine, 18
  D. Simon S., 38
  Daniel L., 19
  David, 7
  David R., 12
  David Y., 4
  Deborah M., 15
  Donald Lee, 7
  Donna LEe, 7
  Dorothy, 6
  Dwight, 4
  E. C., 80 E. H., 35
  Edith R., 7
  Edna F., 4
  Edward M., 37
  Edwin M., 17
  Eliz, 38
  Eliza H., 20
  Elizabeth, 4, 28, 30(2), 32, 34, 47
  Elizabeth A., 17
  Elizabeth M., 12
  Ellen, 35
  Elmer M., 14
  Emma, 38, 39, 46
  Emma K., 7
  Emma Lottie, 12
  Emma M., 16, 28(2)
  Emma Matilda, 12
  Emma R., 16(2)
  Enos M., 4
  Enos O., 43
  Ephraim, 35(3), 36
  Ephraim A., 35
  Erwin G., 6
  Erwin Y., 36
  Esther, 31
  Eugene M., 7
  Evelyn, 16, 20
  Florence, 12(2), 20
  Florence B., 14
  Frances, 28
  Franklin M., 32

MOYER, continued:
  Garwood R., 4
  George A., 161
  George E., 161
  Gideon, 19(2)
  Gideon S., 19
  Glenn R., 54
  Grace C., 18
  Grace Elaine, 17
  Grace H., 152
  Grace S., 53
  H. Warren, 3
  Hannah, 43
  Hannah H., 31
  Hannah R., 28
  Hannah W., 26
  Hans, 3
  Harry H., 4
  Harvey, 20
  Harvey R., 20
  Heinrich, 32(2), 43
  Henry, 24, 30, 39, 43
  Henry C., 15, 27, 28
  Henry D., 151(2)
  Henry G., 27
  Henry H., 30
  Henry R., 12
  Henry S., 36
  Henry Y., 24
  Hester, 31
  Hiram C., 16
  Howard B., 47
  Howard E., 7
  Howard H., 20(2)
  Howard M., 17
  Ida, 33
  Ida D., 13
  Ida H., 12, 157
  Ida M., 8
  Ida May, 35
  Infant, 7, 30
  Irene, 49
  Irwin G., 47
  Irwin M., 142
  Isaac, 43
  Isaac H., 28, 34(2)
  Isaiah, 26(2), 47
  Isaiah B., 26
  J. Arthur, 17
  Jacob, 26, 27, 28
  Jacob C., 24(4), 37
  Jacob H., 12(2), 28(2), 35(2) 39, 43(2), 44(2)
  Jacob M., 12, 28
  James A., 17
  James E., 157
  Janelle K., 54
  Jeanne, 7
  Johannes, 29, 119
  Johannes H., 36
  Johannes S., 23
  John, 98, 100
  John M., 98
  John S., 23
  Jonas D., 58(2)
  Joseph, 24, 34, 38(2)
  Joseph, Dr., 79
  Joseph R., 7
  K. Florence, 12
  Kathryn B., 12
  Katie, 12
  Katie B., 6
  Katie K., 8
  Kenneth A., 12
  Kores, 15
  L. Hortense, 161
  Larue M., 13
  Laura C., 17
  Laura S., 8
  Leila, 151
  Leroy M., 13
  Leroy R., 7
  Levi, 47
  Levi N., 22
  Lillie Alice, 30
  Lillie B., 4

MOYER, continued:
  Lillie L., 5
  Lillie M., 32
  Lisa Gaye, 8
  Lizzie, 34
  Lizzie C., 30
  Lois C., 30
  Lovina H., 13(2)
  Lucy Ann, 13(2)
  Lydia, 34
  M. A., 12
  M. D., 37
  Mabel, 16
  Mabel M., 16
  Mabel S., 7
  Magdalena, 44(2), 109
  Magdalena Rickert, 15
  Mahlon D., 23
  Maimie E., 12
  Malon, 47
  Mamie R., 7
  Marcella, 142
  Margaret, 12
  Margaret S., 142
  Marget, 142
  Maria, 29, 32(2), 36(2), 43, 98, 109
  Maria Anna, 43
  Mariann, 36
  Martha S., 170
  Martin,B., 30
  Mary, 22, 24, 26(2), 33(2), 34, 36, 38, 100
  Mary A., 4, 35
  Mary Ann, 3, 14, 17, 31, 35(2) 37
  Mary Ann K., 36(2)
  Mary Estella, 27
  Mary Ettie, 26
  Mary G., 7
  Mary H., 12
  Mary K., 7, 157
  Mary L., 26
  Mary Malinda, 44
  Mary O., 43
  Mary R., 17
  Mayme D., 20
  Maynard F., 50
  Menno H., 170
  Michael, 109
  Mildred, 18
  Mildred M., 7
  Milton, 35(2)
  Missoura, 47
  Myra F., 18
  Myrtle Y., 4
  Nancy, 28
  Norman M., 8
  Paul B., 12
  Paul M., 17
  Pauline, 6
  Rearson K., 4
  Peter L., 3
  R. Walter, 16(2)
  Reuben C., 17
  Reuben H., 31
  Richard M., 16
  Robert M., 53, 100
  Rudolph, 31(3)
  Rudolph H., 31
  S., 36
  S. G., 152, 153
  Saleme, 32
  Sallie, 17
  Sallie E., 44
  Sally, 30
  Salome M., 23
  Salomie H., 4
  Samuel, 28, 30(3), 33, 35, 36(2), 47
  Samuel A., 34
  Samuel B., 43(2)
  Samuel H., 17(2), 23(2), 33, 35(3)
  Samuel K., 47
  Samuel M., 12, 16
  Samuel R., 14

MOYER, continued:
    Sara, Sarah, 27(2), 36, 43
    Sarah Ann, 30
    Sarah E., 17
    Sarah G., 27
    Simon S., Dr., 38
    Stella A., 6
    Susanna, Susannah, 15, 30(2)
        35(3), 39(2)
    Susanna G., 15
    Sylvanus G., 152
    Theodore F., 13
    Titus K., 12
    Tobias, 3
    Tressie S., 3
    Tyrus H., 15
    U. Hester, 31
    Valeria M., 5
    Vernon H., 152
    W. C., 14(2)
    Wallace R., 18
    Walter M., 16
    Wayne W., 157
    William, 22, 27(2)
    William A., 6
    William F., 32(2)
    William H., 5, 35
    William M., 12(3), 13(2), 15, 80
    William O., 5
    William R., 6
    William s., 27
    Willus B., 14
    Wilson H., 35
    Wilson R., 6

MOYERS
    Susanna, 101

MUHE
    Edith Tyson, 57
    Henry L., 57
    Louis S., 57(2)
    Mary A., 57

MULL
    Emma, 150
    Emma E., 150
    Henry E., 150
    Linford Luther, 150
    Luther, 150

MÜLLER
    Arthur C., 161
    Michael, 161
    Pauline, 161
    Regina M., 161

MULLMAN
    Theodore M., 89

MUMBAURER, MUMBOUR
    Allen, 128
    Anna Mary, 147
    Benjamin, 151(2)
    James, 128(2)
    James M., 128
    John, 97
    Margaret W., 128(2)
    Martha, 97
    Mary Wilhelmina, 151

MUSSELMAN
    Bessie L., 16
    Delilah F., 13
    Dianna H., 16
    Edwin, 137
    Edwin R., 137
    Elizabeth, 119
    Emma E., 12
    Hanna, 36
    Henry F., 13
    Henry K., 34
    Henry W., 13(3)
    Jacob G., 16
    Jacob K., 36

MUSSELMAN, continued:
    John F., 16(3)
    Joseph, 34
    Joseph M., 13
    Katie H., 16(3)
    Lizzie B., 13(2)
    Lizzie F., 7
    Lovina, 127
    Mamie, 16
    Mary, 119
    Mary Ann, 16
    Mary Jane, 137
    Mathias, 127(2)
    Malvin M., 7
    Reuben, 34
    Sadie G., 16
    Sally, 12
    Sally M., 12
    Sally W., 12
    Samuel, 34, 119
    Samuel F., 12(3)
    Sarah, 13, 34
    Simon, 34(2)
    Simon M., 16(2)
    Verda M., 12
    William, 36
    William F., 7

MYERS, MEYERS, MYER
    A. B., Dr., 141
    Agnes, 28
    Albert H., 149
    Allen, 104
    Annie H., 17
    Anthony F., M.D., 141
    Bertha K., 149
    Catharine, 42
    Clara M., 14
    Clarence S., 140
    Claude M., 14
    Craig A., 150
    Dora, 104; Daymon M., 156(2)
    Edwin, 104
    Elizabeth, 46
    Elizabeth M., 150
    Emma E., 162
    Emma H., 149
    Emma J., 156
    E. Norman, 17
    Enos W., 34
    Ephia, 147
    Florence, 17
    Fredricka D., 177
    George, 147
    George W., 147
    Hanna, Hannah, 33, 42, 176
    Isaac, 28, 42(2)
    J. Horace, 17
    Jacob, 33
    Jacob H., 46(3)
    John G., 11
    John H., 17
    John L., 176(2)
    Laura, 104
    Lizzie, 24
    Lizzie J., 18
    Lorenzo R., Jr., 149
    Maria, 11
    Marian S., 141
    Marjorie, 53
    Marthella, 104
    Mary, 24(2), 34, 45
    Mary Gill, 61
    Mirriam, 149
    Richard Glenn, 147
    S., Allen, 162
    Salome, Saloma, 45(3), 46
    Samuel, 161
    Samuel A., 14
    Samuel W., 45(2), 46(2)
    Sarah, 11, 46
    Tilghman, 18
    Tobias, 24(2)
    W. Albert, 149
    Walter W., 149(2)
    Wilhelmina S., 141

MYERS, Conrinued:
    William F., 11(2)
    William H., 141
    William S., 150

NACE, NASE
    Aaron, 101
    Alice L., 54
    Amanda Ann Elizabeth, 62
    Amos B., 62(6)
    Annie, 106
    Barb, Barbara, 101, 109
    Chad Richard, 53
    Francis, 37(4)
    Geraldine, 86
    Helen D., 54
    Hester, 106
    Howard M., 62
    Infant, 62
    James, 109
    John, 101, 109(2)
    Jonas, 37(2)
    Jonas M., 37
    Kay F., 161
    Laanna, 109
    Levi, 62
    Lydia, 37, 62(5)
    Lydia N., 62
    Marie, 151
    Mary, 37(3)
    Mary Ann, 37
    Matilda, 37
    Paul M., 54
    Penrose, 62
    Robert C., 151, 161
    Robert M., 54
    William d., 20
    William Franklin, 106
    William H., 106(2)

NAGURNY
    Andrew, 87
    Fannie, 87
    John, 87

NASH
    Elizabeth, 33

NEAVEL
    Anna, 134
    Catharine A., 134
    Henry, 134(2)
    Jane, 134
    John, 112(2)
    Margaret, 112
    Mary, 134

NELSON
    Ida E., 125
    James C., 125

NEMEC
    Rudolph, 84

NESSLER
    Barbara, 154
    Elizabeth B., 154
    Emily, 154
    George, 154
    Josephine, 154
    Liz & Lorenz, 154(2)

NEUBERT
    Elizabeth, 55
    John F., Sr. & John B., 55(2)
    Nancy A. & Robert E., 85(2)

NEUBOLD
    see Newbold

NEUKOMMER
    David, 30

NEWBOLD
    Bernhard F., 105(2)

NEWBOLD, continued:
    Bernhard Tobias, 105
    Catharine, -rina, 99(2), 104
    Johannas, 99(3)
    Joseph, 99, 104(2)
    Mary W., 105
    Ralph W., 105

NEWSOME
    Catherine V., 89
    Harold W., 89
    Irma G., 55

NEYRA
    Julia F., 89

NICE
    Beatrice A., 164
    Dorothy C., 56
    Emma, 164
    Joseph S., 56
    Price P., 164(2)

NISBIT
    David N., 53

NOLTING
    Anna, 163(2)
    Karl, 163

NORDERSHAUSER
    Peter, 34

NOWAKOWSKI
    Anna, 88
    Stanley, 88

NUNNEMACHER, NUNNAMAKER,
    NUNNEMAKER
    Anna, 49
    Catharina Maria, 94
    Maria, 94
    Michael, 94(3)
    Solomon, 49

NYCE
    see Nice
    David Lee, 53
    Lloyd C., 53
    Madeline L., 53

OBERHOLZER, OLBERHOLZER
    Abraham, 49
    Elizabeth, 39
    Isaac, 39(2)
    Maria, 49

OLD
    Annie L., 155
    Moses, 155
    Sallie, 155

O'LEARV [O'LEARY?]
    Denise Marie, 88

OLPP
    Archibald, 124
    Beatrice, 124

OLSEWSKI
    Adam, 88
    Rose, 88

OMMEREN
    see VanOmmeren

OPDYKE
    Jacob H., 21
    Laura M., 144(2)
    Lillie May, 144
    Maria V., 21
    Reuben, 144(3)
    Reuben F., 27

OPP
    Anna Catherine, 111

OPP, continued:
    Catharina, 111
    Hurruhinou, 111
    Lavinia, 111
    Mary, 111
    Peter, 111
    Valentin, 111(3)

OREMUSZ
    John, 162
    Katherine, 83
    Mary, 162
    Stephan, 83

ORTIZ
    Marion L., 146
    Mercedes, 146(2)

OTT
    Alberta M., 137
    Amanda, 109, 137
    Bertha Mae, 155
    Bertha R., 138
    Clinton, 155(2)
    Dick, 156
    Elizabeth, 95, 109, 137
    Elmer, 144, 149
    Elmer, Jr., 149
    Elmer H., 144
    Eva E., 154
    Frank, 146
    Harold Eugene, 155
    Harvey S., 137
    Infant, 156
    Jacob S., 138
    Jacoby, 137(2)
    John, 94
    Malinda, 138
    Maria, 137
    Mary, 94
    Mary Lou, 156
    Monroe, 137
    Norman L., 153, 154
    Raymond, 145
    Raymond O., 139
    Richard T., 156
    Ronald, 154
    Sallie A., 144
    Samuel, 95
    Samuel H., 109(2)
    Silias Paul, 109
    Simon, 109
    Titus, 146
    Titus H., 146
    Verna R., 146

OVERHOLT
    see Overholtzer
    Catharine Hunsberger, 25
    Martin, 25

OVERHOLTZER
    see Overholt
    see Oberholzer
    Alvin, 148
    Alvin D., 148
    Elizabeth, 148

OVERPECK
    Aaron S., 133
    Alice B., 133
    Blanch S., 133
    Elizabeth S., 133

OWEN
    Catherine, 57
    Griffith, 57(2)
    Henry, 57
    Jane, 57
    John, 57
    Owen, 58, 59

OWENS
    Ebenezer, 57
    Elizabeth, 57

OWENS, continued:
    Sarah, 57

P.
    J. M. P., 40

PAGE
    Mary Kalmar, 89
    William J., 89

PALVOCAK
    Stephen G., 84

PARKER
    Robert L., 77

PASSANTE
    Angela Marie, 85

PATTERSON
    Harry J., 60
    Infant, 60
    John, 60(2)
    Lorng, 173
    Rachel F., 60

PEARSON
    Annie, 146
    Harvey, 146
    Jennie, 146

PECKICONIS
    Andrew, 87
    Caroline, 87

PEKAR
    Hedwig, 89
    Jennie, 83
    John, 83
    Mary, 83, 84
    Michael, 84
    Robert, 89(2)

PENNYPACKER, PENNAPACKER
    Amos, 48
    Amos G., 26
    Daniel, 48
    Eliz, 26
    Eliza, 48

PETERMAN
    Albert, 58
    Annie, 58
    Carrie, 58
    Clara, 58
    Frank, 58
    Mary C., 55

PETERS
    Edith, 126

PETERSON
    Loren, 172

PFEFFER
    Jacob F., 104

PHILLIPS, PHILIPS
    -------, 128
    Catharine, 68
    Fannie E., 128(2)
    Grace Greenwood, 74
    Lewis, 128
    Lewis R., 128(2)

PIECUSKI
    Constance, 83
    Frank, 83
    Stanley Helhowski, 83

PIERCEY
    Anna, 131
    John, 131(3)

PIERZCHALA
    Peter, 88
    Theresa, 88

PISCHL
    Vincent, Sr., 84

PLEISS
    Charles, 150
    Charles F., 132
    John F., 150
    Katie Magdalena, 150
    Magdalena, 132
    Rosie M., 150
    Warren C., 150

POHLE
    Harmon, 100

POLK
    Susanna P., 108

POLZER
    Ignatius, 84

POMA
    Jeannette, 83
    Kathie, 83
    Robert, 83
    Robert G., Jr., 83

POSAVEC
    Katherine, 86
    Peter, 86

PRESS
    Eliza, 127
    Eliza Ruth, 127
    Infant, 127
    John, 127
    Mary Edna, 127
    Matilda Ella, 127

PRICE, PREISZ
    Heinrich, 33
    Johann Elizabeth, 33
    Johannes, 33
    Jonathan, 137
    Mary Ann, 137
    Mary D., 142
    William, 137
    William H., 137

PRIESTER
    Anna Maria, 95(2)
    Anton, 95(2)
    Charles, 130
    Heinrich, 95
    Henry G., 118

PRINGLE
    Donald Ray, 170
    Douglas R., 170

PROCTOR
    Catharine, 39
    John M., 41(3)
    Hannah, 41(2)
    Mary, 41
    Thomas, 39(2)

PRYKAZ
    Adam, 89
    Andrew, 87
    Carolyn, 89
    Helen K., 87

PUGH
    Daniel, 72
    Rebecca, 72

QUINTRELL
    Anna Kramer, 141

R.
    B., 45
    F., 27
    J. H., 72
    M., 63, 70
    M. A., 63

RABBONI
    Louise M., 85

RACE
    Anthony E., 176
    Julia A., 141(2)
    Levi, 176
    M. Lewis, 141
    Wilhemina, 176

RAPPOLD
    Alice W., 156
    Cora, 106
    Henry, 158
    Howard J., 156(2)
    John, 106, 158
    John A., 158
    Wilhelmina, 106, 158

RAUSCH
    Agnes Joan, 86
    Helena, 86
    Joseph, 86
    Mary, 86
    Mathias, 86

RAWA
    Adam, 86
    Mary, 86

RAWN
    Edward M., 168
    Ellen L., 168

R?EALER
    Frank, 96
    Girda May, 96
    Hannah, 96

REASER
    Frank, 150, 151
    Frank H., 150(2)
    Kate E., 150

RECHNER, RECKNER
    Catherine, 83
    Frank, 83
    Ida, 86
    Mary, 83(2)
    Stephen, 83
    William A., 86

REDLOW
    Johanna, 65
    William, 65

REED
    Andrew, 175(2)
    Mary, 175

REEDER
    Anna ELiz, 101
    Emma O., 103(4)
    John, 93
    Levi, 103(4)
    Mary, 93

REESE
    -------, 133
    Anna Mary, 135
    John N., 135
    T. Scott, 135

REICHLEY
    Christian, 113(2)
    Margaret, 113

REIDENAUR, REIDENAURER
    Daniel M., 97(2)
    Rachel, 97

REIFF
    Abraham R., 129(2)
    Calvin C., 138
    Clara H., 138
    Daniel Z., 160
    Hannah B., 160

REIFF, continued:
    Harvey Clinton, 160
    Martha A., 160
    Mary M., 129
    Sarah J., 138

REINHARD
    Thomas Rudolph, 88

REINSTICK
    Charles, 55

REINOSO
    Francisco O., 91

RENNER
    Alan C., 150
    Alberta, 148
    Annie Elizabeth, 62
    Catherine, 148(2)
    Catharine H., 42
    Edward A., 103
    Elizabeth, 29(2), 161
    Emanuel A., 146
    Emeline, 103
    Francis, Frank, 62(2)
    Hannah, 98
    Herbert B., 150
    Ida L., 150(2)
    Infant, 103
    Isaac A., 98
    James, 167
    Joe, 161
    Joseph H., 161
    Joseph L., 161
    Laura D., 161
    Leidy, 29
    Mahlon, 29
    Martha H., 103
    Mary A., 146
    Michael, 148
    Michael A., 148
    Michael H., 29(2)
    Oliver D., 161
    S. A., 98(2)
    Sallie A., 104
    Sara, Sarah, 12, 42
    Willie A., 98
    William. 12, 42, 150(3)
    William A., 150

RENOUX
    Juliette E., 65

REPPERT
    Catherine, 112
    Elizabeth, 112(2)
    Eve, 123
    Frederk, 113
    John, 112, 113
    Magdalena, 113
    Margaret, 111
    Peter, 111
    Samuel, 123(3)

REUBA
    Boleslo, 85
    Ona B., 85
    Veronica, 85

REYNOLDS
    Ronald, 51

RHIMER
    Wilson B., 172

RIALE
    David E., 72
    Joel H., 72
    Sarah E., 72

RICE
    -------, 64
    Blanch H., 53
    Elmer D., 53
    Gordon S., 53
    Margaret, 64
    Moses, H., 64

RICE, continued:
    Susan J., 64

RICHENBACK
    Harry, 127
    Harry M., 127
    Matilda, 127

RICHMAN
    Francis, 172, 173

RICK
    Joseph, 49
    Rosa, 49

RICKERT, RICKER
    Abraham, Abram, 34, 43, 45 (2)
    Alifia, 31; Carolyn Lynn, 56
    Catherine, -ina, 45(2)
    Charles, 62
    D. Clayton, 62(2)
    David A., 63
    David R., 31(2)
    Elizabeth, 45
    Emma S., 63
    Enos, 45
    Esther Beatrice, 63
    Florence M., 151
    Glenn Q., 54
    Hannah, 45
    Henry, 45
    Henry F., 21
    Henry R., 45
    Isaac, 45
    J. Allison, 150, 151
    Kathryn, 62
    Linn, 45
    Lloyd, 21
    Lovina K., 20
    Margie A., 54
    Maria, 21(2)
    Peter S., 63
    Reuben H., 20, 21(2)
    Sarah E., 34
    Susan, 21

RIDLEY
    Glenn Q., 54
    Helen L., 54

RITTER
    Frederick William, M.D., 155
    Wil, 155, 157
    Wilhelmina S., 155

RIVEST
    H. Paul, 86
    Kathryn L., 86

ROBERTS
    Catherine Scheip, 159
    Norman Lee, 55
    Titus & Titus A., 159(2), 160

ROCKEL
    Joan Lee, 163
    John, 163

RODEROCK
    Catherine, 115
    David, 115(2)

ROGERS
    Mary A., 11

ROHR
    Abraham, 20
    Abraham H., 20
    Caroline Bigelow, 5
    Catharine A., 104
    Charles B., 31(2)
    Charles M., 5
    Christian Barbara, 102
    Elizabeth K., 21
    Henry, 102
    Jacob H., 103
    Kate S., 20

ROHR, continued:
    Sallie K., 31
    Samuel B., 21
    Sarah A., 103
    Susan, 103
    Walter M., 5

ROHS
    Agnes C., 89
    Anna, 84
    Anna Rose, 84
    Herta M., 85
    John, 84
    Joseph J., 84
    Stephen, 84
    Stephen J., 89

ROJUNSKY
    Florence A., 89

ROMIG
    Angeline, 104(2)
    Charles Franklin, 104
    James A., 104(3)

ROSENBERGER
    Abel, 28
    Abraham B., 28
    Abraham G., 130(3)
    Alice M., 3(2)
    Allen G., 44
    Allen M., 14
    Alvin K., 13
    Amanda L., 172
    Anna F., 32
    Anna Valeria, 32
    Bertha, 32(4)
    Bertha S., 130(3)
    Blanche B., 32
    Carrie, 146
    Catharine, -rina, 39, 44(3)
    Charles F., 44
    Christian, 32
    David D., 119(2)
    Edward, 28
    Edwin C., 171
    Elias, 37
    Elizabeth, 34
    Elizabeth Eckart Snyder, 113
    Ella Nora, 14
    Elmer W., 124(2)
    Emma L., 170
    Erwin G., 44
    Esther K., 13
    Eva L., 168
    Flora, 130
    Flora Estella, 127
    Gertrude, 32
    Harriet, 127(3)
    Heinrich M., 39
    Henry B., bishop, 28(2)
    Henry F., 170
    Henry G., 6
    Howard, 79
    I. Stanley, 3
    Infant, 23, 130, 168, 169
    Isaac, 28(2), 37(2)
    Isaac G., 13
    Isaac R., 127(3)
    Isaiah D., 168
    J. M., 44(2)
    Jacob, 44(3)
    Jacob B., 27
    Jacob M., 44
    Jennie L., 170
    Joel, 79
    Johannah K., 23(2)
    Joseph, 39
    Joseph D., 23(2), 101
    Joseph W., 44
    Katie L., 170
    L. Elaine, 91
    Laura K., 13
    Laura M., 124
    Leidy H., 126
    Lizzie, 168
    Lydia, 119

ROSENBERGER, continued:
    Lydia S., 6
    M. Emma, 5

    Maretta B., 13
    Maria, 141
    Marilyn, 3
    Martha G., 5
    Martha L., 170
    Martin D., 34(2)
    Mary, 28(2), 116(5)
    Mary Alice, 127
    Mary Ann, 28; Mary D., 13
    Mary Godshalk, 28
    Mayme, 171
    Melvin S., 130
    Mildred D., 126
    Monroe S., 130
    Ralph B., 171
    Rodger, 171
    Rodger B., 171
    Sallie, 79
    Samuel, 28, 168(5)
    Samuel H., 172
    Samuel M., 32(4)
    Sara Mae, 14
    Sarah M., 27
    Silronus, 168
    Stanley, 3
    Susanna, 28, 37
    Titus B., 32
    Titus D., 32(3)
    William, 126
    William H., 141(2)
    Wilson S., 130

ROTH
    Anna, 168
    Elias R., 168(2)
    Helen, 161
    Norman T., 161

ROTZEL
    Catharine, 103
    Joseph, 101

ROUNAN
    Anna, 87
    Joseph J., 87

ROWLAND
    Anna, 71
    Anna Maria, 71
    Artemus T., 71(5), 74
    Elizabeth, 73(2)
    Elizabeth Mathias, 73
    Emily, 73
    Emma, 71
    I. Newton, 73(2)
    Joseph, 73
    Justis, 76(2)
    Letitia, 76
    Lydia A., 74
    Mark T., 76
    Martha, 76
    Martha R., 71(4), 74
    Martha Louise, 71
    Mary, 71
    Matilda, 72
    Newton, 73(3)
    Owen, 71
    Rachel, 69
    Sarah, 73
    Sarah A., 74
    Staughton, 73
    Stephen, 71
    T., 73
    Thomas, 69
    William D., 76
    William H., 73(2)

ROWLETT
    Hamilton C., 85
    Margaret A., 85

RUARK
    Ernest & Virginia R., 55

RUCH, continued:
    Guy A. P., 154
    Robert Allen, 154

RUCKER
    Jacob, 44
    Susanna, 44

RUMER
    Amanda, 176
    Hannah H., 176
    Samuel H., 176

RUPERT
    Peter H., 167

RUSH
    Alvin L., 8
    Annie M., 44
    David R., 8
    Mary B., 8
    Remandus, 44

RUSSEL
    Anna, 22
    Eleazer, 22

RUTH
    Ann Mary, 120
    Charles, 136(2)
    Christian, 151
    Cora E., 120
    Edward, 151
    Elmer L., 120
    Emma, 164
    Emma B., 164
    Ernest B., 164
    Jacob R., 120
    John Clinton, 74(3)
    Joseph, 74, 97, 125(2), 157
    Joseph B., 157
    Joseph S., 125
    Leah, 48
    Leidy L., 127
    Lillie Rowland Yost, 74(2)
    Lizzie, 125
    Maggie, 125
    Margaret N., 147
    Mary, 120, 136(2), 151
    Mary Proctor, 74, 97
    Miena, 33
    Rudolph, 151
    Samuel B., 120
    Sarah A. Leidy, 125(3)
    Thomas, 151
    William R., 120

RYMDEIKA
    Frank, 85
    Josephine, 85

RYZNER
    Frank, 158
    Frank V., 158

S.
    C. A., 80
    C. S., 80
    E., 80, 110
    E. L., 25
    J., 46
    L., 110
    T. H., 80
    W., 109

SAHM
    Michael, 124
    Rosena, 124

SAMPEY
    Etta C., 148
    Harvey, 148

SAUDER
    see Souder

SAVACOOL, SABEHUHL, SABELFUHL,
SABELHUHL, SABELRHUHL
    ?uianna, 116
    Catharine, 108
    Elias, 116
    Eliz Anna, 96
    Eliza Ann, 108(3)
    Elizabeth, 116
    Enoch, 116(4)
    Franklin, 108
    Hannah, 116
    Harriet, 108
    Henry, Henrich, 108, 116
    Jacob, 115(2)
    Lydia, 115, 116(3)
    Magdalena, 108
    Mahlon, 96(2), 108(3)
    Margaret, 109
    Maria, 108
    Maria Anna, 116
    Michael, 109(2)
    Susannah, 116
    Wilhelm & Wilhelmina, 116

SCAHLNEELER
    Adam, 115

SCHADL
    Anton & Mary, 86

SCHAFFER
    Sadie M., 162
    Samuel J., 162

SCHEEBER
    Christian, 125
    John & Lovina, 125

SCHEETS
    Aaron, 134
    Andrew, 93(2)
    Catharine, 93
    Emeline M., 134

SCHEIB, SHEIB, SCHEIBIN, SHIVE
    see Sheip
    Abigail, 118
    Barbara, 108
    Catharina, 108
    Elizabeth, 108, 118
    Elva, 143
    George, Georg, 108(2), 118(2)
    Isaiah, 97
    Johannes, 108
    John, 97
    John L., J. L., 97, 98(2)
    Lidla, 107
    Lydia Anna, 24
    Maria, 97(2)

SCHEIDEL
    Gustave G., Jr., 85
    Gustav G., Sr., 85
    Rose B., 85

SCHEINELIN
    Natalena, 112

SCHEIP
    see Shipe, Scheib

SCHEIRENBRAND, SCHREINBRAND
    Elizabeth, 99(2)
    William, 99(3)

SCHENCK
    John H. & Mae, 56

SCHILLING
    Arthur, 177
    Mamie, 177

SCHILLINGER
    Theresia, 83

SCHINLEVER
    David, 97(2)
    Leidy, 98
    Magdalena, 97

SCHLICHTER, SCHLIGHTER
    Andrew, 22

SCHLICHTER, continued:
    Caroline, 22
    Isaac, 38, 40
    Mary, 22, 38, 40

SCHLOPSNA
    Eugene, 158
    Eugene E., 158
    Julia G., 158

SCHLOSSER
    Annie F., 157
    Grace, 143
    Henry F., 157(2)
    John, 103(2)
    Jonas, 143
    Jonas F., 143
    Lizzie M., 143
    Sarah, 103

SCHMELL
    Betty Anne, 7
    Jean, 7
    Samuel S., 6
    Stella, 6
    Wilmer L., 7

SCHMIDT
    Fritz A., 84
    George C., 155(2)
    John P., 162
    Joseph J., 89
    Winnie, 155

SCHMOYER
    Henry, 93
    Mary Ann, 93

SCHNABLE, SCHNAVEL, SCHABLE
    Abram G., 105(3)
    Abraham B., 105
    Abraham G., 120
    Amelia J., 120
    Florence W., 105
    Jonathan Franklin, 93
    L., 105
    Lucyanna, 105(2)
    Magdalina, 105(3)
    Morvan E., 105
    Rachel, 93
    Raymond B., 105
    Sabina G., 105(2)
    Sammuel, 105
    Titus E., 105

SCHNEIDER
    see Snyder
    Bertha R., 130
    Catharina, 115
    Conrad, 115(2)
    Hanna, 112
    Jacob Adam, 112
    Johannes, 95
    Joseph, Sr., 130

SCHOLL, SCHOOL
    Amanda, 94(2)
    Annie, 154
    Cath, Catherine, 94, 97
    Edgar, 94
    Edith S., 154
    Hannah, 116
    Infant, 116
    J., 116
    Jacob, 148
    Jacob C., 146
    Lavina, Lovina, 146, 148
    Lea, 94
    Leidy, 94(2)
    Magdalena, 27
    Maria Hannah, 115
    Paul Andrew, 55
    Phares M., 146
    Sallie A., 116
    Sarah M., 146
    Simon, 116(2)
    William, 94(2), 155
    William H., 154

SCHRAMM
   George C., 87
   Katherine F., 87

SCHWAGER, SCHRAGER
   Catharine, 49
   Hannah R., 7
   Jacob, 48(2)
   Jacob, Jr., 48
   Magdalena, 48
   William M., 7

SCHWARTZ
   see Swartz
   Anthony, 161
   Joseph, 161
   Maria, 161
   Nicholas, 161

SCHWENK
   Susanna, 109

SCOTT
   Agnes W., 155
   Jane Lewis, 75
   Laird B., 155
   Luella J., 155
   Mica, 75

SEARCH
   John, 62
   John Henry, 62

SEHER, SHERER
   Albert A., 100(2)
   Anthoni, Anthony, 100(5)
   Anton, 112(2)
   Auguste, 100
   Emily, 100
   Fensner, 100
   Jacob, 100,
   Maria, 100

SEIBEL
   see Seiple
   Anna, 103
   Elizabeth, 110
   Jacob, 103(2)
   Johan Hendrich, 23
   John, 110(2)

SEIDEL see Sidel
   see Scheidel
   Charles, 151
   Katie M., 151
   William, 151
   William M., 151(2)

SEIPLE
   see Seibel
   Enos B., 111(2)
   Henry F., Rev., 124
   John B., 103(2)
   Lillian Salome, 124
   Louisa, 111
   Salome Gross, 124
   Sarah, 103
   William A., 104

SEITZ, Anna C., 153
   George, 153
   George M., 153
   George Seeberger, 153
   Jacob, 156(2)
   Katie, 156

SELLERS, SELLER
   Abram, Abraham, 111(2)
   Amanda, 120
   Ann Mary, 111
   Catharine, 74(2), 111, 120
   Catharine A., 80
   Charlotte, 61
   Daniel, W., 127
   David, 79(30
   Elizabeth, 79(2), 80, 111(2)

SELLERS, continued:
   Elizabeth C., 127
   Elizah, 111
   Elmina, 119(4)
   Emmaline, 74
   Ephraum, Ephrim, 79(2), 111(3)
   Francis, 119(5)
   Gilbert S., 80
   H. Linford, 127
   Hannah, 79
   Isaiah, 119
   Joel J., 72
   John, 74(3), 111
   Johny C., 80
   Josiah, 80(3)
   Laura E., 127
   Mahler, 79
   Mary, 119
   Mary Eleanor, 119
   Michael, 72(2)
   Phila Ann, 120(3)
   Reuben, 120(3)
   Samuel, 72
   Sarah, 79(2)

SEMMERN
   Charles, 171
   Ella, 171

SEMPEY
   Flora, 125
   Harvey, 125

SENIOR
   Peter J., 87

SENTMAN
   Ella G., 21
   George C., 21
   Henry M., 21

SENSINGER
   Elizabeth J., 158
   Evelyn, 160
   Howard S., 158
   Lillian H., 160
   Sherwood, 160
   Stan, 160
   Stanley, 158
   Steward, 158
   Truman E., 160

SHADDINGER, SHATINGER, SHATTINGER
   Anna, 26
   Catharine, 26
   Edward, 26
   Emma H., 6
   Griffith, 15
   Henry R., 6
   Jacob, 37
   Jennie, 15
   John L., 26(2)
   M., 65(2)
   Mary, 65
   Mathias, 65
   Samuel M., 65
   Sarah, 37
   Susan, 26
   William, 65

SHAFFER
   see Schaffer
   H., 116
   M. L., 116

SHALLCROSS
   Edna, 53
   Leonard R., 53

SHAMAL
   Conrad, 112
   Emanuel, 112

SHAW
   Catharine, 128(2)
   Robert, 128(2)

SHAW, continued:
   Sarah W., 128

SHEARER
   Annie L., 149
   B. Ellen, 137(2)
   Clayton, 149
   Grier M., 137(3)
   Infants, 137
   J. Theodore, 149

SHEIP, SCHEIP, SCHEIPP
   see Scheib
   Anna, 159(2)
   Anna ALbright, 160
   Anna M., 160
   Anne, 95
   Beulah Lee, 131
   C. Clinton, 96
   Catherine, 159
   Charles Pierce, 131
   Charlotte, 124
   Elizabeth, 132
   Ellen M., 131
   Florence Elizabeth, 131
   Franklin P., 131
   George W., 124
   Hannah, 126
   Hannah B., 126
   Infant, 96
   J. L., 96
   J. Stanley Hartzell, 126
   John, 115, 126
   John L., 124
   Leidy, 96, 140, 142
   Lydia, 124
   Maria, 124
   Mary Ann, 129
   Mary Elizabeth, 96
   Noah, 129, 132(2)
   Noah S., 129
   Susanna, 96
   Susanna E., 142
   Titus A., 160
   William F., 160

SHELLENBERGER, SCHELLENBERGER
   Henry, 107(3)
   Johannes, 108
   Mary A., 107
   Phillip, 110
   Racher M., 107
   Sarah, 107(3)
   Sussanna, 110

SHELLY
   Abraham D., 170
   Annie L., 63
   Clara, 163
   Clara E., 163
   Cora A., 5
   Erwin M., 5
   Henry, 134
   Infant, 7
   Irene S., 6
   John, 176
   Jonas, 176
   Levi, 63(2)
   Lizzie F., 163
   Maggie, 134
   Matilda, 170
   Susan, 176
   Wilmer B., 6

SHEPHERD
   Emma, 117

SHERER
   see Serer

SHERM
   Annie M., 154
   Barbara, 94
   Caroline, 134
   Christina, 146
   Christianna, 146

SHERM, continued:
    Elizabeth, 134
    Elizabeth L., 134
    Frank, 154
    Franklin, 154
    Jacob, 146
    John, 94(2)
    John B., 134(3)
    John Claude, 154
    John G., 146
    Neri B., 133
    William, 133, 134(2)
    William H., 134
    William S., 92

SHILLING
    Annie, 159
    Jacob, 159
    Jacob M., 159

SHIRE
    Barbara, 111
    George, 111
    Maria, 111

SHIVE
    see Scheib, Sheip

SHOEMAKER
    Charles, 96
    H. Annie, 96
    M., 96

SHOLL
    see Scholl
    Adam, 115
    Hannah, 115(2)
    Simon, 115(2)
    William Henry, 115

SHULICK
    Andy, 87
    Julia, 87

SIDEL
    see Seidel
    Infant, 88

SIEGRIED
    Anna K., 89
    Ellwood M., 89

SIGAFOOS
    Howard C., 77

SILFUSS
    Elizabeth, 42

SIMMON
    Matilda, 57

SIMONS
    Florence M., 88
    Gerald L., 88
    Joseph L., 88
    Sarah M., 88

SINE
    Anna, 79
    Eliz. F., 106
    George, 79(2)
    John G., 106(2)
    Mary, 85
    Sam, 85

SION
    Christopher, 112

SLEAR
    Reno J., 89
    Sarah R., 89

SLEIFER
    see Slifer

SLEIGHT
    Harry A., 71

SLEIGHT, continued:
    Margaret E., 71
    Mary Elizabeth, 71
    Rowland, 71
    Samuel, 71

SLICK
    Jacob, 109
    John, 109(2)
    Mary, 109

SLIFER, SLIFFER, SLEIFER
    Abraham, 60
    Anna Mary, 102
    Catharine M., 139
    Charles H., 139(4)
    Christian, 177(2)
    Daniel, 95
    Elizabeth, 118
    Elladora, 102
    Elmer C., 152
    George, 118
    Hannah, 177
    Henry, 105
    Infant, 139
    Irwin C., 152
    Jacob, 60
    Juliann, 139
    Mary, 177
    Mary Ann, 102, 105(2)
    Sam N., 105(2)
    Sammuel, 102(4)
    Wilhelmina, 102

SLUTTER
    Henry T., 125
    Jacob, 119(2)
    John A., 125
    Sarah, 119
    Sophia F., 125

SMITH
    Adam. 127(3)
    Adam G., 127
    Adeline A., 63
    Adella, 24
    Amanda, 24
    Amanda O., 25
    Anna E., 5
    Annie, 106, 145
    Annie B., 145
    Annie C., 172
    Anthony Gross, 125
    Barbara, 147
    Bernard D., 172
    Bertha L., 130
    Charles R., 63
    Clara S., 156
    Clayton D., 25
    Clifford E., 127
    Conrad, Conart, 106(3)
    Donald, 148
    Dorothy, 106(3)
    Edward L., 145
    Ellen Jane, 127
    Elsie M., 4
    Elvin A., 63(2)
    Emaline, 147
    Evelyn S., 156
    Frances, 177
    Frank, 151
    Frany, 34
    Frederick, 101(2)
    Harvey D., 5
    Henry, 101, 147
    Henry B., 21
    Henry F., 132
    Henry K., 21
    Ida A. Hellerman, 63(2)
    Ida G., 132
    Infant, 6, 14, 63
    J. Matthew, 172
    Jacob, 34, 130
    Jacob H., 130
    Jacob K., 13, 14(3)
    John, 106, 111, 155
    John Allen, 172

SMITH, continued
    John F., 125(2)
    John L., 49
    John M., 14
    John R., 25
    Joseph M., 172(2)
    Laura H., 8
    Leidy D., 8
    Leroy E., 145
    Lizzie, 147
    Lizzie Mae, 172
    Lydia, 101
    Lydia Ann, 18
    Maggie, 14(2)
    Maggie H., 4
    Margaret, 101
    Margaret K., 13
    Mary Ann, 125
    Mary D., 25(2)
    Mary M., 176
    Matilda, 127
    Maurice, 156
    Merrie, 172
    Morris, 156
    Nora J., 134
    Oliver D., 24, 25
    Paul L., 176
    Pearl C., 6
    Robert S., 130
    Samuel, 176, 177(2)
    Stanley, 148
    Susan, 111
    T. H., 80
    Thomas S., 130
    Tobias H., 80
    Walter B., 4
    Walter J., 6
    Walter P., 172
    Wilhem, 88
    William R., 18, Wilmer, 154

SMITHERS
    Frances L. & James, 56

SMOLA
    Edna K. & John T., 85

SNOVEL, SNAVEL
    see Schnable
    Abraham, 102(2)
    Annie O. 106(2)
    Frank, 106(3)
    Henry, 114
    Infant, 106
    Isaiah A., 159
    Jonas, 102
    Jonathan, 93
    Lillian M., 159
    Magdalena, 102
    Maria, 114
    Mary, 106
    Mary Y., 159
    Miria, 102
    Monroe, 104
    Robert, 159(2)
    Russell, 106
    William, 114

SNYDER
    see Schneider
    --------, 67, 116
    Abram, 112
    Amanda, 128
    Amanda B., 128
    Amanda R., 147
    Anna, 116
    Anna E., 126(2), 155
    Anna M., 157
    Bertha T., 140
    Blanche A., 157
    Carey, 93
    Caroline, 116
    Catharine, 132
    Charles C., Rev. 148(2)
    Charles Clinton, 142
    Clara J., 149
    E., 93
    Elias, 132(2)

SNYDER, continued:
    Elizabeth, 112, 132
    Elizabeth Martin, 112
    Elizabeth Rosenberger
        Eckhart, 112
    Ella F., 154
    Ella R., 141, 142
    Ella Virginia, 112
    Elmer R., M.D., 147
    Emaline Lucinda, 112
    Emeline, 116
    Emily L. 138(3)
    Emma L., 131
    Enos, 132(2)
    Enos D., 157
    Eve Reppert, 115
    Flora May, 138
    Francis, 116(5), 126(2)
    Francis K., 131
    Francis S., 116
    Franey Yost, 147
    Franklin, 94, 137, 147
    Franklin B., 147
    Franklin P., 128
    Frany, 112
    George, 112(5), 149
    George D., 157
    George S., 149, 150
    Hanna M., 95
    Hannah, 130, 147
    Harriet L., 154
    Hattie, 154
    Harvey, 130
    Helen M., 141
    Henry, 147
    Henry H., 147
    Ida C., 138
    Ida F., 155
    Ida S., 131
    Infant, 94
    Isaik F., 93
    Isaiah, 126
    Isiah F., 155
    Isiah S., 126, 155
    Jacob, 109(2), 116, 143, 155
    Jacob Adam, 112
    Jacob B., 147
    Jacob R., 155
    James Erwin, 132
    John, 95
    John W., 130
    Laura Catherine, 163
    Leidy, 149, 150
    Leidy F., 138
    Letitia M., 131
    Levi S., 131
    Lydia, 112, 140
    Lydia Ann, 116
    M---, 115
    Maria, 95
    Marion H., 154
    Marrian, 155
    Mary, 95, 112, 116(5)
    Mary E., 159
    Mary R., 156
    Mary S., 126
    Michael, 112(2), 116(2)
    Milton, 140
    Milton H., 140
    Miriam E., 126
    Monroe, 163
    Olivia, 140
    Penrose D., 156
    Peter L., 95(2)
    Ralph M., 154
    Ruth D., 126
    Sallie E., 148
    Sarah, 154
    Sarah J., 131
    Sarah Jane, 126
    Simon, 116, 140(2)
    Simon, Jr., 141
    Simon Landis, 138
    Simon S., 130
    Susannah, 109
    Susie Idessa, 138
    Wesley A., 154

SNYDER, continued:
    William, 154
    William Henry, 112
    William D., 154
    William R., 138(4)

SOBOCINSKI
    Ignacz, 86

SOLIDAY
    Walter, 91

SOUDER, SAUDER
    Abraham, 36(2)
    Jonas, 98
    Mahlon A., 6
    Ruth M., 6
    Sarah J., 98

SOWERS, SOWER
    Adam F., 126
    Cath., 131
    Edith S., 126
    Harvey F., 131
    Magdalena, 126
    Mary Jane, 131
    Samuel, 131
    Wilmer, 126

SPANGLER
    Amanda, 96
    Franklin, 96

SPANNINGER
    Laura G., 18

SPIEGELHATTER
    John, 49
    John S., 49
    Mary, 49

SPRINGER
    Abram D., 47
    Charles H., 139
    Elizabeth, 46
    Frank, 156(2)
    Hannah, 47, 156
    Jesse, 47(2)
    Maggie, 139
    Margaret, 139

STAEHLE
    Ann M., 88

STAHR
    George, 175
    John C., 175

STAUFFER
    Edwin S., 53

STEAD
    see Steer

STEEB
    Cari A., 103
    Frederick, 103(2)
    Frederick G., 103
    Louise H., 103(2)

STEED
    Elizabeth, 110(2)
    Mary Ann, 110
    Sabastian, 110(2)

STEELEY
    Susan N., 144

STEEP
    Anna, 142
    Frederick, 142

STEER, STEAR, STIER, STYER,
    STEIR, STIERIN
    Andreas, 110
    Annie, 136
    Catharina, 110

STEER, continued:
    Christiana, 99
    Christine, 110
    Edgar E., 160(2)
    Elisabeth, 110
    Ella M., 160
    George R., 160
    John Andrew, 136
    Mary, 98
    Noah, 136(3)
    Philip, 99(2)
    Tobias, 98(2)

STEINBACH
    Catharina, 94
    Elizabeth, 112
    Frank, 94
    Michael, 112
    William H., 94

STEINLY, STINLEY
    Infant, 5
    J. Clarence, 8
    Margaret D., 5(2)
    Marvin M., 5(2)
    Virginia C., 8

STEVENS
    Amanda A., 130
    John R., 130(2)

STEVER
    Abraham S., 126
    Norman F., 156(2)
    Vestilla, 126

STINE
    Elizabeth, 28
    Philip, 28

STIPE
    Catherine, 102(2)
    Christian, 102(3)
    Laura, 102

STOCK
    Albert, 163
    Albert C., 163
    Albert D., 163
    Susan E., 163
    Wilson, 163
    Wilson A., 163

STONE
    Eliza & James S., 172(3)

STOPKA
    Irene H. & Robert Harry, 55

STOUT
    Anna M., 160
    Henry M., 160(2)
    Howard B., 168
    Infant, 168
    Isac, 150
    Raymond A., 168(2)
    Sarah M., 168(2)

STOVER
    Abram M., 4
    Alice M., 19
    Allen, 18
    Allen F., 18, 26
    Amanda N., 19
    Artemus M., 4
    Barbara M., 5
    Calvin M., 5
    Catherine, 25
    Catherine H., 25
    Dorothy, 5
    E. K., 25
    Edwin F., 16
    Ella, 26
    Ellis L., 19
    Ellis S., 18
    Emma K., 31
    Ephraim G., 25(3)
    Gideon, 47(3)

STOVER, continued:
    Gideon S., 47(2)
    Hannah D., 47
    Howard, 19
    Ida, 47
    Ida H., 16
    Infant, 5
    Katie M., 25
    Laura B., 4
    Laura M., 19
    Lizzie, 18
    Lizzie K., 18
    Mattie, 19
    Milton F., 19, 25, 31
    Nora, 4
    Reuben D., 47
    Salome F., 25
    Samuel, 5
    Sarah, 47(4)
    Vena E. Martin, 16

STROHM
    Elizabeth, 167
    Noah F., 167
    Peter R., 167

STRONG
    Catherine M., 85
    Charles D., 85
    Emeline, 131

STRMER
    Charles, 146

STROUSE
    Francena, 91
    William H., 91

STRUG
    Adela H., 87
    Anna, 87
    John, 87

STYER
    see Steer

SUMMERS
    Ann, 114
    Christianna, 115
    E., 96
    Eliza, 67
    Elizabeth, 67
    Elizabeth G., 67
    Emma, 114
    Enos, 114(4)
    Enos M., 67
    Isaac, 114
    John, 67
    L., 96
    Lizzie, 96
    Lydia, 114(4)
    Nicholas, 114
    Noah, 115(2)

SWALLOW
    Annie, 143
    George W., 143

SWARTLEY
    A., 128
    Abraham D., 103(2)
    Alma A., 133
    Annie L., 153
    Bertha A., 133
    Charles R., 95
    Elizabeth, 128
    Elmer A., 155
    Elmer D., 22
    Howard A., 133
    Jesse, 157(2)
    John K., 157(2)
    M. Elizabeth, 155
    Mabel, 133
    Mary A., 157
    Mary Ann, 95
    Melvin A., 133
    Rosella, 155

SWARTLEY, Continues:
    Sallie J., 133(3)
    Sarah, 103, 157(2)
    Susanna, 103
    William, 133, 134
    William R., 133(3)

SWARTZ
    see Schwartz
    A. Lincoln, 75
    Abraham O., 21
    Allen, 100
    Annie H., 4
    Amanda E., 14
    Christiana, 100
    Elias, 100
    Elizabeth, 100
    Ella Amanda, 75
    Frank R., 104
    I. Frank, 14
    John, 177
    John O., 4
    Katherine, 144
    Licinda B., 100
    Maimie C., 75
    Margaret, 144
    Mary, 161, 177
    Mary Ann, 21
    Nicholas, 161
    Raymond B., 21
    Sallie B., 100
    Samuel, 100(3), 144
    Sarah, 100(3), 144
    Sarah , 104
    William, 144

SWILER
    Carrie R., 100
    Charles, 100
    Mary Hecken, 100

SWINK
    Amos, 178
    David, 178
    Elvia A. G., 176
    Elwood B., 26
    Fanny, 176(3)
    Hannah, 26(2)
    Henry B., 26(2)
    Irwing H., 51
    Jacob, 175, 176(2)
    Mary, 175
    Mary C., 26
    Sarah E. F., 176
    William, 175

SWOYKOWSKI
    Josephine, 38

SZYMANSKI
    Martha S., 153
    Matthew, 153

T.
    E., 115(2)
    E. H., 36
    J., 115
    M., 115
    S., 38

TANNER
    Margaret, 130
    George, 130(2)

TAYLOR
    Anna, 131
    Asenarth R., 73
    Bertha W., 156
    Blanche, 160
    Blanche Rosenberger, 160
    Grace H., 146
    Irene, 131, Irene A., 55
    Lamuel, 73
    Maidell, 131
    W. Theodore, Rev., 55

TEASDALE
    Charles W., Rev., 77

TEASDALE, continued:
    Elva P., 77

TEMOSHCHUK
    Mary D., 65
    Michael, 65

TERTERSY
    Dennis Paul, 172

TEXTER
    Anna Grace, Gracie 62(2)
    Ida Helen, 56
    Ralph, 62
    Susan L., 62(2)
    William H., 62(2)

THIEROLF, THEROLF, THIEROFF
    Adam, 102(2), 120
    Author, 153
    Dalton R., 153
    Ervin, 102
    Infant, 153
    Margaret, 120
    Mary, 102(2)
    Pierson, 102

THOMAS
    Abner, 70
    Alivia, 73
    Ann, 70(4), 71(2)
    Asa, 69(2)
    Benjamin, 70
    E., 70
    Eber, 70
    Eli H., 38
    Elizabeth, 70, 71
    Elizabeth P., 38
    Elias, 70, 71(2)
    Ephraim, 70(2), 71
    Infant, 70
    Issachar, Essachar, 70(4), 71(2)
    Job, 71
    John, 69, 73(5)
    John Edward, 73
    John, Rev., 70
    Jonathan, 70
    Joseph, 70
    Josiah, 71(2)
    Levi, 75(2)
    Lillie S., 177
    Livia, 73(2)
    Mahlon, 71
    Malinda, 70
    Manasseh, 70
    Margaret, 73(2)
    Maria, 69, 70
    Martha, 69
    Mary, 71
    Melinda, 75
    Rebecca, 70
    Sarah, 69, 70(3)
    Sidney, 70 (2)
    Silas, 69(2)
    William, minister, 71(2)

THOMPSON
    Mary S., 54
    Robert E., 54

THOMSON
    James C., 87

TICE
    Annie, 114
    Carl R., 161
    Charles W., 156(2)
    Conrad, 114(2)
    Ella A., 114
    Elmer S., 163(2)
    Emma B., 156
    Frank S., 161(2)
    George, Jr., 157
    George M., 157
    Ida C., 157
    Ida G., 157

TICE, continued:
    Laura E., 163
    Magdalena, 114(3)
    May, 161
    Norman W. & Wilmer B., 156

TITUS
    Joseph O., 56

TOMLINSON
    Alfred, 56

TRABER
    Carl B., 170
    Charles & Rosa, 170

TRAUGER
    Adaline & Agnes, 107
    Mary, 107
    Sarah N. & Solomon 107(3)

TREACY
    Dorothy M., 84
    William E., 84

TREFFINGER, TREFINGER
    Allen, 140(2)
    Allen G., 140
    Caroline, 99(2)
    Clayton S., 140
    Frederick, 99(2)
    Frieterick, 118
    Harriet, 131
    Lewis F., 131
    Mary E., 99
    Mary L., 140
    Reuben, 98

TREICHLER
    Van J., 130

TRIEWIG
    Andren, Andrew, 111, 112
    Christina, 112
    Jacob, 117

TRIMBEE
    Catharine, 68

TRINKLEY
    Aaron Wilson, 100
    Anna, 100(2)
    Martin, 100(2)
    Mary, 100

TROUT
    Charles H., 164(2)
    Phoebe S., 164

TROXEL, TROXELL
    Elizabeth, 109
    Jacob, 109(2)
    Joseph, 109
    Sarah, 109

TYSON
    Abraham, 151
    Clayton M., 152
    Eugene, 151
    Eugene A., 151
    Hannah Albright, 136
    Henry A., 136
    Martin A., 136
    Mary M., 152
    May A., 151
    Warren M., 152(2)
    William, 136

U.
    R. C., 118

UHLIG
    Olga Lisa, 91

UHRICH
    Deborah Darline, 65

ULMER
    Anna M., 143
    Hannah, 143
    Jacob, 143
    Jacob S., 143

UMSTEAD
    -------, 163
    Eliza Ann, 79
    Estella A., 153
    Everard R., 153
    Richard, 79(2)

UNDERCOFFER, UNDERCODDLER
    Mary M., 162
    William, 162
    Wilmer, 162

UNGERCH
    David, 38
    Elizabeth, 38

URBANCHUK
    -------, 165

URSALIS, USALIS
    Adam, 83
    Ursula, 83

VAIL
    Catherine, 59
    Irene, 59
    Peter K., 59

VANHOOK
    -------, 133
    Peter, 133, 135
    Verna M., 133, 135

VANKLEEF
    Peter, 88

VANOMMEREN, OMMEREN
    Ada, 138
    Alida, 127(2)
    Amanda, 138
    Anna Elizabeth, 133
    Emma, 138
    Emma Rose, 159
    Frank, 138
    J. V., 127(2)
    John, 125
    Malinda Ott, 138
    Maria, 138
    Peter, 138
    R., 133
    Susannah, 159
    Yost, 159

VANTHUYME
    -------, 159

VARWIG
    Edna S., 132
    George B., 132

VASTINE
    Martha, 71

VIEBEL
    Benedict, 103

VENETZ
    Bermetta E., 89
    Helen M., 85
    John J., 89
    John L., 85

VETCH
    Eva H., 140
    Hugh A., 140

VIDT
    Valeria S., 127

VITKUS
    Edward J., 87
    Helene, 87

VOCK
    Christian, 120
    Magdalene, 120

VOGEL
    Christian, 155
    Edna H., 153
    Magdalena, 87, 155
    Peter, 155
    Russell C., 153
    Steven, Stephen, 87, 155(2)

VOID
    Bertha, 104
    Della, 104
    Edith C. 159
    Edna C., 104
    Elsie C., 158
    Frederick, 104(3)
    Fredrick R., 158
    Mabel, 104
    Mary, 104(3)
    Mary A., 158

VOLPE
    Anne L., 86
    Anthony J., 86

W.
    A., 58
    E., 118
    H., 118

WACK
    Charles C., 163(2)
    Donald, 164
    Elizabeth B., 163
    Ellemina, 163
    Paul M., 163(2)

WAGNER
    Anton, 85
    Erik, 88
    Hannah, 115
    Herman B., 84
    John, Jr., 147
    John, Sr., 147
    John N., 147
    Josephine, 89
    Katie B., 147
    Leontina, 85
    Maria, 147
    Richard S., 89

WALCH
    Frank J., 86
    John I., 86
    Josephine, 86

WALDSPURGER
    Davida, 85

WALLIS
    Edna A., 169

WALTERS
    Albert F., 85

WAMBOLD
    Maria, 54
    Oscar H., 54

WARD
    Claire T., 56
    Ira B., 56

WARREN, Joseph C., 129

WASSER
    Ann Maria, 112
    Elizabeth, 112
    John, 112(2)

WATZ
    John, 45
    Magdalena, 45

WAYNE
    Lillian M., 150
    Thomas S., 150

WEAND
    Clarence E., 101
    Emma, 101
    Eugene, 101
    Joel, 131(2)

WEAVER, WEEBER, WEBER
    C. Catharine, 96
    Catherine, 8
    Christina Catharina, 95
    Christianna C., 96
    David J., 8
    George F., 96
    George Frederick, 95
    R. Barbara, 96

WEEKS
    J. Freeman, 151
    Laura C. Dimmick, 151

WEIKLE, WEIKEL
    Aramanda, 104
    Hannah, 118(2)
    Hannah Maranda, 104
    Henry, 104
    John, 123
    Mary, 118
    Peter, 118, 123(3)
    Rachel, 123(3)

WEISEL, WEISELL
    see Wetzel
    Aaron, 94(2)
    Catherine, 126
    Dianna, 94
    George l., 113
    Harry, 113(2)
    Henry, 136(2)
    J. George, 126
    John George, 113
    Levi, 94
    Margaret, 113
    Maria, 94(2), 113(2)
    Maria L., 136
    Mary Ann, 126
    Mary Lucinda, 113
    Michael, 126
    Samuel, 138

WEISS
    Alfred, 103
    Catharine, 128
    Charles, 128(2)
    Charles H., 106
    Charles Henry, 100
    Charles S., 100(3)
    Debra S., 100
    Eliz G., 106
    Hannah, 100
    Harrison F., 132
    Jacob, 132
    Joseph, 102
    Katy Elizabeth, 100
    Laura M., 132
    Mary, 132
    Michael L., 100(2)
    Rachel, 102
    Richard D., 151
    Russell C., 151
    Russell L., 151
    Ruth C., 151
    Sarah, 100
    Timothy Edward, 56
    William E. S., 132

WELDER
    Juliann Gross, 138

WENDTLAND
    Carol A., 91
    Mary J., 91
    Sherry Shiela, 91
    William B., 91

WENGER
    Elizabeth L., 50
    Ethel R., 8
    Henry H., 33
    Sallie R., 33

WERNER
    Irvin K., 21
    Rachel Lehigh, 54

WERMAN
    Robert, 157

WERT
    Robert W., Sr., 160

WESSMAN
    Hugh, 163
    Hugo C., 163

WETZEL
    see Weisel
    Aaron, 94
    Maria, 94
    William Francis, 94

WHINNEY
    Charles B., 135
    Isabella M., 135

WHITE
    Eleanor, 106

WHODARCZYK
    Antonia L., 83
    Walter L., 83

WIDMANN
    Mary T., 87
    Paul J., 87
    Reinhold, 87

WIETECHA
    Caroline, 87
    Thomas J., 87

WILKINSON
    Kathryn Fretz, 5

WILLAUER
    George J., 131
    Mary A., 131

WILLIAMS
    Amy, 59
    Betty, 65
    Cora J., 126
    Eleanor, 60
    Eliza, 178
    Jones, 60
    Raymond, 139
    Thomas, 60(2)
    William, 60

WILSON
    George, 157
    George W., 157
    Lena H., 157

WILWERT
    Anthony, 83
    Eva, 83
    Nick, 83

WIMMER
    Joseph, 114(3)
    Mary, 114
    Nancy, 114

WINKLER
    Elizabeth, 57
    Elizabeth A., 57
    Eyre, 57
    Jesse, 57(5)
    Josephine, 99
    Lizzie, 57
    Lizzie Ann, 57
    Margaret, 83
    Ralph E., 65
    Raymond, 65
    Raymond R., 65
    Richard C., 83
    Thomas, 100
    Tobias M., 99
    William Henry, 57

WISMER
    Abram M., 6
    Anna Mary, 169
    Aquilla, 6
    Christian, 169(4)
    Eva S., 169
    Joel, 44, 169(3), 170
    Joel H., 169(2)
    Martha S., 170
    Mary, 44(2), 169(5), 170
    Mary S., 169
    Sallie, 44
    Sarah, 169

WISNIEWSKI
    Laura M., 89

WISSLER
    Rebecca D., 168

WIREMAN
    Henry S., 177

WITMER
    Katherine M., 173
    Levi B., 172

WITTMAN
    John George, 114
    Margaret, 114
    Sophia Matilda, 114

WOLF
    Anna, 83
    Anna ELizabeth, 115
    Franklin, 115
    Margaret, 114, 115(3)
    Peter, 83
    Pierson, 114, 115(2)
    Samuel, 114, 115(3)
    William, 115

WOOD
    Elmer L., 77

WORTHINGTON
    Charles A., 65
    Catharine, 64
    Helen C., 156
    Iva B., 65
    Iva C., 65
    Jonathan, 60
    Mary Ellen, 4
    Melvin H., 156
    Sallie C., 154
    Sarah, 60
    Seth, 60, 61
    Stacy T., 4
    William H., 64(2), 154

WRIGHT
    Edwin, 72
    Jacob, 72

WURSTER
    Christian, 163
    Harriet F., 50
    William, 50

WYDOMINICK
    Alexander, 63
    Mary, 63

WYNNE
    THomas, 155

YEAKEL, YAKEL, JEEFEL, JÖKEL
    Abraham, 47
    Anna, 46
    Catharine, 22, 29
    Christiana, 29
    Elizabeth, 29
    Emaline, 29
    Henry M., 29, 49
    Jacob, 22(2)
    Louis, 47
    Samuel, 46
    Samuel S., 46
    Sarah, 29, 47, 49

YEARICK
    Adaline, 93
    Angeline Christina, 93
    Calvin H., 93
    John N., 93
    Levi Edward, 93
    Philip Harpel, 93
    Susannah M., 93
    Talitha Ann, 93
    Wilhelmina B., 93
    William R., Rev., 93(3)

YOCUM
    Barrilla, 58
    G., 58
    S. M., 58

YODER
    Abraham L., 15
    Adaline A., 63
    Amanda, 19
    Amanda M., 3
    Anna, 45
    Annie, 31
    Annie A., 20
    Annie D., 29
    Bessie M., 3
    Charles E., 124
    Christian, 34(2)
    Christian B., 34
    Edith A., 8
    Edna D., 20
    Edna G., 19
    Emeline, 27
    Ervin, 27
    Hannah M., 42
    Henry L., 44
    Henry M., 44, 45
    Howard E., 124
    Irene D., 20
    Jacob, 29, 31
    Jacob A., 29(2)
    Jacob L., 44
    Johannes, 31
    John D., 18
    Joseph, 32
    Joseph D., 124(3), 140
    Leah, 32
    Levi, 32(3), 35
    Levi M., 3
    Lizzie, 31, 44
    Lizzie S., 44, 45
    Maria, 31(2)
    Mary Ann, 42(2)
    Mary Emma, 32
    Mary L., 40
    Norman L., 3
    Oscar, 29
    Peter, 42
    Peter Y., 42
    Rebecca, 124
    Reuben, 31(2)
    Reuben A., 45
    Reuben M., 31

YODER, continued:
    Rosa Emma, 19
    Rosa M., 15
    Sadie C., 3
    Samuel M., 19, 34
    Samuel Y., 27
    Sarah, 32, 34, 35
    Stella M., 18
    Susanna, 34
    Susanna N., 34
    Susie L., 3
    Warren D., 8
    William A., 172
    William D., 20, 63
    Wilmer L., 44
    Wilmer R., 19

YORK
    Stanley E., 89

YOST
    Remandus, 74(2)
    Sarah A., 74(2)

YOTHERS
    Abram K., 5
    Annie R., 5
    Edna M., 6
    Harvey K., 4
    Henry R., 6
    Ida Mae, 4
    Richard H., 6

YOUNG
    Benjamin, 105
    Carrie Kline, 141
    Harvey, 69
    John, 69(2)
    Lillian, 160(2)
    Mary, 69
    Sarah, 98
    Thomas A., 160

ZEHNER
    Christian M., 162(2)
    Christopher, 162
    Minnie, 162
    Minnie M., 162

ZELLWEGER
    Anna J., 123
    Jacob, 123

ZETTLEMOYER
    Anna Arndt, 105
    C. J., 104(2), 105
    William, 104

ZIEGEN, ZIEGENIN
    A., Rev., 177
    Andrew, 175
    John, 175
    Mary A., 175
    Mary Ann, 175

ZIEGLER, ZEIGLER
    Daniel F., 169
    Ella F., 56
    Emma M., 169
    George W., 56
    Jacob B., 22
    Rosina, 98

ZILL
    John 105(3)
    Sarah 105(2), 106

ZOELLER
    Emma L., 86
    William J., 86

ZOLLER
    Caroline, 117, 153
    Caroline G., 153

ZOLLER, continued:
    Elizabeth, 153
    Elmer, 153
    Frank J., 53
    George H., 153
    Hannah, 153
    Henry, 117, 153(2)
    Jacob, 117

ZUKOW
    Paul J., Jr. 56